RATIONAL CHOICE IN AN UNCERTAIN WORLD

RATIONAL CHOICE IN AN UNCERTAIN WORLD

ROBYN M. DAWES
Carnegie Mellon University

Under the General Editorship of
JEROME KAGEN
Harvard University

HARCOURT BRACE JOVANOVICH, PUBLISHERS

San Diego   New York   Chicago   Austin   Washington, D.C.
London   Sydney   Tokyo   Toronto

In memory of Hilly Einhorn, whose decision to work in the
field of behavioral decision theory under unfavorable circumstances
made such a difference, and Clyde Coombs, whose lifetime of
accomplishments and leadership in this field was based
on his thorough enjoyment of the work.

PREFACE

The greatest enemy of truth is very often not the lie—deliberate, contrived, and dishonest—but the myth—persistent, pervasive, and unrealistic.

John F. Kennedy

Many authors claim that a major reason for their writing a textbook is that their students have been particularly enthusiastic when the materials in it were covered in classes. The implications are that the reader as well will find the content absorbing and that the author is generally skilled at organizing and communicating such material.

I have a more compelling rationale. It is based not just on student response to my courses in behavioral decision making, but on a comparison of the response to these courses as opposed to the response to others I have taught—in areas of statistics and social psychology. In all my courses I collect numerical ratings of student satisfaction. The resulting numbers I receive from my decision-making classes are not just higher than those from my other classes; there is very little overlap. In three consecutive years of teaching courses in rational decision making (first at the University of Oregon and then at Carnegie Mellon University), I attempted to present basic ideas in as nontechnical a way as possible, and the students liked the results. I hope that the reader of this book will as well. Another major reason for writing this book is my belief that an understanding of the principles of rational decision making can help people improve the quality of their choices and, by extension, their lives.

The book is divided into three sections. Chapters 2 through 4 explain principles of rationality that allow us to evaluate the consequences of alternative choices. Chapters 5 through 7 explain principles of rationality that are used to evaluate probabilities when the results of choice are uncertain. Chapters 8 through 12 explain systematic ways of making decisions in a rational manner and discuss general issues in decision making. Finally, three appendixes present the basic concepts of probability theory and statistics.

Throughout I compare basic principles of rationality with actual behavior in reaching decisions. There is a discrepancy. Moreover, this discrepancy is due not to random errors or mistakes but to "automatic" thought processes that influence how decision problems are conceptualized and how future possibilities in life are evaluated. The overall premise is that our thinking processes are limited in systematic ways, and I cite research to support this premise.

And I am, throughout, opinionated. *I attempt to present as clearly and forcefully as possible the thrust and implications of the relevant research.* Perhaps subsequent research will show that some of the conclusions reached in this book are incorrect or that they require modification, but I take the position that research—not anecdote, not "plausible" belief, not common sense, and not our everyday experience—should be the basis for understanding and evaluating our decision making.

Nevertheless, I have used anecdotes liberally as a teaching device. For many of the same reasons that we do not think wholly rationally, anecdotes are a powerful way of conveying information and making it believable and memorable. I have tried, however, not to reason from anecdotes to conclusions (for example, "my great-aunt Matilda was once told she had terminal cancer and then went for a walk by the lake on a moonlit night and the cancer went into remission; therefore . . ."); rather, I use anecdotes to reinforce the conclusions reached from theory and research. Over the years, I have collected many anecdotes that illustrate how our thinking about decision problems systematically deviates from principles of rationality.

The theme of limited cognitive capacity often conflicts with our preconceptions about how smart we are. While many of us are willing to accept the idea that our unconscious (for Freud) or "animal" (for Plato and Aristotle) desires may interfere with our reasoning when we are faced with an important choice, the idea that thinking per se is a flawed and limited process is an unpleasant one. Moreover, many people object to the view that thinking is flawed on the grounds that our evolution to superior species status is related to our cerebral capacity, as evidenced by technologically advanced human civilizations. This common-sensical argument is flawed in several respects.

First, although evolution is often phrased in terms of the "survival of the fittest," its actual mechanism is better described as "survival of the fitt*er*." Animals that have a high*er* probability than their competitors of surviving to adulthood and reproducing ("reproductive fitness") in a particular environment have a high*er* probability of dispersing their genes to future generations. Successful animals need not be optimal when compared to some physical or mathematical criterion of optimality, but only "one-up" on competing animals—and even that relative superiority is defined relative to the particular demands and survival tasks of an environment. If indeed the human cerebral cortex is responsible for our ascendancy over competing species, that does not imply it is the optimal thinking device.

Nor does our technological development attest to the brilliance of our thinking as single human beings. Rather, it attests to the human ability to communicate knowledge, often across generations. A single human could not have created relativity theory, a symphony, or a hydrogen bomb without building on knowledge "borrowed" from living others and from the past. Such borrowing involves recognizing what has been intelligently concluded and produced—and recognizing a valuable intellectual result is far easier than creating it. When faced with an important decision in our lives, in contrast, we are often "on our own" to think through what we might do and the probable consequences of the behaviors we might choose.

I must also counter the misconception that decision making is important simply because of the vastness of the choices with which we as individuals and as a species are faced today. It is true that few of our great-grandparents seriously considered the option of divorce and that few of their political leaders considered risking the annihilation of the human race in order to achieve an international political objective. Nor were engineers of that day asked to produce energy by constructing complicated plants that could poison vast areas of the earth as a result of a few minutes or hours of a few individuals' bad judgment (as at Chernobyl). But despite the much larger set of options available to us than to our ancestors, our decisions are probably not more *difficult* than theirs were. We experience our current subjective state according to principles of human adaptation. We adapt to whatever decisions must be made, and to their consequences, as normal. Such adaptation is both a blessing (as when the individual in the worst prison camp can experience near ecstasy over eating a single piece of bread or cultivating a single weed) and a curse (as when people whom others regard as "having it made" accept their current situation as nothing more than normal and find themselves on a "hedonic treadmill"[1]). The subjective weight of decision making has always been a heavy one; philosophers throughout the centuries have discussed the process of

[1]For an astute analysis of the "hedonic treadmill" see Brickman, P., and Campbell, D. T. (1971). Hedonic relativism and the good society. In Appley, M. H. (ed.). *Adaptation-Level Theory: A Symposium*. New York: Academic Press.

decision making and suggested ways in which it is good or bad. The new knowledge that underlies the field of decision making and this book is knowledge about simple principles that define rationality in decision making and knowledge about our cognitive limitations that lead us not to decide rationally.

A word about format. Both references and tangential remarks are placed in footnotes.[2] In addition, a bibliography at the end lists books and papers that discuss basic ideas in a nontechnical manner. Omission of a referenced work from this list does not mean that I consider it unimportant; rather, the purpose of the bibliography is to suggest further reading to the person who is interested in behavioral decision making but is not a specialist in the area.

Mathematical material requiring knowledge beyond elementary algebra also has been relegated to footnotes. Nevertheless, as mentioned earlier, three appendixes cover the basic concepts of probability and statistics. The presentation in these is concise, without the elaborations or exercises that would be necessary in an exposition for a reader totally unfamiliar with the field. I hope the appendixes will serve as a refresher for those who have taken a statistics course and as an outline for mathematically sophisticated readers who have not been exposed to probability or statistics. Others need not be concerned with the appendixes.

Finally, I express my intellectual indebtedness to many colleagues whose ideas appear throughout this book. To name a few (in alphabetical order), they are Clyde Coombs, Ward Edwards, Hillel Einhorn, Baruch Fischhoff, Ken Hammond, Danny Kahneman, James March, Paul Meehl, Richard Nisbett, Howard Raiffa, Herb Simon, Paul Slovic, and Amos Tversky. That list is not exhaustive. As I have indicated, I believe that all our minds are more limited than we might wish, and I want to make clear that most of the ideas and principles found in this book are ones I have learned from others, mainly from outstanding thinkers and researchers such as those listed above. When I refer to empirical findings of specific studies, the reader should understand that the ideas as well as the findings are those of the authors. The interpretations of these ideas and their implications are, of course, my own responsibility.

[2]Occasional quotations not directly referenced are from Rogers, M. (ed.) (1983). *Contradictory Quotations*. Burnt Mill, Harlow, England: Longman Group, Ltd.

I also thank people who have helped me directly with this book. Clyde Coombs, Baruch Fischhoff, Reid Hastie, Jay Kadane, Danny Kahneman, Pat Larkey, and James Shanteau all critiqued earlier versions, as did many students too numerous to mention. I also thank Carole Hallenbeck, the Harcourt Brace Jovanovich (HBJ) manuscript editor, most especially for her suggestions on how to "tone down" certain sentences and passages without vitiating their impact, and Marcus Boggs of HBJ for his enthusiastic support of the project. Most importantly, I thank Carole Deaunovich, my secretary, for her unerring success and remarkable cheerfulness in transforming impossible demands into possible ones.

ROBYN M. DAWES

C O N T E N T S

CHAPTER

We consider ourselves distinguished
from the ape by the power of
thought. We do not remember that it
is like the power of walking in the
one-year-old. We think, it is true, but
we think so badly that I often feel it
would be better if we did not.

Bertrand Russell
in *Faith and Mountains*

Introduction

1.1 DECISION MAKING AND SWIMMING

People, groups, organizations, and governments make choices. Sometimes the consequences of their decisions are desirable, sometimes not.

This book is about choice. It is not about what to choose, but about how to choose. Choosing wisely is a *skill*, which like any other skill can be improved.

The conclusions in the book follow from a body of research about how people actually make choices and decisions—people ranging from medical and financial experts to college freshman subjects in psychological experiments. The basic finding is that diverse people in such different situations often think about their choices in the same way. They have a common set of cognitive skills. But they also bring with them a common set of modes of thought that make their choices far from optimal. The purpose of this book is to characterize and explain these self-defeating thinking styles, and to suggest others that will improve the decision maker's skill.

Let me draw an analogy with swimming. When most of us (infants excepted) enter the water for the first time, we come with a common set of muscular skills that we use to keep ourselves from drowning. We also, however, have one important bias: we want to keep our heads above water. Because the orientation of the head in large part determines the orientation of the rest of the body, that bias leads us to assume a vertical position, which is one of the few possible ways to drown. Even if we "know better," in moments of panic or confusion we may attempt to keep our heads wholly free of the water, despite the obvious effort involved compared to that of lying flat in a horizontal position, or in a "jellyfish float." (Decisions, too, are often made in moments of panic or confusion.) The first step in helping people learn to swim, therefore, is to make them feel comfortable with their heads under water. (I invented a game in which children were to tell me the number of fingers I held up beneath the surface.) Then, anybody who has managed to overcome the head-up bias can survive for hours by simply lying forward on the water either prone or with arms and legs down—and crooking his or her neck only when it is necessary to breathe (provided, of course, the waves are not too strong or the water too cold). Ordinary skills are modified to cope effectively with the situation by removing a pernicious bias.

Thus I have conceived this book in the spirit of Benjamin Franklin, whose letter of advice about a pressing decision to his friend Joseph

Priestley (1772) began: "I cannot, for want of sufficient premises, advise you *what* to determine, but if you please, I will tell you *how*." I will attempt to detail self-defeating modes of thought in order to advise you how to improve your choices. I will not advise you of what your goals, preferences, or aspirations ought to be when you make these choices, however. The purpose of this book is not to improve taste, or preferences, or ethics—or to provide advice about how to implement decisions once you have made them. Nor (unlike many other books written in this style) does it advise you about how to feel good about yourself. Rather, this book's purpose is to increase your skill in *thinking about* decisions and choices. (I do not wish to derogate the importance of *what* is chosen, or of values; in fact, as will be pointed out in Chapter 8, one goal of choice may be to discover your own value system, or even to create it. My emphasis will be on how, not what.)

1.2 THINKING: AUTOMATIC AND CONTROLLED

So what is thinking? Briefly, it is the creation of mental representations of what *is not* in the environment. Seeing a green wall is not thinking; imagining what that wall would be like if it were repainted blue is. Noting that a patient is yellow is not thinking; hypothesizing that the patient may suffer from liver disease or damage is. Listening to a suicidal client is not thinking; attempting to establish the similarity between that client and previous ones who have or have not made suicide attempts is. (As will be indicated later in this book, matching with specific memories is not a particularly productive way of thinking.)

Sir Frederick Bartlett, whose work fifty years ago helped create much of what is now termed "cognitive" psychology, defined thinking as the *skill* of "filling gaps in evidence."[1] Michael Posner defines it as "the achievement of a new representation through the performance of mental operations."[2] Thinking tends to be primarily visual or verbal, and there are very clear individual differences in the degree to which people use either mode. Thinking often involves some type of "mental

[1]Bartlett, F. C. (1958). *Thinking: An Experimental and Social Study*. New York: Basic Books.
[2]Posner, M. I. (1973). *Cognition: An Introduction*. Glenview, Ill.: Scott, Foresman.

effort," although we have never been able to measure that very well. Sometimes it does not.

To oversimplify, there are basically two types of thought processes: automatic and controlled.[3] The terms themselves imply the difference. Pure association is the simplest type of automatic thinking. Something in the environment "brings an idea to mind." Or one idea suggests another, or a memory. As the English philosopher John Locke (1632–1706) pointed out, much of our thinking is associational.

At the other extreme is controlled thought—in which we deliberately hypothesize a class of objects or experiences and then view our experiences in terms of these hypothetical possibilities. Controlled thought is "what if" thinking. The French psychologist Jean Piaget (1896–1980) defined such thinking as "formal," in which "reality is viewed as secondary to possibility."[4] Such formal thought is only one type of controlled thinking. Other types include visual imagination, creation, and scenario building.

To distinguish these two broad categories of thinking, let me give an example that I will discuss at greater length in a later chapter. Many of my colleagues in psychology are convinced that *all* instances of child abuse, no matter how far in the distant past and no matter how safe the child is presently, should be reported, "because one thing we know about child abuse is that no child abusers stop on their own." How do they know that? They may have seen a number of child abusers, and of course none of those they have seen have stopped on their own. (Otherwise, my colleagues wouldn't be seeing them.) The image (representation, idea) of what a child abuser is like is automatically associated with those they have seen. These people did not "stop on their own," so child abusers do not. The conclusion is automatic.

Controlled thinking, however, indicates that the logic of this conclusion is flawed. There *could* be a set of child abusers who stop on their own, but they are not referred to psychologists (by definition, those referred would not have "stopped on their own"); consequently, the experience of psychologists seeing child abusers is irrelevant for determining whether any child abusers stop on their own. A dissident psychologist pointing out the flaw in colleagues' reasoning does not do so on the basis of what comes to mind (the clients he or she is seeing),

[3]Kahneman, D. Presentations at the University of Oregon and the Oregon Psychological Association Fall Conference, November 1983.
[4]Inhelder, B., and Piaget, J. (1958). *The Growth of Logical Thinking from Childhood to Adolescence*. New York: Basic Books.

but quite literally *pauses* to ask "what if." Such thinking corresponds to Piaget's definition of "formal." The sample of people that are observed (child abusers who have not stopped on their own) is regarded as one of two possible sets, and the practicing psychologist does not have the people in the other set available for observation.

The prototype of automatic thinking is the thinking involved when we drive a car successfully. We respond to stimuli not present in the environment—for example, the certainty that the light will be red before we get there. Our responses to the stimuli are so automatic that we are usually unaware of them. We "move the car" to obtain a desired position without being aware that what we are doing is turning the steering wheel a certain amount so that the car will respond as we desire. It is only when we are learning to drive that we are aware of the thought processes involved, and in fact we have really learned to drive only when we cease being aware of them. While much of driving involves "motor programs" as opposed to "mental representations," we nevertheless do "think." This thinking is so automatic, however, that we can carry on conversations at the same time, listen to music, or even create prose or music "in other parts of our head." When automatic thinking occurs in less mundane areas, it is often termed "intuition."

In contrast, a prototype of controlled thought is scientific reasoning. While the original ideas may arise intuitively (for example, the benzine ring, which may or may not have originated in a dream about a snake swallowing its own tail), they are subjected to rigorous investigation by consideration of *alternative* explanations of the phenomena the ideas seem to explain. (In fact, one way of characterizing Piaget's idea of formal thought is that it is scientific thinking applied to everyday situations.) *Conceivable* explanations are considered, and most of them are systematically eliminated by experimentation, observation, or mathematical reasoning.[5] (There are historical instances of ideas

[5]Some cognitive psychologists maintain that controlled thinking simply consists of "higher-level associations" (an entire set of mental procedures) and that sufficiently sophisticated versions of associative networks eventually will describe such thinking. Other psychologists create artificial intelligence simulations of such thought through computer programs that yield automatic access to "executive" (planning) components at certain points in a problem-solving task. The success or failure of such attempts lies in the future. The important point here is that controlled thinking involves (literally) pausing to consider a problem independent of the immediate associations that "spring to mind."

later regarded as correct being eliminated as a result of poor experimentation; Schrodinger's equations describing the behavior of the hydrogen atom is an example. The physicist Paul Dirac later claimed that Schrodinger had paid too much attention to the experimentation, and not enough to the intuition that his equations were "beautiful.")

Occasionally, the degree to which thinking is automatic rather than controlled is not clear until the process is examined carefully. For example, business executives often claim their decisions are "intuitive" but when questioned demonstrate that they have "thought through" the alternatives involved quite thoroughly before deciding which "intuition" to honor. At the other extreme, the thinking of chess grand-masters has been shown to be much more automatic than most of us novices believe it to be. When, for example, a grand-master's visual search across the chess board is traced by an "eye camera," it often indicates that the grand-master looks at the best move first. Then, the eye pattern indicates checking out alternative possibilities—most often only to come back to the original and best one. Moreover, the grand-master is not distinguished from the expert by the number of moves he "looks ahead" (anticipates); the eye-camera indicates that *both* experts and grand-masters look ahead only two or three moves, with a maximum of five. Additionally, masters and grand-masters can look at the twentieth position in a grand-masters chess match for five seconds and then reproduce it almost perfectly (approximately 90% accuracy). Experts and novices cannot do that, and no one can do it for pieces randomly placed on the board (the ability thus having nothing to do with skill at visual memory per se). These findings have been observed by Herbert Simon and William Chase; the original work was done by Adrian D. de Groot, himself a master chess player.[6] The conclusion is that grand-masters are more familiar with positions in grand-masters' games, that in five seconds they can code entire patterns of pieces as being ones familiar to them—with perhaps a displacement or two—and that they know from experience (estimated at 50,000 hours) what constitute good and bad moves from such patterns. As Chase and Simon summarized their findings, "the most important processes underlying chess mastery

---

[6]de Groot, A. D. (1965). *Thought and Choice in Chess* [translated from 1946 *Het denker van der schaker*]. The Hague: Morton. See also de Groot, A. D. (1966), Perception and memory versus thought: Some old ideas and recent findings. In Kleinmuntz, B. (ed.). *Problem Solving*. New York: Wiley, 19–50.

are ... *immediate* visual-perceptive processes rather than the subsequent logical-deductive thinking processes" (italics added).[7] Such immediate processes are automatic, like the decision to brake to avoid a collision.

The basic point of this book is that we often think in automatic ways about choice situations, that these automatic thinking processes can be described by certain psychological rules ("heuristics"), and that they systematically lead us to make poorer choices than we would by thinking in a more controlled manner about our decisions. Basically, I will present advice about how *not* to make a choice—that is, how to avoid certain automatic thought processes. As mentioned previously, this advice is based on a wide variety of research in cognitive psychology and decision making over the past thirty years.

1.3 QUALITY OF CHOICE: RATIONALITY

But what is a poor choice? The quality of a decision cannot be determined unambiguously by its outcome. For example, most of us believe it would be very silly to accept an even wager that the next time we throw a pair of unloaded dice we will roll "snake eyes." Moreover, we would regard the person who accepted such a gamble as foolish—even if he happened to roll snake eyes. On the other hand, if that person were in danger of physical harm or death at the hands of a loan shark, and if the wager were the only one available to raise enough money to avoid that harm, then the person might not be so foolish. What this example illustrates is that it is the potential outcomes, their probabilities, and their values to the decision maker *at the time the decision is made* that lead us to judge a particular choice to be wise or foolish. A general who is losing a war, for example, is much wiser to engage in a high-risk military venture than is a general who is winning a war. The failure of such a venture would not reflect unfavorably on the decision-making ability of the losing general; it is more "rational" for the losing general to take a risk. (As is pointed out in Appendix 1, many ancient Greeks and Romans, who believed that the outcomes of risky actions were determined by the gods, did not judge the wisdom of decisions in the same manner that we do.)

So what is "rationality?" Often the term is used in a purely evalua-

---

[7]Chase, W. G., and Simon, H. A. (1973). The mind's eye in chess. In Chase, W. G. (ed.). *Visual Information Processing*. London: Academic Press, 215.

tive sense: decisions I make are "rational"; those of which I disapprove are not. Occasionally, we adopt a broader perspective, and judge rationality not just in terms of approval but in terms of the "best interests" *of the person making the decision*—"best interests" as defined by *us*. Thus, for example, some of Adolph Hitler's decisions may be viewed as rational and others as irrational, despite the fact that we may disapprove of all of them.

In this book, "rationality" has a much narrower meaning; it will nevertheless provide the criterion by which we will judge the wisdom of choices. A *rational* choice can be defined as one that meets three criteria:

1. It is based on the decision maker's *current* assets. Assets include not only money, but physiological state, psychological capacities, social relationships, and feelings.
2. It is based on the possible consequences of the choice.
3. When these consequences are uncertain, their likelihood is evaluated without violating the basic rules of probability theory. (And whatever our philosophical positions about determinism versus indeterminism or free will, the consequences of our choices from our perspective are usually uncertain.)

Don't we all make decisions like that? Decidedly not. Chapter 2 will detail how it is that we are affected not only by our present state but *how we got to it*. The past is over and cannot be changed, but we often let it influence our futures in a totally irrational manner. In Chapters 3 and 4 I will show how we are sensitive not just to the possible consequences of our decisions but also to the way in which we *frame* these consequences. The second section of this book (Chapters 5 through 7) are devoted in large part to the cognitive heuristics (mental "rules of thumb") we use to judge future likelihood—heuristics that systematically violate the rules of probability theory. Then the final chapters (8 through 12) specify some ways of reaching decisions that avoid the problems specified in the previous sections.

In fact, there are common decision making procedures that have no relationship to these criteria of rationality, and hence no relation to the content of this book. They include:

1. habit
2. tradition ("That is what I/we choose.")
3. making whatever choice (you think) most other people would make

4. choosing on the basis of (your interpretation of) religious principles or mandates

5. making whatever choice led to a good outcome in the past in similar circumstances (a learning-based choice that is difficult to differentiate from one based on superstition)

6. imitating the choice of successful people you admire (Robert Boyd and Peter Richardson have pointed out that imitation of success can be quite adaptive in general, though not, for example, if it is imitation of the drug use of a particular rock or baseball star.)[8]

The three criteria of rationality have a philosophical basis. If any are violated, the decision maker can reach contradictory conclusions about what to choose—even though the conclusions are based on the same preferences and the same evidence. That is, the person violating these principles may decide that a course of action is simultaneously desirable and undesirable, or that choice A is preferable to choice B *and* choice B is preferable to choice A. For example, a business executive who attends not just to the current assets of the company but to the fact that they have been increasing or decreasing in the past could conclude both that it is wise and unwise to continue to finance a losing venture. For example, a doctor whose probabilistic reasoning follows automatic thinking principles rather than the rules of probability could decide that a patient both should and should not have an operation. By the logical *law of contradiction*, reasoning processes based on the same evidence that reach contradictory conclusions are irrational.[9] And because reality cannot be characterized in contradictory ways, irrational thinking is erroneous thinking. A proposition about reality cannot be both true and false.

Note that the characterization of rationality in the preceding paragraph is basically a *negative* one. Thinking processes that lead to contradictions are irrational, and thought that violates any of the

---

[8]See Boyd, R., and Richardson, P. J. (1982). Cultural transmission and the evolution of cooperative behavior. *Human Ecology, 10,* 325–351; and Richardson, P. J., and Boyd, R. (1984). Natural selection and culture. *BioScience, 34,* 430–434.

[9]The law of contradiction should be distinguished from the "law of the excluded middle," which asserts that either a conclusion is true or its negation is true. "Tri-value" logics deny this latter law; for example, modern mathematicians have concluded that some mathematical assertions are neither true nor false, but "undecidable."

three criteria will lead to contradictions. Rationality, then, dictates what *cannot* be concluded, *not* what can. As mentioned previously, this is not the view of "rationality" that appears in everyday language. In fact, it is not the view that has been most prevalent throughout history in Western culture. Plato, for example, believed that rationality can determine what we *should* do—for example, "hold our appetites in check."[10] His famous example was that of a thirsty person who for some reason decides not to drink. He argued that because there is clearly an "appetitive" level of the soul desiring water, there must for that person be a "rational" level of the soul countermanding this appetitive level. It is therefore "rationality" that stands in opposition to animal desires. Plato's view that rationality per se is involved in the suppression of desires was continued in the philosophy of Aristotle (for whom the "rational," and only the "rational," level of the soul is immortal), the Roman Catholic Church, Freud, and even Nazism. (Some "good Nazis"—such as Rudolph Hoess, the commandant of Auschwitz—claimed to have made "heroic" efforts to keep their gut-level sympathy for the victims of their horrific brutality from getting in the way of their rational devotion to their duty.[11]) In everyday talk we hear of persons "being overcome by irrational desire," but the view endorsed in this book—the one most accepted by modern philosophers—is that rationality leads us only to avoid trains of thought that lead to contradictions, not to particular conclusions.

1.4 SPECIFIC HISTORY: VON NEUMANN AND MORGENSTERN

Where does this idea of rationality come from? In the Western world, it began in Renaissance Italy (see Appendix A.1). The most recent impetus, however, comes from the book published in 1944 entitled *Theory of Games and Economic Behavior*[12] by mathematician John von Neumann and economist Oskar Morgenstern. Von Neumann and

---

[10]Cornford, F. M., translator (1941). *The Republic of Plato*. London: Oxford University Press.

[11]Hoess, Rudolf (1959). *Commandant at Auschwitz: Autobiography*. London: Weidenfeld and Nicholson.

[12]von Neumann, John, and Morgenstern, Oskar (1944). *Theory of Games and Economic Behavior*. New York: Wiley.

Morgenstern provided a theory of decision-making according to the principle of maximizing *expected utility*. The book says nothing about behavior per se; it is rather a purely mathematical work that discusses utility theory's relevance to optimal economic decisions. Its relevance to noneconomic decisions was assured by basing the theoretical development on *utility* (read *personal value*) rather than monetary outcomes of decisions.

This criterion of expected utility may most easily be understood by analyzing simple gambling situations. Consider, for example, a choice between two gambles:

(a)   with probability .20 win $45, otherwise nothing

(b)   with probability .25 win $30, otherwise nothing

The *expected value* of each is equal to the probability of winning multiplied by the amount to be won. Thus, the expected value of gamble (a) is .20×$45, or $9, while that of gamble (b) is .25×$30, or $7.50. People need not, however, prefer gamble (a) simply because its expected value is higher. Depending upon their circumstances they may find $30 to have more than ⅘ths the *utility* of $45, in which case they would—according to the theory—choose gamble (b). For example, an individual may be out of money at the end of a week and simply desire to have enough money to eat until the following Monday. In that situation, the individual may find the difference in utility between $30 and $45 to be negligible compared to the difference between a ¼th and a ⅕th chance of receiving any money at all. Such a preference is represented in the von Neumann and Morgenstern theory by the conclusion that .25 times that individual's utility for $30 is greater than .20 times that individual's utility for $45. Note the algebraic equivalence with concluding that $30 has more than ⅘ths the utility of $45; for let the utility of $30 be symbolized U($30) and that of $45 be symbolized U($45); then .25 × U($30) > .20 U($45), which is true if and only if U($30)/U($45) > .20/.25 = ⅘.

In point of fact, most people when asked prefer gamble (a). But when faced with the choice between the following two gambles, most prefer the one with the $30 payoff.

(a′)   with probability .80 win $45, otherwise nothing

(b′)   win $30 for sure

An individual who preferred (a) to (b) yet (b′) to (a′) would *violate* the von Neumann and Morgenstern principle of choosing according to expected utility. Using the same algebraic symbolism as before, a choice of (a) over (b) implies that $.20 \times U(\$45) > .25 \times U(\$30)$, or $U(\$45)/U(\$30) > .25/.20 = \frac{5}{4}$. A choice of (b') over (a'), however, implies that $.80 \, U(\$45) < U(\$30)$, or $U(\$45)/U(\$30) < 1/.80 = \frac{5}{4}$.

Another possible violation of expected utility theory would occur if a person were willing to pay more for one gamble than another, yet preferred the other gamble when given a choice. For example, such a person might prefer the sure $30 of alternative (b') yet—realizing that (a') has a higher expected value ($36 vs. $30)—be willing to pay more to play it than to play (b'). The theory equates the utility of each gamble with the utility of the maximal amount of money paid for playing each. The result is that by preferring the gamble for which he or she was willing to pay less, this hypothetical individual has implicitly indicated a preference for less money over more. Assuming any positive utility at all for money, that is irrational—because the greatest amount of money is equal to the lesser amount plus some more. The conditions then can lead to such contradictions that will be discussed in Chapters 6 and 8.

What is important here, however, is not just that some choices can contradict expected utility theory, but that the three criteria of rationality listed in section 1.3 are *preconditions* for the development of expected utility theory. It is based on the consideration of all alternative courses of action in terms of their possible consequences, and when the likelihood of these consequences is assessed probabilistically, the assessment is made within the rules of probability theory. (Again, there is nothing in the theory that mandates what needs a decision maker should wish to satisfy—i.e., that mandate what the utilities for various outcomes should be.) Rationality is a necessary condition for following the von Neumann and Morgenstern rules in decision making, but it is possible to be rational and make choices on a somewhat different basis, as would the person preferring (a) to (b) yet (b') to (a')—so long as that person based that choice on the amount to be won (the potential consequence) and its probability.

Theory of Games and Economic Behavior inspired a lot of work on utility theory; many mathematically oriented researchers published work that drew out consequences of maximizing expected utility that were not present in the initial formulation. Others suggested that the basic formulation might be in error, but they did not advocate abandoning the three criteria of rationality; instead, often supported by examples that were "intuitively compelling," they suggested that rational decision makers might choose according to some principle other than maximizing expected utility.

These initial works concerned the *normative* question of how decision makers *should* choose. Soon, however, people became interested in the *descriptive* question of how decision makers—people, groups, organizations, and governments—*actually* choose. Do actual choices conform to the principle of maximizing expected utility? The answer to this question appears to have depended in large part on the field of the person asking it and (relatedly) on the phenomena the person investigated. Many traditional economists, looking at the aggregate behavior of many individual decision makers in broad economic contexts, are satisfied that the principle of maximizing expected utility does describe what happens. The catch is that by specifying the theory in terms of utility rather than monetary value, it is almost always possible to *assume* that some sort of maximization principles work and then to define utilities accordingly. This is analogous to the assertion that all people are "selfish" because they do, by definition, what they "want" to do. (As James Buchanan points out, many aspects of standard economic theory tend to be "vacuously true" when phrased in terms of utilities, but demonstratively false if money is substituted for utility.[13]) At best, the only real evidence that these principles don't work in the aggregate would be a demonstration of out-and-out irrationality according to one or more of the three criteria. "The market" is not irrational in that sense, presumably because buying and selling mechanisms have evolved that prevent or counteract irrationality.

Psychologists and behavioral economists studying the decision making of individuals and organizational theorists studying single groups tend to reach the opposite conclusion. Not only do the choices of such unitary decision making units tend to violate the principle of maximizing expected utility, they are often patently irrational. (Once more, recall that irrationality as discussed here has nothing to do with the *goals* of the decision maker.) What is of more interest is that they are not just irrational, but that they are irrational in *systematic* ways—ways related to peoples' automatic thinking patterns. What is most intriguing to many of us in the field is that the systematic irrationalities can be found both in the thinking of (socially defined)

[13]Buchanan, J. M. (1978). *Cost and Choice: An Inquiry in Economic Theory*. Chicago: University of Chicago.

experts reaching decisions in their specialty areas and in the choices of subjects in psychological experiments presented with hypothetical problems. The first seven chapters of this book are devoted to a discussion of these systematic irrationalities.

1.5 GENERAL HISTORY: FROM PSYCHOANALYTIC THEORY AND BEHAVIORISM BACK TO THOUGHT

Finally, much of the work discussed in this book has been done in the last thirty years. Why? because until the mid 1950s, psychology was dominated by two traditions: psychoanalytic theory and behaviorism. Although psychologists in the 1800s studied processes involved in thinking, neither of these traditions—which became preeminent in the early 1900s—treated thought as a particularly important determinant of human behavior.

Unconscious needs and desires were the primary stuff of psychoanalytic theory; even defense mechanisms, by which these unconscious impulses could be channeled into socially acceptable—or neurotic—behaviors, were largely unconscious, and hence beyond the awareness of the individual. (People who claimed to be aware of their own defense mechanisms were denying their problems through "intellectualization"; only the analyst could figure them out.)

Although dogmatic acceptance of psychoanalytic theory still lingers on in some settings, skepticism concerning its scope was enhanced by its failure to explain one of the most important aberrations of the twentieth century, Nazism. A strong implication of the theory was that the Nazi leaders, who engaged in such monstrous activities, *had* to be suffering from the types of pathologies postulated by the theory; moreover, these pathologies had to be related to pathologies and traumas of childhood, which—according to the theory—are crucial to the development of adult disorders. "The child is father to the man."[14] In fact, a 1943 United States Office of Strategic Services

---

[14]By this statement, Freud may not have meant—as has been widely interpreted—that childhood problems necessarily lead to adult neurosis or psychosis, but rather that such problems were a *necessary condition* for such adult disorders (brought about by the "return of the repressed"). Freud was well aware that many people experienced the same childhood trauma his patients did without becoming neurotic or psychotic.

report, by Walter C. Langer, was devoted to an analysis of Adolf Hitler and a prediction of his future actions based on his "psychosexual perversion," which was later found not to exist.[15] (Supposedly incapable of normal sexual intercourse, Hitler was believed to achieve sexual release through urinating and defecating on his mistress. Moreover, Langer wrote that Hitler survived World War I by granting homosexual favors to his officers; there is no historical evidence of any such behavior. In fact, applying his philosophy of the valuelessness of the individual human life to his own as well as to others, he served without hesitation in the particularly dangerous position of "runner" [messenger], declining promotion to a safer position.) No mention was made of Hitler's basic cognitive assumptions about the world, his thinking style, the ways in which he framed problems, or the heuristics he used for solving them. Instead, the future of the world was to be predicted on the basis of his ambivalent hatred of his brutal father and his unconscious identification of Germany with his mother. Except for making the somewhat obvious prediction that Hitler wouldn't succeed, this psychoanalytic approach didn't work. Hitler did not, for example, die on the battlefield. Moreover, careful study of the defendants at the Nuremberg war crimes trials—complete with Rorschach inkblot tests—failed to reveal any particularly extraordinary psychosexual disorders or childhood problems. These men were ordinary people, much too ordinary. Years later, studying Eichman in Jerusalem, the late Hanna Arendt coined the phrase "banality of evil."[16, 17]

A strategic retreat was called. The Nazis suffered not from blatant pathologies but from a subtle "intolerance of ambiguity," one nurtured in the "German character" by the strict, authoritarian, paternalistic upbringing prevalent in German families. Scales were developed to assess such intolerance so that these ambiguity-intolerant people ("authoritarian personalities") could be distinguished from the rest of us. That didn't work either. While scores on authoritarian personality scales were correlated to behavior that might be termed "fascistic,"

[15] See Langer, W. C. (1972). *The Mind of Adolf Hitler: The Secret Wartime Report*. New York: Basic Books.

[16] Arendt, H. (1963). *Eichmann in Jerusalem: A Report on the Banality of Evil*. New York: Viking Press.

[17] It is possible that one of the psychological appeals of psychoanalytic theory is its denial that banality really is banal.

the relationship was weak.[18] Then in 1963 Stanley Milgram[19] published his striking and controversial experiments on "destructive obedience"; in them he demonstrated that a variety of subjects would administer extremely painful and potentially lethal shocks to strangers as part of a psychological experiment provided that: (1) they were urged to do so by an authority figure who "took responsibility," and (2) the victim was physically distant from them. (The shocks were not actually administered to the stranger, but the subjects thought that they were.) In effect, Milgram asked not, How were the Nazis different from us? but, How are we like the Nazis? and he was able to answer the latter question better than others had answered the former. So much for the psychoanalytic explanation for the most serious pathological behavior of the twentieth century (thus far, anyway).

According to the behavioristic approach, in contrast, the reinforcing properties of the rewards or punishments that follow a particular behavior determine whether the behavior will become habitual. Awareness is—as in the psychoanalytic tradition—unimportant; at most it is an "epiphenomenon." It was only in the late 1950s and early 1960s that a number of ingenious experimenters (for example, Don Dulaney[20] and Glen Sallows[21]) demonstrated that awareness of "reinforcement contingencies" were not only important in determining whether behavior would be repeated, but that in many areas—such as verbal behavior—such awareness was crucial. This finding contradicted the "law of effect," which maintains that the influence of a reward is automatic, although not denying that people may interpret the reward in different ways.

An ingenious experiment by Gordon Bower and Tom Trabasso

[18] Adorno, T. W.; Frenkel-Brunswick, E.; Levinson, D. J.; and Sanford, R. N. (1950). *The Authoritarian Personality*. New York: Harper and Row.
[19] Milgram, S. (1963). Behavior study of obedience. *Journal of Abnormal and Social Psychology*, *67*, 371–378.
[20] Dulaney, D. E. (1968). Awareness, rules, and propositional control: A confrontation with S-R behavior theory. In Dixon, T. R., and Horton, D. R. (eds.), *Verbal Behavior and General Behavior Theory*. Englewood Cliffs, N.J.: Prentice-Hall.
[21] Sallows, G. O.; Dawes, R. M.; and Lichtenstein, E. (1971). Subjective value of the reinforcer (RSv) and performance: The crux of the S-R vs. cognitive mediation controversy. *Journal of Experimental Psychology*, *89*, 274–281.

illustrates the necessity of postulating an active human mind in order to understand behavior.[22] The experiment involves a task termed *concept identification*. In this task, subjects are presented with stimuli that vary on many attributes—most often geometric figures that vary in size, shape, color, and various pattern characteristics. The subject's task is to sort these stimuli into two categories (most often by placing them in one of two piles) and by so doing, identify the rule (or "concept") that the experimenter has used as the basis for sorting. For example, the rule may be that deeply colored patterns are to be placed on the left and pastel ones on the right (a difficult rule to learn, given subjects' natural inclinations to attend to shape, size, and pattern). Subjects are simply told "right" or "wrong" (or "correct" or "incorrect") when they sort each stimulus, and they are judged to have identified the concept (or rule) when their sortings are always correct.

Behavioral analyses of responses to this task focused purely on the reinforcement (being told "right" or "wrong") for the subjects' choices. Awareness, to the degree to which it exists, was assumed not to affect sorting choice. Some early results appeared to support such analyses. For example, some subjects were able to achieve perfect sorting without being able to verbalize the experimenter's rule (although it turned out that they could if "pressed" but they were unsure of themselves), and in some tasks subjects did not achieve the perfect learning that would be predicted from intellectual insight (but the experimenter's rules themselves—e.g., "unitary" designs versus "multiple" ones—were ambiguous). Moreover, *average* success in concept identification *across subjects* appeared to increase gradually, much like the learning of an athletic skill.

Bower and Trabasso's experiments indicated that learning in such tasks was in fact not gradual but "all-or-none," the type of learning predicted on the basis of a hypothesis-testing mind that continually searches for the correct rule whenever the experimenter indicates that an incorrect sorting has been made. First, these investigators analyzed each subject's responses separately and determined the pattern of correct and incorrect sortings *prior to the last error*. If learning was gradual, as predicted by most reinforcement theories, the proba-

---

[22]Trabasso, T., and Bower, G. (1964). Presolution reversal and dimensional shifts in concept identification. *Journal of Experimental Psychology, 67,* 398–399.

bility of a correct sort should increase from .50 (the chance probability of being "correct"). Instead it was *stationary* at .50. The gradual increase found earlier was an artifact of averaging across subjects who had identified the correct concept at different points of time in the experiment. Moreover, an error was—in the terminology of Frank Restle[23]—a *recurrent event*. Patterns of sorting after each error were indistinguishable irrespective of the point in the experiment at which the error occurred. By making an error the subject indicated that she or he "didn't get the idea"; hence, performance was at the chance level prior to each error. An error indicated that the subject had no knowledge of the rule the experimenter wished him or her to learn.

Note that the recurrent event property of errors indicates that the subjects were limited, rather than perfect, information processors. If they had remembered each hypothesis they tested and rejected it as the result of an error, then—because there are only a limited number of *possible* hypotheses—they would have had a higher and higher probability of selecting the correct hypothesis after each error. But they did not. (In effect, they "sampled" each hypothesis "with replacement.")

However, reinforcement may work in mysterious ways. Things termed "response tendencies" may increase but only evidence themselves in all-or-none overt behavior. The recurrent event property of errors appears to contradict that possibility, but there may be a way around that as well.

Thus Bower and Trabasso devised an ingenious procedure they termed the *alternating reversal shift* procedure. Every *second* time the subject made an error, the rule was reversed. For example, subjects who had initially been told "correct" when they placed deeply colored figures on the left and pastel ones on the right were told they were correct the second time they put a pastel figure on the left (or a deeply colored one on the right), and were subsequently told correct or incorrect according to this reversed rule—until they again made a second error, at which point the rule was reversed again. Except for subjects lucky enough to identify the concept without making two errors, all would be "reinforced" a roughly equal number of times for placing pastel and deeply colored figures on the same side. If the effect

[23]Restle, F. (1962). Selection of strategy and cue learning. *Psychological Review, 69*, 329–343.

of reinforcement were automatic, subjects should never identify the concept. But in fact they do. As a group they identify the concept after being told they are incorrect (a "called error") roughly the same number of times as do those in comparison conditions where the rule is never reversed. Performance prior to the last error is stationary, and called errors—as well as "real" ones—are recurrent events.

It is not possible to explain these results without hypothesizing an active, hypothesis-testing mind mediating between the reinforcement provided by the experimenter and the behavior in the sorting task. Moreover, the mind we hypothesize is a limited mind. For example, subjects who perfectly recalled all of their previous choices and the experimenter's responses to them would be totally confused by the alternating reversal shift procedure (and suspicious that the experimenter was doing something bizarre—because they were told they were wrong much less than half the time before identifying the concept). It is precisely such a limited, hypothesis-testing mind that this book is about, and for.

Neither the psychoanalytic nor the behavioral tradition regarded individuals or groups as decision-making units that consciously weighed the consequences of various courses of action and then chose from among them. Needs associated with the Second World War and the advent of the computer has begun to focus attention on decision making prior to the experiments just described. Pilots, for example, must make fast and crucial choices among alternatives, and it became necessary to understand their thinking processes—in particular the limits of those processes under conditions of wartime stress—in order to design cockpit instrumentation with which they could cope. (Childhood experiences were irrelevant and relying on "reinforcement" could, literally, be fatal.) Intelligence and aptitude tests, which had been used since the early 1900s, became important tools for determining how each of the millions of men drafted might best fit into the war machine (not that fit was the predominant consideration in all choices). Then as computers developed after the war, it became necessary to talk about "information processing," and what psychologists of the 1800s had referred to as "thinking" was slowly subsumed in this concept. It is now legitimate for psychologists to talk about thinking, choice, mental representations, plans, goals, mental hypothesis testing, and "cognitive biases." (People such as Sir Frederick Bartlett, who studied these phenomena in the 1930s, were truly exceptional.) This book uses such concepts in discussing decision and choice.

CHAPTER

My colleagues, we have come too
far to waver now, we have accomplished too much to give up now, we
have struggled too long to fail now.
Speaker of the House Thomas P.
O'Neill, Jr., arguing in favor of
tax reform, September 25, 1986

2

The Future
and the Past

2.1 CONFUSION ABOUT CURRENT MONETARY ASSETS: SUNK COSTS

Would you rather pay $100 to be where you wanted to be or where you didn't want to be?[1] The answer to this question seems obvious. Now let's rephrase the question.

You and your companion have driven half-way to a resort. Responding to a reduced-rate advertisement, you have made a nonrefundable $100 deposit to spend the weekend there. Both you and your companion feel slightly bad physically and out of sorts psychologically. *Your assessment of the situation is that you and your companion would have a much more pleasurable weekend at home.* Your companion says it is "too bad" you have reserved the room because you both would much rather spend the time at home, but you can't afford to waste $100. You agree. Further, you both agree that given the way you both feel, it is extraordinarily unlikely you will have a better time at the resort than you would at home. Do you drive on or turn back? If you drive on, you are behaving as if you prefer paying $100 to be where you don't want to be than to be where you want to be.

Look at the problem another way. The moment you paid the $100 your net assets decreased by $100. That decrease occurred several days before your drive half-way to the resort. Is the fact that your net assets have decreased by $100 sufficient reason for deciding to spend the weekend at a place you don't want to be?

The point is, you reiterate, that if you turn back you will have *wasted* the $100; waste not, want not. Perhaps you are slightly obese due to the same reasoning. Once you have paid for your food, you feel compelled to eat it all in order to avoid wasting it—even though the outcome of that particular policy is to decrease your dining pleasure and make you fat.

If the $100 could be refunded, you would certainly return home; otherwise you must remain a slave to the check you wrote (or to your credit card number). What does that imply? Once the deposit was made, you had a certain net asset level. Now, if you could only get a refund and thereby *increase* your net assets by $100, you would be willing to do what you prefer to do—otherwise not. That's rational?

The $100 *you have already paid* is technically termed a *sunk cost.* Rationally, sunk costs *should not effect decisions about the future.*

---

[1]I am indebted to my daughter Molly Dawes, who was 15 years old at the time, for this phrasing of the question.

When you behave as if your nonrefundable deposit is equivalent to a current investment, you are *honoring* a sunk cost. You certainly would not send the resort a check for $100 for the privilege of staying home. That, too, would be irrational, because you would simultaneously conclude that $100 is worth more to you than nothing, a price for which you could remain at home. You are not paying *now* for the opportunity to go to the resort, although *at the time* you did so it might have been a very wise decision. Now, however, the only choice available that avoids the contradictions specified earlier is the one you judge to be the more valuable—turning back. Honoring sunk costs is irrational. (I'm excluding the possibility that you have motives *other* than enjoying yourself for going to the resort, or that you wish to create the impression you are at the resort when you actually are not. The information presented in the examples in this book is to be taken as the total information available to the decision maker. Naturally, if there is other information, or if there are other reasons for engaging in a behavior that are not specified in the examples, then the choice might be different.)

People honor sunk costs:

"To terminate a project in which $1.1 billion has been invested represents an unconscionable mishandling of taxpayers' dollars." —Senator Jeremiah Denton, November 4, 1981

"Completing Tennessee–Tombigbee is not a waste of taxpayers' dollars. Terminating the project at this late stage of development would, however, represent a serious waste of funds already invested." —Senator James Sasser, November 4, 1981[2]

Both senators were responding to critics who had pointed out that the total value of the Tennessee–Tombigbee Waterway Project, if completed, would be *less than the amount of money yet to be spent completing it.* Of course, these statements may be mere rationalizations for continued expense that will create employment in the state. The point, however, is that both senators believed that the arguments presented were compelling—or they would not have made them. (I'm assuming that politicians do not present public arguments they believe the listeners will categorize as inane or stupid.) I am criticizing the logic of the argument, not the possibility of ulterior motives for presenting it.

[2]See Arkes, H. R., and Blumer, C. (1985). The psychology of sunk cost. *Organizational Behavior and Human Performance, 35,* 129–140.

The irrationality is clear. The federal budget deficit was $1.1 billion more than it would have been had the project not been started. That is used as a justification for spending money to create something worth less than the money yet to be spent. Clearly, like lost lives, dollars must not be spent in vain. Limiting concern to the *future* consequences of choices is the best way to avoid honoring sunk costs. Conversely, honoring sunk costs violates the first criterion of rationality—that decisions should be based only on future consequences. As illustrated by the example, such violation yields contradictions.

2.2 THE SUNK COST PROBLEM: OTHER ASSETS

If the irrational "payment" of sunk costs were limited to money, it might be possible to educate business and laypeople to ignore them. Irrationality fails, for reasons we discussed in Chapter 1; and the rational abandonment of sunk costs often succeeds—as, for example, when Lockheed stock jumped 7¾ points in 1981 the day after it finally abandoned its thirteen-year-old Tristar L1011 program into which it had sunk $2.5 billion.[3]

Concern with sunk costs is pervasive in other domains of our lives as well. We do not wish to *invalidate* the past, particularly our own pasts, by ignoring sunk costs. It is not just vanity that keeps us from admitting that we have invested our past resources—monetary and psychic—in a venture that we should now abandon. We wish to view our lives as cohesive. People who turn back due to discomfort without being affected by the fact they have already paid the resort $100 may be regarded not just as financially wasteful, but as disordered or silly. Businesspeople who abandon an unprofitable line may be regarded not as wise, but as vacillating—certainly not the "dynamic" type we all admire.

For example, Ford Motor Company wisely abandoned the Edsel as not suitable to American taste and later marketed the popular Mustang. In the 1964 presidential elections, however, the Republican candidate, Barry Goldwater publicly chided the former president of Ford, then the Secretary of Defense, for having first promoted and then abandoned the Edsel—even though it could equally well be maintained that the Edsel venture provided Ford with invaluable

---

[3]Referenced in Staw, B. M. (1982). Counterforces to change. In Goodman, P. S. (ed.). *Change in Organizations*. San Francisco: Jossey-Bass, 87–121.

information that led to the tremendous success of the Mustang. This same Secretary of Defense showed a much greater commitment to a sunk cost in Southeast Asia—as did the subsequent Secretary of State, who wrote: "We could not simply walk away from an enterprise involving two administrations, five allied countries, and thirty-one thousand dead as if we were switching off a television channel."[4] The kindest interpretation of these commitments is that because the leaders of *other* nations honor sunk costs, the United States would have suffered a severe blow to its prestige had it failed to do so.

If, indeed, abandonment of a sunk cost negatively affects reputation, then it may be wise not to do it. Reputational damage, however, leads to *future* problems, and it is only with respect to such future consequences that honoring sunk costs should make a difference. If the future cost to reputation outweighs the cost of paying a sunk cost, it is rational to pay it.

Consider, now, our beliefs about addictions. "Knowledgeable" people confidently maintain that it is *impossible* to stop the course of an addiction until the addict has reached "the bottom of the bottle." Why? To my knowledge, no studies, have demonstrated this. In fact, studies that are conducted examine people who are *already* in the advanced stages of addiction—perhaps comparing them to people who claim not to be addicted at all—so it is logically impossible to estimate the number of people who stop somewhere along the way. Of course it is possible to study people *prospectively*; such a study would begin with people who are not addicted but might become so (anyone—or perhaps people presumed to have a genetic disposition to an addiction); then, and only then, would it be possible to see whether people stop before reaching "the bottom," and how many people do so. Such studies are rare. The fact that such studies are "classics" when they are done—for example, those by George Vaillant—attests to their rarity. (Asserting that no one stops half-way is like the assertion discussed in Chapter 1 that child abuse will not stop without intervention. Given that these colleagues' evidence is based entirely on contact with a "clinical" population—that is, with people who haven't stopped—it is logically impossible to reach this conclusion.)

So why the belief? Consider the problem from the point of view of the person wishing to kick an addiction. By definition, the addiction has been ongoing and has led to distress and suffering—or the person

---

[4]Referenced in Howard, M. (1984). *The Causes of War*. Cambridge: Harvard University Press, 232.

would not wish to stop. If, however, it is possible to stop now, why was it not possible to stop earlier, for example, before trouble arose? That's a reasonable question, which remains unanswered *unless* being at rock bottom is a necessary precondition for stopping. Conversely, if it was not possible to stop earlier, why should it be possible now? Again, without the belief, that question is perfectly reasonable—and perhaps haunting.

Consider, now, the assessment of the addicted person who does *not* believe in the necessity of reaching the bottom but who has some hope of quitting:

1. I can quit now.
2. I could have quit earlier, but didn't.
3. My addiction has caused me—and perhaps others—significant distress, or worse.

This is a very painful set of beliefs. From a sunk cost perspective, the past has been "wasted" if the addict does now indeed quit. One possible way of justifying such costs is to conclude that one is simply a victim, couldn't quit, and can't (a not very petty or pretty consistency).

In contrast, the assessment:

1. I can quit now.
2. I couldn't quit earlier because I hadn't reached rock bottom.
3. My addiction has caused me—and perhaps others—significant distress, or worse.

provides the addict with no sunk costs. In fact, previous addicted behavior is now assessed as a *benefit*, because it put the addict in a position to quit. ("Thank God, I'm an alcoholic!") I am not maintaining that the "bottom of the bottle" hypothesis is false, just that the evidence for it is not there, and that it is explicable in terms of our irrational need to justify sunk costs (and may therefore be "therapeutic" even if false).

Of course, there is an alternative assessment:

1. The past cannot be changed.
2. Today is the first day of the rest of my life.
3. Trying to quit can't hurt and might help.

A final explanation for our devotion to sunk costs lies in our belief not just in coherent behavior but in *committed* behavior. ("Love is not love which alters when it alteration finds." —Shakespeare.) If I have made sacrifices for a reason, I should continue doing so. To behave otherwise would be cowardly. But while love may not be love that alters when it alteration finds, behavior that doesn't is just plain stupid.

2.3 THE RATIONALITY OF CONSIDERING ONLY THE FUTURE

Emphasis on merely ignoring sunk costs has arisen only with modern decision theory, which in turn is based on probabilistic thinking that arose in the Italian Renaissance. This thinking is based on the idea that probabilities can be assessed properly only with reference to *future* events. For example, consider a fair coin that has been tossed four times and is to be tossed a fifth time. The probability of its landing heads is ½. The pattern of previous results is irrelevant because they have already occurred and do not affect the way in which the coin is handled when it is tossed for the fifth time. For example, four previous heads do not make a fifth head unlikely—even though in general four heads and a tail is an outcome five times more likely than five heads. Given four heads have already occurred, a fifth head is as likely as a tail.

That the idea of limiting such probability assessment to future possibilities was not intuitively obvious prior to the Italian Renaissance can be inferred from answers proposed to a famous problem in Fra Luca Paccioli's *Summa de arithmetica, geometrica, proportioni e proportionalita*, published in 1494. The problem: "A and B are playing a fair game of *balla*. They agree to continue until one has won a total of six rounds. The game actually stops when A has won five rounds and B three rounds. How should the stakes be divided?"[5] Paccioli's answer: 5:3.

One problem with this answer—dividing the stake proportionally to the number of games won—is that it implies A should get the entire stake whether he has won one, two, three, four, or five games in a row, although he clearly is in a much better position the more simultaneous games he has won. Further, it implies that there would be a sudden discontinuity in the rule for dividing the stake if A were to move from leading 5:4 to winning 6:4 (in which case the stake is split 1:0). Moreover, it implies that A is more deserving when he is ahead 2 to 1 than

---

[5]The history of this problem is discussed in Chapter 4 of David, N. (1962), *Games, Gods, and Gambling*. London: Charles Griffin.

ahead 5 to 3, even though it is clear that he has a much better chance of winning six games from the latter lead. Proposals based on the differences between the number of games won have, *mutatis mutandis*, the same problems.

It was not until 64 years later that G. F. Peverone proposed a solution that doesn't have any of the problems listed above (or others). According to Peverone's solution:

1. The more consecutive games won the higher the proportion of the stake;

2. The same rule is applied once a player has won six games as is applied earlier; and

3. A player ahead 5 to 3 receives a higher proportion of the stake than does a player ahead 2 to 1.

The solution is based on two principles. First, where p is the probability that A will be the first person to win six games, p is the proportion of the stake that should be given to A. Second, p is computed by analyzing the number of games *remaining* before A or B wins a total of six. Peverone actually miscomputed p. The correct computation begins by noting that when A is ahead 5 to 3, the only way B can win six first is to win three consecutive games. Since the game is fair, that probability is $(½) \times (½) \times (½)$, or ⅛. Hence, A's probability of winning is ⅞; A should receive ⅞ths of the stake. (Peverone concluded ⅝ths.)

Similar calculations can be used to determine A's proportion of the stake when A has won five consecutive games, when A is ahead 2 to 1, and so on. When, of course, A has won six, he has the probability of 1 of having won, and hence, receives the whole stake.

In general, the past is relevant, *only for estimating current probabilities and the desirability of future states*. It is rational to conclude that a coin that has landed heads in 19 of 20 previous flips is probably biased, and that therefore the probability it lands heads on the 21st flip is greater than ½. It is not rational to estimate the probability of a head on the 21st toss by assigning a probability to the entire pattern of results *including those that have already occurred*. (Again, the probability of five straight heads when tossing a fair coin is 1/32; in contrast, the probability of a fifth head *given* four heads in the past is ½.) *Rational estimation of probabilities and rational decision making resulting from this estimation are based on a very clear demarcation between the past and the future.*

That people do not naturally make this demarcation in their own lives is evidenced by the recent success (circa 1958 on) of *attribution theory* in social psychology. Briefly, attribution theory examines the conclusions people reach about their own and other people's characteristics and the *effects* of these conclusions on future judgment and choice—as one early attribution theorist put it, "what we say to ourselves about ourselves and what that does to ourselves" (and to others). For example, one finding of this theory is the "fundamental attribution error," by which we attribute others' behavior largely to personality factors and our own behavior largely to situational factors to which we respond.[6] Thus, for example, a candidate for parole who explains the situational factors leading to his crime may be judged either to be lying or to be lacking insight into his character defects, even though he is truthfully explaining the reasons for the crime as he views them. In contrast, a candidate who duplicitously claims to have seen the reasons as residing in his own past antisocial characteristics—which have now changed (e.g., through a religious conversion)—may be believed.

The relevance of attribution theory is that attributions ("schemas") are *not* of the form

"When confronted with this type of situation in the past, I have (he has) done X; therefore, it is probable that in the future in this situation . . . ."

but of the form

"When confronted with this type of situation in the past, I have (he has) done X; therefore, I *am* (he *is*) the *type* of person who *will* . . . ."

This distinction is not trivial. If, for example, I have acted weakly in a situation in the past, it is rational to conclude that I have a high probability of acting weakly again in a similar situation in the future. But that is a half-full/half-empty glass, because this probability assessment may in fact forewarn me to take precautions *against* acting weakly. If, in contrast, I conclude that since I have acted weakly in the past I *am* a *weak person*, then I have woven myself a verbal straightjacket that may actually increase the probability I behave in a way I

---

[6]Jones, E. E., and Nisbett, R. E. (1972). The actor and the observer: Divergent perceptions of the causes of behavior. In Jones, E. E.; Kanouse, D. E.; Kelley, H. H.; Nisbett, R. E.; Valins, S.; and Weiner, B. (eds.), *Attribution: Perceiving the Causes of Behavior*. Morristown, N.J.: General Learning Press.

wish not to behave.

> "Whoever observes himself arrests his own development. A caterpillar that wanted to know itself well would never become a butterfly." — André Gide, *Les Nouvilles Nourritures*, 1935
>
> "Life could not continue without throwing the past into the past, liberating the present from its burdens." —Paul Tillich, *The Eternal Now*

Attributions of stable characteristics—which forge an inappropriately strong link between past and future—can easily become self-fulfilling prophecies. (Not all prophecies are self-fulfilling; there must be a *mechanism*. Some prophecies may even be self-negating— for example, the prophecy of reckless drivers that "nothing bad can happen to me.")

The point here is that attribution theory describes some significant aspects of human behavior quite well. We continually make attributions about ourselves and others. For example, when asked to describe themselves, first-graders in one U.S. school system used roughly 86% action verbs (describing what they *do*) and only 14% state-of-being verbs (describing what they *are*). The percentage of being verbs used increased steadily over grade levels until the ratio was 50–50 by the senior year of high school.[7] The unfortunate thing about such attributions is that they not only reflect perceived sunk costs ("I am; therefore I must continue"), but that they are highly malleable as well. Social psychology experimenters have been able to change subjects' attributions (at least temporarily) with minimal manipulations such as mumbling "good job," "hmmm," "that's not quite as good as average," and the like. More dramatic manipulations have convinced male subjects that they were more attracted to some *Playboy* "playmates" than to others by giving them phony feedback about their heart rates as they viewed the magazine pictures,[8] or that they have "homosexual

---

[7]McGuire, W. J. (1984). Search for the self: Going beyond self-esteem and the reactive self. In Zucker, R. A.; Aronoff, J.; and Rabin, A. I. (eds.), *Personality and the Prediction of Behavior*. New York: Academic Press, 73–120.

[8]Valins, S. A. (1966). Cognitive effects of false heart rate feedback. *Journal of Personality and Social Psychology*, 7, 345–350. In fact, male heart rate decreases (and peripheral blood volume increases) with sexual arousal, but most people don't know that, and the subjects were presented with phony feedback that their heart rate *increased* more when they viewed some pictures than when they viewed others.

tendencies" by having a needle that supposedly indicates unconscious libidinal tendencies deflect sharply when they view a photograph of a nude man. (Such experimentation is now considered unethical.)

One possible implication is that people with negative self-attributions (for example, "I am a vulnerable, sick, weak, incompetent person") should not be encouraged to develop positive ones ("I am an invulnerable, well, strong, competent person," at which point the changed person is elected President and starts a nuclear war), but to abandon the self-attribution process altogether. "Shut up to yourself about yourself. What you say might be a trap, and it probably isn't true anyway." Given that we have been constantly bombarded with verbal descriptions—usually evaluative—of ourselves throughout our lives, that's a hard prescription.

In summary, rational decisions are based on an assessment of future possibilities and probabilities. The past is relevant only insofar as it provides information about possible and probable futures. Rational decision making demands the abandonment of sunk costs, unless such abandonment creates future problems outweighing the benefits of abandonment. Today really is the first day of the rest of our lives.

Before concluding this chapter, it is necessary to point out again that any "loss of face" involved in abandoning sunk costs may be a *real* cost for the decision maker. In fact, such a change in reputation is a *future* cost that one might choose to bear in abandoning a sunk cost. The auto maker who abandons the Edsel may be derided for making a "gutless" decision. The alcoholic who quits drinking without finding God may be reviled by drinking companions and viewed with suspicion by the "therapeutic establishment." Such costs are perfectly reasonable costs to consider in determining whether or not to abandon a particular course of action. The sunk cost per se should not be a factor, however. So long as other people believe in honoring sunk costs, the person who does not may be regarded as somewhat aberrant. (A student once stated that after taking a course on decision making she found it more difficult to discuss decisions with her friends, and sometimes her friends thought her something of a kook.) The point is to deal with the possibility of mindless social disapproval as a potential consequence of your decisions. (A suggestion for doing so is given at the end of Chapter 3.) And as will be argued in Chapter 11, our concern with derogation for abandoning sunk costs may be grossly exaggerated anyway. It is not rational to honor sunk costs mindlessly.

CHAPTER

For there is nothing either good or
bad but thinking makes it so.
William Shakespeare,
Hamlet

3

Framing
Consequences

3.1 EXAMPLES OF FRAMING EFFECTS

Imagine that I have given you $200. I now offer you more, in the form of one of two options:

Option 1. I will give you an additional $100.

Option 2. I will toss a fair coin. If it lands heads, I will give you an additional $200; if it lands tails, I will give you no additional money.

Most people select option 1 of this hypothetical offer.

Now consider a variation of this. I begin by giving you $400, but there is a slight penalty involved. You must choose one of two penalty options:

Penalty Option 1. You must give me back $100.

Penalty Option 2. I will toss a fair coin. If it lands heads, you must give me back $200; if it lands tails, you may keep all the money I gave you.

Presented with this hypothetical choice, most people select penalty option 2.

These two situations are not just variations of each other; they are identical. In both, you are presented with a choice between a certainty of $300—either by taking the additional $100 or by giving back the $100—versus a 50–50 chance of obtaining $200 or $400. The choice that most people make is inconsistent. When they are presented with the problem phrased in terms of *gaining* money, they tend to choose the "sure thing"—to be *risk-averse* in the technical terminology. When the options are presented in terms of losses, however, people tend to avoid certainty; they are *risk-seeking*.

Now consider the following choice, which is much more like the ones that social policy makers must make, for they often do in fact face choices involving life and death. Imagine that the U.S. is preparing for an outbreak of an unusual Asian disease that is expected to kill 600 people. Two alternative programs to combat the disease have been proposed. Scientific estimates of the consequences of the programs are as follows:

If program A is adopted, 200 people will be saved.

If program B is adopted, there is a 1/3 probability that 600 people will be saved and a 2/3 probability that no people will be saved.

Which program would you favor?

That question was posed to university students by Amos Tversky and Daniel Kahneman. Seventy-two percent chose program A. As in the first example, the alternatives were presented in terms of gains— lives saved—and the subjects were risk-averse. A second group of respondents, however, was presented with the same situation but a different formulation of the alternative programs:

If program C is adopted, 400 people will die.

If program D is adopted, there is a 1/3 probability that nobody will die and a 2/3 probability that 600 will die.

Which program would you favor?

Only 22% of the students chose program C, while 78% chose program D. Yet program C is identical to program A (400 people dying being equivalent to 200 living), and program D is equivalent to program B. The difference in the way the programs were presented led to a whopping 50% difference in their endorsement.

This is irrational—the second criterion of rationality is that choice be made on the basis of the consequences of behavior—yet with identical consequences people choose different courses of action. The way in which a consequence is presented is termed its *frame*. While competent debaters have always realized that such framing is a very important component of persuasion, it is only within the last ten years that psychologists have been investigating *framing effects* systematically.

Moreover, psychologists have discovered that framing effects are particularly strong in matters regarding life and death. Why? Because the first life saved is the most important, just as is the first life lost. Thus, decision makers are risk-averse when questions are framed in terms of saving lives and risk-seeking when the identical questions are framed in terms of losing lives. The number of lives lost plus the number of lives saved, however, must equal the number of people at risk for death. Hence, the contradiction.

In fact, the contradiction concerning saving versus losing lives is even deeper than indicated by the inconsistent responses. Researchers such as Baruch Fischhoff, Sarah Lichtenstein, and Paul Slovic have asked people not only to make such hypothetical choices, but also to enunciate general policies concerning death from various causes. A typical study is that in which members of the League of Women voters were asked both to make hypothetical choices and to state their overall philosophies. With great consistency, they opted for avoiding risk when questions were framed in terms of saving lives. However, when they were asked to state how serious it would be for various numbers of people in society to lose their lives, they consistently indicated that such seriousness *accelerated* with the number of lives lost. Thus, a large airplane accident was seen as more than twice as serious as a small one with half the number of fatalities (which presumably would have less than half the disruptive effect on society). In a more extreme situation, it is probable that most of us would agree that a nuclear attack involving 80 million casualties would be more than twice as bad as one involving 40 million, and, at the greatest extreme, a nuclear war annihilating all life on earth would be more than twice as bad as one annihilating "only" half.

The same accelerating concern for possible deaths is implied by parents who fly on separate airplanes when their children are not with them. By doing so, they reduce the probability that both of them will be killed, while simultaneously increasing the probability that *at least one* of them will be—since the probability that one of two planes will crash is greater than the probability that either alone will crash. As will be rigorously demonstrated in Chapter 8, this choice to fly on separate planes also implies, according to the von Neumann and Morgenstern theory, that the implicit *dis*utility of both dying is more than twice as great as the disutility of one of them dying.

These positively accelerating concerns for loss of life are totally inconsistent with risk aversion for saving lives. For example, if 600 deaths is more than three times as bad as 200, then it is contradictory to opt for 200 of 600 people being "saved" for sure rather than a 1/3 chance of saving all 600. Nevertheless, people appear consistently risk-averse when presented with *single* choices in which the alternatives are phrased in terms of lives saved.

3.2 THE CONSISTENCY OF FRAMING EFFECTS

Is framing verbal trickery? The answer is no, for two reasons. First, people who make such contradictory choices often stand by them when the inconsistency is pointed out. Second, framing effects can be explained by simple psychological principles. This first result was demonstrated by Scott B. Lewis in 1985. Lewis noted that when previous researchers had demonstrated contradictions, they had typically done so by asking the same question framed in two ways to two different groups of people. (Primarily interested in demonstrating the existence of these effects, these researchers had perhaps avoided making the contradiction obvious to their subjects by asking them to respond to the same question framed in different ways.) What Lewis did was to take six pairs of questions that had been shown to be susceptible to framing effects in the previous literature, and to present both frames of each pair to a group of undergraduate subjects (although there were always at least two other intervening questions between each pair). His subjects, nevertheless, were inconsistent in the manner of the two examples we have discussed: they were *risk-averse* when the alternatives were stated positively, and risk-prone (*certainty-averse*) when the alternatives were stated negatively. (When Lewis's subjects made contradictory choices, 75% of those choices were consistent with risk aversion for gains and certainty aversion for losses.) Lewis pointed out these inconsistencies to his subjects, and almost all of them recognized that they had in fact been inconsistent, but when he gave them the opportunity to change their responses in order to achieve consistency, they did so only half of the time. Moreover, when they were presented with new pairs of logically equivalent questions framed to elicit different choices, the rate of inconsistency dropped only from 52% to 47%.

Eric Johnson, Scott Hawkins, and I have replicated the result that framing effects can lead individuals to make such inconsistent choices. We found, for example, that over half of our subjects were inconsistent in the life versus death problem we presented, and our sample of students was four times the size of Lewis's. Most importantly, we found that the degree of inconsistency was as high within single subjects (who responded to identical questions framed in two different ways within five minutes of each other) as between subjects. Whereas verbal tricks lose their effectiveness once they are understood, framing effects are stable.

3.3 HISTORY: FROM THE JUST NOTICEABLE DIFFERENCE TO PROSPECT THEORY

Framing effects are not only resistant to change; they are consistent with fundamental psychological principles. Understanding the theory and research on which these principles are based can be enhanced by a brief historical description, going back to the 1850s.

In that period, many psychologists asked a simple question: how much must the physical intensity of a stimulus be augmented for people to notice the difference? For example, if people are first given a one-gram weight, how much heavier must another weight be for them to notice that it is in fact heavier? Psychologist Max Weber (1795–1878) noted that, in general, the amount the stimulus must be incremented (or decremented) physically for people to notice a difference is proportional to the stimulus itself; that is, it must be incremented (or decremented) by a certain *fraction* of its physical intensity in order to achieve what is technically termed a *just noticeable difference*, or *j. n. d.* (The standard procedure currently used for determining the *j. n. d.* is to require people to judge which of two stimuli is more intense, and to define this noticeable difference as occurring whenever the subjects are correct 75% of the time; that figure is chosen by defining the *j. n. d.* as the intensity at which people can note a difference 50% of the time, and assuming that when they cannot note it they guess correctly 50% of the time; 50%+[50% of 50%]=75%.)

The proportion that stimuli must be incremented or decremented to obtain a just noticeable difference in intensity has been termed a *Weber fraction*. The Weber fraction for weight, for example, is approximately 2.8%. The fact that this fraction is more or less constant for any particular type of intensity has been termed *Weber's law*. It does not hold exactly over all dimensions and ranges of intensity, but the fact that deviations from it are not large has allowed considerable research since it was first proposed. It is useful as a rough approximation.

In the 1880s, the psychologist Gustav Fechner (1801–1887) proposed that just noticeable differences could be conceptualized as units of *psychological* intensity, as opposed to physical intensity. It immediately follows that psychological intensity is a logarithm of physical intensity.[1] The proposal that psychological intensity is the logarithm

---

[1] Why a logarithm? Consider weight. What is desired is that the psychological difference between 1.028 times any weight X and that weight X is equal to the difference between 1.028 times Y and Y for any other weight Y. The logarithm of 1.028X is equal to the logarithm of 1.028 plus the logarithm of X, while the logarithm of X is, of course, simply the logarithm of X. Taking the difference between these two logarithms therefore yields a constant value, the logarithm of 1.028, which is the same value obtained by taking the difference between the logarithm of 1.028Y and the logarithm of Y. In contrast, the difference between the unmodified values of 1.028X and X versus 1.028Y and Y is dependent on the values of X and Y themselves, as are the squares of the values, the square roots of the values, and so on. In general, when a transformation is desired that translates the difference between aX and X to be equal to the difference between aY and Y, the logarithmic function is mandated.

of physical intensity became known as *Fechner's law*. Again, it does not hold over all dimensions and ranges of intensity, but it is a good approximate rule. In fact, it has been so well accepted that when the psychological intensity of noise was measured in bells and decibels, these units were defined as the logarithm of the physical amplitude. (A *bell* is a tenfold increase in physical amplitude, while a *decibel* is an increase of 1.26; $1.26^{10}=10$; hence, the logarithm of $1.26^{10}=10$ times the logarithm of 1.26; that is, 10 decibels to a bell.) This logarithmic function is illustrated in Figure 3.1.

The logarithmic function follows what may be termed the "law of diminishing returns," or the "law of decreasing marginal returns." Independently, economists have proposed that this law also characterizes the *utility* (again read "personal value") of money and possessions for individuals. Two million dollars would be worth less than twice the value of $1 million to the reader of this book—even when these two amounts refer to money after taxes. This diminishing-return characteristic of what is termed the *utility function* for money need not yield a precise logarithmic pattern.[2]

Figure 3.1 Illustration of Fechner's law

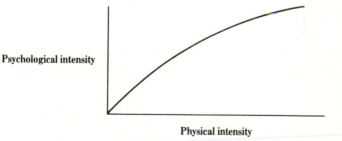

Psychological intensity

Physical intensity

----

[2]This law can be characterized quite simply in calculus terms by noting that the slope of the function diminishes over amount; that is, the second derivative is negative. Knowledge of calculus is not assumed for readers of this book. The essential idea can be illustrated with the phrase "the rate of inflation is down." What is meant by this phrase is that inflation is continuing—dollars are still becoming worth less and less—but that the *degree* to which this is happening is diminishing; for example, a previous inflation rate of 7% has been cut to 3%. A function (graph) whose degree of increase is always decreasing is, by definition in calculus, one with a negative second derivative.

In the late 1970s, Kahneman and Tversky proposed what they term *prospect theory*. A basic tenant of this theory is that the law of diminishing returns applies not only to intensity but to *good and bad quantitative consequences of decisions*. There are many components of this theory, but only two of them need concern us here in order to understand framing effects:

1. An individual views monetary consequences in terms of changes from a *reference* level, which is usually the individual's *status quo*. The value of the outcomes for both positive and negative consequences of the choice then has the diminishing-returns characteristic.

2. The resulting value function is steeper for losses than for gains.

Now consider the first problems presented in this chapter. A gain of $100 has, by the diminishing-returns characteristic of the value function, greater than half the value of a gain of $200; hence, people prefer the certainty of $100 to the 50% chance of $200. But at the same time, a loss of $100 is more than half as negative as the loss of $200, so the people prefer a 50% chance of giving back $200 to a certainty of giving back $100. The irrational contradiction occurs because people do not look at the final outcomes of their choices, but rather allow the reference level to change. When they have been told they are given $200, they accept that status quo as their reference level; when they are told they have been given $400, they accept that. Thus, they make contradictory choices even though the final outcomes are identical in both problems. Prospect theory likewise explains the contradictory choices in life-or-death decisions. Two hundred lives saved is more than 1/3 as valuable as 600, while 400 lost is more than 2/3 as bad as 600 lost.

As Kahneman and Tversky point out, the psychological justification for viewing consequences in terms of the status quo can be found in the general principle of *adaptation* (discussed briefly in the preface to this book). They write:

> Our perceptual apparatus is attuned to the evaluation of changes or differences rather than to the evaluation of absolute magnitudes. When we respond to attributes such as brightness, loudness, or temperature, the past and present context of experience defines an adaptation level, or reference point, and stimuli are perceived in relation to this reference point. . . . Thus, an object at a given temperature may be experienced as hot or cold to the touch depending on the temperature to which one has

adapted. The same principle applied to non-sensory attributes such as health, prestige, and wealth. The same level of wealth, for example, may imply abject poverty for one person and great riches for another—depending on their current assets.[3]

The difference between prospect theory and the standard economic theory of diminishing marginal utility is that the latter assumes that decision makers frame their choices in terms of the *final* consequences of their decisions. For example, as mentioned earlier, it is quite reasonable for a general who believes that he is losing a war to take a very large risk because he sees his current state as negative, while it is not very reasonable for a general winning a war to do so. The diminishing-return shape of the utility function guarantees that any gamble between two negative outcomes is *less* negative in terms of utility than the corresponding certainty, and the utility for gambles between the positive outcomes is also less. (Ironically, stock brokers often advise poorer people to be conservative and wealthier ones to take chances, which makes no sense at all from this framework—especially given that poorer people who invest their money conservatively are virtually destined to remain poor, while the wealthy have nowhere to go but down.) Figure 3.2a presents the prospect theory analysis, and Figure 3.2b illustrates the standard economic analysis of the gamble that begins this chapter.

Recall that the choice is between a final outcome of $300 versus a 50–50 chance of $200 or $400. These final outcomes form the basis of the expected utility theory analysis. If there is marginal decreasing utility for money, the average of the utility for $200 and that for $400 is less than the utility for $300. This average is indicated by a point on the line connecting the $200 point and the $400 point; the shape of the curve dictates that this line will always lie entirely *beneath* it. If the decision maker has a positive asset level that is added to the options in determining final consequences, the line connecting these points still lies entirely beneath the curve—as they are moved to the right—so the certainty of $300 is still preferred. In fact, a line connecting *any* two points will lie entirely beneath the curve.

Now consider the choice framed in terms of being given $200 and then asked for a preference between $100 more for sure versus a 50–50

[3]Kahneman, D., and Tversky, A. (1979). Prospect theory: An analysis of decision under risk, *Econometrica*, *47*, 263–291; quote on page 277.

Figure 3.2 (a) Standard utility analysis versus (b) prospect theory analysis

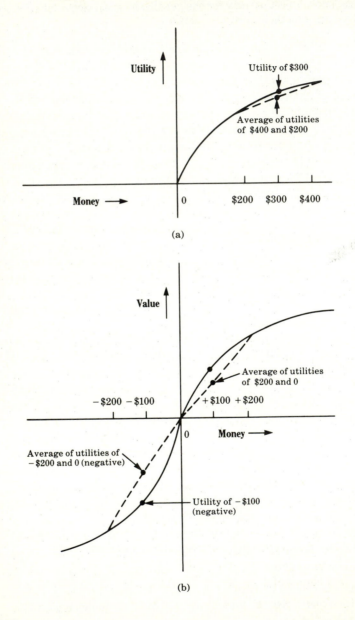

chance of $200 more or nothing. According to prospect theory, the decision maker does not look at the final outcomes ($300 versus a 50–50 chance of $200 or $400) but rather views each choice between options in terms of gains or losses from his or her status quo (reference level). The $200 has been incorporated into that reference level, and because the shape of the utility postulated by prospect theory is also marginally decreasing, the decision maker again opts for the additional certainty of $100.

Suppose now that the choice is framed in terms of being given $400 and being required to either give back $100 or take a 50–50 chance of giving back nothing or $200. The final outcomes remain the same. According to prospect theory, however, the decision maker analyzes the options in terms of losses from the status quo (now including the $400). Given the (hypothesized) marginally decreasing utility function for losses as they get *more* severe (Figure 3.2b), the average of the disutility of −$200 and nothing is not as bad as the disutility of −$100. (This result is illustrated by the point on the line connecting the relevant outcomes; on the negative side, a marginally decreasing utility function will guarantee that the line connecting any two points lies wholly *above* the curve.) The choice, according to prospect theory, is for the 50–50 gamble, and that is in fact the most common choice when people are presented with this hypothetical problem.

Before discussing examples outside a gambling context, I will illustrate prospect theory predictions with the example used in Chapter 1 to illustrate expected utility theory. It involved choice between two pairs of gambles:

(a)   with probability .20 win $45, otherwise nothing, versus

(b)   with probability .25 win $30, otherwise nothing,

and

(a′)   with probability .80 win $45, otherwise nothing, versus

(b′)   win $30 for sure.

As pointed out in Chapter 1, options a and a′ have higher expected *values*, than options b and b′, respectively. (For example, the expected value of a is $9, while that of b is $7.50.) Nevertheless, the marginally decreasing shape of an individual's utility function may lead to a choice of b and b′. What is incompatible with expected utility theory is a choice of a and b′ or of b and a′. It is still possible, however, to choose a and b' or b and a' without violating the three criteria of rationality presented in section 1.3.

Now consider a choice between two options:

(a″) with probability .75 fail at stage I of the gamble and receive nothing, but if stage II is reached win $45 with probability .80, otherwise win nothing, versus

(b″) with probability .75 fail at stage I of the gamble and receive nothing, but if stage II is reached receive $30.

If "stage II" becomes a functional status quo, prospect theory predicts that b″ may be chosen in preference to a″ by subjects who would choose b' to a'—and in fact most subjects do. But a″ is logically equivalent to a (because .25×.80=.20) and b″ to b (because .25×1=.25), so that a choice of a and b″ or of b and a″ violates rationality itself. In the research described earlier, such choices are common. The phenomenon has been labeled *pseudocertainty*; the prospect theory explanation is that the chooser adopts a particular stage or hurdle in a probabilistic process as a psychological status quo and consequently becomes risk-averse for gains and risk-seeking for losses following it. If the stage is actually reached, there is nothing irrational about preferring the $30 certainty (b' to a') while prior to reaching it preferring the uncertain option with the higher expected value (a to b). That violates only expected utility theory. The irrationality here is that pseudocertainty leads to contradictory choice prior to knowledge of the outcome—depending upon whether the choice is viewed in its totality (which might lead to a choice of a in preference to b) or sequentially (which might lead to a choice of b″ in preference to a″).

Prospect theory is meant to describe behavior; thus, it incorporates irrationality when it occurs. Prospect theory is a successful descriptor, however, not just because it incorporates irrationality, but because it predicts the *direction* of irrationality when it occurs. It does not describe everyone's decision-making behavior all the time; for example, some people some of the time will not make the contradictory choices resulting from the pseudocertainty effect. Subjective expected utility theory, in contrast, can be interpreted as a normative theory of how we *should* choose. That is the interpretation I will supply in Chapter 8, modified somewhat by maintaining that while we should not be bound by the theory's implications, we should be aware of them and violate them only self-consciously for a compelling reason.

A central thesis of this book is that our automatic thinking processes can lead us to choose one alternative while controlled rational thought leads us to choose another. Prospect theory describes choices made as the result of automatic processes—for example, as the result of accepting our status quo as a basis for our choices, rather than framing them in terms of potential changes from our (most often positive) asset level. If we could not choose differently "upon reflection," there would be little point in studying decision making.

A few everyday examples may further illustrate the role of the status quo in prospect theory. People buy insurance. Why? The easiest explanation is that when considering insurance they no longer view their status quo as neutral, but rather they view their possessions on the positive side of zero (and a good salesperson encourages that view); hence, they are willing to take a small financial loss in order to avoid a risk of being wiped out. Again, the principle is that the expected utility of the gamble when dealing with positive amounts will always be less than the expected amount defined in monetary terms. In fact, defined purely in monetary terms, individuals expect to lose when they purchase insurance; after all, insurance companies make money.

Now consider people's unwillingness to use automobile seatbelts unless state or national legislation requires them to do so. According to prospect theory, people tend to adopt their status quo as the reference point. Due to the shape of the value function, small gains become very important. People believe that not wearing seatbelts yields a small gain in comfort. On the other hand, due to the diminishing-returns shape of the value function for negative outcomes, the "objective" consequences of a catastrophic auto accident are undervalued. Hence, viewed in prospect theory terms, not wearing seatbelts appears to be a reasonable behavior.

The point is that people's decisions may be changed by changing the reference level. As Norman Gutkin has pointed out, people might be more willing to use seatbelts if their status quo was made positive.[4] Instead of emphasizing all the terrible things that could result from an accident, seatbelt campaigns might better be framed in terms of how well off people are prior to the drive, in which case they would regard seatbelt use as a form of insurance—insurance that they remain in

[4]He did so in a term paper for a course of mine on decision making.

their happy state. Gutkin suggested that seatbelt advertising should not emphasize the terrible results of a serious automobile accident, but should rather show a happy and affluent young couple reminding themselves that they don't wish to lose their pleasant lives as a result of an avoidable injury.

A similar analysis can be made of propaganda from peace groups who wish to change people's attitudes about nuclear armament and proliferation. While these groups typically show films of how awful nuclear war would be, the psychological impact of objective awfulness diminishes—according to Fechner's law, prospect theory, and the entire tradition of "diminishing returns" utility. For example, the fact that nuclear winter may last two years rather than six months can hardly have much psychological impact. In contrast, if these groups emphasized how well off most Americans are—that is, portrayed us as *above* the reference level provided by the life of most people in the world—some limitations on armaments, and consequently power, would constitute only the type of small loss involved in buying an insurance premium. Currently, it is those opposed to the philosophy of such groups who have successfully sold nuclear buildup as a form of insurance.

Given our propensity to avoid sure losses, insurance sales pitches must be carefully framed. As one of my colleagues points out, a campaign advertising lower premiums that begins, "Reduce your sure loss," would not be likely to sell insurance. I speculate that at least some people buy insurance in part because—*in prospect*—they can imagine themselves to be "small winners" vis-à-vis the insurance company if disaster does occur; they have won a low-stakes, low-probability-of-big-payoff bet against that company. Fully aware that the expected value of this bet is negative, they make it to assure "peace of mind" in contemplating what *might* happen; for example, "at least my children will be able to make it through college if the wing falls off." The same prospective contemplation of possible outcomes may be a motive for buying lottery tickets with full knowledge of negative expectation.

Of course, sometimes insurance coverage pays off. Reuven Brenner notes that purchases of both insurance policies and lottery tickets may be explained when they are framed in terms of *relative* rather than *absolute* wealth, given that wealth relative to other people's wealth is generally not altered by the small amounts spent on the premiums and tickets. Brenner writes:

They [people] perform both acts for the same reasons: in both cases individuals expect to lose relatively small amounts, either the price of the lottery ticket or the insurance premium. But these small amounts are worth losing since these are the only ways by which people can either change or avoid changing their relative position in the distribution of wealth. Thus people gamble in order to try to become richer and change their relative position in the distribution of wealth, and they insure themselves in order to prevent becoming poorer, thus avoiding a change in their relative position.[5]

To end this chapter on a clearly upbeat note, I will point out that social problems that arise after abandoning a sunk cost can be ameliorated by a type of framing. The framing consists of explaining that one is not forsaking a project or enterprise, but rather wisely refusing "to throw good money after bad." Rationally, that is exactly what is involved in abandoning a sunk cost, and of course it involves forsaking a project or enterprise. Using this phrase, moreover, tends to enhance the credibility of the speaker, who is then relieved of the necessity to explain in any detail the irrationality of honoring such sunk costs.

This "good money after bad" framing focuses the listener's attention on the *present* as the status quo and phrases the abandonment of a sunk cost as the *avoidance* of a sure loss (which is good). In contrast, honoring a sunk cost involves framing a *past* state as the status quo and abandoning it as the *acceptance* of a sure loss (which is bad). As pointed out throughout this chapter, frames are malleable. The person who abandons a sunk cost benefits from behaving rationally and if the present is effectively framed as the status quo, he or she also enjoys the approval of others. Remember that President Kennedy achieved the height of his popularity shortly after he abandoned the Bay of Pigs venture.

[5]Brenner, R. (1983). *History of the Human Gamble*. Chicago: University of Chicago Press.

CHAPTER

The beauty of a Beneficial National Bank USA Money Management Account is that it costs you nothing to join. In fact, the only fee is a $2.50 monthly usage charge which only applies during months when your account is in use or has an outstanding balance.

author's unsolicited mail,
July 16, 1986

4

Ordering and Grouping of Alternatives, Assets, and Consequences

4.1 ORDERING ALTERNATIVES

We cannot think of our decision options—and their possible consequences—simultaneously; we must do so sequentially. The resulting order in which we consider options and consequences may have profound effects on decision making. Because many of the ways in which we order alternatives in our minds are automatic, irrational choices are common. Let me give a very simple example.

Richard Nisbett and Timothy Wilson asked people to state their preference from an array of merchandise (dresses and stockings).[1] The items were arranged in a single row facing the subject. Nisbett and Wilson discovered that no matter where the particular items were placed, the subjects tended to choose the item at the far right. The subjects were not aware that the positioning of the items had an effect on their choice, and certainly they would have rejected a decision rule to "choose whatever happens to be on the far right."

Nisbett and Wilson observed that most subjects scanned the products from left to right—a habit that may well be related to the fact that we *read* from left to right. (It would be interesting to repeat the experiment in Israel, given the right-to-left orientation of Hebrew writing.) Why did the subjects tend to prefer the product on the far right? One possibility is that each new product seen possesses desirable characteristics that the one previously scanned does not, and that there is no product on the right of the one to the far right to bring attention to desirable characteristics that it lacks. (This interpretation is bolstered by the plausible assumption that any product must have a desirable characteristic that others don't in order to be on the market—for long anyway. I suggest this interpretation most tentatively, however, because as will be pointed out in Chapter 11, the argument that "what is plausible is therefore probable" is a weak one.)

In Nisbett and Wilson's experiment, people at least looked at all the alternative choices. A very severe problem with the ordering of alternatives is that it may *exclude* consideration of certain possibilities. Herbert Simon made a strong impact in the fields of individual and organizational decision making by demonstrating that far from

[1]Nisbett, R. A. and Wilson, T. (1977). Telling more than we can know: Verbal reports on mental processes. *Psychological Review, 84,* 231–259.

making optimal choices, organizations often search through the set of possible alternatives until they find one that satisfies an aspiration level, and then they terminate their search. Such a procedure yields a satisfactory decision but not necessarily an optimal one. Simon introduced the term *satisficing*—as opposed to *optimizing*—to describe this process.

The tendency to search through possible alternatives only until a satisfactory one is found has extremely important implications in the study of the rationality of choice. The *order* in which people search may be of paramount importance, but order can be determined by many factors having very little to do with the consequence of choice (for example, left-to-right bias), or can even be manipulated by a clever person with control of the agenda of a discussion. The procedure we are discussing is not fully rational, because it operates independently of considerations of the desirability of the consequences of alternative choices. A search in one manner may lead to one decision, while a search in another may lead to a different decision.

Decisions that would be rational if they were not influenced by factors not directly tied to consequences—such as the order in which alternatives are considered—have been termed *bounded* by Simon. Decision theorists now speak of "bounded rationality" to characterize a *wide range* of choice processes that do not adhere strictly to principles of rationality but may or may not approximate them.[2] In later work, Simon has pointed out that such bounds on rationality are often the most important determinants of choice.

Bounded rationality can, nevertheless, have desirable consequences. First, there are situations in which it is not possible to

---

[2]Simon, H. A. (1956). Rational choice and the structure of the environment. *Psychological Review, 63*, 129–138. For a more recent explanation of his ideas, see Simon, H. A. (1979), Rational decision making in business organizations, *American Economic Review, 69*, 493–513; and Simon, H. A. (1985), Human nature in politics: The dialogue of psychology with political science. *American Political Science Review, 79*, 293–304. When Simon first introduced the term, he was referring mainly to procedures that are not *optimal*. The position taken in this book is that all of the currently proposed criteria for defining the optimality of a decision require rationality, as defined by the three criteria in section 1.3. Hence, discussion will focus on forms of bounded rationality that violate them.

specify all of the alternatives and their consequences in advance. In such a situation, a very reasonable strategy is to collect information in a predetermined manner over a specified period of time and then select the alternative that appears best. This strategy, however, is not as reasonable as one that constantly revises the manner and time frame of the search on the basis of the information as it is gathered, which is another form of bounded rationality that does not consider all the alternatives. Second, the consideration of all relevant possibilities and consequences involves *decision costs*, which are very difficult to integrate with the costs and benefits of payoffs, because they are of a qualitatively different type. Let me give two examples; first, one of decision costs.

A visiting professor is contemplating three job offers of well-paying professorships, all of which would provide considerable time and support to do the research he loves. From the information he has gathered thus far, there is a clear ranking of how good the offers are, but he needs to collect more information. The situation is complicated by the fact that the offer that appears now to be best is one he must accept or reject within a month; he can postpone a choice between the other two (and any other alternatives that might appear in the mean-time) for half a year. How much time should he spend collecting information, evaluating possible consequences and their probabilities, and attempting to integrate the information and potential results in order to reach a decision? There are other things he wishes to do with his time, and there is a deadline; moreover, such decision making is emotionally draining. Should he, as some friends have urged, begin by "bounding" his search by rejecting what appears to be the weakest offer? That clearly has the advantage of allowing him more time and energy to evaluating the other two, but it has the disadvantage of eliminating an option before a thorough evaluation of it. Should he make a "higher-level" decision about how to decide— for example, by adopting a criterion for the decision to reduce the set of three alterna-tives to two? These questions are not as easily answered as are those in choices between gambles. What makes this choice particularly difficult, however, is the incomparability of the benefits and costs involved in making the decision with those involved in the jobs them-selves. Given the professor's bounds on time and "computational ca-pacity," he cannot consider the decision costs in a fully rational manner—even if he had some way of integrating them with the consequences of the decision. And then, somewhat paradoxically, even if he could figure out a way to do that, he would have to take into account the probable time and effort involved in figuring it out in order to determine whether he should attempt to do so in the first place! The rationality of whatever decision he makes will be "bounded." Nonetheless, he must decide something.

An example of not considering all possibilities is that of someone hiring a secretary for the first time. In some areas of this country it is not uncommon for as many as 100 applicants to apply for such a position. The decision is particularly difficult for someone who has only second-hand knowledge of what is required of secretaries and how to evaluate secretarial skills. Applications pour in over days. Should the employer wait until a hundred applications have arrived and evaluate these in as thorough a manner as possible? That would require an enormous amount of time. Should the employer evaluate all 100 quickly in a superficial manner, and then evaluate twenty in depth? Could better information be gained by evaluating a few in depth (with the help of interviews—a procedure to be discussed in Chapter 10)? Let us suppose the employer uses a very bounded strategy: evaluate the first twenty applicants in depth and choose the one that appears to be best. How bad is this decision-making procedure relative to one of judging all 100 in depth?

We can evaluate one aspect of this strategy quite specifically. Let us suppose that the employer would be quite satisfied with any of the five best applicants. How likely is it that out of the potential 100 one of these five will appear in the first twenty? Assuming the order of applications is random with respect to secretarial quality (that is, that there is not some systematic bias by which the better secretaries apply earlier or later), the probability is .68. In fact, there is a probability of slightly over one-half that one of these good secretaries will be among the first fifteen applicants.[3] So while the strategy of evaluating only the first twenty in depth does not satisfy the criterion of looking at all possible alternatives in terms of their consequences, it

---

[3]There are $\binom{95}{20}$ sets of twenty applicants not including the top five and $\binom{100}{20}$ sets of twenty applicants. The probability of not evaluating any of these top five is therefore $\binom{95}{20}/\binom{100}{20} = .319$. Hence, the probability of evaluating at least one is .68. Similarly, $\binom{95}{15}/\binom{100}{15} = .436$.

does not do badly—at least on the criterion of having access to a top-notch secretary. (Whether the employer will correctly judge the worth of one of these applicants is another matter.) It has the advantage of cutting down on the decision time and effort, and it allows the employer to find out what the applicant pool is like in order to determine what qualities should be considered in evaluating applicants.

A similar procedure is to examine fifteen randomly chosen applicants and then continue the search until finding one that is better than any of those. Doing so would result in a probability of .83 of picking one of the top five, with an expected search length of 29 subsequent applicants.[4] (It is a well-known result of combinational analysis that if 37% [=1/e] of applicants are randomly scanned from a pool and the search is continued until one better than any of these is chosen, the probability of choosing *the best* is .37 [=1/e].)

If, of course, the employer knew in advance how to judge the qualifications of potential secretaries, he or she could simply search until finding one in the top five percent. An average of seventeen applicants would have to be screened.

As pointed out by Amitai Etzioni, all three of the search procedures just described are "boundedly rational" or "satisficing."[5] The first involves simply truncating the search, because there are too many alternatives to consider; the degree to which that procedure is desirable depends upon the degree of truncation, the trade-off (difficult to specify) between the costs of reaching the decision and the costs and benefits resulting from the decision itself, and the degree to which the chooser can avoid a pernicious bias in conducting the search. The second procedure involved using the first part of a search to determine what constitutes a desirable alternative, and the third involves a predetermined "aspiration level." The desirability of the latter two procedures is determined by the same three factors as that of the first one.

According to Cyert and March, organizations as well as individuals often use bounded search procedures to arrive at "good" solutions to "problems."[6] Moreover, the characteristics that define the "goodness"

---

[4]Eric Gold computed these values.

[5]Personal communication, November 3, 1986.

[6]Cyert, R. M., and March, J. G. (1963). *A Behavioral Theory of the Firm.* Englewood Cliffs, N.J.: Prentice Hall.

of a solution may consist of a mix of those chosen at the beginning of the search and those that become more noticeable as it proceeds.

Another procedure for reducing a search procedure involves concentrating on *aspects* of alternatives rather than the alternatives themselves. Specifically, as Amos Tversky has proposed, decision makers often *eliminate* alternatives by aspect.[7] The *elimination by aspect* procedure involves choosing a desirable aspect, eliminating all alternatives that do not have it, then choosing another desirable aspect and eliminating all those alternatives not containing it, and so on, until either a single alternative is left or so few are left that they can be evaluated thoroughly. In the secretary choice, for example, familiarity with word processing and willingness to take dictation might be aspects by which to eliminate candidates.

If the aspects are considered in the same order as their desirability, this form of bounded rationality results in reasonably good choice—although it involves no compensatory (weighting) mechanism. If the aspects are chosen probabilistically in proportion to their importance (one of Tversky's "models"), the procedure is somewhat less satisficing. If they are chosen ad hoc on the basis of the ease with which they "come to mind," it is a decidedly flawed procedure.

Is there a contradiction between the bounded rationality of terminating searches and the findings of Nisbett and Wilson? No, because there is a crucial difference in the choice problems. In the Nisbett and Wilson study, the subjects were necessarily aware of all the choices. (The items were physically lined up in front of them.) The problem with the satisficing procedure is that certain alternative choices may not even be considered, including those that may be the best one or better ones for the decision maker (with greater or lesser probability depending on the procedure).

A problem arising in a sequential search when alternatives must be created rather than scanned was identified years ago in the context of group choice by organizational psychologist Norman R. F. Maier. Maier noted that when a group faces a problem, the natural tendency of its members is to propose possible solutions as they begin to discuss the problem. Consequently, the group interaction focuses on the merits and problems of the proposed solutions, people become emo-

---

[7]Tversky, A. (1972). Elimination by aspects: A theory of choice. *Psychological Review, 79,* 281–299.

tionally attached to the ones they have suggested, and superior solutions are not suggested. Maier enacted an edict to enhance group problem solving: "do not propose solutions until the problem has been discussed as thoroughly as possible without suggesting any." It is easy to show that this edict works in contexts where there are objectively defined good solutions to problems.

Maier devised the following "role playing" experiment to demonstrate his point. Three employees of differing ability work on an assembly line. They rotate among three jobs that require different levels of ability, because the most able—who is also the most dominant—is strongly motivated to avoid boredom. In contrast, the least able worker, aware that he does not perform the more difficult jobs as well as the other two, has agreed to rotation because of the dominance of his able co-worker. An "efficiency expert" notes that if the most able employee were given the most difficult task and the least able the least difficult, productivity could be improved by 20%, and the expert recommends that the employees stop rotating. The three employees and a fourth person designated to play the role of foreman are asked to discuss the expert's recommendation. Some role-playing groups are given Maier's edict not to discuss solutions until having discussed the problem thoroughly, while others are not. Those who are not given the edict immediately begin to argue about the importance of productivity versus worker autonomy and the avoidance of boredom. Groups presented with the edict have a much higher probability of arriving at the solution that the two more able workers rotate, while the least able one sticks to the least demanding job—a solution that yields a 19% increase in productivity.

I have often used this edict with groups I have led—particularly when they face a very tough problem, which is when group members are most apt to propose solutions immediately. While I have no objective criterion on which to judge the quality of the problem solving of the groups, Maier's edict appears to foster better solutions to problems.

4.2. GROUPING ALTERNATIVES

As mentioned in the preface and section 3.2, *adaptation* is one of the basic processes of human life. It affects judgment and decision—for example, in framing alternatives relative to a status quo. Another basic phenomenon that affects judgment and decision is sensitivity to *context effects*. Just as a particular visual stimulus (for example, a grey ring) appears different in different contexts (perhaps surrounded by a yellow or blue background), a particular alternative may appear different to a decision maker when it is considered in different contexts. Specifically, it may appear more or less desirable. In fact, the more judgmental the evaluation, the greater is the importance of context effects. For example, despite the differences with which we perceive a color depending on the colors surrounding it, we experience a great deal more "color constancy" than would be expected from a simple analysis of light frequency on an object and its surroundings; specifically, the light that illuminates an object does not have much effect on our perception of the object's color. When evaluating an alternative course of action and its possible consequences, however, we often do not experience such constancy. In fact, the influence of competing alternatives can lead to a contradictory choice, even when the competing alternatives are not chosen. Such alternatives are truly irrelevant. One principle of rationality that most theorists accept is that choice should be *independent of irrelevant alternatives*. That is, if alternative A is preferred to alternative B when the two are considered alone, then A should be preferred to B when alternative C is considered along with them; the existence of alternative C should be irrelevant to the choice between A and B. Of course, if C is the preferred alternative in the set consisting of A, B, and C, we have no way of knowing whether its existence has reversed the preference for A over B. Hence, to demonstrate that choice may violate this principle of rationality, we must show that the choice of A over B is reversed in a situation where C is not chosen. Can that happen? Yes, and its occurrence is due to context effects. Such a reversal was illustrated by Harrison and Pepitone.[8]

Student subjects were asked to train a rat by administering electric shocks. In one condition, only two alternatives were available: shocks labeled "mild" and "slightly painful." In the others, however, a third shock level labeled either "moderately painful" or "extremely

[8]Harrison, M., and Pepitone, A. (1972). Contrast effect in the use of punishment. *Journal of Personality and Social Psychology, 23*, 398–408.

painful" was available. The subjects were told not to use this more severe level, and none did; thus, the only two alternatives were "mild" and "slightly painful." Nevertheless, while the "slightly painful" shock level was chosen only 24% of the time when no (irrelevant) third alternative appeared, it was chosen 30% of the time in the presence of the irrelevant "moderately painful" alternative and 36% of the time in the presence of the irrelevant "extremely painful" alternative. Thus, by changing contexts with the introduction of an irrelevant alternative, the experimenters changed the frequency of choice between the relevant alternatives. (What are a political "moderate's" choices?)

4.3 GROUPING ASSETS—"BUDGETING"

People—particularly less affluent ones—are urged by various real and purported financial experts to budget their money. Such budgeting may occur "concretely" in a family ledger; occasionally, it is "psychic." A certain amount is to be set aside for food, a certain amount for shelter, a certain amount for entertainment, and so on. Insofar as budgeting helps people to meet their needs, such budgeting advice is fine. It can, however, lead to irrationality—for both individuals and organizations. (For starters, it would not be very rational to buy a Ferrari because the automobile budget is in a state of excess, while simultaneously depriving oneself of warm clothes during a northern winter because the clothing budget has been depleted.)

Consider, for example, an individual whose budget—psychic or concrete—has a certain amount for automobile expenses and a certain amount for entertainment. The automobile budget will, unless an individual is quite affluent, be larger than the entertainment one. Now, the question is whether to buy a new, dealer-supplied radio cassette for the new car. Viewed in terms of the automobile budget, the additional expense of $250 to $500 does not appear to be very substantial. The buyer, however, would be totally unwilling to spend $250 to $500 from the entertainment budget to buy a radio/cassette system of the same low wattage, fidelity, and tone quality of the dealer-supplied radio. Most of us expect to spend vastly different amounts of money on automobiles than on stereo systems. The irrationality occurs because if we had been *given* the automobile, we might not be willing to spend the additional amount we pay the dealer for the stereo system we get. (Dealers apparently are aware of this form of irrationality, and in fact a careful analysis of their profit margin indicates that a large percentage of their profit comes from such added features, rather than from the sale of the automobile itself—which typically has a markup of 8% to 10%.)

For the same accounting reason, most individuals would not drive across town to buy an identical car for $25 less, but would to save $25 on an identical vacuum cleaner, as pointed out by Richard Thaler.[9] The conclusion is that saving $25 both *is* (if a vacuum cleaner is being bought) and *is not* (if a car is being purchased) worth a trip across town.[10] Another interesting example that shows people do not view their assets in terms of their totality is the fact that few people will buy new tickets to a concert or football game if they lose their tickets, whereas if they should lose that amount of money in cash they would not even consider cashing in those same tickets.

As pointed out in the discussion of the irrational contradictions derived from prospect theory, the rational way to view assets is in terms of their *totality*. (Here again, we are considering physiological, social and psychological assets as well as monetary ones.) In the automobile radio example, the person's asset level would be reduced by $250 to $500 by the purchase of an inferior piece of equipment.

Psychic accounting may also be an important factor in the consistency with which many people lose on gambling excursions in Atlantic City, Las Vegas, and Reno. They set aside a certain amount of money with which to play, and quite disciplined, they stop after losing that amount. They have, however, no equivalent rule for stopping gambling when they are ahead. Filled with fantasies of the big payoff, they continue to gamble, and because the odds favor the house, they eventually lose. Now consider the situation of a friend of ours who had budgeted $250 for the gambling occasion but by luck gets ahead by $1,000. At that point, our friend's total asset position is $1,000 more than before gambling. Had that $1,000 been obtained by some means

---

[9]Thaler, R. (1985). Mental accounting and consumer choice. *Marketing Science, 4,* 199–214.

[10]Ironically, the major objection my students give to this example is that it ignores the greater sunk costs of time and effort in negotiating with a car dealership than in buying a vacuum cleaner.

other than gambling, our friend would *still* have been willing to invest only $250 in the excursion. ("Blow $1,250 at the tables? You're kidding! I can't afford that!") But by framing the $1,000 as different from other money, this friend has no compunction about losing all of it, plus— of course—the $250 already budgeted for the process. It's a sure way to lose, while simultaneously congratulating yourself on your "discipline."

Organizations, whose budgets tend to be more formal than those of individuals, can also behave irrationally as a result of accounting rather than considering their overall assets. For example, a unit that has overspent must nevertheless be supported if it is crucial to the goals of the organization. (To use an analogy, excess lung capacity does not compensate for a failing liver.) Nevertheless, organizations will often "scrimp" in ways that hurt themselves badly as a result of "not having enough money" for certain purposes or units—despite being in better financial shape overall. For example, Lyndon Johnson announced a "hiring freeze" for government positions shortly after he became President. This freeze created severe anxiety in the Veterans Administration hospital where I was doing research, and the hospital administrators immediately instituted procedures to "get around" it. The motive was not that they wished to spend money, or a fear that the treatment of patients would diminish as a result of the freeze. The motive was fear that such a freeze would *cost* the hospital a considerable amount of money. For example, the opinion of specialists who visited various hospitals and made rounds once or twice a week was necessary before discharging many patients. If any such specialists retired, quit, or died, and the number rotating through various hospitals was diminished by the freeze mandating no replacements, the time such patients would have to remain hospitalized before discharge would increase dramatically, with a concurrent dramatic increase in costs. Even putting a "cap" on the budget for such specialists may not have been cost-effective, and a policy of diminishing that budget would have been "counterproductive" if it had been instituted. (Fortunately, the "freeze" was more verbal than real in the hospital in which I worked.)

Of course, just as bounded rationality can have salutary effects, so can budgeting. It discourages overspending without having to consider the financial consequences of each purchase in detail; it can also involve certain "traps" we will discuss in Chapter 9—for example, the potential disastrous results of allowing small expenditures because they involve only a small fraction of your total assets.[11]

4.4 GROUPING CONSEQUENCES

Not just alternatives, but their consequences can be affected by the context in which they are embedded. Such effects are illustrated by an example described by Richard Smith.[12]

Since members form interpretations as a result of limited search and oversight, opposing advocates may have opportunities to overturn existing interpretations (and positions) by making members aware of alternative, more appealing interpretations. As an example, consider an incident reported by Eric Redman (1973, pp. 206–207),[13] involving the Senate's consideration of an amendment offered by Senator Warren G. Magnuson of Washington to block a proposed shipment of nerve gas from Okinawa through the Pacific Northwest. The amendment appeared destined for defeat. Redman writes: "I prepared a memorandum cataloging the arguments he (Magnuson) had marshalled against the shipment and took it to him at his desk on the Senate Floor. He surveyed the memo cursorily, then handed it back with annoyed "no, no, no!"

[11]The standard advice to consumers buying an automobile is first to decide how much money they are willing to budget for it and then to look at models within the respective price range. I seriously suggest reversing the procedure; life is too short not to enjoy possessions we can afford. If the desired car is "over-budget," then the consumer must decide what is more important; if the desired car is within the budget, so much the better. I suggest that the same principle should be applied to "dieting." First decide whether you want to eat the particular food and *then* decide if it is worth the calories. This way, you needn't say "never again," or, more usually, "never again starting tomorrow." Gluttonize occasionally if that is truly desired, but *never* eat food simply "because it is there," or to avoid "wasting" it (section 2.1).

[12]Smith, R. A. (1984). Advocacy, interpretation and influence in the U.S. Congress. *American Political Science Review, 78,* 44–63 (excerpt is from pp. 47–48).

[13]Redman, E. (1973). *The Dance of Legislation.* New York: Simon and Schuster.

Bewildered, I retreated to the staff couch and waited to hear what argument he intended to use instead of familiar ones of possible sabotage, dangerous sections of track along the proposed route, and populations that would have to be evacuated as a precaution against leakage. When the time came, he took a wholly novel and ingenious approach. The issue, he told his colleagues, was not one of the people versus the Pentagon, as the news media seemed to assume. Instead, it was another case of the President versus the Senate. The Senator from West Virginia (Robert C. Byrd) had recently offered a resolution, which the Senate had passed, stating that the Senate expected the President to keep it informed throughout the treaty negotiations with the Japanese government on the subject of Okinawa. The President's sudden decision to move the nerve gas off Okinawa must reflect some aspect of those treaty negotiations, Magnuson insisted—and the Senate had not yet been informed of, much less consented to, any such agreement. To allow the nerve gas shipment under such circumstances, he asserted, would be to abandon the Byrd resolution and to abdicate the Senate's rightful role in treaty making generally. The President, Magnuson said, might get the idea that he could ignore the Senate and its Constitutional prerogatives whenever he wished. Jolted by this reasoning, the Senator from West Virginia and his Southern colleagues—friends of the Pentagon almost to a man, but vigilant guardians of the Senate's Constitutional responsibilities—voted down the line with Magnuson. The amendment, which had been doomed a few minutes earlier, passed overwhelmingly.

Magnuson succeeded by embedding two alternatives (vote for or against) in a context of foreign policy rather than of civilian risk versus military priorities. Such context changes can change choice.

4.5 INSTABILITY

Framing effects, the ordering and grouping of alternative choices, and budgeting—actual or psychic—influence decision. While some of these effects can be justified by considerations of information search and decision costs, others are arbitrary. Studying them can leave one with an uneasy feeling about the "course of history"—both personal and social—and the uneasiness is not diminished by considerations of the magnitude of the effect of certain choices in our technologically advanced (nuclear) world. The feeling is enhanced still more by the finding—to be documented in Chapter 10—that when we attempt to predict the future of individuals we do so much worse than we believe ourselves capable of doing. Perhaps framing, ordering, and grouping partly explain this lack of predictability. People make choices every day, and many of these choices have important consequences (even ones that are considered trivial at the time—like whether to go to a party where you might "happen" to meet someone who will have a profound effect on your life). To the degree to which choices are influenced by factors other than considerations of their consequences, they are arbitrary. Hence, they and their effects cannot be predicted. How rational are our choices if we can be swayed by a $2.50 per month "use" fee as opposed to a $30 per year "service" fee (or use our credit cards so long as the difference between cash payment and credit-card payment is referred to as a "cash discount" rather than a "credit-card surcharge")? And when our choices are influenced by irrational factors, how can they be very predictable?

CHAPTER

This is definitely a case where one
plus one equals more than three.
Charles S. Rogers, M.D.,
February 6, 1979

5

Representative
Thinking

5.1 EXAMPLES

I will begin this chapter by asking two questions that I asked practic-ing clinical psychologists at a workshop I once conducted. The answers require probabilistic judgments about hypothetical people described by scenarios (adapted from the work of Amos Tversky and Daniel Kahneman). Such scenarios, of course, yield much less detail than most of us—particularly clinical psychologists—desire in order to make a probabilistic judgment, but in fact we often make predictions and reach conclusions on the basis of just such sparse information; for example, professionals working in clinics and hospitals often make judgments on the basis of much *less* detailed knowledge. Further-more, in everyday life we are often constrained to reach conclusions on the basis of very little information. That is one reason our conclusions are, in fact, probabilistic. (As will be pointed out in Chapters 10 and 12, we might be wise to keep our judgments probabilistic rather than certain even when we are provided with a great deal of information.)

The instructions to the clinicians read as follows: "Please answer these questions as best you can. They are hypothetical, and the information is sparse, in 'scenario' form. Nevertheless, they are the types of questions that are often asked in written or oral examina-tions, and they involve variables in situations about which psycholo-gists are expected to have opinions."

Question 1. T. D. had been a good student until eighth grade, when he suddenly failed several courses. He was sent to a school psychologist, who interviewed him, gave him a W.I.S.C. [the standard intelligence test for children], a Rorschach [the inkblot test], and a sentence-comple-tion test. The school psychologist concluded that T. D. had an I.Q. of 125, was basically stable, but had been having social problems with peers and family—from whom he was somewhat distant. He had withdrawn into such pursuits as stamp collecting and reading, at which he spent an inordinate amount of time. The psychologist speculated that this withdrawal would probably be tem-porary, because there was no strong evidence of schiz-oid characteristics [lack of interest in other people and social interaction] or of gross pathology. The school psychologist concluded that T. D. nevertheless had little sympathy or feelings for other people.

In fact, T. D. did well in high school, went on to college to graduate cum laude with a major in history and minors in computer science and sociology and entered a master's program in graduate school. Please make a probability judgment about which of two fields he entered:

A. library science

B. education

Question 2. You have two clients, each of whom experiences an anxiety attack about once every two days. Your attempts to determine the environmental or self-generated triggers for such attacks have been unsuccessful. You decide, therefore, to look at their pattern across days, to determine if this pattern appears random or structured in a way that might suggest some factor you've overlooked. You monitor each client for twenty days and obtain the following sequences—an X indicating a day of an attack and O a day free of an attack. Which sequence appears less random (more "structured") to you?

OXOXOXOOXOOXOXXOXOXX
XOOXXXOOXOOOXXOOXXOO

Most of the psychologists—and I trust most readers—believed that T. D. probably entered library science, and most chose the second sequence as being more structured.

I then asked the clinicians these questions about the T. D. example:

1. Estimate the ratio of the number of people in M.A. education programs to the number in M.A. library science programs.

2. What do you know about the background and expertise of the school psychologist described?

3. How well can you predict the occupation of someone age twenty-two from personality characteristics at age thirteen?

4. How well can these personality characteristics be assessed on the bases of an interview and W.I.S.C., Rorschach, and sentence-completion tests?

I then invited the psychologists to change their answers. Most did so, now believing that T. D. was more likely to be in a master's program in education than one in library science. Moreover, several expressed embarrassment at their previous answer. A few expressed annoyance that they had been "tricked" or "suckered" by a description that sounded so much like someone who would opt for a job involving technical skills rather than social interaction—when in fact they knew that they could not reasonably make this judgment given the unreliability of the data, the time frame involved, and the much larger proportion of people in education.

I also asked them to reconsider their answer to the second question by noting the degree to which the X's and O's alternated: "If the X's and O's are randomly chosen, with probability equal .50, what is the probability of *alternation*—of an O following an X or vice versa? Check out the actual number of alternations in the two sequences (there are 19 possible)."

The first sequence, which most of the workshop members chose as a random one, in fact contains 15 alternations out of the 19 possible—whereas the second contains only 9, which is roughly the expected 50%. (In fact, I constructed both sequences by rolling a die; the second one was constructed on a purely random basis with probability .50 by putting down an X whenever the die rolled 1, 2, or 3, and putting down an O otherwise; the first symbol in the second sequence was determined in the same manner, but then I alternated if the die came up a 1, 2, 3, or 4 and otherwise repeated.)

5.2 REPRESENTATIVE THINKING

The purpose of these examples was to demonstrate (1) that probability estimates are often based on the degree to which characteristics are *representative* of schemas or other characteristics, and (2) that such representativeness does not necessarily reflect an actual contingency.

What is *representative* judgment? The English empiricists such as John Locke (1632–1704) maintained that thinking consists of the association of "ideas." (*Cognition* derives from the Latin *cognito*, "to shake together.") While this assertion led to considerable debate about whether such ideas were primarily visual or verbal—or some "imageless" combination—and whether some might be "innate," the basic thesis that thought is primarily an *associative* process has gained wide acceptance. More sophisticated forms of thinking such as numeration, logical deduction, and scientific hypothesis testing, are, according to this thesis, based on associations. While such a reductionistic approach has faced considerable empirical challenge, the conclusion that *a great deal* of thinking is basically associative appears firm.[1]

In the language of modern cognitive psychology, *characteristics access schemas*, which may in turn access other characteristics (all through association). The following article describing the decision-making process of a college admissions committee provides an example of such access.

> The next morning, the admissions committee scans applications from a small rural high school in the Southwest. It is searching for prized specimens known as neat small-town kids. Amy is near the top of her class, with mid-500 verbals, high-600 math and science. She is also poor, white, and geo—she would add to the geographic and economic diversity that saves Brown from becoming a postgraduate New England prep school. While just over 20% of the New York State applicants will get in, almost 40% will be admitted from Region 7—Oklahoma, Texas, Arkansas, and Louisiana. Amy's high school loves her, and she wants to study engineering. Brown needs engineering students; unfortunately, Amy spells engineering wrong. "Dyslexia," says Jimmy Wrenn, a linguistics professor. After some debate, the committee puts her on the waiting list.[2]

The problem with making decisions on the basis of representative thinking is clear. Misspelling *is* symptomatic of dyslexia; the schema is accessed. But, of course, there are many more of us who cannot spell well who are *not* dyslexic than who *are*. Nevertheless, the schema has been accessed and Amy pronounced dyslexic. So much for Amy, and the goal of diversity among Brown students. It is neither *relevant* nor ethical to consider dyslexia in making such a decision, but as a member of graduate admissions committees, I have observed similar judgments. For example, when asked for "other information that the admissions committee might find important," an applicant wrote in 1972 that "being a Capricorn, I will be a careful experimenter."

"We don't want any of these astrology nuts around here!" the clinical professor on the committee snorted, and the applicant—who

---

[1]See Starkey, P. R. (1980), Perception of numbers by human infants, *Science*, *210*, 1033–1035, for evidence that very young infants have a concept of number (1, 2, 3, many) years prior to learning enumeration.
[2]*Time*, April 9, 1979, 73.

ranked second out of more than 700 on a linear combination of GRE and GPA—was rejected. In 1972, more applicants who knew their sun sign were *not* "astrology nuts" than *were*, but once again, the associated schema ("astrology nut," i.e. "hippie") was accessed.

The basic problem with making probability judgments on the basis of representative characteristics is that the schema accessed may in fact be *less* probable, given the characteristic, than one not accessed when the schema not accessed has a much greater *extent* in the world than the accessed one. For example, the categories "nondyslexic" and "nonhippie" are much larger in reality than those of "dyslexic" and "hippie"; thus, the misspeller is more likely to be a nondyslexic than a dyslexic, and the applicant who knew his sun sign more likely to be nonhippie than a hippie. There is, however, no corresponding mental intuition of the extent of a schema *tied to the schema itself.* When the schema is accessed automatically, its extent is not. That requires a second, self-reflexive judgment: "How prevalent is this category?" (for example, dyslexic or hippie). Such a judgment invites the evaluation of *base rates, independent of the characteristic.*[3] For example, the point of the first "second thought" question about T. D.'s graduate-school major was to force the reader to consider reflectively the extent (base rates) of library science majors and education majors.

5.3 THE RATIO RULE

In contrast to representative judgments, accurate judgments can be made by using the simplest rules of probability theory. Let c stand for a characteristic and S for a schema (category). The degree to which c is representative of S is indicated by the conditional probability $p(c|S)$—that is, the probability that members of S have characteristic c. (In my examples, this conditional probability is high.)

The probability that the characteristic c implies membership in S, however, is given by the conditional probability $p(S|c)$, the probability

---

[3]See Meehl, P. E., and Rosen, A. (1955). Antecedent probability and the efficacy of psychometric signs, patterns, or cutting scores. *Psychological Bulletin, 52,* 194–201; Dawes, R. M. (1962). A note of base rates and psychometric efficiency. *Journal of Consulting Psychology, 26,* 422–424; Tversky, A., and Kahneman, D. (1974). Judgments under uncertainty: Heuristics and biases. *Science, 185,* 1124–1131.

that people with characteristic c are members of S, which is the *inverse* of $p(c|S)$. Now, by the basic "laws" of probability theory

$$p(c|S) = \frac{p(c \text{ and } S)}{p(S)} \tag{5.1}$$

that is, the extent that c and S co-occur divided by the extent of S. Similarly,

$$p(S|c) = \frac{p(S \text{ and } c)}{p(c)} \tag{5.2}$$

But, $p(c \text{ and } S) = p(S \text{ and } c)$; it therefore follows that:

$$\frac{p(c|S)}{p(S|c)} = \frac{p(c)}{p(S)} \tag{5.3}$$

And in general,

$$\frac{p(A|B)}{p(B|A)} = \frac{p(A)}{p(B)} \text{, or} \tag{5.4}$$

Ratio Rule: *The ratio of inverse probabilities equals the ratio of simple probabilities.*

This simple ratio rule provides a logically valid way of relating $p(c|S)$ to $p(S|c)$. To equate these two conditional probabilities in the absence of equating $p(c)$ and $p(S)$ is simply irrational. Representative thinking, however, does not distinguish between $p(c|S)$ and $p(S|c)$ and consequently introduces a symmetry in thought that does not exist in the world. Associations are symmetric; the world generally is not.

Statements and beliefs about the relationship between pot smoking and hard drug addiction provide a rich source of such irrationality. For example, a headline in the *Redwood City* (California) *Tribune* of December 11, 1970, reads "Most on Marijuana Using Other Drugs." The first line of the story that followed read, "Almost without exception, drugs are used by high schoolers in combination with marijuana when drugs are used at all, according to the findings. . . ." Whereas the text clearly states that of the students who use drugs most use marijuana, the headline asserts the reverse.

The ratio of pot smoking given drug usage to drug usage given pot smoking is large because the ratio of smoking pot to drug usage is large, and these two ratios are equal. Thus, the survey found that the former conditional probability—smoking pot given drug usage—is quite high, in accord with our everyday observation. But that does not imply that the latter is high also. The ratio rule indicates that the latter probability—of drug use given pot smoking—is much smaller than the former, so that a large value for the former does *not* indicate that "most on marijuana [are] using other drugs." Nevertheless, two years previously the Democratic candidate for President, in response to an election-eve phone call, termed marijuana "what we in the pharmaceutical profession call a kicker."

In most writings about confusion of the inverse, authors give funny examples. For instance, on August 27, 1967, *This Week* magazine published advice on how to stay alive in a car over Labor Day weekend ("This Quiz Could Save Your Life Next Weekend").[4] In it the author asserted that "the farther one drives from home the safer he is," because most deaths occur within twenty-five miles of home. That is a confusion of the probability of death given distance with the probability of distance given death; its invalidity is clear by invoking the ratio rule and noting that the probability of driving close to home is *much* greater than the probability of being killed. It is easy to make fun of that confusion. (Most deaths occur within twenty-five miles of people's homes because that is where they do most of their driving. By confusing the inverse, one might be tempted to tow one's car to the freeway.) When, however, identical irrationality is used as a justification—or sometimes even as a reason—for enforcing harsh prohibitions against marijuana, the confusion is not so funny. For while an individual arrested may view the arrest as a natural consequence of government by the vindictive, uptight, and exploitive, many people approve of such arrests because they believe—with the late Hubert Humphrey—that marijuana is "a kicker."[5] Neither is it amusing when state hospitalization in a locked ward is recommended for a patient because "she gave a typical schizophrenic response; therefore, she must be schizophrenic." Nor is the example discussed in the next section amusing.

[4]Barns, L. R. (1967). This quiz could save your life next weekend. *This Week*, August 27, 10–11.

[5]Ironically, ascribing inept social judgments and policies to intellectual confusion or stupidity rather than to unpleasant motives is often considered "cynical."

5.4 A MEDICAL EXAMPLE

BAY CITY, MICHIGAN, 1979: A surgeon here is one of a handful in the country who is taking a pioneering approach to the treatment of breast cancer. Charles S. Rogers, M.D., is removing "high-risk" breasts before cancer has developed.

The risk factor is determined by mammogram "patterns" of milk ducts and lobules, which show that just over half of the women in the highest-risk group are likely to develop cancer between the ages of 40 and 59. The mammogram patterns are the work of Detroit radiologist John N. Wolfe, M.D.

The surgery, called prophylactic (preventive) mastectomy, involves removal of the breast tissue between the skin and the chest wall as well as the nipple.

Reconstruction of the breast with the remaining skin is usually done at the time of the mastectomy. Silicone implants and replacement of the areola (the pigmented skin around the nipple) leave the patient "looking like a woman," according to the surgeon.

He has performed the surgical procedure on 90 women in two years. . . .

The rationale for the procedure is found in *Rogers's interpretation* of studies by Wolfe. The newspaper article continues:

In his research Wolfe found that one in thirteen women in the general population will develop breast cancer but that one in two or three DY (highest-risk) women *will develop it between the ages of 40 and 59.* [Italics added, Wolfe did *not* find that; what he discovered is explained in the next paragraph.]

The low-risk women (NI) account for 42 percent of the population, but only 7.5% of the carcinomas. By examining the DY women and those in the next-lower risk groups, P1 and P2, Wolfe felt that 93% of the breast cancers could be found in 57% of the population.

Using these figures, it is possible to construct results for 1,000 "typical" women; see Table 5.1. No other numbers satisfy the constraints. Note that $499+71=570$ or 57% of the population, which is the stated proportion in the high-risk category. Also, $71/(71+6)=.92$. Thus, as stated, 92% of the cancers are discovered in 57% of the population. The overall breast cancer rate of the population is $(71+6)/1000=.077$, which is approximately 1/13. And so on.

But, *while it is true that 93% of the cancers are found in the high-risk group, the estimated probability that someone in this group will*

Table 5.1

		CANCER	
		No	Yes
BREAST RISK FACTOR	High	499	71
	Low	424	6

develop a cancer is only 71/570 or .12. (Remember, these calculations are based on the proportions cited by Rogers.)

The .12 figure can be determined even more easily by applying the ratio rule. According to Wolfe's figures, $p(\text{cancer})=.075$, $p(\text{high risk}|\text{cancer})=.93$, and $p(\text{high risk})=.58$. Thus,

$$\frac{p(\text{cancer}|\text{high risk})}{.93} = \frac{.075}{.580} \text{ therefore,}$$

$$p(\text{cancer}|\text{high risk}) = .12$$

The most informative information is negative—the estimated probability of developing breast cancer if the woman is from the low-risk group being 6/430, or .014. It is not possible based on the newspaper article to evaluate the claim about the very highest risk group, DY.

Dr. Rogers does not stress the value of a negative inference. After urging *all women over 30* to have an annual mammography examination, he is quoted as saying:

> The greatest danger is in having a mammogram without a medical exam by a doctor. There are too many times when the surgeon feels a lesion that wasn't picked up on a mammogram. . . . This is definitely a case where one plus one equals more than three.

Agreed. Incidentally, his mammogram advice is also based on a confusion of inverse probabilities. At the time, roughly 20% of cancers were not detected by mammography—that is, surgeons discovered a lesion "that wasn't picked up on a mammogram." But that is much different from the percentage of times women have cancer given a normal ("negative") mammogram result; $p(cancer|negative)$ $\neq p(negative|cancer)$. In fact, this former figure at the time the article was written was approximately .5% (1 in 200)—which most of us would not regard as a "great danger"—according to figures from the Hartford Insurance Project that had just been completed and published. (In fairness to Rogers, it must be pointed out that the article did not specify how seriously high risk the "high-risk" breasts would have to be before Rogers would operate. The point of this critique is that his *reasoning* used to justify the procedure *at all* should—from a rational perspective—be highly unpersuasive.)

5.4 OTHER EXAMPLES

Occasionally, people assert dependency—and its direction—without considering either base rate, as illustrated in the following item from *Management Focus*.[6]

> Results of a recent survey of 74 chief executive officers indicate that there may be a link between childhood pet ownership and future career success.
>
> Fully 94% of the CEOs, all of them employed within Fortune 500 companies, had possessed a dog, a cat, or both, as youngsters. . . .
>
> The respondents asserted that pet ownership had helped them to develop many of the positive character traits that make them good managers today, including responsibility, empathy, respect for other living beings, generosity, and good communication skills.

For all we know, *more* than 94% of children raised in the backgrounds from which chief executives come had pets, in which case the direction of dependency would be negative. But perhaps a better psychological analysis can be found by relating success to tooth brushing during childhood. Probably all chief executives did so, which would clearly imply that the self-discipline thus acquired led to their business success. That seems more reasonable than the speculation that "communication skills" gained through interacting with a pet generalize to such skills in interacting with business associates.

[6]*Management Focus* (November–December 1984), 2.

Examples are not always so humorous. For example, in an article entitled "Airline Safety: The Shocking Truth" David Nolan presents "some tips from experts on how to improve your chances of surviving."[7] "Know where the exits are and rehearse in your mind exactly how to get to them. Harry Robertson, who has interviewed almost 200 survivors of fatal airline accidents, reports that more than 90% had their escape routes mentally mapped out beforehand." Unfortunately, there is no evaluation of what percentage of *all* airline passengers do that (90%?), and of course, Robertson did not interview any passengers who did not survive.

Clinical psychology is not immune to such judgments. For example, Nathan Branden writes, "I cannot think of a single psychological problem—from anxiety and depression, to fear of intimacy or of success, to alcohol or drug abuse, to spouse battery or child molestation—that is not traceable to the problem of poor self-esteem."[8] In other words, $p(c|S)$ is high, where c refers to poor self-esteem and S to problems. To state that these problems are "traceable" to poor self-esteem, however, is to assert that $p(S|c)$ is high, which we do not know—because *clients come to Branden because they have problems*. Branden's experience is with people who want help with their problems—that is, his experience is conditional on S. Even if we found a high $p(S|c)$, we could not make a causal inference: peoples' self-esteem may be poor *because* they have such problems as Branden lists. Branden concludes:

> There is overwhelming evidence, including scientific findings, that the higher the level of an individual's self-esteem, the more likely that he or she will treat others with respect, kindness, and generosity. People who do not experience self-love have little or no capacity to love others. People who experience deep insecurities or self-doubts tend to experience other human beings as frightening and inimical. People who have little or no self have nothing to contribute to the world.

Following Branden's "I cannot think" style, I cannot imagine *any* "scientific study" in which the dependent variable was "nothing to contribute to the world." And it does *not* follow that since people with

---

[7]Nolan, D. (1986). Airline safety: The shocking truth. *Discover 7*, October, 30–58, quote from p. 58.

[8]Branden, N. (1984). In defense of self. *Association for Humanistic Psychology Perspectives*, August–September, 12–13.

problems have (in Branden's experience) poor self-images that, there-fore, such problems have a high probability given "deep insecurities and self-doubts"—a characteristic that may not be that uncommon. While the word *deep* is sufficiently ambiguous that a clear statistical refutation of Branden's position is impossible, using representative thinking to communicate to a mass of people that they "have nothing to offer to the world" is—in my opinion—intellectually irresponsible. In fact, Branden's observations are consistent with a conclusion that having low self-esteem is *good* for people who have problems (e.g., abuse children), for otherwise they wouldn't be motivated to seek change (e.g., enter therapy).

Fortunately, not everyone is prone to confuse inverse probabilities all of the time. For example, Bertrand Russell was not. His grand-mother, in an effort to dissuade him from marrying his first wife, had impressed upon him how much insanity there was in his family. Nine years later, he was considering having children and consulted a doctor about the hereditary component of insanity. His biographer Clark writes:[9]

> Four days later he saw his doctor, "who said it was my duty to run the risk of conception, the fear of heredity being grossly exaggerated. He says 50% of insane have alcoholic parentage, only 15% insane parentage. This seems to settle the matter." Settle, that is, until Russell, the potential parent, was overtaken by Russell the statistician; the footnote in his journal reads: "But he didn't say what proportion of the total population are insane and drunken respectively, so that his argument is formally worthless."

As head of a department with a clinical psychology program, one of my goals was to help students learn to think like Russell. But that is an ideal, because most of our thinking most of the time is governed by that most ubiquitous "law of thought," association, and hence we make representative connections, particularly when we assess proba-bilities. Even Russell, in this example, can be faulted for a degree of "mindlessness." Why, for instance, should he take the 50% and 15% figures so seriously at the outset?

The symmetry between characteristic and schema also character-izes "McCarthyite thinking" and several forms of thought labeled

[9]Clark, R. W. (1976). *The Life of Bertrand Russell*. New York: Knopf, 96–97.

"paranoid."[10] When, for example, Dan Smoot (a not very eminent ultraconservative thinker) asserts that all liberals are communists and all communists are liberals, he is simply referring to a symmetry that exists in his mind, but not in the world of political activists. Moreover, it is not necessary to be suffering from some form of psychopathology (ranging from a poor self-image to paranoia) to engage in such thinking. All people do it at least some of the time. In my doctoral dissertation I demonstrated that "paranoid-like" distortions from asymmetric to symmetric relationships occur when normal people attempt to understand emotionally neutral reading material. In addition, people are quite confident about their distortions—to the point of being more confident when their judgments are wrong but simplistic than they are when their judgments are correct but complicated.

The problem is that to avoid such confusion, it is necessary to *hypothesize* classes of objects or events with which one has had little experience; for example, women with high-risk breasts who do not develop cancer and child abusers who stop abusing without seeking help from others. Then to estimate a conditional probability value, one must estimate the extent of this class, despite the lack of experience with its members. Doing so involves controlled "scientific" thinking—in Piaget's terms, regarding the actual (instances I observe) as a set of the possible (instances I *could* observe) rather than vice versa.

[10]Liberal psychologists, psychiatrists, and other social scientists have been quick to discover the presence of such thinking in political reactionaries and schizophrenics. In schizophrenia, for example, it has even been elevated to a "principle" of psychotic thought: reasoning according to the Von Domarus principle. The principle refers to establishing identity through a common predicate—as, for example, the belief of a schizophrenic woman that she was the Virgin Mary because she was a virgin.

The irony of this analysis is that the conclusion that people who reason in a representative way must be paranoid is itself based on representative thinking; that is, the automatic access of the schema (paranoid) given the characteristic (confusion of inverses). Roger Brown, a psychologist and linguist, lived for a sabbatical year among hospitalized mental patients, mostly psychotics, to determine how their thought patterns differed from those of the others. He found no great differences. The people he studied thought and talked the same way other people do, except that they had certain "crazy" beliefs—for reasons, Brown concluded, unknown. (See Brown, R. (1973). Schizophrenia, language and reality. *American Psychologist, 28*, 395–403.)

In concluding this section, I would like to venture an opinion: *education does not necessarily help.* That is, education—at least as practiced in this country in elementary and secondary schools—may actually train automatic thinking. The reason is that so much of what passes for education consists of memorizing connections between words, phrases, and images. These words, phrases, and images may or may not, in turn, have any mental link to external reality.[11] ("I always just thought of fractions and decimals as two different types of numbers, but sometimes you refer to probabilities with fractions and sometimes with decimals, so I guess they're connected somehow. How do you go from a fraction to a decimal?" —college junior)

Let me give an example. In elementary school, most of us were expected to learn how to multiply one-digit numbers in our heads. A multiplication that posed some difficulty was $8 \times 7 = 56$, or is it 57 or 54 or 53? If all that is required is memorizing the right product, there is no reason the product should not be 57 or 54 or 53. Some fortunate students, on the other hand, are taught *not* to memorize the product, but to derive it rationally. These students are taught to think:

> When multiplying 7×8 it is easy to "get to" 5×8 because that's $10 \times 8 = 80$ divided by 2, which is 40. There's 2×8 "left over," which is 16. (Because 8 is "2 down" from 10, 2×8 must be "4 down" from 20.) So the product is $40 + 16 = 56$.

A student asked to memorize $8 \times 7 = 56$, in contrast, is simply being asked to form an association. To the degree that "education" consists of merely forming such associations, we can expect "educated" people to confuse inverses, often with great ease. For example, consider the relegation of Amy to the college admission waiting list. Although it is never possible to be sure what would have resulted if something else

---

[11]B. F. Skinner has proposed that the speed of education could be doubled if students were individually programmed to proceed at their own rates. I believe that's fine, *provided* what they are being programmed to do is to learn something about the world. It is too easy, however, to construct programs simply to form associative links between schemas and words without any link to reality. What happens then is that the student is trained to elicit the "correct" (uprooted) response in a manner that is maximally efficient and minimally painful; i.e., elicited in the most "mindless" possible manner. See Skinner, B. F. (1984). The shame of American education. *American Psychologist, 39,* 947–954.

had happened, it is reasonable to speculate that if the committee members had not known that misspelling is symptomatic of dyslexia Amy's fate might have been different.

5.6 HOW TO THINK ABOUT INVERSE PROBABILITIES COHERENTLY

Words are poor vehicles for discussing inverse probabilities. It is clear that some verbal links are not symmetric; for example, "roses are red" does not mean that all red flowers are roses. Other verbal links however, are symmetric; "zeppelins with hydrogen gas are the type that explode" means as well that the type of zeppelins that explode are filled with hydrogen gas. It is easy to confuse symmetric and asymmetric verbal links. In fact, linguistic links are notorious for their ambiguity. (Does "the skies are not cloudy all day" mean that the skies are cloudy for only a portion of the day?) And it is possible to affirm sincere belief in a linguistic phrase without knowing what it means.[12] (How many school children singing our national anthem know that *o'er* refers to "over" rather than "or"? How many Christians reciting Corinthians know that the word *charity* translates to "love" in modern English?)

But it is difficult for many people to think without words. In fact, some eminent thinkers maintain that it is virtually impossible. "How do we know that there is a sky and that it is blue? Should we know of a sky if we had no name for it?" (Max Muller). "Language is generated by the intellect and generates intellect" (Abalard). "The essence of man is speech" (the Charodogya Upanishad). "In the beginning was the word . . ." (Genesis 1:1).

More to my liking is the advice of the Lankavatara Sutra: "Disciples should be on their guard against the seduction of words and sentences and their illusive meaning, for by them the ignorant and dull-witted become entangled and helpless as an elephant floundering around in deep mud." Perhaps we should cultivate nonverbal thinking

---

[12]Or a newspaper headline "two women hospitalized by accident" (the paramedics were klutzes?) or "they are drinking companions" (*they* referring to vampires?). More seriously, compare the zeppelin statement to: "University administrators are the type who. . . ."

patterns such as those of Albert Einstein, who wrote: "The words or language, as they are written or spoken, do not seem to play any role in my mechanism of thought."[13]

Concrete visual images are no better than words, however. For example, the expert's image of a breast cancer victim is indeed of a woman with high-risk breasts, because most breast expert's cancer victims have high-risk breasts.

Fortunately, there is a third alternative—a systematic one proposed by the nineteenth-century mathematician and logician, Venn (1834–1923). Intersecting circles can be drawn to represent sets of objects or events. Such circles are called Venn diagrams. The area of each circle represents the simple probability that an outcome is from it, and the overlap of the circles represents the probability that the outcome is from the corresponding compound event. Conditional probabilities are thereby represented by the ratio of the area in the overlap to the area in the large circle representing the "given" event. Clearly, then, conditional probabilities are not symmetric; moreover, their ratio is equal to the ratio of the area in the two "given" probabilities—expressed algebraically by the ratio rule. The Venn diagram in Figure 5.1 expresses the relationship between pot smoking and hard drug usage. Clearly, being a pot smoker does not imply with high probability being a hard drug user, but being a hard drug user does have such an implication for pot smoking.

5.7 OTHER IRRATIONALITIES OF REPRESENTATIVE THINKING

Yet another pernicious result of representative thinking is that it implies structure ("nonrandomness") where none exists. This implication occurs because a representative view of randomness involves *too much* alternation—often to the point that we could make a clear statistical inference that the generating process is *not* random. (The question in the demonstration of which sequence is random is the one that is best at yielding the wrong answer.) For example, Russel Vaught and I have noted that many people believe airplane accidents

[13]These examples are taken from pp. 307–308 of Davis, P. J., and Hersh, P. (1981). *The Mathematical Experience.* Boston: Birkhauser.

Figure 5.1 Hypothesized Venn diagram of pot smokers and hard drug users

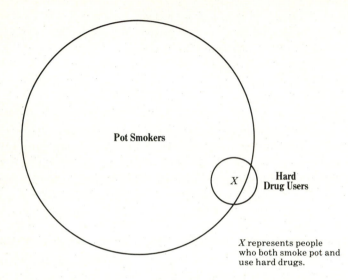

Pot Smokers

X

Hard Drug Users

X represents people who both smoke pot and use hard drugs.

happen in "bunches"—usually "threes." (One clinical psychologist I know cites such "coincidences" as evidence for Jungian "synchronicity.") Vaught and I obtained data from the FAA describing all commercial airline crashes between 1950 and 1970. We plotted (examined) the number of days between the occurrences of the crashes. A totally "random" model begins with the assumption that the probability of a crash on any given day is a constant, p. Hence, the probability of a crash occurring the day following another crash is p. The probability the next crash occurs on the second day subsequent to a crash is $(1-p)p$, because there must be no crash on the succeeding day and then a crash on the next one. (Note that $(1-p)p$ is *less* than p, a result that some people find counterintuitive.) Similarly, the probability that the next crash will occur on the third day following a crash is $(1-p)(1-p)p=(1-p)^2p$; and in general the probability that the next crash will occur on the nth succeeding day is $(1-p)^{n-1}p$.

Examining all crashes and fatal crashes separately, Vaught and I discovered that the fit to the theoretical prediction based on a constant p was almost perfect. Yet crashes tend to occur in "bunches." Why? Because $(1-p)^j>(1-p)^kp$ when $j < k$. Hence, random sequences contain "bunches" of events, as in the truly random pattern in the second question in section 5.1. The problem is that representative thinking leads us to conclude that such random patterns are *not* random. Instead, we hypothesize such positive feedback mechanisms as "momentum" to account for them. (Those of us hypothesizing Jungian "synchronicity" are in a minority.) While, for example, the maxim that "nothing succeeds like success or fails like failure" *may* be true, phony "evidence" for it can be found in the bunching of successes in patterns of people or organizations with high probabilities of success, and of failures in those with high probabilities of failures—even when the pattern is of independent events. A particular example of this maxim is that of the "hot hand" in basketball—which is not meant to refer to the phenomenon that some players are more accurate shooters than others but to the positive feedback supposedly governing all players that makes them more likely to score after scoring and to miss after missing. (Note that the *same* term—a "hot hand"—is used to describe successful crap shooters, despite general acknowledgment that at well-run games they cannot control the outcome of a roll.) Gilovich, Vallone, and Tversky have demonstrated empirically that the "hot hand" does not exist; that a success following a success is just as likely for an individual player as a success following a failure.[14] At least, neither the floor shots of the Philadelphia '76ers, the free throws of the Boston Celtics, or the experimentally controlled floor shots of men and women on the Cornell varsity basketball teams show evidence of a hot hand. The players' *predictions* of their success showed a "hot-hand" effect, but their performance did not. As these authors conclude (p. 295): "The belief in the hot hand and the 'detection' of streaks in random sequence is attributable to the general misconception of chance. . . ." It's representative thinking.

Do four good weeks in a row indicate therapeutic success with a patient? Do four bad weeks indicate failure (or, more sanguinely, "coming to face the problems")? No, no more than four heads in a row within a sequence of coin tosses indicates that the coin is biased. Yet, knowing the patient's base rate for good weeks—and expecting more alternation than in fact occurs if these weeks are totally *unrelated* to therapy—makes the temptation to impute causal factors to such

---

[14]Gilovich, T.; Vallone, R.; and Tversky, A. (1985). The hot hand in basketball: On the misperception of random sequences. *Cognitive Psychology*, *17*, 295–314.

strings almost overpowering, especially causal factors related to therapy—that is, to the therapist's own behavior.

Why do we expect too much alternation? Tversky and Kahneman ascribe this expectation to the belief that even very small sequences must be representative of populations—i.e., the proportion of events in a small frame must match ("be representative of") the proportion in the population. When, for example, we are tossing a fair coin, we know that the entire population of possible sequences contains 50% heads; therefore, we expect 50% heads in a sample of four tosses. That requires more alternation than is found when each toss is independent. (At the extreme, 50% heads in a sequence of two tosses requires that each head is followed by a tail and vice versa.) Here, representative thinking takes us from schema to characteristic, rather than the reverse. Again, however, the basic belief is due to matching, that is, association.

Occasionally, this belief in alternation in random sequences (the "gambler's fallacy") reaches ludicrous extremes. Consider, for example, the beginning of a letter to "Dear Abby":[15]

> DEAR ABBY: My husband and I just had our eighth child. Another girl, and I am really one disappointed woman. I suppose I should thank God that she was healthy, but, Abby, this one was supposed to have been a boy. Even the doctor told me the law of averages were [sic] in our favor 100 to one.

The final problem with representative thinking that I will discuss is that it leads to nonregressive predictions. To understand why, it is necessary first to understand regressive prediction.

Consider very tall fathers. On the average, their sons are shorter than they are. Also, the fathers of very tall sons are on the average shorter than their sons. That may seem paradoxical at first, but it can be understood by looking at Figure 5.2. What you see is a simple averaging effect. Because the heights of fathers and sons are not perfectly correlated (for whatever reasons), there is *regression*.[16]

Perhaps it is easiest to understand regression by considering the

---

[15]*Universal Press Syndicate*, June 28, 1974.

[16]The clearest exposition of regression effects I have found is Furby, L. (1973). Interpreting regression toward the mean in developmental research. *Developmental Psychology, 8*, 172–179.

Figure 5.2   An example of regression

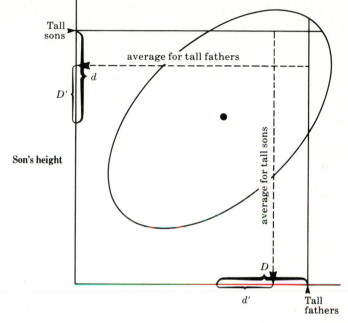

Father's height

extreme case in which we obtain perfect regression. Toss a fair coin 8
times; now toss it another 8 times. No matter how many heads
are obtained in the first sequence of tosses, the expected (average)
number of heads in the second sequence is 4. Because the coin is fair,
the number of heads in the first sequence is totally uncorrelated with
the number in the second—hence, the average of 4. That is total
"regression to the mean." As variables become more predictable from
each other, there is less regression; for example, on the average the
sons of very tall fathers are taller than the average person, but not as
tall as their fathers. It is only when one variable is perfectly predictable from the other that there is no regression. In fact, the (squared
value of the) standard correlation coefficient can be defined quite
simply as the degree to which a linear prediction of one variable from
another is *not* regressive.

On the other hand, when we match the predicted extremity of one variable from the extremity of another, we make a *nonregressive* prediction. Some of the subsequent errors can be quite subtle. For example, when Kahneman [Daniel Kahneman, referenced throughout this book] was explaining to Israeli Defense Force flight instructors in the mid 1960s that reward is a better motivator than punishment, he was told that he was wrong.[17]

> With all due respect, Sir, what you are saying is literally for the birds. I've often praised people warmly for beautifully executed maneuvers, and the next time they almost always do worse. And I've screamed at pupils for badly executed maneuvers, and by and large, the next time they improve. Don't tell me that reward works and punishment doesn't. My experience contradicts it.

This flight instructor had witnessed a regression effect. People tend to do worse after a "beautifully executed maneuver" because performance at one time is not perfectly correlated with performance the next (again, for whatever reason). They also tend to "improve" each time after "badly executed maneuvers"—once more, simply because performance is not perfectly correlated from one occasion to the next. (The easiest way to obtain an award for "noted academic improvement" is to be right near the bottom of the class the semester prior to the one for which such awards are given, and the way to be labeled an "underachiever" is to score brilliantly on an aptitude test.) Unfortunately, as the Kahneman anecdote illustrates, teachers who do not understand regression effects may be systematically rewarded (by regression to better performance) for punishing students and punished (by regression to worse performance) for rewarding them. (A "deep" explanation of people's general preference for punishment over reward as a means of behavior control may be unnecessary.)

The rational way of dealing with regression effects is to regress when making predictions. Then, if there is some need or desire to evaluate discrepancy (e.g., to give awards for "overachievement" or therapy for "underachievement") compare the actual value to the *predicted* value—not to the actual value of the variable used to make

---

[17]Reported in McKean, K. (1985). Decisions. Two eminent psychologists disclose the mental pitfalls in which rational people find themselves when they try to arrive at logical conclusions. *Discover*, June, 22–31.

the prediction.[18] For example, to determine patient "improvement" by comparing MMPI profiles at time 1 and time 2, first correlate the profiles to determine a (regressed) predicted score for each patient at time 2; then compare the actual profile with this predicted score, not to the score at time 1. Otherwise, patients who have high ("pathological") profiles at time 1 may be mistakenly labeled "improved" ("nowhere to go but down"), while those with more normal MMPI profiles may be mistakenly regarded as unresponsive to treatment. Representative thinking, in contrast, leads to comparing discrepancies without regressing first, and the results are predictable. For example, "Of particular significance was the fact that those scoring highest on symptom reductions after SD were those whose symptoms were initially more severe, and who were the less promising candidates for conventional types of therapy."[19] (While I was a clinical trainee, I asked the psychologists and psychiatrists at the hospital where I was training to dichotomize patients whose improvement was above average at discharge and those whose improvement was below average. Those they categorized as above average in improvement had higher scores on most of the MMPI scales on admission—significantly higher on the major "clinical" ones.)

A final pernicious result of representative thinking is the *compound probability fallacy*, which will be discussed at length in Chapter 7.

5.7 EXPERIMENTAL EVIDENCE

The study of psychology often consists of an unclearly mixed combination of informal observation, the attempt to establish simple "theoretical" explanations or principles that work on at least a statistical basis, and controlled experimentation. This chapter has emphasized informal observation and theory. In addition, a great deal of experimentation on representative thinking has been conducted (generally with college students as subjects), and it has been uniformly confirmatory. For example, naive subjects do not distinguish between $p(A|B)$ and

[18]Technically, such a discrepancy is termed a *residual* score, as opposed to a *discrepancy* score.
[19]*Behavior Today*, May 16, 1977, 3.

$p(B|A)$ in most circumstances, and when given one conditional probability they attempt to estimate the other without reference to the base rates $p(A)$ and $p(B)$, which must be considered according to the ratio rule.

There is one important exception to the generalization about not attending to base rates. If people ascribe some *causal* significance to discrepant rates, they often incorporate them into their reasoning. For example, the belief that one bus company has more accidents than another *because* its drivers are more poorly selected and trained will influence (hypothetical) jurors to take this difference in accident rate into account in evaluating eyewitness testimony; belief that a bus company has more accidents simply because it is larger will not.[20] Study after study has shown that when these rates are "merely statistical" as opposed to "causal" they tend to be ignored. (Of course, how the $p(A)$'s and $p(B)$'s in the right-hand side of the ratio rule happened to come about is irrelevant; rationality demands their use.) For example, when subjects are given descriptions of hypothetical people and asked to make probability judgments that these people are either engineers or lawyers, their judgments are the same whether the descriptions are said to be drawn randomly from a pool predominantly of engineers or predominantly of lawyers. Someone, for instance, who is described as being unsociable, disinterested in politics, and devoted to working on his boat in his spare time *sounds like* an engineer, and the same probability judgment is made whether the pool from which he is purported to be drawn is 70% engineers or 70% lawyers. When no description at all is given, subjects correctly judge that someone drawn randomly from a pool of 70% engineers and 30% lawyers has a .70 probability of being an engineer, whereas someone from a 30% engineer versus 70% lawyer pool has a .30 probability. When a description is presented, however, subjects tend to ignore the rates. Even when the description is *totally irrelevant* (such as, "has a wife and two children and is well liked by his friends") the base rates are ignored. (The modal judgment is .50 whether the pool is 70% engineers or 70% lawyers.) Note that this power of irrelevant information was illustrated in Question 1 at the beginning of this chapter. Even though the clinical psychologists readily admitted that they knew

---

[20]Bar-Hillel, M. (1980). The base rate fallacy in probability judgments. *Acta Psychologica, 44,* 211–233.

nothing about the school psychologist and that it is extraordinarily difficult to judge future occupation from characteristics of a thirteen-year-old, they *still* used the school psychologist's report to make a prediction that was totally counter to their own base-rate judgments that many more people enter master's degree programs in education than in library science.

Experimental evidence for expecting alternation in random sequences and for non-regressiveness of prediction is also ample. When asked to pick which sequences in pairs of sequences are random, subjects consistently pick those sequences with *too many* alternations.[21]

The explanation that these irrationalities are due to representative thinking is supported by the finding that when people are asked to rate "resemblance" or "similarity," they make the *same* judgments that they make when asked to assess probability.[22] This tendency is unfortunately true even in contexts in which people *simultaneously* acknowledge that the information on which they are making these matching judgments is unreliable, incomplete, biased, flawed, or even nonpredictive (e.g., "has a wife and two children and is well liked by his friends").

---

[21] The first experimental demonstration of this effect was Ronald Pickett in his 1962 doctoral dissertation at the University of Michigan.

[22] See, for example, Tversky, A., and Kahneman, D. (1982). Judgments of and by representativeness. In Kahneman, D.; Slovic, P.; and Tversky, A. (eds). *Judgment under Uncertainty: Heuristics and Biases*. London: Cambridge University Press; and Shweder, R. A., and D'Andrade, R. G. (1980). The systematic distortion hypothesis. In Shweder, R. A. (ed.). *Fallible Judgments in Behavioral Research*. New Directions for Methodology of Social and Behavioral Science, no. 4. San Francisco: Jossey-Bass.

CHAPTER

Experience is a dear teacher, but
fools will learn from no other.
Benjamin Franklin

6

Other Heuristics in Evaluating Probabilities

6.1 AVAILABILITY TO MEMORY

Consider a psychotherapist whose client threatens to commit suicide. If the "best professional judgment" of the therapist is that the threat is a serious one, most ethical codes require the therapist to act to prevent an attempt (regardless of the therapist's personal ethical view toward people's rights to terminate their own lives). How is a therapist to exercise that judgment?

One method would be to search his or her memory for experiences with similar clients who have made similar threats. Which instances are likely to "come to mind"? Those that were serious—specifically any in which a client did attempt suicide (especially if the attempt had been successful after the therapist had not intervened). Those instances are *salient*, and they are also readily available to memory due to the circumstances that follow an attempt, particularly a successful one. (As Willem Wagenaar points out, events are readily recalled when other events are associated with them; e.g., a report to the police associated with a robbery.)[1] Those instances in which the threats were idle, or in which clients quickly overcame their self-destructive feelings are much less apt to be recalled; in fact, they may be totally forgotten. It follows that if the therapist estimates the probability of an actual attempt on the basis of the instances most available to memory, he or she will overestimate the probability. But it is precisely that probability—whether it is estimated explicitly or integrated implicitly by the therapist's "intuition"—that may determine whether or not the therapist takes action.

Other considerations—for example, the therapist's own views about the ethics of suicide, his or her fear of a lawsuit, concern about reputation among colleagues or potential clients, and so on—all enter into the consideration of how high the probability should be before the therapist intervenes. The point here is simply that the probability of an attempt is likely to be overestimated due to the *availability* of the instances in the therapist's memory of threats followed by attempts versus those not followed by attempts. The therapist is likely to hospitalize the client, even when the probability of a suicide attempt

---

[1]Wagenaar, W. A. (1986). My memory: A study of autobiographical memory over six years. *Cognitive Psychology, 18*, 225–252.

(based on the *actual* frequency of attempts following threats among the therapist's clients) is low. Note that this bias exists from salient instances in the *therapist's own experience*; whether this experience itself is biased, and hence serves as a poor basis for estimating the probability of an attempt, introduces a whole other set of problems, discussed in section 6.4.

Or consider the current widespread belief that much of the "home-lessness problem" in the United States is due to the "deinstitution-alization" of mental patients, which simply releases them into the streets without the ability to obtain or hold jobs. This belief was thoroughly expounded in the January 6, 1986, cover story of *Newsweek*, which began with the provocative headline ABANDONED (and subsequently failed to recount a single instance of an emotionally disturbed individual requesting psychiatric hospitalization and being denied it). The homeless are "America's castoffs—turned away from mental institutions and into the streets. Who will care for them?" The story continues by quoting from a number of eminent psychiatrists and mental health workers: "It is true that up to 65% of the liberated mental patients have successfully adapted to life outside, but as any psychiatrist can testify, 'success' among the long-term mentally ill is a very sometimes thing." (My own observation is that "success" for *all* of us is a "sometimes" thing.)

What do actual surveys of the homeless show? Estimates of the proportion who are mentally ill vary from locality to locality, but the average is about one-third—with the criteria for categorizing some-one as "mentally ill" being either current mental distress or a history of psychiatric hospitalization. The vast majority of the homeless are poor, just plain poor.[2] So why do so many people (and a usually

---

[2]See Morrissey, J. P., and Dennis, D. L. (eds.). *NIMH-Funded Research concerning Homeless Mentally Ill Persons: Implications for Policy and Practice*. Proceedings of the Third Annual Meeting of NIMH-Funded Researchers Studying Homeless Mentally Ill Persons. Sponsored by Division of Education and Service Systems Liaison, National Institute of Mental Health, July 24–25, 1986. NIMH Administrative Document, Public Health Service, Alcohol, Drug Abuse, and Mental Health Administration, Dec. 1, 1986. See also Levine, I. S. (1984). Homelessness: Its implications for mental health policy and practice. *Psychosocial Rehabilitation Journal, 8,* 6–15.

responsible national publication) accept the conclusion that homelessness is due to deinstitutionalization of mental patients? Search your memory for the homeless people you saw most recently. What were they like? The unobtrusive homeless person is easily forgotten. We tend to remember the person who sings on the bus, who accosts strangers with stories of lost fortunes, who is drunk, or who is obviously high on some drug. Moreover, we may prepare ourselves to behave in certain ways if such a person approaches us, such preparation being exactly the type of ancillary event that—as Willem Wagenaar points out—enhances recall of the event leading to it. Hence, our view of "the homeless" is one of people whose emotional and physical debilitation is so severe that it suggests that homelessness and poverty alone cannot be the cause of their problems. The judgment quoted earlier of "any psychiatrist" is in addition subject to a selection bias. Unlike family doctors, psychiatrists do not see their patients for periodic check-ups. They see their former patients, if at all, only when subsequent emotional problems develop. This selective sampling is particularly severe for psychiatrists who work in mental institutions, because discharged patients tend to be very disturbed when a former psychiatrist sees them upon readmission.

Why, for example, do many people believe that they are particularly prone to getting into the slow line at a bank when they are in a hurry, that it is more likely to rain if they do not carry an umbrella, that sportscasters have "jinxed" athletes by praising them directly prior to an error, and so on? Given that there can be no logical connection between these events, such superstitious beliefs are based on pure summaries of "experience." Those summaries, however, are affected by what we remember, and those instances of agitation in the bank line, getting soaked, and "jinxing" are particularly memorable (available).

Many more examples could be given. The principle is simple. When we have experience with a class of phenomena (objects, people, or events), those with a particularly salient characteristic are those that most readily "come to mind" when we think about that class. It follows that if we estimate the proportion of members of that class with whom we have had experience and who have that characteristic, we tend to overestimate it. Our estimate will be systematically higher than the one we would obtain if we explicitly coded whether each member of that class did or did not have that characteristic (e.g., by paper-and-pencil, mechanical counter, or computer). This bias is termed *availability*; in this context, availability to our memories. As illustrated by the homelessness example, availability can lead to a very large misestimate of proportion—and a consequent misunderstanding of the nature of a serious social problem. (It is also serious to clients who find themselves hospitalized after uttering an idle threat during a transitory mood of despondency.)

6.2 VICARIOUS AVAILABILITY

Which is more common: murder or suicide? Statistics indicate that many more people commit suicide than are murdered (and the ratio is probably even underestimated, due to the ambiguity of such causes of death as single-car accidents—which are ascribed to alcohol if the individuals had been drinking even when evidence indicates that they may have been drinking to "get up the guts" to kill themselves). Yet most people estimate that murder is more common. Why? The simplest explanation is that murders get more publicity. Whereas suicides of people who are not well known are rarely reported in newspapers, murders are, irrespective of the identity of the victim. This explanation has been supported by research findings of Barbara Combs and Paul Slovic; peoples' estimates of frequency of causes of death are correlated with the frequency with which such causes appear in newspapers independent of their actual frequency.[3]

What proportion of people on welfare have adopted welfare as a "way of life"? Once again, we must rely on the news, because we cannot know which people we see on the street are on welfare (as opposed to being able to make a judgment that they are impoverished and probably homeless). Stories of "welfare queens" abound. Moreover, people read articles about "the underclass" (to be discussed later). What do the statistics show? A careful study by Mary Corcoran, Greg Duncan, Gerald Gurin, and Patricia Gurin of people on government assistance (welfare) programs between 1969 and 1978 showed that only 2.2% of American families were on such programs for the entire eight-year period; in contrast, a full 25% of American

[3]Combs, B., and Slovic, P. (1979). Newspaper coverage of causes of death. *Journalism Quarterly*, *56*, 832–849.

families received government assistance at *some* time during that interval.[4,5]

What proportion of crimes are committed by "ex-mental patients"? By blacks? When a former mental patient commits a crime—particularly a violent one—the fact that that person has been in a mental hospital is often mentioned by the news media. But when someone has never been in a mental hospital, that is never mentioned. ("Archibald Smith, who has never been in a mental hospital, was convicted of a heinous. . . .") News reports also often mention race. For example a news item, broadcast by the Cable News Network on November 29, 1986, described a kidnapping as follows: "Mr. Esquavale left his motor running while he paid for the gas, and a black man jumped into the car and drove off with his children." This reporting is not necessarily ill-motivated. We all tend to code and mention characteristics that are unusual (that is, that have low rates), and fewer people have been in mental hospitals than haven't, are black than white, are left-handed than right-handed. (I mentioned the last, seemingly trivial, example, because there is evidence that even in describing *themselves*, left-handed people will mention that they are left-handed, whereas right-handed people will not "bother" to mention that they are right-handed.[6]) But once again, the result is that the frequency of these unusual characteristics among the class of people considered tends to be overestimated. The overwhelming majority of people on welfare are *not* "welfare queens"; that leads to publicity for "welfare queens" that are discovered, which leads to overestimation of the number of people who are. Thus, bias due to *vicarious availability* leads to the same overestimation of unusual characteristics as does

---

[4]Corcoran, M.; Duncan, G. J.; Gurin, G.; and Gurin, P. (1985). Myth and reality: The causes and persistence of poverty. *Journal of Policy Analysis and Management*, *4*, 516–536.

[5]Another problem that leads to the overestimation of the people chronically on welfare arises from *Simpson's paradox*, which is discussed in Appendix A2. Families on welfare for brief periods of time are less likely to be sampled at a particular point in time than are those who are on welfare for longer periods of time; hence, an estimate of the proportion of families who are long-term welfare recipients *on the basis of a single sample* is higher than the actual proportion.

[6]McGuire, W. J., and McGuire, C. V. (1980). Salience of handedness in spontaneous self-concept. *Perceptual and Motor Skills*, *50*, 3–7.

the estimation of relative frequency from availability in experience. (Most people who threaten to commit suicide do not make an attempt; most people who are homeless are not mentally ill.) Both these availability biases are augmented by yet another: the particular salience of socially *negative* information either from one's own experience or from external sources—for example, that someone once behaved violently. (The salience of negative information may be adaptive, for we must know what to avoid in order to survive—although not necessarily in order to procreate, which combined with survival defines "inclusive fitness.")

Vicarious instances can have a profound effect even when the person supplied with them knows that they have been generated in an arbitrary or biased manner. For example, students shown a videotape of a prison guard talking about his attitude toward prisoners generalize to all prison guards when answering a questionnaire about the "criminal justice system"—even when they are told, and recall, that the guard they have seen was picked specifically to be *different from* other prison guards. In the study demonstrating this effect, Ruth Hamil, Timothy Wilson, and Richard Nisbett presented one of two videotapes to their subjects: one of a guard (an actor) who was compassionate and concerned with rehabilitation, the other of a guard (also an actor) who scoffed at the idea of rehabilitation and constantly referred to the prisoners as "animals."[7] Some subjects were given no information about how the guard for the interview was chosen; others were told either that he was typical of guards in that particular prison or that he had been chosen because he was *unlike* most of the guards there—for example, that he was "one of the three or four most humane [inhumane] out of sixty." Subsequent testing revealed that the subjects remembered how the guard was chosen in the latter two conditions. Nevertheless, their subsequent beliefs about the attitudes of prison guards were strongly related to those expressed by the guard they had witnessed—whether he was one chosen as typical or one chosen as atypical. (There was a slight difference in the direction of being more influenced by the typical guard, but it was slight.)

A single instance is a poor basis for a generalization, and it is a

[7]Hamil, R.; Wilson, T. D. C.; and Nisbett, R. E. (1980). Insensitivity to sample bias; generalizing from atypical cases. *Journal of Personality and Social Psychology*, *39*, 578–589.

particularly poor basis when the instance is known to be atypical. Nevertheless, such generalization occurs—often with great ease. It is especially likely to occur when the instance is salient; for example, a non-Arab who believes that he or she has been cheated by a single Arab merchant may readily generalize to form a negative view of all Arabs. (Why Arabs and not merchants is a fascinating question, but one that lies beyond the scope of this book.) As Richard Nisbett and Lee Ross point out, while logic requires a generalization from the universal to the particular (e.g., taking account of base rates—see Chapter 5), but not from the particular to the universal, we are prone to do the exact opposite.[8]

We can easily make such generalizations about socially important topics even when it is clear that a particular sample was chosen in a highly biased manner (as in the Hamil, Wilson, and Nisbett experiment). For example, in his well-known articles about "the underclass," Ken Auletta stated quite explicitly that the group of people he reported about in detail were chosen in a highly selective manner:[9]

> To be eligible for BT-27 [a basic typing course], and for the other classes at Wildcat, which are part of a national experiment, a person must satisfy one of four sets of criteria: be an ex-offender who has been released from prison within the last six months; be an ex-addict who has recently been or is currently in a treatment program; be a female who has been unemployed and on welfare for thirty of the preceding thirty-six months; or be a youth between the ages of seventeen and twenty who has dropped out of school (half of the dropouts must be delinquents).

As pointed out in the Corcoran, Duncan, Gurin, and Gurin article, such people are *not* typical of "the poor." What Auletta does, however, is to intersperse concrete and anecdotal histories of the particular people he studied in BT-27 with a general (often quite scholarly and thoughtful) analysis of the problem of poverty in our country. Whatever Auletta's intentions, the impression is created that the "poor" in general are like the people he describes in detail. At least, that is the conclusion reached by people I know who have read the article.

[8]Nisbett, R., and Ross, L. (1980). *Human Inference: Strategies and Short-comings of Human Judgment.* Englewood Cliffs, N.J.: Prentice-Hall.
[9]Auletta, K. (1981). A reporter at large: The underclass. *The New Yorker,* November 30.

6.3 AVAILABILITY TO THE IMAGINATION

How many seven-letter English words have the form

$$\_\ \_\ \_\ \_\ \_\ n\ \_$$

Not many? How many seven-letter English words have the form

$$\_\ \_\ \_\ \_\ ing$$

More? When Amos Tversky and Daniel Kahneman asked subjects to make estimates, they judged seven-letter words ending in -*ing* to be much more frequent than seven-letter words with *n* in the sixth position. It is easier to think of the seven-letter words ending in -*ing*— for example, *playing*. It is even possible to go through the alphabet: *Abiding*, *bribing*, and so on. It is much more difficult to think of seven-letter words with *n* in the sixth position, unless the ending -*ing* "springs to mind." Moreover, it is even possible to *estimate how difficult* it would be to generate seven-letter words into two different types.

There are, of course, more seven-letter words with *n* in the sixth position than seven-letter words ending in -*ing*. In fact, it is logically necessary that there are more, for every word ending in -*ing* has *n* in the sixth position, while there are in addition seven-letter words with *n* in the sixth position that do not end in -*ing*—for example *turbans*.

Or consider a group of ten people. Make an intuitive estimate of the number of *pairs* of people—that is, "committees of two"—that can be formed from this group. Now make the same estimate of the number of committees of eight people that can be formed. Most subjects asked estimate the former number to be much larger than the latter one. The hypothesized reason is that it is much easier to imagine "picking out" pairs of people from the set of ten than groups of eight. Once again, it is not necessary to form all such pairs mentally; it is possible to estimate the ease of doing so without an exhaustive search, and in particular to estimate that it is easier to form pairs than to form committees of eight.

In fact, there are exactly the same number of committees of eight as there are committees of two. Again, this conclusion can be reached by pure logic. Each time a unique pair is chosen from the group, a unique committee of eight remains. It follows that there is a one-one relationship between committees of two and committees of eight; it is not even necessary to have recourse to formulas to conclude that their numbers are equal.[10,11]

In both of these examples, *availability to the imagination* influences our estimates of frequency. The problem that arises, just as with the availability of actual instances in our experience or availability of vicarious instances, is that this availability is determined by many factors other than actual frequency. Although the current psychology literature contains only hints of starts toward defining and studying the "difficulty" of various types of thinking, it is quite clear that some types are "easier" than others and that some types of ideas "come to mind" more readily than others. Moreover, it is also clear that this difference is not based entirely upon past experience. (For example, how many of us have had experience generating words, or forming committees of size two or eight?) The resultant ease of availability does in fact bias our estimates of frequency, and hence our judgments of probability based on such frequency. Currently, psychologists are limited to presenting "obvious" examples of this ease. A general theory about such ease—and about what constitutes "difficulty" of thinking—does not yet exist.[12]

The availability of imagination is a serious biasing factor, for it leads to "the compound probability fallacy" and "scenario thinking," which will be discussed at length in the next chapter. In addition, it leads to "dearly held hypotheses," which will be discussed in Chapter 11.

6.4 THE PROBLEM OF "LEARNING FROM EXPERIENCE"

The sayings of Benjamin Franklin are widely quoted in our culture, particularly as justification for this or that action or decision. One is especially interesting because it has come to mean the exact opposite

---

[10]The number of committees in each instance equals $10!/8!2! = 45$.

[11]The examples in the preceding three sections are from Tversky, A., and Kahneman, D. (1974). Judgment under uncertainty: Heuristics and biases, *Science*, *185*, 1124–1131.

[12]That has always struck me as somewhat paradoxical, given that many scholars fail because they find intellectual work "too hard" or they are unable or unwilling to "put forth the mental effort" to master it.

of what Franklin intended. This saying is that "experience is a dear teacher," which is usually stated as "experience is the best teacher." By *dear* Franklin meant "expensive," and he went on to observe, "yet fools will learn in no other [school]." (The meaning of *dear* is clear from the context of the sentence, which immediately follows a discussion of the life of Job. The exact quote is, "experience keeps a dear school. . . ."[13]) Learning from an experience of failure, for example, is indeed "dear," and it can even be fatal. (As pointed out in Chapter 1, an airplane pilot in a war has no wish to learn what to avoid doing "from experience"; in fact, the whole point of extensive training prior to combat is to *avoid* "learning from experience.") Moreover, experiences of success may have negative as well as positive results when people mindlessly "learn" from them. For example, an individual who has succeeded through just plain luck may repeat the behavior with disastrous results; people who are extraordinarily successful—or lucky— in general may conclude from their "experience" that they are invulnerable and consequently court disaster by failing to monitor their behavior and its implications—as apparently happened to many of the major players in the Watergate drama (a type of arrogance described vividly by John Dean).[14] Factors leading to success in the past may be irrelevant to the present, or worse yet, lead to failure (as when generals "fight the last war").

Because learning from experience is an idea so ingrained in our culture, I will outline eight problems with it here. My conclusion, however, is that it is very difficult *not* to learn from experience. My hope is that the reader will come to appreciate all the problems involved with such learning, or at least these eight.

Availability

As outlined in sections 6.1 and 6.2, the degree to which experience— either direct or vicarious—is available to us is influenced by many factors other than its actual occurrence. As we "dig in to our memories" for instances of this or that, we come up with a biased sample. Yet if we have taken no precautions against such bias—for example, by

---

[13]Franklin, Benjamin (1757/1773). *Poor Richard's Almanac.* New York: David McKay, Inc., 31.
[14]Dean, John W., III (1976). *Blind Ambition.* New York: Simon and Schuster.

systematically collecting frequencies by methods external to their own mental processes such as paper and pencil and computer—we have only this biased sample on which to base our conclusions. Biased sampling yields incorrect conclusions. There is no way out of that problem, because it is impossible to "think in a way that we do not think."[15]

Biased Generation of Experience

My colleagues who claim to know that no child abusers stop on their own do in fact have experience with abusers. The problem is, of course, that these therapists' experience is limited to those who have *not* stopped on their own, and since their experience is in treatment settings, these abusers cannot *by definition* stop without therapy. What happens as a result is that the very nature of my colleagues' experience *precludes* contact with the subset of people whose extent is at issue: child abusers who stop on their own. But that is not realized. A similar problem arises from the generalizations of Dr. Branden that were discussed in Chapter 5. He sees only people who are in therapy. They have all engaged in negative social behaviors, and they all have a negative self-image. He concludes that this self-image problem is at the basis of the behavior. It can equally well be concluded, however, that the self-image problem leads people to therapy, or even that the negative self-image is *valuable* to these people because otherwise they would not be motivated to change their behaviors. Or consider the assertion of the former president of the American Psychological Association in his inaugural address that "all alcoholics are obsessive-compulsive when sober." Again, who are the alcoholics with whom he has had contact? Those in a treatment setting.

---

[15]Edward Lichtenstein has pointed out that it is possible to imagine a physical debilitation (e.g., blindness) or enhancement (e.g., the ability to swim more rapidly), or even to place ourselves deliberately in a situation in which we might experience that vicariously (e.g., using a blindfold or swimming fins). That experience will not, of course, be identical with that of the person who actually has the disability or unusual ability, but it may at least provide cues to that experience. In contrast, it is very difficult to imagine ourselves less or more intelligent than we are; that is, to "think in a way that we do not think." When trying, we may immediately imagine *consequences* of such a change, but not the change itself.

A great deal of thinking is associational, and it is very difficult indeed to ignore experience that is *associationally relevant* but *logically irrelevant*. Such discounting involves Piagetian thinking of reality as a subset of possibility rather than vice versa, and most people do not think that way most of the time. It is very difficult to have had extensive contact with a particular type of person, issue, or problem and to regard that experience as irrelevant because it is biased in a particular manner by the way it was generated. That type of "controlled thinking" is difficult and unusual. (See footnote 9 of section 6.3.) The problem is not that the availability of instances may be biased, but that the entire basis of the experience may be; the external constraints generating it may result in its being partially or even totally irrelevant.

A particularly humorous example of such irrelevance, and failure to appreciate it, can be found in the work of Lee Ross, Teresa Amabile, and Julie Steinmetz.[16] They constructed an experiment in which two people were randomly assigned the roles of "questioner" and "contestant." The questioner was instructed to ask the contestant "ten challenging but not impossible questions." Other subjects observed the question–answer interaction. Not surprisingly, the contestants did not do well; all of us have knowledge of some areas about which most other people are ignorant, and the questioners naturally chose questions from the areas of their special knowledge. After the contestant had done poorly on the ten-item "test," the questioner, the contestant, and the observers were all asked to make ratings of the general knowledge of the questioner and of the contestant.

Knowing how the "quiz" was arranged, we can predict with some confidence that even the most knowledgeable contestant would not answer many questions correctly; hence, failure to do so cannot rationally lead to a conclusion that the questioner has a greater level of general knowledge than does the contestant. Nevertheless, the observers rated the contestants as much less knowledgeable than the questioners. So did the contestants themselves! Only the questioners, who had access to the degree to which they had chosen questions with

[16]Ross, L. D.; Amabile, T. M.; and Steinmetz, J. L. (1977). Social roles, social control, and biases in social-perception process. *Journal of Personality and Social Psychology, 35*, 485–494.

a low probability of being answered correctly, failed to "learn" that the contestants lacked general knowledge, and that they themselves were particularly knowledgeable.

The Superannuation Problem

Experiences are necessarily of the past. Situations change. (Whether life is changing "more rapidly" in present generations than in past ones is a difficult judgment to make, particularly given the ubiquity of adaptation.) The difficult problem is to determine how a situation has changed, and how it has not. Conflicts arise—both within the single individual who has "learned" one way to behave but simultaneously perceives that the demands of the environment have changed, and across generations, where the argument is between the relative virtues of the "wisdom of age" versus the "new knowledge and approaches" (see, for example, Pearl Buck's *The Good Earth*). What is clear, however, is that a knee-jerk reaction to apply the "lessons of the past" in a mindless manner courts disaster. For example, some high-level executives who have been very successful at developing their organization behave in the same ways after the organization has become established as they did during the period of rapid growth. Having "learned" to ignore the doubting Thomases who point out the potential problems involved in their plans, they have built the financial base of the organization and succeeded in attracting talented people to it. But these talented people will leave if *their* advice and insights concerning problems are ignored. Moreover, it is rationally compelling that people or organizations that are well-off should not adopt high-risk strategies ("nowhere to go but down")—just as generals who are winning wars with the preponderance of manpower and material support on their side would be foolish to engage in bold military actions that have low probabilities of high payoffs. (Given the difference in their assets, both General Grant's "war of attrition" and General Lee's daring maneuvers were reasonable strategies during the American Civil War, although this difference is often ascribed to style or personality.) In fact, highly successful experience of any sort will of necessity *change the situation*, as well as actions that will lead to success or failure. It follows that these same actions in a different situation will not have the same consequences. Once again, past experience tends to be partially or wholly irrelevant, because the conditions have changed.

Creating One's Own Experience

Several years ago I had a long, unpleasant telephone conversation with a friend and colleague who had resigned his position with great anger and publicity. Toward the end of the conversation, he screamed at me, "The only way you get anywhere in this world is to push, push, push, push!"

This observation was true, for him. He had behaved in such an aggressive manner over the previous several years that no one was willing to engage in joint problem-solving with him, compromise with him, or regard his heart-felt wishes as anything but obnoxious demands. He had, in effect, dug a "social trap" for himself (see Chapter 9). Hostility begets hostility. As John F. Kennedy observed about the Cold War in 1963: "Suspicion on one side breeds suspicion on the other, and new weapons begat counter weapons."

This possibility of creating experience is not just an everyday observation; research evidence backs it up. For example, in an extensive social psychological literature on behavior in repeated games that may be played either competitively or cooperatively (the "prisoners' dilemma," see Chapter 9), the most replicable finding is that when one of two individuals playing the game behaves cooperatively, the probability that the other will cooperate in the future is enhanced, while if one individual plays competitively the probability that the other will cooperate is diminished.[17] Observations in natural settings also have supported this principle. For example, as Harold Rauch observed, both normal children and children with pathological hostility toward others tend to respond to hostility with hostility, the difference being that the disturbed children have a much higher probability of responding to friendliness with hostility than do the normal ones; the result is a cycle of hostile interaction, given the universal tit-for-tat response to hostility.[18]

It is very difficult to appreciate the role of our own behavior in *creating* our own experience. As pointed out in Chapter 2, we tend to

[17]This literature, as well as two computer simulation "tournaments" of such game-playing behavior is discussed in Axelrod, R. (1984). *The Evolution of Cooperation.* New York: Basic Books.

[18]See Rauch, H. L. (1965). Interaction sequences. *Journal of Personality and Social Psychology, 2,* 487–499.

view our behavior as responding to situational demands and the behavior of *others* as being determined primarily by personality factors. Consequently, it is difficult to understand the self-imposed bias in our own experience. It is perhaps even more difficult to understand the influence of past decisions on current ones; for example, having considered certain factors weighing against a decision we made in the past, we may simply ignore those factors when making a choice in similar circumstances "because we thought about that before, and it did not influence us then." Yet it is the *repeated* decisions we make that most bias our current reality. The friend who screamed at me had developed his own social trap only by adopting his "aggressive stance" on so many occasions that others came to expect it, to discount it, and to respond in kind. As this type of behavior is repeated, it ceases to have the subjective quality of decision, but merely that of a "natural reaction" to the circumstances, which become increasingly grim. With repetition, this grimness is less and less apt to be attributed to one's self.[19]

Biases of Retrospection

> Memory belongs to the imagination. Human memory is not like a computer which records things; it is part of the imaginative process, on the same terms as invention.—Alain Robbe-Grillet[20]

While memory from our experience is introspectively a process of "dredging up" *what actually happened*, it is to a large extent determined by our current beliefs and feelings. This principle has been well established both in the psychological laboratory and in surveys. What we have at the time of recall is, after all, only our current state, which includes fragments ("memory traces") of our past experience; these fragments are biased by what we now believe (or feel) to be true to an extent much greater than we know consciously. Moreover, the organi-

---

[19] I have been increasingly struck over the years by the congruence between the implications of behavioral decision theory and those of existentialism. The research evidence has born out many of the speculations of modern existentialists, particularly that of the degree to which we create our own reality.

[20] Robbe-Grillet, Alain (1986). The art of fiction XCI. *The Paris Review*, Spring, 46.

zation of these fragments of past experience into meaningful patterns is even more influenced by our current beliefs and moods—especially if we are particularly depressed or elated. Memory is basically a "reconstructive" process. Thus, our experience is often recalled inaccurately, even that selectively biased and possibly irrelevant experience discussed in the previous sections. The problem is particularly acute because our recall is often organized in ways that "make sense of" the present—thus reinforcing our belief in the conclusions we have reached about how the past has determined the present. We quite literally "make up stories" about our lives, the world, and reality in general. The fit between our memories and the stories enhances our belief in them. Often, however, it is the story that creates the memory, rather than vice versa.

For example, Greg Markus studied stability and change in political attitudes between 1973 and 1982.[21] Specifically, a national sample of 1,669 high school seniors in the graduating class of 1965, along with at least one parent in nearly every case, was surveyed in 1965, 1973, and in 1982. Fifty-seven percent of the parents (64% of those still living) and 68% of the students (70% of those alive) were personally interviewed all three times. All subjects were asked to indicate on a seven-point scale (with verbal anchors at the end) their attitudes toward five issues: guaranteed jobs, rights of accused people, aid to minorities, legalization of marijuana, and equality for women. In addition, they were asked to characterize their political views as generally liberal or generally conservative. Most important for analysis of the retrospective bias, Markus asked the respondents in 1982 to indicate how they had responded to each scale in 1973. The results were quite striking. With the exception of the ratings on the overall liberal-conservative scale, the subjects' recall of their 1973 attitudes in 1982 was more closely related to their rated attitudes *in 1982* than to the attitudes they had *actually* expressed in 1973. Retrospecting, they believed that their attitudes nine years previous were very close to their current one, much closer than they in fact were. This bias was so strong that an equation set up to predict subjects' recall of their 1973 attitudes gives almost all weight to their 1982 attitudes, and virtually none at all to the attitudes they actually expressed in 1973 (with the important exception of the students' overall liberal versus conservative ratings).

[21]Marcus, G. B. (1986). Stability and change in political attitudes: Observe, recall, and "explain." *Political Behavior, 8,* 21–44.

In addition, what discrepancy there was between 1982 attitudes and recall of 1973 attitudes could primarily be explained in terms of stereotypic beliefs about how general attitudes in the culture had changed; the subjects believed that they had become more conservative in general, but that (again in general) they had favored equality for women all along. Subjects whose attitude had changed in the direction counter to the general cultural change tended to be unaware of such change. Finally, the parent group attributed much more stability to their attitudes than did the student group, which is compatible with the belief that the attitudes of older people change less. In fact, however, the attitudes of the parent group were *less* stable.

Attitudes are, of course, somewhat amorphous and difficult to determine. Linda Collins and her colleagues found quite similar results for actual behaviors when they surveyed high school students about their use of tobacco, alcohol, and illegal "recreational" drugs.[22] They repeated the survey after one year and again after two and one-half years. At each repetition, the students (many of them then in college) were asked how much usage they had reported on the original questionnaire. (Collins and her colleagues had established strong rapport with this group and had reason to believe that their guarantees of confidentiality, which they honored, were in fact believed.) Again, the subjects' belief in lack of change introduced severe retrospective bias. For example, the recall of alcohol use for those subjects whose drinking habits had changed over the two-and-one-half-year period was more highly related to their reported use at the time of recall than to the reports they had made two and one-half years earlier.

Thus, change can make liars of us, liars to ourselves. That generalization is not limited to change in an undesirable direction. As George Valliant, who has studied the same individuals for many years throughout their adult lives, writes: "It is all too common for caterpillars to become butterflies and then to maintain that in their youth they had been little butterflies. Maturation makes liars of us all."[23]

[22]Collins, L. N.; Graham, J. W.; Hansen, W. B.; and Johnson, C. A. (1985). Agreement between retrospective accounts of substance use and earlier reported substance use. *Applied Psychological Measurement*, *9*, 301–309.

[23]Vaillant, G. E. *Adaptation to Life*. Boston: Little, Brown and Company, 1977.

(Recall the quote about caterpillars and butterflies from André Gide in Chapter 2.)

But not always. Sometimes, when our belief is in change, we recall change even when it has not occurred. In order to make our view compatible with this belief, we resort (again not consciously) to changing our recall of the earlier state. We can, for example, reinforce our belief in a nonexistent change for the better by simply exaggerating how bad things were before the change. Certainly there have been times before a religious or psychiatric conversion, for example, when the individual was badly off (we all are at times), and memories of those times persist; recall can be organized around the traces of these memories. A dieter who has not succeeded in losing a single pound can certainly recall periods of time prior to embarking on a diet when he or she was heavier than when he or she completes the ineffective diet; by carefully not recording his or her weight before starting the diet, those times can be recalled as an evidence for its success.

Experimental evidence supports the contention that when we believe a change has occurred we are apt to distort the past in the direction compatible with the change. For example, in two separate but similar experiments, Conway and Ross randomly selected participants for a university program designed to improve study skills and a control group of students who had indicated a desire to be in the program and were on the waiting list for it. Participants and controls were questioned before the study skills program began and at its conclusion. At both times, they were asked to assess their study skills (e.g., how much of their study time was well spent, how satisfactory their note-taking skills were, etc.) and the amount of time they studied. At the second interview they were also asked to recall what they reported during the first session concerning their skills and study time.[24]

At the initial interview, participants and controls did not differ significantly on any measure of skill, study time, or other variables. Both groups performed equally well and—most important to the study—the program itself was not found to improve study skills. Nor did it improve grades. When asked to recall their situations before the program started (or before they were put on the waiting list), how-

[24]Conway, M., and Ross, M. (1984). Getting what you want by revising what you had. *Journal of Personality and Social Psychology, 47,* 738–748.

ever, the subjects did differ. There was no difference between the two groups in their memory of the amount of time they spent studying, but their recall of their skills was markedly different. Program participants recalled their study skills as being significantly *worse* than they had initially reported, while on the average, waiting-list subjects recalled their skills as being approximately the same as they had reported initially. Thus, program participants exaggerated their improvement in a direction consistent with their beliefs of what *ought* to be (improved skills due to taking the course), not by exaggerating their current skills, but rather by reconstructing their memory of the past to fit with the belief that they should have improved. In short, they recalled themselves as having been worse off before they entered the program than they had in fact been. There was no such distortion on the part of the subjects who had been put on the waiting list.

Mood also affects recall. It has, for example, been strongly established experimentally by Gordon Bower and others that recall of material learned in a particular mood is facilitated by recreation of that mood.[25] Does the same principle apply to our recall of our own lives? Is our recall of events that occurred when we were in a bad mood—which are usually negative events—facilitated by a current bad mood, and vice versa for good moods? The answer is yes.

Lewinsohn and Rosenbaum studied the recall of parental behavior by acute depressives, remitted depressives (that is, people who had once been depressed and were no longer depressed), nondepressives (people who had never been depressed), and "predepressives" (people who were to become depressed) in a group of 2,000 people over a three-year period. One focus of this research was on the relationship between current mood states and memory; one possibility is that recollections of one's parents are influenced by a current state of depression or nondepression; another is that people who are *prone* to depression recall their parents differently from those who are not (the nondepressives). Theories that depression follows from childhood problems would predict that the childhood of those of us who are depression-*prone* is different from that of those who are not and hence would be recalled differently, while theories about the effect of current mood on past recall predict that the primary difference in recall should be between people who are *currently* depressed and those who

---

[25]Bower, G. (1981). Mood and memory. *American Psychologist, 36*, 129–148.

are not. The results were consistent with the hypothesis that recollection of one's parents as rejecting and unloving is strongly influenced by current moods; it is not a stable characteristic of depression-prone people. "Whereas the currently depressed subjects recalled their parents as having been more rejecting and as having used more negative control than the normal controls, the remitted depressives did not differ from the never depressed control in their recall of parental behavior. Similarly, the subjects who were about to become depressed shortly after the initial testing did not differ from the controls in their recollections of the degree to which their parents used negative control methods."[26] One particularly important aspect of this study was that the subjects were drawn from the general population; they were not sampled on the basis of having any particular psychiatric problems.[27]

This study of depression is particularly important in that it casts doubt on the degree to which adult problems are related to childhood ones. Given a biasing effect of mood on memory, people who are distressed as adults tend to remember distressing incidents in their childhood. One result is the view that the sources of the problems encountered lie in early life is reinforced. To the degree to which the people accept this view, it may serve as an organizing principle for even greater distortion of recall, which in a circular way reinforces the "child is father to the man" view of life. (Freud himself emphasized

---

[26]Lewinsohn, P. M., and Rosenbaum, M. (1987). Recall of parental behavior by acute depressives, remitted depressives, and nondepressives. *Journal of Personality and Social Psychology 52*, 611–620.

[27]There is no way of determining the *accuracy* of this recall. It is possible, for example, that when the depression-prone people become depressed, their memory of their parents' behavior loses the "rosy glow" that appears to be a concomitant of "good mental health," and that the reports are in fact more accurate than when the people are not depressed. Some evidence supports that depressed people are more accurate in their perceptions—of themselves anyway—than are people judged to be in good psychological health; these latter people tend to have a "Pollyannish" view of themselves and their abilities—in fact, depressed people tend to become "Pollyannish" as they get over their depression. See Lewinsohn, P. M.; Michel, W.; Chaplin, W.; and Barton, R. (1980). Social competence and depression: The role of illusory self-perceptions? *Journal of Abnormal Psychology, 89*, 203–212.

that he knew people who had childhood problems similar to those of his patients but who never became distressed. One view of Freudian psychology is that when adults become distressed, the form of the distress will mirror childhood problems. That is not the same, however, as saying that these childhood problems *cause* adult distress. These problems may even be necessary for adult neurosis and psychosis, but again that does not make them sufficient. The idea that childhood problems necessarily lead to adult ones [i.e., are sufficient to cause adult problems] is due much more to the neo-analytic followers of Sigmund Freud than to Freud himself—particularly those who have popularized their view of neo-Freudian psychology; see, for example, Harry Overstreet's book *The Mature Mind*.)[28]

Finally, our retrospective bias that we (usually) haven't changed can lead us to expect that we will not change with changing circumstances; in particular, that our intentions and motives—which, as pointed out in Chapter 2 and the previous section, serve as background in our judgment of our experience—will not change. For example, consider the statement, "You have nothing to fear from me now that I have this power over you; I have always been benign." (Reagan administration officials assert that the Soviets have nothing to fear if "we" develop an invulnerable "star wars" defense, because "our" intentions have always been peaceful, mainly defensive. First, we must remember that we are not always the best judges of our own intentions, particularly not of what they have been in the past. Second, intentions can change as capacities do, and the person who changes is often "the last to know." Third, and most importantly, the Soviets have no way of knowing who the "we" in charge of U.S. policy will be when and if such a defense system is ever perfected; nor do *we*.)

The Probabilistic Relationship between Events and Outcomes

As I stressed from the beginning, the wisdom of decisions cannot be evaluated fully by their outcomes. Again, an individual gambler who accepts 50–50 odds that the next roll of fair dice will be snake-eyes makes a foolish decision, even when snake-eyes subsequently occur. Pure luck—good or bad—is a partial determinant of many conse-

---

[28]Overstreet, Harry (1949). *The Mature Mind*. New York: W. W. Norton. See particularly Chapter 10, "The home as a place for growth." Earlier, Overstreet alleges: "The human individual is a fairly tight-knit pattern of consistency" (p. 73.).

quences, as are a great many factors that are beyond the decision-maker's control (or sometimes even knowledge). Nevertheless, in an attempt to learn from experience, we often focus on the consequences of decisions we have made as if they follow inevitably. The result is that we "overlearn" from experience, believing that what appeared to be wisdom in the past is *in fact* wisdom, and that what appeared to be folly is in fact folly. That is not necessarily so. As we will see in Chapter 12, we tend to derogate the influence of luck, often to our own disadvantage. Moreover, a social stigma is attached to attributing failure to "bad breaks" (although we may make that claim internally), and our supporters try to dissuade us from the modest-appearing attribution that our successes might also be due to factors beyond our control. ("Oh no, you really *deserved* that promotion; the fact that your competitor was killed in an airplane crash had very little to do with the choice.") By viewing consequences as inevitable results of choice, we create a phony coherence in our experience, and if we believe in that coherence too much, it offers a poor basis for making decisions about the future.

The Lack of Comparison in Experience

Briefly put, we do not know what would have happened if something else had happened first. This is not a failing on our part; it is a necessity, because only one set of events occurs in our experience at a particular time. In fact, it is precisely the lack of such knowledge that makes the methodology of social science and psychology necessary for investigating our social and internal worlds. This methodology is based on *comparative* investigations, which by necessity elude us in our own experience. We cannot know what would have happened if something else had happened first.

We often agree with that principle when it is stated in the abstract and then ignore it when contemplating our own experience. We believe, for example, that certain decisions we have made are good ones because the consequences were desirable, but yet we have no way of knowing what the consequences would have been had we decided to do something else. We may castigate ourselves for certain decisions, such as for having a "fender-bender" accident on an uncleared side road during a snowy evening, when for all we know we might have been killed if we had decided to take the main highway. (Consider the most trivial of decisions while driving, whether to stop for a yellow light or speed through the intersection; now we will change the entire driving pattern for the rest of our trip, a pattern that may not only have different consequences in itself, but might "snowball" into different courses of our life as we reach our destination at different points in time.) We just don't know what would have happened *if*, and we have no way of knowing. Trivial changes can have profound consequences ("for want of a nail . . .").

But we think about our experience as if we *can* make comparisons:

> "I couldn't be happier [or more miserable]."
> "Being with you is the best [or worst] decision I have ever made in my life, dear [or you lousy . . .]."

Regardless of the romantic experience of this couple, they have no way of justifying their statements. (Such statements are often good [or bad] ones to make anyway, the point being that we tend to *believe* them.) To claim never to have been happier (or more miserable) is one thing (and again subject to the seven distortions listed), but to say that a decision is good or bad (or optimal or pessimal) is another. Nevertheless, experience is the basis on which we often make such judgments, and society at large does as well. Consider, for example, the number of governmental decisions based on the *testimonials* of people who have had particular experiences, such as having become addicted to drugs or alcohol and then having changed "as a result" of a particular program or experience. There is no way logically to use such statements to evaluate the reality; nevertheless, our government and others ascribe great weight to such experience—particularly that of legislators or other decision makers themselves. (For the decision makers, who are often older people, the experience may be out-dated as well as ambiguous.) Governments "learn" from the past, even though the past cannot be manipulated in any way in order to reach the comparative judgment about what might have happened had things been different. During the Vietnam War, for example, our leaders cited "the lessons of Munich" so often that it was sometimes unclear whether we were fighting Ho Chi Minh or Hitler, despite the fact that our leaders had no knowledge of what would have occurred had the Munich agreement not been negotiated. Such "learning" can be pernicious, especially for governmental policy makers who treat current problems as if they were past ones.[29]

---

[29]See May, E. R. (1973). *Lessons of the Past: The Use and Misuse of History in American Foreign Policy.* New York: Oxford University Press.

Post Hoc Ergo Propter Hoc Causal Reasoning

This Latin phrase refers to the conclusion that one event caused a second event because it preceded it. It is possible to ridicule such reasoning with ludicrous examples (e.g., brushing teeth causes addiction to heroin, birth is a primary cause of death, Aunt Matilda's walking along the lake in the light of a full moon caused her remission from cancer). Nevertheless, it is a common form of causal reasoning in which all of us engage on occasion—often without awareness. Sometimes it makes great sense; for example, failure to study for an examination caused a poor grade. (Perhaps the individual would have attained a poor grade anyway, and we could just as well attribute the causality to the deviousness of the instructor in writing the questions.) In fact, the whole process of attributing causality in everyday life tends to be one of *post hoc ergo propter hoc* reasoning. (See Chapter 2 for a discussion of "attribution theory.") The reason is that there is no other basis most of the time on which to make such causal judgments.[30]

Often, regression effects (discussed in Chapter 5) make such *post hoc ergo propter hoc* "learning" particularly dubious. We take action when something goes wrong. If that problem occurs in a relatively "steady state" environment, the statistical expectation is that the problem will be less serious at time 2 than at time 1 simply because the severity of problems at time 2 is not perfectly correlated with such severity at time 1—just as the son of an extremely tall father is most likely to be less tall than the father, as is the father of an extremely tall son, because the correlation of heights between fathers and sons is not perfect. (See section 5.7.) Cohen and Marsh illustrate this problem well in the context of managers' learning from their decisions about how to treat subordinates who have problems.[31]

---

[30]Bertrand Russell argues that causality has little place in scientific theorizing; see, for example, Russell, B. (1913). On the notion of cause. *Proceedings of the Aristotelian Society, 13*, 1–26. Causality certainly plays a role in everyday thinking, however. I would go one step beyond Russell and claim that we might be much better off if we were to diminish that role. As pointed out in Chapter 2, our causal attributions can be punishing as well as rewarding, and since they have very little logical basis to begin with, we might be better off without them.

[31]Cohen, M. D., and Marsh, J. G. (1974). *Leadership and Ambiguity: The American College President.* New York: McGraw-Hill.

We can illustrate the phenomenon by taking a familiar instance of learning in the realm of personnel policies. Suppose that a manager reviews his subordinates annually and considers what to do with those who are doing poorly. He has two choices: he can replace an employee whose performance is low, or he can keep him in the job and try to work with him to obtain improvement. He chooses which employees to replace and which to keep in the job on the basis of his judgment about their capacities to respond to different treatments. Now suppose that, in fact, there are no differences among the employees. Observed variations in performance are due entirely to random fluctuations. What would the manager "learn" in such a situation?

He would learn how smart he was. He would discover that his judgments about whom to keep and whom to replace were quite good. Replacements will generally perform better than the men they replaced; those men who are kept in the job will generally improve in their performance. If for some reason he starts out being relatively "humane" and refuses to replace anyone, he will discover that the best managerial strategy is to work to improve existing employees. If he starts out with a heavy hand and replaces everyone, he will learn that being tough is a good idea. If he replaces some and works with others, he will learn that the essence of personnel management is judgment about the worker.

Although we know that in this hypothetical situation it makes no difference what a manager does, he will experience some subjective learning that is direct and compelling. He will come to believe that he understands the situation and has mastered it. If we were to suggest to the manager that he might be a victim of superstitious learning, he would find it difficult to believe. Everything in his environment tells him that he understands the world, even though his understanding is spurious.

Note that the regression problem in such learning is closely related to the failure to appreciate the role of random variation in experience. But chance fluctuation is just one reason regression occurs. *Whenever* there is an imperfect prediction from one variable to another—*for whatever reason*—the best prediction is regressive; that is, the value predicted will on the average be closer to its mean than is the value from which it is predicted. It's a simple averaging effect. (Again, see Figure 5.2.)

Governments also engage in the *post hoc ergo propter hoc* method of causal inference (and psychotherapists *must*, insofar as they make judgments on the basis of their interaction with a particular client rather than on the basis of scientific principles). For example, the

Rogers Commission investigating the space shuttle disaster of January 1986 relied entirely on information about what led up to it in order to criticize the decision making of NASA.[32] This retrospectively based information taken from people who we could expect to be motivated to remember the past in ways that would protect their reputations and careers. The Commission concluded that a number of decisions made prior to the final one to launch the *Challenger* failed to address the evidence that there had been deterioration of the O-rings on previous flights. What the Commission *did not* do was develop information that would allow it to make a *comparative* judgment—either by *contrasting* the decision making leading to the *Challenger* launch with decision making leading to more successful launches within NASA, or to the decision making in programs that had not experienced such a disaster (e.g., the Nuclear Submarine Program). For example, the Commission placed great weight on the memoranda from Morton Thiokol engineers warning of possible problems with O-rings, one of which began with the single word *HELP!*, but no effort was made to determine how many similar memoranda were sent from engineers to management people responsible for making decisions—in particular, memoranda about potential problems that turned out to be unimportant. (That is the "base rate" problem discussed in Chapter 5.) In fact, from all that can be gathered from the Commission's report, the particular engineer started the memorandum with "HELP!" as a matter of personal style. (I'm not saying that he did, just that we don't know.) Nevertheless, the Commission concluded that in addition to the physical causes well documented with photographs and engineering analyses, NASA's "poor" decision making was also a causal factor in the disaster.

In contrast, the whole thrust of social science research is to search for some comparison—whether from within existing groups or across them, or—most rigorously—from randomly constituted experimental and control groups. I do not wish to be unduly harsh on the thinking processes of the Commission members, because they are typical of people not trained in social science methodology, and because in this context there is no opportunity for the type of precise comparison desired. They did, however, have a distressing tendency to ignore questions of base rates.

But trained experts are giving the government advice about

[32]Rogers, W. P. (1986). *Report of the Presidential Commission on the Space Shuttle Challenger Accident.*

"street people," and even such trained experts occasionally fall prey to the *post hoc ergo propter hoc* fallacy. For example, the "causal role" of mental illness is investigated by defining people as mentally ill if they are *either* currently distressed *or* have a history of psychiatric hospitalization. The sum of these two percentages (less the percentage of people that are classified in both ways) is then used as an estimate of the proportion of the people on the streets who are "chronically mentally ill." (For references, see footnote 2 in section 6.1.) The first problem with such an estimate is that it assumes that people who have been hospitalized and who are now on the streets are necessarily mentally ill now. While "any psychiatrist" can claim that success for such people is a "sometimes thing" (again, as it is for *all* of us), the proportion of people who leave a hospital and then become sufficiently disturbed to need to return may be overestimated by hospital personnel—because they are the only former patients of whom they learn. Former patients who do well drop from their sight (availability of instances). Thus, not only is the "if ever, then now" syllogism logically inappropriate, the actual proportions involved are skewed. More importantly, the conclusion that homeless, impoverished, mentally ill people are homeless and impoverished *because* they are mentally ill is a particularly destructive form of *post hoc ergo propter hoc* reasoning. Would impoverishment improve the mental health of any of us? ("There but for fortune go I.")

The "scientifically rational" way to determine the degree to which mental illness is a factor in leading people to live on the streets would be to provide the opportunity for food, safe shelter, and a job to everyone and then determine what proportion of people were so disoriented that they would continue to live on the streets. Ironically, the very belief—*post hoc ergo propter hoc*—that such homelessness is due to mental illness is a factor preventing the implementation of such a social policy, or even its consideration.

Let me give an example of the difficulty of establishing causality on a *post hoc ergo propter hoc* basis from even the most systematic analysis of experience, one involving prolonged periods of time and many people. John Howard and I analyzed two different samples of daily activity reports of distressed and nondistressed heterosexual couples and found that couples who were happy made love more and fought less than did couples who were unhappy.[33] That did not sur-

---

[33] Howard, J. W., and Dawes, R. M. (1976). Linear prediction of marital happiness. *Personality and Social Psychology Bulletin, 2,* 478–480.

prise us. What was striking, however, was that in one of these samples *all* the distressed couples had fights more often than they made love, and that in the other sample the rate of intercourse per week minus the rate of fighting was the best predictor we had of self-assessments of married (or coupled) happiness. Later, Thornton replicated this finding and, systematically comparing this difference with variables suggested by theory and marital counselors, found it to be superior to all.[34] (Thornton had the couples report their behavior first and then assess their happiness—reversing our order. It is possible that what his subjects discovered when they monitored their behavior may have affected their ratings; for example, one subject decided she wanted a divorce when she discovered that she was fighting more than she was loving.)

Our colleagues, of course, interpreted this finding as indicating that psychological factors leading to happiness or unhappiness also lead to differential rates of intercourse and fighting. That's "obvious." In contrast, Howard and I occasionally joked about setting up a marital counseling service—or at least an experiment—consisting of the simple manipulation of requiring subjects to make love more often. ("Try it. You'll like it.") The point is that *given only these data*, it is impossible to distinguish between the interpretation that unhappiness causes less love making and more fighting and the interpretation that less love making and more fighting cause unhappiness. My own speculation, counter to both that of my colleagues and our hypothetical treatment proposal, is that the relationship is one of "reciprocal causation"—with the consequence that happiness or unhappiness tends to be augmented through the positive feedback that results.

The Hindsight Bias

In a series of ingenious studies, Baruch Fischhoff demonstrated that people who know the nature of events *falsely* overestimate the probability with which they would have predicted it.[35] In his initial studies,

---

[34]Thornton, B. (1977). Linear prediction of marital happiness: A replication. *Personality and Social Psychology Bulletin, 3*, 674–676.

[35]See, for example, Fischhoff, B. (1980). For those condemned to study the past: Reflective on historical judgment. In Schwede, R. A., and Fiske, D. W. (eds.). *New Directions for Methodology of Behavioral Science: Fallible Judgments in Behavioral Research*. San Francisco: Jossey-Bass, 79–93.

Fischhoff simply asked people to predict what would happen before particular events occurred (e.g., Nixon's visit to China) and then to recall what they had predicted. Their recall was biased in the direction of having predicted what actually happened. It follows, as Fischhoff points out, we are "insufficiently surprised" by experience. One result is that we do not learn effectively from it.

Note that this "hindsight bias" is not reducible to a "knew-it-all-along" attempt to appear more omniscient than we are. People actually *make mistakes* in their recall of what they thought would happen, even when they are motivated to be as accurate as possible. Memory fits knowledge. While this "creeping determinism"—to use Fischhoff's phrase—is well-documented, the exact mechanism or (more likely) mechanisms accounting for it are still under investigation.

Overview

The degree to which we can really "learn from experience" is suspect, for the reasons just discussed as well as others. But our experience is the stuff of reality. We have only our personal experience; even the vicarious experience that we believe we possess is based on our own personal contact with it. We are stuck. We cannot, for example, conduct controlled experiments to determine how things would be different *if* something else had happened or we had done something differently; only one thing happens at a particular time, and we are constrained to make only one decision in a particular circumstance. In fact, we cannot even make sloppy and ad hoc comparisons. The point of this section is to instill caution, particularly to show why we must guard against mindless extrapolation from the past to the present and the future. It may well be true that "those who do not remember the past are condemned to relive it" (George Santayna), but it is also true that we often avoid making *exactly* the same mistake twice—even when it would not be a mistake the second time. (As James Thurber once pointed out, we often fall on our face because we have previously fallen on our ass.[36]) I have no simple solution to the problems raised here. My desire is simply to introduce what I hope is a healthy skepticism about "learning from experience." In fact, what we often must do is to learn how to *avoid* learning from experience.

[36]Thurber, J. (1945). The bear who let it alone. In *The Thurber Carnival*. New York and London: Harper and Brothers, 214–215.

6.5 ANCHORING AND ADJUSTMENT

Often, our estimates of probabilities and of the desirability of consequences are vague. Even when they are not, they may be influenced by such factors as framing, grouping, representative thinking, and availability. In ambiguous situations, a seemingly more trivial factor may have a profound effect: an "anchor" that serves as an orienting point for estimating probabilities or outcomes. What happens is that people will adjust their estimates *from* this anchor but nevertheless remain close to it. We "underadjust." For example, if we know (individually or vicariously) a particular professional football player, we expect other professional football players to be a lot like him. If we have had a good meal in a particular restaurant, we expect the restaurant's other offerings to be equally tasty (and are often disappointed, due to regression effects). If we know a coin to be fair, we expect two heads in four tosses (even though the probability of that particular occurrence is ⅜).

Such anchors may be entirely arbitrary. For example, in 1972 Daniel Kahneman and Amos Tversky asked student subjects to estimate the percentage of African countries that were in the United Nations. (The correct answer was 35%.) Prior to making the estimates, however, the subjects were requested to make a simple binary judgment of whether this percentage was greater or less than a number determined by spinning a wheel that contained numbers between 1 and 100. The wheel was in fact rigged so that the number that came up was either 10 or 65. Subjects who first judged whether the percentage was greater or less than 10 made an average estimate of 25%; those who first judged whether it was greater or less than 65 made an average estimate of 45%. Thus, 10 and 65 served as anchors for the estimates *even though the subjects were led to believe that these numbers were generated in a totally arbitrary manner*. What happened was that the final estimates were "insufficiently" adjusted away from these anchors. (The finding of such insufficiency is general; in this particular example, the reader may question—as I do—whether knowledgeable subjects could be expected to know that the actual percentage was as low as 35.)

Let me give another example of an arbitrary anchor, this one implicit rather than explicit. Subjects were asked, again by Kahneman and Tversky, to estimate the magnitude of "8!" ("8 factorial," which means $8 \times 7 \times 6 \ldots$; the correct answer is 40,320.) The subjects were expected to know neither the answer nor the factorial terminology, and the problem was presented in two different ways. Some subjects were asked to estimate the product $8\times7\times6\times5\times4\times3\times2\times1$, while others were asked to estimate the product $1\times2\times3\times4\times5\times6\times7\times8$. Kahneman and Tversky argued, from other psychological literature indicating the importance of "primacy" in judgment, that the first number presented would serve as an anchor. Indeed, it appeared to do so. The median judgment of the subjects presented with the numbers in the ascending sequence ($1\times2\times3\times$ . . .) was 512, whereas the median estimate for those presented with the descending sequence ($8\times7\times6$ . . .) was 2,250. (Note, however, that in both formats subjects tended to underestimate the true product: 40,320.)

The "classic" studies on anchoring and adjustment were conducted using choice versus pricing between gambles by Paul Slovic, Sarah Lichtenstein, and Baruch Fischhoff.[37] They studied such choice and pricing in two discrepant contexts: survey experiments in which college-student subjects made hypothetical choices and provided hypothetical monetary values for the gambles, and actual choices at a casino in Las Vegas in which gamblers played—and bought or sold the gambles—for substantial amounts of real money. The results were the same.

The gambles consisted simply of probabilities to win or lose certain amounts of money. Subjects were requested to respond to these gambles in one of two ways: either they were asked how much money they would accept in lieu of playing the gamble, or they were asked which of two gambles they would prefer to play. To encourage subjects to state as their "selling price" the true monetary worth of the gamble to them, the experimenters used a device that determined a random "counterbid." If this counterbid was lower than the stated selling price, the subject played the gamble; if it was higher, the subject was given the amount of the counterbid. Now consider any subjects who state a selling price that is *less* than the true monetary value of the gamble to them. If the randomly determined counterbid falls *between* the stated selling price and the true monetary value, the subjects are

[37]See, for example, Slovic, P.; Fischhoff, B.; and Lichtenstein, S. (1982). Responsibility, framing, and information-processing effects in risk assessment. In Hogarth, R. (ed.), *New Directions for Methodology of Social and Behavioral Science: Question Framing and Response Consistency* (No. 11). San Francisco: Jossey-Bass.

given the amount of the counterbid when in fact they would prefer to play the gamble. Also consider subjects whose stated selling price is *higher* than the true monetary value to them. If the randomly determined counterbid falls between their true monetary value for the gamble and their stated selling price (which is then higher), these subjects would have to play a gamble when in fact they would prefer to receive the amount of the counterbid. Thus, subjects who state a selling price that is either too high or too low can be put in a position where they receive one alternative (the privilege of playing the gamble or the counterbid) although they would prefer the other. This procedure was thoroughly explained to the subjects, and when they appeared to understand its logic, the experimenters commenced.

Consider two such gambles. Gamble A has an $^{11}/_{36}$ probability of winning $16 and a $^{25}/_{36}$ probability of losing $1.50; Gamble B has a $^{35}/_{36}$ probability of winning $4 and a $^{1}/_{36}$ probability of losing $1. (The expected values are both approximately $3.85; see Appendix A2.) Subjects given the choice between these two gambles have a strong tendency to choose the second, which has the higher probability of winning—people like to win. When asked for their selling prices, however, these very same people produce a larger dollar equivalent for the first—it has a higher payoff. The hypothesis is that when people think of winning versus losing, they *anchor* on the probability of success; higher probabilities are more desirable. They then insufficiently modify their judgment on the basis of the amount to be won or lost. When they are asked to produce a monetary equivalent (through the selling price procedure), however, they first anchor on the monetary amounts and the outcomes. Again, they insufficiently adjust in terms of the probabilities involved. The result is that the very same subject at different parts of the interaction with the experimenter may prefer Gamble A to Gamble B, but state a higher selling price for Gamble A. That can turn such a subject into a "money pump."[38] The experimenter "sells" the first gamble to the subject for the amount specified. Then, given a choice between the two gambles and selecting the second, the subject trades the second for the first. Now the experimenter buys back the second gamble for the selling price specified by the subject. Because this amount is less than the previous amount, the experimenter has made a profit—while the subject is left

---

[38] As will be illustrated in Chapter 8, any inconsistent set of preferences can turn the person holding them into a "money pump."

with the original gamble he or she bought. The experimenter can repeat the sequence in order to "pump" the subject for money; in fact, the experimenter can even begin by giving the subject one of the two gambles and still make an infinite profit (hypothetically anyway). Interestingly, people who have this pattern of preferences and selling prices will engage in this buying, choice, and selling procedure repeatedly—even though they realize while doing so that the experimenter is making a profit. Comments such as "I just can't help it," and "I know it's silly and you're taking advantage of me, but I really do prefer that one although I think the other is more valuable," are common.[39]

Such *preference reversals* challenge standard economic theory, which equates the utility (personal value) of an object with the amount of money people are willing to pay for it. Two "experimental economists," Charles Plott and David Grether, "rose to the challenge" by conducting a series of experiments using real monetary payoffs in which they examined every possible "artifactual" explanation for such reversals. They concluded that the finding was robust; they found no artifacts.[40]

Anchors need not consist of extreme values. For example, people often use an average as an anchor. We all know such people, those habitual compromisers who always say "six" when one person says "one" and another says "eleven." In fact, such behavior has even been observed in a subcommittee for educational funding of a state legislature. No one at the meeting could remember exactly how much money the staff had recommended budgeting for continuing education. Two members had quite discrepant ideas about the amount, but neither was sure of the figure. These amounts were simply averaged, and the committee members proceeded to discuss whether or not the resulting figure should be raised or lowered.

The most common anchor, of course, is the status quo. While we are not constrained mentally—as we are physically—to begin a journey from where we are, we often do. Changes in existing plans or policies more readily come to mind than do new ones, and even as new alternatives close to the status quo are considered, they, too, can

---

[39]Professor S. Lichtenstein has a particularly amusing tape of one such subject.

[40]Grether, D. M., and Plott, C. R. (1979). Economic theory of choice in the preference reversal phenomenon. *American Economic Review, 69,* 623–638.

become anchors. This generalization is true of organizations as well as of individuals. As Cyert and March write, firms "search in the neighborhood of the current alternative."[41]

Finally, bounded search procedures can be directed *toward* a satisficing alternative or *away from* an undesirable alternative. Again, the status quo or the currently considered alternative can serve to anchor the search. Sometimes asking what is desired *without* considering what is currently possessed is superior. The probable consequences of the possible alternatives define their desirability; rationality demands that evaluation be made in terms of these consequences. A search procedure that limits the considered alternatives and consequences through anchoring is at best "boundedly" rational. To the degree to which such anchors are arbitrary, they encourage irrational choice.

---

[41]Cyert, R. M., and March, J. G. (1963). *A Behavioral Theory of the Firm*. Englewood Cliffs, N.J.: Prentice-Hall, 121.

CHAPTER

To leave Vietnam to its fate would
shake the confidence of all these
people in the value of an American
commitment and in the value of
America's word. The result would
be increased unrest and instability
and even wider war. . . . The battle
would be renewed in one country
and then another.

Lyndon B. Johnson
April 7, 1965

7

Scenario Thinking

7.1 INTRODUCTION

Ask a person how likely it is that an alcoholic tennis star who starts drinking a fifth a day will go on to win a major tournament eight months later, and he or she will probably answer that it is extremely unlikely. Now ask another person how likely it is that an alcoholic tennis star who starts drinking a fifth a day will join Alcoholics Anonymous (AA) a month later, quit drinking, and win a major tournament eight months later. To most people that seems not quite as unlikely.

It is logically necessary, however, that the first outcome (winning the tournament) is more likely for the alcoholic star who starts drinking a fifth a day than is the second (joining AA *and* quitting *and* winning the tournament). The probability of three events *must* be less than the probability of one of them alone. In this example, there are ways in which the star could win the tournament without joining AA (for instance, quitting drinking on his own, bribing the other players, even just being extraordinarily lucky). Hence, winning the tournament must be more likely than winning it after the specific action of joining AA, which in turn is followed by the specific action of quitting. But joining AA creates a scenario that is *representative* of the ways alcoholic individuals rehabilitate themselves. By *scenario* I mean an ordered sequence of events, each of which is judged to be probable (on a rational or an irrational basis).

Belief in the likelihood of scenarios tends to be associated with belief in the likelihood of their components; believable components yield believable scenarios (and often vice versa as well). That association yields overestimation of the probability of scenarios for two reasons. First, a combination of events may be improbable even though each event in it is probable; the probability of a combination of events $1, 2, \ldots, k$ is $p_1 \times p_2 \times \ldots \times p_k$, where p_1 is the probability of the first, p_2 is the probability of the second *given* the first, p_3 is the probability of the third given the first two, and so on (see Appendix A1). $p_1 \times p_2 \times \ldots \times p_k$ may be quite small, even though each p_i in it is large; for example, $.90 \times .80 \times .85 \times .80 \times .85 \times .90 = .37$ even though $.80$ is the smallest number in this sequence. To estimate the probability of the sequence on the basis of its components' probability (average $= .85$) seriously overestimates this number. Second, any irrational cognitive factors—such as imaginability—that lead to an overestimation of the probability of a component may also lead to an overestimation of the probability of the scenario as a whole. In fact, the imaginability of the entire scenario may lead to *greater* belief in the likelihood of it than in one of its components, as illustrated by the belief that the sequence AA–quit–win is more probable than the single event win.[1]

7.2 THE COMPOUND PROBABILITY FALLACY

It is not even necessary to ask separate people to obtain judgments that pairs of events may be more likely than single events. As part of a general investigation indicating that people generally overestimate compound probabilities, Amos Tversky and Daniel Kahneman have demonstrated that such judgments can be obtained from individual college students and experts.[2] Kahneman and Tversky term the belief that a combination of events can be more likely than parts of that combination the *extension fallacy*. A more precise designation is *compound probability fallacy*.

Kahneman and Tversky asked college students the following question:

> Linda is thirty-one years old, single, outspoken, and very bright. She majored in philosophy. As a student she was deeply concerned with issues of discrimination and social justice and also participated in anti-nuclear demonstrations. How likely is it that:
> - Linda is a teacher in an elementary school.
> - Linda works in a bookstore and takes yoga classes.
> - Linda is active in the feminist movement.
> - Linda is a psychiatric social worker.
> - Linda is a member of the League of Women Voters.
> - Linda is a bank teller.
> - Linda is an insurance salesperson.
> - Linda is a bank teller and is active in the feminist movement.

Fully 86% of 88 undergraduates questioned believed it more likely that Linda is a bank teller *and* active in the feminist movement than that

---

[1]Since $p(A) = p(A \text{ and } B) + p(A \text{ and not-}B)$, $p(A \text{ and } B)$ cannot be greater than $p(A)$.

[2]Tversky, A., and Kahneman, D. (1983). Extensional versus intuitive reasoning: The conjunction fallacy in probability judgment. *Psychological Bulletin, 90,* 293–315.

Linda is a bank teller. The reason? Given the information about Linda, we can imagine her becoming a feminist bank teller, but it is hard to imagine her as merely a (stereotyped) bank teller, *even though feminism was not mentioned in the description of Linda*. (Could she not also have been a very devout fundamentalist Christian in college?) Even when the bank teller alternative was stated as "Linda is a bank teller whether or not she is active in the feminist movement," 57% of an additional 75 students believed that "Linda is a bank teller and in the feminist movement" was more likely.

Kahneman and Tversky also discovered the compound probability fallacy when they asked medical internists questions about symptoms and diagnoses. For example:

> A fifty-five-year-old woman had a pulmonary embolism (blood clot in the lung). How likely is it that she also experiences:
> - dyspnea [shortness of breath] and hemiparesis [partial paralysis]
> - calf pain
> - pleuritic chest pain
> - syncope [fainting] and techycardic [accelerated heart beat]
> - hemiparesis
> - hemoptysis [coughing blood]

On the average, 91% of the 32 internists questioned believed that the combination of a probable symptom (in this case dyspnea) and an improbable one (in this case hemiparesis) was more likely than the improbable symptom alone.

Clinical psychologists as well as physicians make this error. At the workshop described in section 5.1, I asked the clinicians to make a prediction involving single and multiple events.

> B. C. was a top student in high school, but was somewhat withdrawn and asocial. He dated rarely, belonged to no social group, and had few friends. Although he was doing well in his freshman year at his Ivy League college, he became very depressed at the beginning of his second semester. When therapy through the college counseling center failed to help, he was hospitalized with a diagnosis of psychotic depression. After four months with no improvement, he was about to be given ECT when he started getting better. By the following fall, he was out of the hospital, and he returned to college the second semester to complete his freshman year. He took antidepression medication but quit therapy after concluding it was not helping. That June, a significant event occurred in his life. Rank the following possibilities for that event in the order of their likelihood.

_____ B. C. flunked out of college.

_____ B. C. again became depressed and attempted suicide.

_____ B. C. was arrested for shoplifting and attempted suicide.

_____ B. C. made the Dean's List.

_____ B. C. attempted suicide.

_____ B. C. was arrested for shoplifting.

_____ B. C. flunked out of college, became depressed, and attempted suicide.

Many of the participants' answers contained the compound probability fallacy—in several parts of the question. Being arrested for shoplifting was seen as quite improbable, less so than being arrested for shoplifting *and* attempting suicide; being depressed and attempting suicide was generally seen as more likely than attempting suicide alone, and so on. (The most common first choice was that B. C. made the Dean's List.)

Perhaps the compound probability fallacy occurs only in responding to hypothetical questions. To test that possibility, Tversky and Kahneman offered each subject a bet. They would roll a fair die with four green (G) sides and two red (R) ones, and the subject made a choice between betting that the sequence RGRRR or the sequence GRGRRR would occur. This bet cost the subject nothing, and if the chosen sequence occurred the subject received $25. The second sequence is more representative of a die with four green faces because it has more green outcomes. Nonetheless, the second sequence is logically less likely than the first, because RGRRR is part of the sequence GRGRRR. (It is exactly ⅔ as likely if the die is unbiased, because it is identical to the first sequence except it is preceded by a G, which has probability ⅔.) When subjects were asked to make a hypothetical choice for the $25 payoff, two-thirds chose the second sequence. When Kahneman and Tversky actually rolled the die and offered to pay the $25 in hard cash, two-thirds chose the second.

7.3 GENERALITY AND THEORETICAL EXPLANATION

Compound probability violations of rationality are widespread, particularly in thinking about the future. We imagine the future, and the content of our imaginations tends to conform to our intellectual schemas. Thus, many of our scenarios are conjunctions of specific events that we believe are highly probable. Again, such belief is fairly automatic. Those of us whose thought processes are primarily visual, for example, tend to anticipate the future by "seeing" what we and others are likely to do, and our images may be quite concrete. Our knowledge that *almost nothing* turns out exactly the way we imagine does not stop us from imagining the future concretely by building scenarios of sequences of likely events. It is only upon reflection that we attempt to assess the probability of events in isolation and thereby become less vulnerable to the compound probability fallacy. (The conclusion that the likelihood of events can better be considered by viewing them in isolation than as part of a "meaningful," "holistic" probable sequence may be jarring to some readers.)

Why do we think in terms of sequences of particular events? Concrete conjunctions are *available to our imaginations* either because they correspond to stereotypic (representative) beliefs or because they are available through past experience. (Such availability need not be based on actual frequency, as pointed out at some length in the previous chapter.) Thus, both representativeness and availability are involved. *Availability* here, however, refers to availability to our imagination rather than availability in fact—because it is logically impossible for us to experience conjunctions of events more frequently than we experience the individual components of these conjunctions. Imagination is an important determinant of feelings, thought and action. Consider again, as in section 6.3, estimating the probability that a seven-letter word ends in *-ing* versus the probability that it has an *n* in the sixth position. Without seeing or hearing any words, it is easier to imagine—visually or verbally—those ending in *-ing*, even though they cannot be more common.[3]

---

[3]Experimental demonstrations of the compound probability fallacy have involved combining one likely and one unlikely event, with the result that the compound is judged as more likely than the unlikely event but not more likely than the likely one. For example, in the Linda question, being a feminist is judged as likely and being a bank teller as unlikely. See Yates, J. F., and Carson, B. W. (1986). Conjunction errors: Evidence for multiple judgment procedures, including "signed summation." *Organizational Behavior and Human Decision Processes*, *37*, 230–253. In effect, subjects average. One possible exception involves part–whole relationships; for example seven-letter words ending in *-ing* may be judged to be more likely than *both* those having *i* in the fifth position and those having *n* in the sixth.

7.4 THE OTHER SIDE OF THE COIN: THE PROBABILITY OF DISJUNCTIONS OF EVENTS

Consider a set of events 1, 2, . . ., k. Suppose moreover, that these events are *independent*—that is, whether or not one occurs has no effect on whether any of the others occurs, singly or in combination. (For a more precise definition of *independence*, see Appendix A1.) Let the probabilities that the events occur be p_1, p_2, . . ., p_k. What is the probability that *at least one* will occur? That is, what is the probability of the *disjunction* (as opposed to the conjunction) of these events?

The probability of disjunction is equal to one minus the probability that none will occur. But the probability that the first will not occur is $(1-p_1)$, the probability that the second will not occur is $(1-p_2)$ and so on. Hence, the probability that none will occur is $(1-p_1) \times (1-p_2) \times$ . . . $\times (1-p_k)$. (This, also, is explained in Appendix A1.) The product may be quite small, even though each $(1-p_i)$ is quite large, because each p_i is small. For example, let the probabilities of eight events be .10, .20, .15, .20, .15, and .10, respectively. Then the product of the $(1-p_i)$'s is, once again, $.90 \times .80 \times .85 \times .80 \times .85 \times .90 = .37$. So the probability that at least one of these events will occur is $1 - .37 = .63$. Again, the result occurs even though each separate event is quite improbable (the average is .15).

Just as we tend to overestimate the probability of conjunctions of events (to the point of believing in the compound probability fallacy), we tend to *under*estimate the probability of disjunctions of events. There seem to be two reasons for this. First, our judgments tend to be made on the basis of the probabilities of individual components; as illustrated, even though those probabilities may be quite low, the probability of the disjunction may be quite high. Second, any irrational factors that lead us to underestimate the probabilities of the component events—such as lack of imaginability—may lead us to underestimate the probability of the disjunction as a whole. Occasionally, this underestimation problem is well-understood, at least on an implicit basis. For example, in their summations lawyers avoid arguing from disjunctions ("either this or that or the other could have occurred, all of which would lead to the same conclusion") in favor of conjunctions. Rationally, of course, disjunctions are *much* more probable than are conjunctions.

Note, however, that psychologists have *not* discovered a *disjoint probability fallacy* comparable to the compound probability fallacy—

such a fallacy consisting of the belief that a disjunction of events is *less* probable than a single event comprising it. Logically, if the probability of *A* and *B* were higher than the probability of *A*, then the probability of not-*A* would be less than that of not-*A or* not-*B*. This is because the probability of not-*A* is one minus that of *A* and the probability of not-*A* or not-*B* is one minus that of *A* and *B*. So why doesn't the former belief imply the latter? In fact, if we can arbitrarily decide what we call *A* and not-*A* (for example, call *A* not being a feminist and not-*A* being one) and *B* and not-*B* (call *B* not being a bank teller and not-*B* being one), then aren't the two fallacious inequalities equivalent? My answer is that they are logically equivalent, but not psychologically equivalent. We think in terms of categories, not their complements (negations). In fact, the absence of a disjoint probability fallacy can be interpreted as evidence that we do not naturally think of the complements of categories. To a trained logician, not-*A* is as well-defined a category as *A* is, but *A*'s (which may have many associations) rather than not-*A*'s (which tend to have few) crowd our minds. It takes a Sherlock Holmes to understand that the fact that the dog *did not* bark constitutes a crucial clue (implying that the dog was familiar with the person)—that is, to treat not-barking as a category of events.

7.5 SCENARIOS ABOUT OURSELVES

It is widely believed among psychoanalytic clinicians that clients of Freudian analysts have Freudian dreams and clients of Jungian analysts have Jungian dreams. The extension that clients of Freudian and Jungian analysts have led Freudian and Jungian lives, respectively, is a bit more disconcerting, for it implies that the dearly (i.e., expensively) gained insights of these clients may—to some unknown and perhaps unknowable degree—be joint inventions of the clients and analysts. Research on the nature of retrospective memory has reinforced this possibility, for the malleability of such memory implies that mere agreement with the therapist is a poor basis for judging accuracy. Could the therapy process be partly, or even primarily, one of inventing a "good story" about the client's life? If so, could this "story" hinder as well as help to foster free and responsible choice?

Early in 1987 I presented the research on retrospective memory that is summarized in section 6.1 to a group of clinicians and was amazed to discover general agreement with what I reported. (Like most other people, I expect members of an "out-group" to hold a uniform set of beliefs that is quite different from my own.) Many of the clinicians agreed that to a greater or lesser extent they do (*somewhat*) "invent" life stories for their clients, but it is with the purpose of allowing the clients to accept their past distressed behavior as a normal consequence of what had previously occurred in order to reach the decision to abandon this behavior. In contrast, James March, in discussing the problem with "discovering" that one's adult years flow naturally—as part of a good story—from childhood, points out that[4]

> . . . belief in the model seems likely to create a static basis in personal self-analysis. Individuals who believe the "formative years" hypothesis seem quite likely to consider the problem of personal identity to be a problem of "discovering" a pre-existing "real" self rather than of "creating" an "interesting" self. The notion of discovery is biased against adult change.

As I argued in section 2.3, such discoveries can become verbal straitjackets through the attributions they create—for example, "I have come to accept the fact that I suffer from a narcissistic character disorder." (The one person I know who has accepted that "fact" reported that he has been "very struck" in his clinical practice that narcissism "appears to have become a major problem among young and middle-aged men in our culture." He went on to say that most of his male clients were narcissists and that many of them had been told not to "be a cry-baby" as children. Therapy yields insight and acceptance, and I must admit that the clinician has become a much more pleasant and socially connected person with his own, new insight.)

All of the elements for belief in the high probability of our scenarios are there when we view our lives. These include stereotypes derived from family myths, cultural beliefs, literature, plays, movies, and television—and in the case of people involved in psychology or psychiatry, prototypical case histories communicated in textbooks or through contact with others who have an interest or a professional commitment. These sources all provide prepackaged, believable, complex sequences of events for our entertainment, education, and *use*. No wonder some "pop" psychologists have achieved great fame through arguing that we often "act out" preselected "life scripts!" Scenario thinking provides us with such scripts, and they are compelling, but they can forge a chain of bondage. I do not have good evidence

[4]March, J. G. (1972). Model bias in social action. *Review of Education Research, 42*, 413–429.

for this bondage assertion, which lies beyond the scope of this book, and it would be difficult to obtain such evidence. Nevertheless, the conclusion that people form scenarios about their own lives as well as external sequences of events has an empirical basis. (See, for example, Valliant's book of "life histories."[5]) The overestimation of the probability of conjunctions of events—which culminates in the compound probability fallacy—makes such scenarios (irrationally) believable.

7.6 SCENARIO THINKING AND NUCLEAR WAR

We often think of the possibility of nuclear war in terms of scenarios of conflict—clear mental images (visual or verbal) of confrontation: we do this, the Soviets do that, we respond, the Soviets respond, and so on. Currently, most such conflict scenarios focus on a U.S.–U.S.S.R. confrontation leading to war (but there are many other possibilities). So the way to prevent it is thought to be through U.S.–U.S.S.R. negotiation.

Or perhaps the scenario war starts by accident. To avoid that possibility, we develop devices that are "fail-safe" against *particular* accidents that we can imagine by drawing (or having available) a "fault tree." Or perhaps it is started by a lunatic (such as Jack D. Ripper in *Strangelove*). So we submit personnel at missile sites to psychiatric screening and we fire them if (we find out that) they use drugs.

Let me suggest a different scenario. Within a few years, several small countries may have developed nuclear weapons. Iran, Iraq, and Pakistan are candidates. One or more of these countries may be run by a fanatic who incites his people to suicidal missions such as that against the U.S. Marine barracks in Lebanon in 1983. Given that H-bombs are now the size of a child's sled, it would not be impossible to smuggle one into New York or San Francisco. The suicidal fanatics all agree to die in the blast so that they cannot be traced. The city is annihilated, and there have been no missiles, no early warning, no warning of any sort. There is no reason to blame the Soviets, the Cubans, or even the Iranians. The city is simply gone, and various terrorist groups claim responsibility. (The group actually responsible will make sure there are bogus calls as well.) The civil liberties of the citizens of this country disappear soon after the city does.

[5]Vaillant, G. E. (1977). *Adaptation to Life*. Boston: Little, Brown and Company.

Vivid? Yes. (The terrorists are thin, excitable young men with moustaches.)

Likely? No, but not impossible. The point is that there are literally thousands of scenarios leading to nuclear destruction. Yet the *real* availability, accuracy, and delivery speed of nuclear weapons increase year by year, while we concentrate on a few scenarios. For example, roughly sixty percent of the university students in my decision-making class in 1985 believed it was more likely that there would be a Mideast crisis leading to nuclear war between the U.S. and the U.S.S.R. in the next twenty-five years than that such a war would occur for *whatever* reason. When we concentrate on scenarios, we develop a false sense of security by taking precautions against *them*. If the first event of a scenario (perhaps an "intentional crisis" that leads to a confrontation between the U.S. and the U.S.S.R.) does not occur, we believe the rest of the scenario will not occur either (just as we "knew" the tennis star must join AA and quit drinking to win the tournament). Believing events such as nuclear war can occur only in the context of specific scenarios is not thinking rationally.

How probable is nuclear war? Not very—tomorrow, next month, or this year. But the risk is similar to the risk involved in riding in cars. The probability of a person's being seriously injured or killed while riding in an automobile is less than 1 in 50,000 *on any particular trip*, but greater than 1 in 3 in a lifetime. So most people do not wear seatbelts. Only 12% did in the years 1977–79, and 49,999 times out of 50,000 their judgment that they did not need seatbelts was exonerated.[6]

The necessity of controlling nuclear weapons is analogous to that of wearing an automobile seatbelt. A low probability of disaster in any particular small time interval translates into a high one across intervals. By not controlling nuclear weapons, we are in effect playing a game of Russian roulette each day with thousands of empty chambers in the gun, *but we keep playing it*. We are riding without a seatbelt. And just as no automobile accident occurs in precisely the way we imagined we might have one, nuclear war—if it occurs—will come about in a way we have not anticipated. If we keep playing the nuclear game, it is not primarily a question of *if* it will occur, but of *when*. Nevertheless, the overestimation of compound events makes us believe that since it is unlikely a war will start in any particular year, it is unlikely it will occur within a range of years as well. But no matter how

[6]O'Neill, B.; Williams, A. F.; and Karpf, R. S. (1983). Passenger size car and driver seatbelt use. *American Journal of Public Health, 64*, 1071–1080.

small the probability of an event is, the probability than an event will *not* occur in n independent trials, $(1-p)^n$, approaches 0 as n gets indefinitely large, (provided, of course, p remains constant).

Again, what is the probability of a nuclear war? The probability that it will occur in *some* year or other is a disjunctive one, and the probability that it will never occur is a conjunctive one. Thus, for the reasons specified in sections 7.1 and 7.4, the probability of its occurring in some year or other tends to be underestimated, while the probability that it will never occur tends to be overestimated. (It is important to understand that these biases occur independently of any emotional factors involving optimism, pessimism, or horror—and independently of any framing effects as well). Before speculating about possible values of p, let me illustrate the conclusions to be drawn by a simpler example in which we (the American public) have been provided with a value—or rather, an expert estimate. According to experts I have seen on television, the probability that there will be a large earthquake in the Los Angeles area in the next 20 years is .90. Moreover, the earth's plates there are in such a state of tension already that the probability of its occurring in any particular year may be treated as a constant p. Thus, $(1-p)^{20}$, the probability that no such earthquake will occur, is .10, which means that $p=.11$. Note that if the quake has not yet occurred as you are reading this book, that probability remains unchanged, for we have simply experienced a sequence of years in which the event *has not* occurred; the probability is the same for the next 20 years.

What, then, is the probability that a large earthquake will occur in the next 4 years? (This question may reasonably be asked by a student considering a college in Southern California). The probability that it will not is $(1-.11)^4=.89^4=.63$, so the probability that it will occur in the next four years is .37; $1-.63$. Thus, it is slightly over 40% as likely to occur in the next 4 years as in the next 20; I suspect that most people would judge it to be only about 20% as likely to occur. (Note that this analysis is based on the *assumption* that the .90 figure is correct; the important aspect of the analysis is the relationship between single years and sets of years. I am not claiming "objective" accuracy for these numbers.)

How high is p for a nuclear war each year? I am *not* maintaining that it is a constant, merely that it can be approximated with a single value *given* no additional information. Let us suppose, for the sake of analysis, that the probability of nuclear destruction (which *did not* occur) between 1945 and 1984 was 1/3. That means, assuming a constant probability p and independence between years (as rough approximations to reality), that $(1 \pm p)^n = 2/3$, or $p = .01$ per year. Thus, if p remains constant, the probability of having a nuclear war sometime in the next century is $2/3$; $1 - .99^n$. *But p does not remain constant.* If, for example, it were to become twice as likely in each of the next 40 years as the last—and if we accept the 1/3 figure—then the probability of surviving the next 40 years without a nuclear war is only .44.

The probabilistic approach to nuclear war also contains a positive message: *whatever can decrease the probability of a war, by even a small amount, is valuable.* Assume, for example, the probability of .02 per year. As pointed out earlier, the probability of surviving the next 40 years is only .44 (assuming constancy and yearly independence). Now suppose some "small" arms agreement is reached that reduces the probability by 1/3; that is, to .0133. The probability of surviving the next 40 years would then be .58.

If that decrease does not appear important, consider this situation:

A barrel contains 100 balls, 44 of which are green, 14 of which are blue, and 42 of which are red. A single ball is drawn at random. Choose between two options:

A. If a green ball is chosen, you receive $10,000. If a blue or red ball is chosen, you die.

B. If a green or blue is chosen, you receive $10,000. If a red ball is chosen, you die.

Which option would you prefer? When the difference between .58 and .44 is viewed in this manner, the much greater desirability at .58 is evident. (Unfortunately, people tend to assess the magnitude of probability difference in terms of *ratios*—for example, the "mortality ratio" of smokers versus nonsmokers—rather than in terms of actual differences.)

Paul Slovic has emphasized the probabilistic approach to reducing the danger of nuclear war.[7] Small differences in probability for small intervals can yield large differences in broad ones. As Slovic points out, scenario thinking can once again get into the way of a probabilistic assessment. The desirable scenario for most of us would be an agreement resulting in technological control of nuclear weapons to the point that they could not be used in haste or by accident. The least desirable scenario is U.S.–U.S.S.R. confrontation followed by war. As mental

[7]Paper presented at the fall meeting of the Oregon Psychological Association, Salem, Oregon, 1983.

images of what could occur in the next few decades these scenarios are understandable, vivid, and compelling. Thus, we exaggerate the probability of confrontation and of total agreement while we neglect assessing policies that would reduce the probability of nuclear war each year by some small amount.

The first step in resolving a problem is to think clearly about it. Scenario thinking grossly overestimates the probability of scenarios that come to mind and underestimates long-term probabilities of events occurring one way or another. In contrast, probabilistic assessments tend to be more valid. Moreover, probabilistic thinking indicates that "small" changes in likelihood can have "large" long-term effects. Provided we must continue to play nuclear Russian roulette, putting more blank chambers into the gun is preferable to trying to determine which chamber the bullet is in.

7.7 AN OVERVIEW OF IRRATIONAL THINKING

Mental processes that systematically lead us to make irrational decisions include honoring sunk costs, being swayed by framing and grouping effects, systematically misjudging probabilities on the basis of representativeness or availability, and thinking in scenario terms. It is important to note, however, that we do not *always* think irrationally. For example, President Truman did not honor sunk costs when he abandoned the policy of "unconditional surrender" in order to end the Second World War in the Pacific; nor did Charles de Gaulle when he withdrew the French from Algeria in 1956, nor President Kennedy when he abandoned the Bay of Pigs in 1961, nor President Reagan when he withdrew the Marines from Lebanon in 1983. Nor did Lee Iococca, the president of Chrysler Corporation, when in 1987 he reversed his publicly reiterated opposition to reinstating discounts to encourage sales of new automobiles at the end of 1986.

Neither are people necessarily subject to framing effects. In fact, we sometimes use them ourselves quite consciously—as when President Kennedy urged, "Ask not what your country can do for you but what you can do for your country." Nor do we always purchase expensive "add-ons" or estimate probabilities by representativeness; Bertrand Russell did not make such an estimate in his thinking about heredity, alcoholism, and insanity. Furthermore, it is entirely possible that someone on the university admissions committee might have immediately responded to the member's statement about dyslexia by noting that there are a great many more poor spellers than there are dyslexics. Certainly, we are not always mindless slaves to our experience or our memory of particular instances in it; nor do we always act as though we believe scenarios will occur exactly as we imagine them. The point is that when we do think about decisions irrationally, our thinking corresponds to the principles presented in Chapters 2 through 7.

If a theoretical position cannot state when an event will occur, a skeptic might ask what good it is. In fact, a dedicated behaviorist (if any still exist) might critique this entire book on the grounds that since the phenomena discussed are *not* controllable, descriptions of them—and the mechanisms hypothesized—are of no scientific value. The answer is that insofar as we are dealing with mental events and decisions of real people in the "booming, buzzing confusion" of the real world, we can neither predict nor control them with perfect accuracy. The argument of *certeris parabus* ("other things being equal") always applies to these phenomenon. What I have attempted to do is to point out factors and *thinking styles* that lead us all to irrational choices. People will not necessarily engage in these thought processes, any more than a swimmer who panics necessarily attempts to keep his or her head above water.

The uncertainty of predicting actual outcomes in the world is intrinsic to the problem of decision and the consequences of decision. Of course, it may be said that "true scientists" should not investigate such uncertain phenomena—that they should perhaps limit themselves to investigating the rate at which a rat presses a bar in an environment whose only moving part is the bar. (What other than the consequences of manipulating the one thing that can be manipulated could "shape" the rat's behavior?) From a normative perspective, however, becoming able to specify conditions that facilitate or inhibit certain types of behavior, or to distinguish between productive and nonproductive ways of thinking is quite an accomplishment for psychologists or other social scientists. Finally, as will be pointed out with extensive research data in Chapter 10, people who attempt to grasp the totality of situations in order to predict or control exactly what will happen seldom fare as well as those who seek the more modest goal of determining what we can influence. A person who attempts to understand everything can easily end up understanding nothing.

An understanding of irrational forms of thinking is not nothing, even though it does not entail predicting when such irrationality will occur, or controlling it.[8] This view is not very different from that of genetic predispositions with "incomplete penetrance." For example, whereas everyone with the dominant gene for Huntington's disease suffers from the disorder, only half of the identical twins of people diagnosed as schizophrenic become schizophrenic. Something in addition to the genetic disposition influences the development of schizophrenia. Although genetic analysis (of identical twins, fraternal twins, and relatives) cannot specify the other influences on such disorders, that does not detract from the findings of genetic analysis.

7.8 WHAT TO DO ABOUT THE BIASES

Ulysses wisely had himself chained to his ship's mast before coming within earshot of the Sirens. He did so not because he feared the Sirens per se, but because he feared his own reaction to their singing. In effect, he took a precaution against himself, because he knew (or thought he knew) what he would be likely to do if he heard the Sirens. Similarly, the cognitive biases of automatic thinking can lead us astray, in a predictable direction. We must take precautions against the pitfalls of such unexamined judgment.

Attempts to train people not to think representatively and not to be influenced by availability or other biases have not been very successful. Associations are ubiquitous in our thinking processes (although perhaps they are not its "building blocks," as the English empiricists believed). Moreover, making judgments on the basis of one's experience is perfectly reasonable, and essential to our survival. Finally, as pointed out previously, it is impossible for us to think in a way we do not think.

One precaution against our biases is the use of external aids. For example, a clinical psychologist can record instances (e.g., of suicide threats) on paper or computer and then compile the data when he or she wishes to estimate the frequency. Or a simple charting of "good"

---

[8]While I have termed the approach presented in this book that of "shallow psychology," I believe it has some kinship with the interpretation of psychoanalytic theory that maintains that childhood problems are reflected in those of adulthood, rather than that childhood problems necessarily lead to adult ones (which is not supported at all by longitudinal studies). See Dawes, R. M. (1976). Shallow psychology. In Carroll, J., and Payne, J. (eds.), *Cognition and Social Behavior*. Hillsdale, N. J.: L. Erlbaum Associates.

and "bad" weeks can reveal a pattern—or the lack of one. Actually writing down base rates and the ratio rule can help us to avoid irrational judgments.

We can all use a variety of external aids. The greatest obstacle to using them may be the difficulty of convincing ourselves that we should take precautions against ourselves, as Ulysses did. Most of us, like our government leaders searching for the ultimate nuclear weapons and defense, seek to maximize our flexibility of judgment (and power). The idea that a self-imposed external constraint on action can actually enhance our freedom by releasing us from predictable and undesirable *internal* constraints is not a popular one. It is hard to play Ulysses. The idea that such internal constraints can be cognitive, as well as emotional, is even less palatable. Thus, to allow our judgment to be constrained—or even influenced—by the "mere numbers" or pictures or external aids offered by computer printouts is anathema to many people. In fact, there is even evidence that when such aids are offered, many experts attempt to "improve upon" these aids' predictions—and they do worse than they would have had they "mindlessly" adhered to them.[9] Estimating likelihood does in fact involve mere numbers, but as Paul Meehl pointed out, "When you come out of a supermarket, you don't eyeball a heap of purchases and say to the clerk, 'Well, it looks to me as if it's about $17.00 worth; what do you think?' You add it up."[10] Adding, keeping track, and writing down the rules of probabilistic inference explicitly could be of great help in overcoming the systematic errors introduced by representative thinking and availability and other biases. If we do so, we might even be able to learn a little bit from experience.[11]

[9]See Goldberg, L. R. (1965). Simple models or simple processes? Some research on clinical judgment. *American Psychologist*, *23*, 483–496, Also Arkes, H. R.; Dawes, R. M.; and Christensen, C. (1986). Factors influencing the use of a decision rule in a probabilistic task. *Organizational Performance and Human Decision Processes*, *37*, 93–110.

[10]Meehl, P. E. (1986). Causes and effects of my disturbing little book. *Journal of Personality Assessment*, *50*, 370–375.

[11]My impression is that people who regard themselves as experts in a field—or even just as unusually smart—are willing to accept external aids in reaching decisions about situations they regard as "complex," but not about those they regard as "simple." The idea that limits on our mind's "computational capacity" mandate external aids for dealing with vast quantities of information is more acceptable than the idea that these limits mandate such aids for dealing with simple information coherently.

CHAPTER

Reason means truth, and those who are not governed by it take the chance that someday the sunken fact will rip the bottom out of their boat.

Oliver Wendell Holmes, Jr.

8

Subjective Expected Utility Theory

8.1 INTRODUCTION

Previous chapters described principles of rationality and their relationship to the alternatives, consequences, and probabilities of decisions. Values, goals, preferences, or tastes of the decision maker have not been discussed; utility—or personal value—was mentioned briefly in Chapter 1, but only for the purpose of emphasizing that this book is not concerned with *what* is chosen, but with the rationality of choices. Other books about decision making define "rationality" in terms of compatibility between choice and value. As may be clear by the end of this chapter, the question of what constitutes a "value" is not easily answered; even defining the term is difficult. Nevertheless, some very important research in decision theory is concerned with the relationship between decisions and the values of the decision makers. This is the work of John von Neumann and Oskar Morgenstern mentioned in Chapter 1, in particular their classic studies described in *Theory of Games and Economic Behavior* published in 1944. That work is summarized in this chapter. In addition, I will present my own perspective that it can be used as a basis for *improving* the quality of decision making, a perspective continued in Chapter 10.

Von Neumann and Morgenstern's work was purely mathematical. They demonstrated that if a decision maker's choices follow certain rules ("axioms"), it is possible to derive *utilities*—real numbers representing personal values—such that one alternative with probabilistic consequences is preferred to another if and only if its *expected utility* is greater than that of the other alternative. Let us break that up into a series of steps. We begin by assuming that a decision maker's choice among alternatives with probabilistic consequences "satisfies the axioms" (i.e., follows the specified rules). Then it is possible to associate a real number with each possible consequence that can be termed the *utility* of that consequence for the individual. The *expected utility* of a particular alternative is the expectation of these numbers—that is, the sum of the numbers associated with each possible consequence weighted by the probability that that consequence will occur. (See Appendix A2.) The conclusion is that a decision maker will prefer outcome X to outcome Y if and only if the expected utility associated with X is greater than that associated with Y.

It is important to note that there is nothing in von Neumann and Morgenstern's theory that states that the person making the decision has any insight into the utilities. The utilities are purely mathematical entities, and their existence is defined by the axioms—just as the lines and vertices of triangles we study in Euclidian geometry are mathematical entities defined in terms of the axioms of that system. Nevertheless, just as we identify the abstract ideas of points and lines in geometry with the points and lines in the world—or on a piece of paper or pictured in our minds—these utilities are often identified with the "personal values" of the decision maker. Moreover, there is absolutely nothing in the system itself that requires a decision maker's choices to satisfy the axioms, although many decision theorists who concentrate on the relationship between values and action define rationality as making choices that are consistent with these axioms. (A rational decision maker would then be one that prefers alternative X to alternative Y whenever the expected utility of X is greater than that of Y.)

The axioms are crucial to the theory. Before presenting them, however, I would like to emphasize that the work of von Neumann and Morgenstern extended well beyond the material presented in this chapter; for example, they introduced many crucial concepts of "game theory," which is discussed briefly in Chapter 9. I also wish to compare the concept of "utility" as used by von Neumann and Morgenstern with the concept of "personal value" as used in everyday life and language. Finally, before presenting the von Neumann and Morgenstern axioms themselves, I will illustrate the "axiomatic approach" in a simpler context: that of defining and measuring "weights."

The term *value* has come to mean monetary equivalent. In the 1923 edition of *Webster's International Dictionary*, the first definition of *value* is that of a quality of a thing or activity according to which its "worth" or degree of worth is estimated; subsequent definitions concern intrinsic desirability, and later ones talk about market equivalent in terms of "money or goods." In the 1968 edition, in contrast, the first five definitions concern monetary equivalent: "1. A fair or proper equivalent in money . . . fair price. 2. The worth of a thing in matter of goods at a certain time; market price. 3. The equivalent (of something) in money. 4. Estimated or appraised worth or price. 5. Purchasing power." Only the sixth 1968 definition corresponds to the first 1923 definition. Hence, *value* has come to be synonymous with *monetary equivalent*. The degree of worth or desirability specific to the decision maker, as opposed to mere money, is thus better termed *utility*. Even that term is ambiguous, however, because the dictionary definition of *utility* is "immediate usefulness," and that is not what decision theorists have in mind when they discuss "utility." My own preferred terminology is *personal value*—to the decision maker.

When most of us talk about personal value, we have a far broader concept in mind than that found in the von Neumann–Morgenstern theoretical system. For example, we believe that people can verbalize their personal values or value systems; we do not infer these from behavior alone. Otherwise, our language system would not include such concepts as "hypocrisy," which refers to a lack of congruence between a stated value and a particular behavior. Moreover, we believe that values exist independently of both verbalization and behavior. "Logical positivist" philosophers have challenged this belief, while other philosophers consider its implications and justification. Nevertheless, in ordinary language we regard "values" as an important existential dimension on which we can place objects, actions, and other phenomenon. For example, we say "he values freedom" as easily as we say "he went to work yesterday." In fact, we often treat statements of value as if they were statements of fact, even though many philosophers make a very strong distinction between these two types of statements, and only after studying philosophy do most of us become confused by our own beliefs that we or others value certain objects or actions. Perhaps we "should" (another value!) be less cavalier in our everyday thinking and speaking.

Another important characteristic of values is that they transcend particular situations. When we say we "value" something, we are referring to more than our behaviors, feelings, and beliefs in just a particular, specific situation. "He values freedom," for example, refers to a general set of dispositions, actions, and beliefs—and once again, a set that the individual described can at least vaguely verbalize.

As an axiom system that leads to conclusions, specifically derivations of numerical utilities, the von Neumann–Morgenstern theory does not in and of itself imply any of these characteristics of utility (personal value). It is of interest, however, because its conclusions have implications about "decisions" and "values" as we understand these terms in everyday language and life, just as the conclusions of Euclidian geometry can be applied to real-world objects; otherwise, it would be simply a system of rules for manipulating symbols and deriving numbers that would have little interest for most of us.

To explain the nature of a mathematical axiom system and how such a system can be related to real-world objects and phenomena, I will first describe a system that is simpler than von Neumann and Morgenstern's. Specifically, let us consider the weight of objects. Such weights are *positive real numbers*; they can be added together, as when a 1.37-pound weight and a 7.86-pound weight are put together on a scale to yield 9.23 pounds. Such real numbers have important properties, eight of which are elaborated here.

Property 1. Comparability Given any two positive real numbers, one is larger than the other or they are equal. That may be expressed algebraically by letting x and y stand for the numbers. Then either $x>y$, $y>x$, or $x=y$. To avoid expressing all of the following properties in terms of both inequality and equality, I will usually use the "weak" form of comparability: "greater than or equal to," symbolized $\geq$. Thus we can express comparability as meaning that for any two real numbers x and y, $x \geq y$, $y \geq x$, or both, in which case they are equal.

Property 2. Ordering The relationship "greater than or equal to" determines the transitive ordering of the numbers; that is, if $x \geq y$ and $y \geq z$, then $x \geq z$.

Property 3. Additive closure When we add two positive numbers we get a third positive number; that is, if x and y are positive numbers, $z = x+y$ is a positive real number.

Property 4. Addition is associative. The order in which we add numbers is unimportant; that is, $x+(y+z)=(x+y)+z$. "The sum of the sums equals the sum of the sums."

Property 5. Addition is symmetric. The order in which two numbers are added is unimportant; that is, $x+y=y+x$.

Property 6. Cancellation When a third number is added to each of two numbers, the order of the two sums is the same as the order of the two original numbers; that is, $x+z \geq y+z$ if and only if $x \geq y$.

The next property is often termed the *Archemedian* property (although it is credited to Eudoxus, circa 408–355 B.C.). In effect, it asserts that no positive real number is infinitely larger than any other; that is, that no matter how much smaller one number is than a second number, there is some multiple of the first number that is larger than the second number.

Property 7. The Archemedian property Given any two numbers, there always exists an integer-value multiple of one that is larger than the other; that is, if $x \geq y$, then there exists an n such that $ny > x$. Here, ny simply refers to y added to itself n times; this axiom does not involve the general concept of multiplication, since multiplication is unnecessary when we combine integers. (Note that the Archemedian property implies that there is no largest or smallest positive real number: consider any two numbers x and y with $x \geq y$. x cannot be the largest number because there exists an n such that $ny > x$. Similarly, y cannot be the smallest, because $y > x/n$ with that same n.)

Property 8. Solvability If $x \geq y$, there exists a z such that $x < y + z$.

The weights that we attach to objects satisfy all these properties. In 1901, Holder demonstrated something quite profound.[1] Using knowledge from a branch of mathematics called *measurement theory*, he demonstrated that if a system has these eight properties (axioms), then real numbers can be associated with the elements of the system, and these real numbers are unique except for multiplication by a positive constant. That is, he restated these eight properties in terms of axioms in which an abstract relationship R replaced the $\geq$ and an abstract operation $\bigcirc$ replaced addition. He subsequently demonstrated that if the elements of the system related by R and combined by $\bigcirc$ satisfy these eight axioms, then it is possible to associate a positive real number with each such that: (1) the real number associated with $x \geq y$ if and only if $x\ R\ y$, and (2) $z = x + y$ whenever $z = x \bigcirc y$. Moreover, any two sets of real numbers associated in this manner have the relationship that one set is a positive multiple of the other. (For example, the number of ounces is 16 times the number of pounds.) These numbers are termed *measures*; the measure associated with the entity x is often symbolized $m(x)$.

How do we get from that to weight? What Holder recognized is that the way in which objects behave on a pan balance corresponds perfectly to the eight axioms of his system, where $x\ R\ y$ indicates that object x outbalances object y and the operation $\bigcirc$ corresponds to placing two objects together on the same pan ("concatenating" them). Readers should confirm for themselves that the behavior of objects on

[1]Holder, O. (1901). Die Axiome der Quantitat und die Lehre von Mass. *Berichte uber die Verhandlugen der Koniglich Saclisischen Gesellschaft der Wissenschaften zu Leipzig, Mathematisch–Physische Classe, 53*, 1–64.

a pan balance satisfies these eight properties restated as abstract axioms where R refers to the tilt of the balance and $\bigcirc$ refers to placing objects in the same pan. (This correspondence is *conceptual*; any particular pan balance may not be large enough to hold all objects that have weight.) Thus, Holder demonstrated mathematically the correspondence between his axiom system and the positive real numbers and noted the empirical correspondence between the axiom system and the behavior of objects on pan balances. The result is that the behavior of objects on pan balances may be used to assign them real-number measures, which we term *weights*. Just as a 1 is the "unit of measurement" in the real numbers, the "standard gram" or "standard pound" is the unit of measurement for weights. Finally, the fact that we measure weights in pounds, ounces, or grams—all of which are multiples of each other—corresponds to the conclusion that two sets of measures assigned to the entities satisfying the axiom system are positive multiples of each other.

Before proceeding to von Neumann and Morgenstern's axiomatic system for determining "utilities," I must point out that different axiom systems may be equivalent to each other. My choice of the particular eight properties of numbers, and hence the translation into the eight axioms of weight, is based on my judgment of which axioms readers will find easiest to understand. Other authors cite different systems, many of which are more "elegant."

Let me sketch the basic system of the von Neumann and Morgenstern axioms. The basic *entities* can be conceptualized as alternatives consisting of probabilistic consequences—that is, "gambles." The basic *relationship* can be conceptualized as one of "preference," which induces an order on the alternatives. The *operation* for combining the alternatives may be conceptualized as a "probability mixture" of alternatives. Thus, if A and B are alternatives, ApB refers to receiving alternative A with probability p and alternative B with probability $(1-p)$. Because the alternatives specify the consequences with particular probabilities, the probability mixture of alternatives is synonymous with a probability mixture of the consequences; that is, if alternative A consists of consequence x with probability r and consequence y with probability $(1-r)$ whereas alternative B consists of consequence z with probability s and alternative w with probability $(1-s)$, then ApB consists of consequence x with probability rp, consequence y with probability $(1-r)p$, consequence z with probability

$s(1-p)$, and consequence w with probability $(1-s)(1-p)$. An alternative with a particular consequence is conceptualized as one in which the consequence occurs with a probability of 1. What von Neumann and Morgenstern proved is that when their axioms are satisfied, a measure can be associated with each consequence—termed a *utility* of that consequence—and that the alternatives themselves can be ordered according to their expected utility. In other words, the basic result is that a preference between the alternatives can be represented by an ordering of their expected utilities. Because a single consequence can be conceptualized as an alternative in which that consequence occurs with the probability of 1, and vice versa, the axioms can be stated in terms of either consequences or alternatives. I choose to present the axioms as alternatives.

Axiom 1. Comparability If A and B are in the alternative set S, then either $A \gtrsim B$ or $B \gtrsim A$, or both, in which case $A \sim B$.

Axiom 2. Transitivity If $A \gtrsim B$ and $B \gtrsim C$, then $A \gtrsim C$.

Axiom 3. Closure If A and B are in alternative set S, then ApB is as well.

Axiom 4. Distribution of probabilities across alternatives If A and B are in S, then $[(ApB)qB] \sim (ApqB)$.

Axiom 5. Independence If A, B, and C are in S, $A \gtrsim B$ if and only if $(ApC) \gtrsim (BpC)$. This is a very crucial axiom. For example, the *pseudocertainty* effect (section 3.3) constitutes a violation of this axiom, as will be detailed shortly. This axiom is also violated by certain hypothetical choices that will be discussed in the next section of this chapter.

Axiom 6. Consistency For all A and B in S, $A \gtrsim B$ if and only if $A \gtrsim (ApB) \gtrsim B$.

Axiom 7. Solvability For all A, B, and C in S, if $A \gtrsim B \gtrsim C$, then there exists a probability p such that $B \sim (ApC)$. This axiom is crucial to the construction of the utility scale.

If numbers are substituted for the alternatives and probabilities for the p's and q's, then it is clear that these axioms are satisfied whenever the number associated with an alternative is equal to its expectation. What von Neumann and Morgenstern did was prove the converse: if these axioms are satisfied, then it is possible to construct a measure for each alternative equal to its expectation in such a way that the order of the alternatives corresponds to the order of the expectations. Moreover, the origin (0) and unit of these measures are arbitrary (as in the familiar scales of temperature). The number associated with an alternative is termed its *expected utility*; that number associated with a consequence, which is equivalent to an alternative that has that consequence with probability 1, is the utility of that consequence. Because only the origin and the unit of measurement are arbitrary in such utility assignments, any different assignments are related in a linear (straight-line) manner.[2]

The arbitrary origin and unit of measurement allow us to use the solvability axiom to determine the utility of a third alternative whenever the utilities of two others are known. Suppose, for example, $A \gtrsim B \gtrsim C$. We can allow the utility of A to equal 1 and the utility of C to equal 0. Now, according to the solvability axiom, there exists a probability p such that the utility of B is equal to the utility of ApC that is simply p times the utility of A plus $(1-p)$ times the utility of C, which is $p \times 1 + (1-p) \times 0 = p$. Thus, as promised, the solvability axiom is crucial in determining the actual numerical values of these utilities. Because all possible scales and utilities are linear functions of each other, we can simply assign 1 as the utility of the most preferred alternative in each set S, and 0 as the utility of the least preferred alternative, and then solve for the utilities of all the remaining alternatives.

Von Neumann and Morgenstern's system is conceptually beautiful. At the risk of being redundant, I state again that the *utilities* derived from these axioms do not necessarily correspond to our intuitive or verbal notions of "personal value," any more than the measures of weight derived from behavior of objects in pan balances necessarily correspond to our intuitive notions of weight. Nevertheless, just as a concept of weight that did not relate to our intuitions about which objects are heavier than which others would be a very strange notion

---

[2]We can change the origin of that scale by adding an arbitrary constant B which may either be positive or negative and change the unit of measurement by multiplying each number on the scale by a *positive* constant A. The difference between two numbers $a-b$ is then $(Aa+B)-(Ab+B)=A(a-b)$. When the difference between any two points on one scale is equal to a positive constant times that difference on the other scale, the two scales are related in a linear (straight-line) manner.

indeed; the concept of utility is meant to have a relationship. (I do not wish to get into a whole philosophical question of how "science" moves from intuitive concepts to precisely defined concepts according to operations satisfying axiom systems.) In fact, it is because the utilities derived according to the von Neumann and Morgenstern system *do* bear relationship to our notions of personal value that they are of interest. In fact, as promised, I will attempt to explain how they can be used to *improve* our decision-making capabilities.

To indicate the desirability of making choices in accordance with these axioms, I will discuss each in turn, interpreting the $\gtrsim$ as meaning "is preferred to" and the $\sim$ as "is indifferent to." (Note that the interpretation is somewhat rough; a more precise interpretation of $\gtrsim$ is "is not unpreferred to," because both $A \gtrsim B$ and $B \gtrsim A$ are possible, in which case $A \sim B$. However, that usage is quite awkward. To be technically precise, I should distinguish between "strong" preference ($>$) and "weak" preference ($\gtrsim$); the reader wishing such precision can translate by considering weak and strong preference separately.) Now consider the axioms with this interpretation.

Comparability

Axiom 1 states that when faced with two alternatives, the decision maker should have at least a weak preference. The strongest rationale for this axiom is the fact that a decision maker faced with alternatives must choose one of them. But it also equates inability to make such a choice with indifference. Is someone who maintains that he or she cannot choose between two alternatives necessarily "indifferent"? Some alternatives are *incomparable* (such as apples and oranges). Consider, for example, the choice discussed in Chapter 4 of the professor trying to decide what job to take. If he were to conclude that he could not make a choice, would that really mean that he is indifferent, that he does not care? Jay Kadane and Teddy Seidenfeld, for example, maintain that not having a preference is *not* equivalent to being indifferent.

Apples and oranges are, however, fruit, and if one must choose a fruit from a dish of apples and oranges, it will be either an apple or an orange. Could not the choice itself define the "preference?" (Economists refer to such a choice as a "revealed preference.") Moreover, isn't it true that when people maintain that they have "just chosen," subsequent questioning reveals that there really *is* a preference involved. For example, if the professor maintained that he really was incapable of choosing between jobs but "happened to pick" one of them in order to be near (or away) from relatives, would not proximity to relatives be an important consideration in his choice? Perhaps he would be simply unaware of this factor at the time he made the choice—or perhaps embarrassed to discuss it, because he might not consider it a "good" reason for choosing one job over another. My own position is that people really do have preferences, except in such instances as predicting outcome of a coin toss, in which case they are truly indifferent. I do not, however, accept the "revealed preference" position— that the preference is inherent in the choice—for the reasons outlined in the previous chapters. Specifically, choice may be irrational, and hence, contradictory. It follows that there may be a discrepancy between choice and a particular situation and the "preferences" of the individual making the choice.

While "revealed preference" can be rejected on the basis of the cognitive difficulty of choice, the most common reason for rejecting the apparent evidence is that people sometimes do things they do not *want* to do; that is, choose alternatives they do not prefer. For example, William James (1842–1910) noted that people with toothaches often prod the painful area of their mouth with their tongue, although they clearly prefer lack of pain to the pain that results from doing that. (I have yet to find anyone who denies doing that.) Clearly, people do not always do what gives them greatest pleasure, or what they "want" to do.

The counterargument of the revealed preference theorist is that the very act of prodding the area of a toothache indicates that the individual has a greater positive value for the information gained that the tooth is still hurting than negative value for the pain experienced. Such values may appear "stupid," because toothaches tend not to go away on their own without treatment, and when a given part of our mouth is aching we can be more than reasonably sure that it will be more painful if we touch it with our tongue, *without* actually doing so. The revealed preference theorist, however, has the counterargument that *de gustubus non disputandem.* ("There's no disputing matters of taste.") The fact that the sufferer prods the tooth reveals that even such redundant information is worth the pain.

Because what constitutes pleasure and pain to an individual cannot be known unambiguously, the argument that people often do what they "really" dislike doing is fairly ineffective against the revealed preference position. In contrast, knowing that the choices are often contradictory for *cognitive* reasons undermines this position.

Transitivity

The primary justification for axiom 2 is that individuals who violate it can be turned into "money pumps" (section 6.5). Suppose that John Dolt preferred alternative A to alternative B, alternative B to alternative C, and yet C to A. Assume, further, that he is not indifferent in his choice between any of these alternatives. Consequently, he should be willing to *pay something*—perhaps a considerable amount of money or perhaps only a few pennies—to trade a less preferred alternative for a more preferred one. Now suppose John is given alternative B *as a gift*. Because he prefers alternative A to B, he should be willing to pay the gift giver something to have A instead. Subsequently, John should be willing to pay something to have alternative C substituted for A, and finally to pay for the substitution of B for C. Then John will have paid for the privilege of ending up with the alternative he was given in the first place. By repeating this cycle indefinitely, John (hypothetically anyway) would pay an indefinite amount of money to get nowhere.

The response to the money pump argument is that an individual with intransitive preferences would simply refuse to play that game. Choices are, after all, not made repeatedly, but in a particular context. A choice between two alternatives does not have to be one by which the individual is bound for all time and in all circumstances. One noted economist is quoted as saying that his concern in a particular decision-making situation is to satisfy himself "and let the axioms satisfy themselves." For example, consider the hiring of a new secretary. Suppose that the employer has three criteria for making a job offer: (1) clerical skills, (2) organizational ability, and (3) willingness to take dictation and do other jobs not specifically in the position description. Suppose that the rank of prospective secretaries A, B, and C on clerical skills is A, B, C; on organizational ability is B, C, A; and on willingness is C, A, B. Thus applicant A is superior to applicant B on two of these three dimensions (clerical skill and willingness), B is superior to C on two (clerical skill and organization), and C is superior to A on two (organization and willingness). A decision based on the principle that one applicant is preferred to another whenever that applicant is superior on two of three dimensions results in intransitivity. What will happen is that the *order* in which the applicants are considered will be crucial, with *the applicant considered last* being the one chosen.[3]

Is this consequence necessarily a bad one? Even though the employer could in principle become a money pump, no one is going to make her one—by giving her one of the secretaries and then demanding payment for subsequent substitutions.

---

[3]Majority votes in democracies can easily result in such intransitivities. Consider, for example, a "society" consisting of three people with the same preferences between alternatives A, B, and C as in the secretary example: ABC, BCA, and CAB; that is, two of the three prefer A to B, B to C, and C to A. The possibility of such cycles led Kenneth Arrow to question whether there was *any* social decision system for amalgamating individuals' rank orders to arrive at a social choice that did not have the potential of being "dictatorial" (i.e., determined by a single individual). In Arrow's famous "impossibility theorem," he proved that no such system can exist. What happens when such cycles exist in actual majority vote in society is that people maneuver to have their preferred alternatives considered *last*—because, as in the secretary example, intransitivity implies that there is always some alternative that will defeat a competing one. For example, before the "civil rights revolution" in the early 1960s, Southern senators used that tactic to block civil rights legislation. A sufficient number of like-minded Southern senators chaired committees (due to the seniority system), which allowed them to manipulate the order of voting. I once witnessed the defeat of a moderate civil rights bill on the Senate floor in 1960 because it was first compared to a much stronger one, which defeated it with the help of Southern senators. Then this new alternative in turn was defeated, and a much weaker bill was passed in its place. Specifically, the "Lauche Amendment" (named after the senator from Ohio) was attached to the original bill; according to this amendment, it would have been a federal crime to "attempt to circumvent a federal court order," which many government officials in the South at the time were doing when they tried to block the integration of schools mandated by the Supreme Court in 1956. The "Southern bloc" arranged to have this amendment considered prior to a weaker version of the bill, and as a bloc voted *for it*. (Of course, if it ultimately had become law, many of these senators would have gone to jail.) As a result of such "insincere voting," they were able to present the Senate with a final choice that was unacceptable. Senator Margaret Chase Smith of Maine saw quite clearly what was happening and gave an eloquent speech urging her colleagues to vote against the amendment even if they approved of it in principle. She did not prevail, and the bill was subsequently defeated.

I will argue in the latter part of this chapter and in Chapter 10 that individuals' choices *should* be transitive. This idea is part of a general argument that choice is superior when it is made as if the decision maker *were* bound by that choice in a broader context and across time. This argument is basically that of Immanuel Kant (1724–1804), who proposed that individuals should make choices as if they are formulating *policy* for all people at all times. I will enhance that argument with empirical evidence showing that when there is a criterion available according to which we can decide whether choices are good or bad, choices made in accord with Kant's principle are in fact superior to those made in the narrower context of considering only the options immediately available. In Chapter 12 I will try to relate ethical principles to quality of choice in uncertain situations. (Kant was primarily concerned with the ethics of choice, rather than the desirability of consequences; I attempt to demonstrate that his "noninstrumental" approach to ethics yields desirable consequences—probabilistically.)

Closure

Axiom 3 simply requires that the decision maker is capable of conceptualizing a probability mixture of alternatives as itself an alternative. If people were incapable of doing so, there would be little point in theorizing about decision making.

Distribution of Probabilities across Alternatives

Basically, axiom 4 requires that people are capable of following the rules of probability theory. While von Neumann and Morgenstern discuss probabilities as if they were "objective," their theory and axioms were extended by Edwards to cover "subjective probabilities," and I have not made a distinction between the two types in this chapter.[4] What is required is simply that choice be rational in the sense defined in this book; that is, whenever the decision maker attempts to deal with future uncertainty by making probability assessments, these must be made according to rules of probability theory. (See Appendix A1.) To dispute this axiom is to dispute rationality itself. Of course, people may violate it without disputing it; for example, it is violated by the person who reacts differently to a conse-

[4]Edwards, W. (1954). The theory of decision making. *Psychological Bulletin, 51,* 380–417.

quence of receiving $45 with probability .20 than to a two-stage consequence in which the person receives nothing with probability .75 in the first stage and then receives $45 with .8 if the second is reached. (Since $[1.00 - .75] \times .8 = .20$, the distribution axiom requires that the two lotteries be *identical*.)

Independence

Axiom 5 is crucial. In fact, many decision theorists have investigated at length the effects of violating it, or of omitting it from a set of rules governing choice. At first reading, it appears innocuous. If one alternative is preferred to another, shouldn't that preference remain even though the decision maker with some specified probability receives neither, but a third instead? That is all this axiom states. Consider, again, the "pseudocertainty" effect discussed in section 3.3. Most people prefer a .20 probability of receiving $45 to a .25 one of receiving $30, yet simultaneously prefer $30 for sure to an .80 probability of receiving $45. Now let A be the alternative of receiving $30 for sure and B be that of receiving $45 with the probability of .80. A is preferred to B. Let C be the alternative of receiving nothing. Now let p equal .25. Then, (A .25 C) is an alternative consisting of receiving $30 for sure with probability .25 versus receiving nothing with probability .75, which—by axiom 3—is just the alternative of receiving $30 with probability .25. In contrast, (B .25 C) is the alternative consisting of a .25 probability of receiving $45 with probability .8 and a .75 probability of receiving nothing; that is, receiving $45 with probability $.8 \times .25 = .20$. Therefore, the preference pattern elicited by the pseudocertainty effect violates the independence axiom.

The pseudocertainty effect describes choices that are influenced by the way the consequences are framed, rather than solely by the consequences themselves. Is such irrationality the only reason for violating the independence axiom? I believe there is another reason. Axiom 5 implies that the decision maker cannot be affected by the *skewness* of the consequences, which can be conceptualized as a probability distribution over personal values. Figure 8.1 shows the skewed distributions of two different alternatives. Both distributions have the same average, hence the same expected personal value, which is a criterion of choice implied by the axioms. These distributions also have the same variance. (For a description of the mean (average) and variance of probability distribution see Appendix A2.)

Figure 8.1

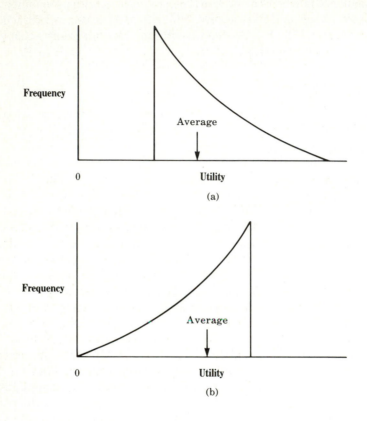

Two skewed distributions with the same average and variance

If the distributions in Figure 8.1 were those of wealth in a society, I have a definite preference for distribution a; its positive skewness means that income can be increased from any point—an incentive for productive work. Moreover, those people lowest in the distribution are not as distant from the average as in distribution b. In contrast, in distribution b, a large number of people are already earning a maximal amount of money, and there is a "tail" of people in the *negatively skewed* part of this distribution who are quite distant from the average income.[5] If I have such concerns about the distribution outcomes in society, why not of the consequences for choosing alternatives in my own life? In fact, I believe that I do. Counter to the implications of prospect theory, I do not like alternatives with large negative skews, especially when the consequences in the negatively skewed part of the distribution have negative personal value.

Consistency

Axiom 6 states that if we prefer one alternative to another, then we prefer at least some chance of receiving that alternative rather than the other one. This axiom appears indisputable.

Solvability

Axiom 7 is similar to the Archemedian property in the context of numbers and weight. What it states in effect is that no alternative is so much better or worse than another that some probability mixture of alternatives on either side is not regarded as equivalent to the original alternative. Consider, for example, three alternatives A, B, and C with the preference order ABC. The axiom states that there will be *some* probabilistic way of combining A and C such that the individual is indifferent to choosing B or this combination. Now if A were incomparably more attractive to the decision maker than any of the other alternatives, then *any* probability of receiving A rather than C might lead to a preference for ApC over B. The same argument would hold *mutatis mutardis* if alternative C were incomparably worse than B. The axiom states that no such alternatives exist.

Well what about death? Or conversely, eternal bliss in Heaven? Would not any alternative involving even the slightest probability of eternal bliss be preferred to some other alternative with drabber consequences—so that the individual could never be indifferent in choosing between the drab alternative and a probability mixture involving such

---

[5]One common objection to "Reaganomics" is not that a number of wealthy people have become even wealthier through such measures as income tax reduction, but that it has introduced a negative skew in the distribution; the number of people "below the poverty line"—especially children—has increased. That is not represented in the "average income" or "gross national product" of the society, which are characteristics analogous to expected utility in the von Neumann and Morgenstern theory.

bliss? Do we not eschew completely those alternatives involving some probability of death? I cannot discuss eternal bliss, because I cannot even conceptualize it. (Being a human, I am subject to adaptation level effects). But it is clear from our behavior that we dread death and attempt to avoid it, at least for as long as we even have hope that the positive aspects of life and the future outweigh the negative. Do we not, then, avoid all alternatives that involve some probability of death? The answer is no. Everyday life involves some risk of death, even such trivial actions as crossing a street to buy a newspaper. Sometimes this probability is more salient than at other times—as when people who despise airplane trips travel tens of thousands of miles a year.[6] But it is always there. Even staying in bed all day to avoid what appears to be the risk of death would involve a severe risk of physical deterioration, perhaps leading to death. In addition, there are clear examples of thoughtful decisions that involve a rather high probability of death—for instance, a decision to join an underground resistance movement during an occupation.

All of the axioms appear quite reasonable. In fact, if we assume comparability, we can violate only the independence axiom without becoming outright irrational. The axioms, however, have strong implications, as do other mathematical results. Believing the Pythagorean theorem, for example, we anticipate the length of a third side of a right triangle when we know the length of two sides. If physical measurement does not confirm our expectations, we conclude that the triangle is not a right triangle; we rarely or never conclude that the theorem is true—that the triangle has a right angle and our measurements are correct, but that the logic of mathematical deduction just doesn't apply. The demanding aspect of the von Neumann and Morgenstern axioms is that if we accept them, we are bound to evaluate alternatives in a choice situation in terms of their expected utility. That is, numbers exist—just as do weights of objects—that describe the utility of each consequence of alternative choices. (Such numbers are—once again—those associated with alternatives that have that particular consequence with probability of 1.) These can be determined by some

---

[6]As the airlines are fond of pointing out, such travel is safer *per mile* than automobile travel; most of us, however, live per second rather than per mile, and in addition we simply would not take a trip across country by automobile for a single weekend.

choices, using the solvability axiom; they then require that other choices as well be made in terms of the expected utilities computed. Other characteristics describing the distribution of consequences, for example their skewness, are irrelevant.[7]

8.2 TRADITIONAL OBJECTIONS TO THE AXIOMS

As pointed out in the previous section, actual behavior often violates one or more of the axioms. The axioms however, were not presented as descriptions of actual behavior, but rather as conditions of *desirable* choice. Are they? After the publication of von Neumann and Morgenstern's book, several theorists suggested that the axioms placed unreasonable constraints on choice behavior and that they should *not* be satisfied. The best-known objections consisted of two "paradoxes." One of these objections was raised by the economist Maurice Allais and the other by the decision theorist Daniel Ellsberg (who, with reporter Neil Sheehan, achieved notoriety by releasing the "Pentagon Papers," which outlined the United States government's secret objectives in the Vietnam War).[8]

The Allais Paradox

The Allais argument is that the expected utility principle that results from the axiom system is inadequate because it is too restrictive. Consider, for example, the choice between alternatives A and B involving millions of dollars:

Alternative A: Receive 1 million dollars with probability 1 (i.e., for certain).
Alternative B: Receive 2½ million dollars with probability .10, 1 million with probability .89 and nothing with probability .01.

---

[7]Skewness is *not* invariant over probabilistic combination with other alternatives; hence no transformations on the utility scale can account for a skewness preference consistently. Proof of this assertion lies beyond the scope of this book.

[8]Allais, M. (1953). Le comportement de l'homme rationnel devant le risque: Critique des postulats et axiomes de l'ecole americaine. *Econometrica*, *21*, 503–546.

When presented with this (hypothetical) choice, most people choose alternative A. That means that if they abide by the axioms, it is possible to assign utilities to the consequences of receiving 1 million dollars, 2½ million dollars, or nothing in such a way that the choice of A implies a higher expected utility for it than for B. Specifically,

$$U(1 \text{ million dollars}) > .10 \ U(2\frac{1}{2} \text{ million dollars})$$
$$+ .89 \ U(1 \text{ million dollars}) + .01 \ U(\text{nothing})$$

By the solvability axiom we can set U(2½ million dollars)=1 and U(nothing)=0. The conclusion then is

$$.11 \ U(1 \text{ million dollars}) > .10$$

Now consider the choice between these two alternatives:

Alternative A′: 1 million dollars with probability .11, otherwise nothing.

Alternative B′: 2½ million dollars with probability .10, otherwise nothing.

The expected utility of alternative A′ is .11 U(1), while that of alternative B′ is .10, because we have set the utility at 2½ million dollars equal to 1. Thus, the choice of A over B requires the choice of A′ over B′. Allais argued that it was nevertheless reasonable to choose A over B and B′ over A′, which is in fact the choice most people make when presented with this pair of decisions. Why accept a one-in-one-hundred chance of receiving nothing when you can receive a million dollars for sure? Conversely, given that the most probable outcome in the second choice is to receive nothing at all, why not take a one-one-hundredth risk of getting nothing in order to increase the potential payoff by a factor of two and one-half times?

Lee (Jimmy) Savage made a compelling response to those questions.[9] Consider his suggestion that the probabilities of the various outcomes are brought about by randomly drawing a chip out of a bag containing 100 chips. One of these chips is black, 10 are blue, and 89 are red. Alternative A can then be conceptualized as paying off 1 million dollars no matter which chip is drawn. In contrast, an individual choosing alternative B receives a million dollars if a red chip is drawn, 2½ million dollars if a blue chip is drawn, and nothing if the black chip is drawn. Now it does not matter to the decision maker which alterna-

[9]Savage, L. J. (1954). *The Foundations of Statistics.* New York: Wiley.

tive is chosen if a red chip is drawn, because in either case he or she receives a million dollars; hence, a choice of A over B implies that the possibility of receiving a million dollars rather than nothing if the black chip is drawn from the 11 chips that are not red is preferred to the possibility of receiving 2½ million dollars rather than nothing if one of the 10 blue chips is drawn. But that preference is *violated* if the individual also chooses B' over A'. Once again, the outcome will be the same if a red chip is drawn, but the individual is now indicating a preference for receiving 2½ million dollars if a blue chip is drawn and nothing if the black one is drawn over receiving 1 million dollars if either a blue or the black is drawn. Savage's example is basically a restatement of the independence axiom in concrete terms, and—for me anyway—it makes this axiom quite compelling. Savage's argument is illustrated in Figure 8.2.

The Ellsberg Paradox

Consider two bags, each with 100 poker chips in it. The first bag contains 40 white chips, 30 yellow, and 30 green. The second bag contains 40 white chips and 60 chips that are either yellow or green,

Figure 8.2

		BALLS		
		89 Red	1 Black	10 Blue
CHOICE	A	$1 million	$1 million	$1 million
	B	$1 million	nothing	$2.5 million
CHOICE	A'	nothing	$1 million	$1 million
	B'	nothing	nothing	$2.5 million

Illustration of Savage's analysis

with the number of yellow ones and the number of green ones being unknown. Now consider three alternatives:

Alternative D: Receive 1 million dollars if a white or yellow chip is drawn from the first bag.

Alternative E: Receive 1 million dollars if a white or yellow chip is drawn from the second bag.

Alternative F: Receive 1 million dollars if a white or green chip is drawn from the second bag.

Which alternative would you prefer? Most people prefer D. If we choose this alternative, we estimate that the probability that we will receive a million dollars is .70. If, however, we were to choose E or F, our probability of receiving the million-dollar payoff could be as low as .40. Moreover, most people are not indifferent in the choice between D and E or between D and F (but they are indifferent between E and F). Such a preference order violates the axioms. Because we strictly prefer D to E, the axioms imply that .7 of our utility for a million dollars is greater than $(.40+p)$ of that utility, where p is the probability of drawing the yellow chip. That implies that p is less than .30. But if p is less than .30, then we should prefer alternative F to alternative D, because the probability of receiving the million dollars will be greater than .70.

Despite that argument, the choice of D is compelling. The counterargument is that in situations of ambiguity we cannot be expected to estimate probabilities; consequently, a pessimistic stance toward the *possibilities* involved is most reasonable. In fact, many decision theorists have attempted to incorporate such ambiguity into theoretical positions, in particular to modify the von Neumann and Morgenstern axioms to incorporate pessimism in ambiguous situations. Note that in the present example, such a modification would involve having the probabilities of sampling a white, yellow, or green ball add up to less than 1 when considering alternatives E and F. However, since the ball drawn must be white *or* yellow *or* green, a fundamental rule of probability theory (see Appendix A1) would be violated by this modification, and while most decision theorists interpret probabilities subjectively rather than objectively—as von Neumann and Morgenstern did— failure to adhere to the rules of probability theory still results in irrationality.

Situations of ambiguity can often be resolved by introducing a nonambiguous factor; for example, consider an alternative G in which a coin is flipped and a decision maker is subsequently presented with alternative E or F, each with probability .50. A preference for D over both E and F implies a preference for D over G. But *whatever* assumptions one makes about the relative frequency of yellow and green balls in the second bag, a 50–50 mixture of alternatives E and F is equivalent to alternative D, by axiom 4 (which we have not questioned).[10] The problem is that the assumption of pessimism implies the belief that one's choice somehow effects the probabilities of the consequences, and the introduction of a random element into that choice makes such influence impossible. (For example, I cannot rationally believe that airplanes on which I fly are more likely to crash than others if I make my choice of flight on a random basis—*unless* I believe that some malevolent force determines the outcome of this random choice or that the outcome itself determines the physics of the airplane trip. Few of us would be quite that irrational.)[11]

8.3 THE SHOULD'S AND DO'S OF THE SYSTEM

Of course, people do not always choose in accord with von Neumann and Morgenstern's axioms, for several reasons. First, there are the irrationalities of decision that have been described in the previous chapters of this book. Second, without being irrational in the sense defined in this book, people often make choices that contradict the axioms—as when they are faced with the Allais and Ellsberg paradoxes. In fact, Savage noted in discussing these paradoxes that his own initial choices sometimes violated the axioms. It follows that since we do not necessarily satisfy the axioms in our actual choice behavior, we do not *behave* as if we assign utilities to consequences and alternatives and then pursue the alternative that has greater expected utility—or greater subjective expected utility when our estimates of probability are "subjective."

Should we make only choices satisfying the axioms of the system? My answer to that question is a qualified yes. The qualification is that

[10]Whenever I estimate the probability p of drawing yellow from the second bag to be, the probability of winning given alternative G is, $.4+.5p +.5(.60-p)=.70$.

[11]I first became aware of the effect of systematically introducing a random event to determine choice in ambiguous situations through the work of Teddy Seidenfeld, although I myself have always used a quasi-random device for scheduling airline trips.

although we should not be *bound* by the axioms, we should *consider* them when making choices. While it is difficult to determine whether a particular decision per se satisfies or violates an axiom or a set of axioms, the fact that the axioms are true if and only if choices are made according to expected utility provides a method for considering alternative decisions. Let me give an example. I stated in the first chapter that the decision of the husband and wife with children to fly on separate airplanes indicated (according to the theory) that the couple felt that the death of both of them would be more than twice as bad as the death of either one alone. We will analyze this example within the von Neumann and Morgenstern framework.

There are three distinct consequences: both die, one dies and one lives, neither dies. Because the assignment of two utility values is arbitrary (given that all utility scales are related to each other in a linear manner), we can arbitrarily assign the utility -1 to the consequence that both die and 0 to the consequence that neither dies. Now let p be the probability that *an* airplane crashes; whether we estimate this probability "objectively" by looking at the airline's safety statistics or on the basis of our subjective hunch, our conclusion is that the probability that both airplanes independently crash is $p \times p$ or p^2. This is the probability that both parents will die if they fly separately. In contrast, the probability that they both will die if they are in the same airplane is simply p. Now let the utility that *exactly one* of them dies be symbolized x (which, like the utility that both die, will be a *negative* number). The choice of flying separately is interpreted within the von Neumann and Morgenstern framework as

$$p(-1) < 2p(1-p)x + p^2(-1)$$

The first term on the right side is x times the probability that one parent will survive the trip and the other will not (which is equal to the probability that the first plane will crash and the second will not *plus* the probability that the first one will not and the second one will; that is, twice the probability that only one plane will crash). The second term is the probability that both will die on independent trips multiplied by -1, the arbitrarily assigned utility of that.

Dividing by p and rearranging terms yields $x > -\frac{1}{2}$. (After the p is canceled out, move the remaining $-p$ on the right side to the left side, which yields $p-1 < 2(1-p)x$; dividing by $(1-p)$ yields $-1 < 2x$. $x > -\frac{1}{2}$ means that the death of exactly one has less than half the negative utility of both dying.

My advice is that the couple might be well advised to consider whether the death of one of them is less than half as bad as the death of both. In this example, that would probably not change the decision; in fact, such consideration would most likely reinforce it. Note that what I have done in this example is to assume that people have at least *partial* appreciation of the utility as specified by the framework. As I repeatedly emphasize, there is nothing in the framework itself that requires such insight—just as there is nothing in the framework for measuring the weight of objects that requires that the numbers obtained should correspond to our subjective ideas of which are heavier than which. Nevertheless, just as weights measured by pan balances *do* correspond—at least partially—to our subjective experience of these weights, so might the utilities in the system correspond to our subjective conceptions of personal value. In fact, if there were no such correspondence in either case, there would be little reason to be interested in the axiom systems.

Let me give another example, this one from a medical context involving the diagnosis of a renal cyst versus a tumor on the basis of X-ray evidence.[12] In his doctoral dissertation, Dennis Fryback studied decisions at a university hospital to test whether a kidney abnormality that appeared on an X ray was a cyst or a tumor. The standard procedure was for patients who appeared to be suffering from a kidney disorder to be X-rayed, and if an abnormality appeared, the radiologist interpreting the X ray made a probability judgment about whether that abnormality was a cyst or a tumor. Then the patient would be tested directly by an invasive procedure. No procedure existed at that time, however, that tested for both a cyst and a tumor. Moreover, because there was always the possibility that an X-ray abnormality is a "normal variant," a negative result on the test evaluating one of these two pathologies required a subsequent test for the other. The question Fryback studied was a decision of which test to do first. This decision was important to the patient, because the nature of the tests is quite different.

[12]See Fryback, D. G. (1974). Use of radiologists' subjective probability estimates in a medical decision-making problem. The University of Michigan Mathematical Psychology Program, NNPP74-14; and Fryback, D. G., and Thornbury, J. R. (1976). Evaluation of a computerized Bayesian model for diagnosis of renal cysts versus tumor versus normal variant from exploratory urogram information, *Investigative Radiology, 11,* 102–111.

A test for a cyst is termed *aspiration*. It consists of inserting a large needle through the patient's back to the location of the abnormality and determining if fluid can be drawn from it; if fluid can be drawn, the abnormality is a cyst. The procedure can be accomplished in a doctor's office with a local anesthetic; the risk of a blood clot is very low; the cost is not great.

The test for a tumor is termed *arteriography*. A tube is inserted into the patient's leg artery and manipulated up to the kidney, at which point a device on the end of the tube removes a sample of tissue from the suspected spot; this tissue sample is then subjected to a biopsy. At the time of Fryback's study, this procedure required one day of hospitalization in preparation for the operation and at least one day's hospitalization after the operation. The probability that a blood clot would develop was approximately ten times as great as that with the aspiration procedure; the patient experienced considerable discomfort in the days following the operation, and it was much more costly than the aspiration test.

Fryback found that in general the aspiration test was done first if the radiologist believed that the probability was greater than .5 that the abnormality was a cyst rather than a tumor; otherwise, the arteriography test was conducted. In addition, however, he also noted that the patients, doctors, and "potential patients" from the general public he questioned all thought that the arteriography test was at least ten times worse than the aspiration test. (Interestingly, discomfort, lost work days, and probability of formation of a blood clot were the major determinants of this judgment; cost was considered irrelevant (perhaps given the assumption that "insurance pays"), which is why I do not specify the cost difference in the above description.) Fryback then conducted an expected utility analysis on the assumption that the disutility of the arteriography test was ten times that of the aspiration test. For the purposes of this analysis, we can "conditionalize" probabilities on the assumption that the patient has *either* a cyst or a tumor, even though the requirement that the second test be given if the first is negative arises because the patient may have *neither*; that is, we can let p be the probability that the patient has a tumor *given* the abnormality is not a "normal variant," and hence, $(1-p)$ is the probability that the patient has a cyst given that the abnormality is not a normal variant. Again, we can arbitrarily set the utility of no test at all at 0; then setting the utility of the aspiration test at -1, the utility of the arteriography test is -10.

Now let the probability that the radiologist interpreting the X ray believes the problem to be that of a tumor be p. If the arteriography test is done first, the expected disutility of the entire testing procedure is

$$p(-10) + (1-p)(-11)$$

The second term in the expression occurs because both tests are required if the abnormality is not a tumor. In contrast, the disutility of doing the aspiration test first is

$$(1-p)(-1) + p(-11)$$

The expected utility of doing the arteriography test first will be greater than that of doing the aspiration test first (i.e., the disutility will be *less negative*) whenever:

$$-10p - 11(1-p) > -(1-p) - 11p$$

this is true if and only if:

$$11p > 10$$

$$p > 10/11$$

In other words, doing the arteriography test first is better in an expected utility framework—or rather, subjective expected utility framework, given that the radiologist's readings were certainly "subjective"—only under those conditions in which the probability of a tumor relative to that of a cyst is greater than 10/11; that is, when a tumor is ten times more likely. Recall that the people questioned believed that the disutility of the arteriography test was *at least* ten times that of the aspiration test; it follows that the 10/11 figure is a *lower bound*. Yet, the procedure at the hospital was to test for arteriography first whenever the judged probability was greater than .50. Again, this example involved at least a partial equating of the "utilities" in the von Neumann and Morgenstern system with the personal values expressed by people when asked. Nevertheless, believing people can assess such utilities seems to be quite reasonable; in fact, when this conclusion was communicated to the hospital physicians, the procedure was changed. An interesting sidelight is that when the radiologists' probability judgments were checked against the actual frequency with which cysts and tumors were found upon testing, these judgments turned out to be quite accurate. Simultaneously, however, the analysis indicated that they were also quite irrelevant, because it implied that the aspiration tests should be done first irrespective of the judged probability, except in those rare cases in which the radiologist was at least ten times more certain that the aberration was a tumor rather than a cyst.

In fact, the new (since 1970) field of "applied decision analysis" often makes use of the von Neumann and Morgenstern approach in an attempt to aid decision makers in their choices. It is based on the premise that people do in fact have some insight into their personal values, but that these values may not be reflected in single choices within a particular context—especially those that tend to be made automatically or according to a standard operating procedure. What the "applied decision analyst" does is question the decision maker or decision-making unit at length about values and probabilities in hypothetical contexts as well as the context in which the choice of interest is to be made. After having done so, the analyst proposes an expected utility analysis that would allow the decision makers to systematize the alternatives in making subsequent choices. Such applications can have a profound effect, as when the hospital decided to change its order of tests.

Yet another example is provided by a man who owned a company in a small town and was considering automation. His family had owned the company for many years, and the factory provided employment to a substantial number of people in the community. After receiving an economic report on the probable increase in profits that would follow automation of many of the factory jobs, he was "uneasy" about implementing automation and he was not sure why. He hired a consultant who works as an applied analyst in such situations. After questioning the business owner at length, the consultant concluded that the owner's "real" utilities in running the business had very little to do with the profit he made. Instead, he derived great pride and satisfaction from providing employment to so many people in the town; doing so provided him with status and a feeling of doing something important for the community. According to the consultant's analysis of expected utility, automation would be a very poor choice, one that would decrease rather than increase the utility this man derived from running his business. When the owner was presented with the results, his response was "aha!" He understood that providing employment was exactly what he wanted to do. In fact, his reluctance to automate in face of rather conclusive data that it would increase his profits was, he now understood, due to that desire. In addition to reinforcing his "gut impression" that something was amiss with the automation plan, the consultant's analysis provided him with a rationale for explaining his refusal—both to himself and to those who might regard him as a poor businessperson for having bypassed the opportunity to increase his profits.

Such decision analysis is a form of therapy because it helps people change behavior—to be consistent with their "basic values." The von Neumann and Morgenstern framework does not dictate what choice *must* be made, but it is an important tool for such therapy. Moreover, it can help prevent more basic irrationalities, because a decision made within this framework cannot be irrational. Consider, for example, an individual who is reluctant to abandon a sunk cost; because expected utility analysis concerns only the expectation of *future* consequences, concern for sunk costs is not mirrored in the analysis. In effect, the individual who is tied to the sunk costs broadens his or her framework in such a way that the original motive—the perception of "waste" in abandoning the sunk costs—disappears when he or she realizes that honoring sunk costs conflicts with the more important motive of behaving in an economically rational manner.

The decision analyst starts with the assumption that there are conflicts between dispositions in individual decision-making contexts and general dispositions, analyzes the conflicts, and then hopes that the client can resolve them in a manner more compatible with his or her "basic needs." This procedure is analogous to what the psychoanalytic therapist does, for example, in analyzing "Dora's" coughing fits as simultaneously an unconscious wish to engage in fellatio with her father and a revulsion at that desire. Once the conflict is (gently and appropriately) explained to the client, it can be resolved in a manner that is beneficial to the client (although not always). Thus, just as Dora can deal with her incestuous feelings toward her father by recognizing them intellectually and replacing the debilitating coughing fits with other activities, people can abandon sunk costs when they see them as irrational. Likewise, the factory owner can feel that he has made a very fine decision in choosing to forego the additional profits he could achieve through automation. Chapter 10 will present research that supports the basic ideas underlying decision analysis and the use of the von Neumann and Morgenstern framework as a therapeutic tool.

8.4 SOME BUM RAPS FOR DECISION ANALYSIS

A popular misconception is that decision analysis is unemotional, "dehuman," and obsessive because it uses numbers and addition and multiplication in order to arrive at important life decisions. Isn't this "misquantification"? Aren't the "mathematicizers" of life, who admittedly have done well in the basic sciences, moving into a context where such uses of numbers are irrelevant and irreverent? Isn't this turning over important human decisions "to a machine," particularly the computer—which now picks our quarterbacks, our chief executive officers, and even our lovers? Don't we suffer enough from the "tyranny of numbers" when our opportunities in life are controlled by scores on aptitude tests and numbers entered on rating forms by interviewers and supervisors? In short, isn't the human spirit better expressed by intuitive choices than by "crunched" numbers? Or even by rationality itself?

The answer to all these concerns is an unqualified no. There is absolutely nothing in the von Neumann and Morgenstern theory—or in fact in this book—that requires the adoption of "inhuman" values. In fact, the whole idea of utility is that it provides a measure of what is truly important to individuals reaching decisions. As presented here, the aim of analyzing expected utility is to help us achieve what is really important to us. As James March points out, one goal in life may be to *discover* what our values are.[13] That goal might require action that is "playful," or even arbitrary. Does such action violate the dictates of either rationality or expected utility theory? No. Upon examination, an individual valuing such an approach will be found to have a utility associated with the existential experimentation that follows from it. All that the decision analyst does is help to make this value explicit so that the individual can understand it and incorporate it into action in a noncontradictory manner.

Nor is decision analysis an obsessive activity. In fact, some conclusions will mandate action rather than thought. For example, as mentioned earlier, there is a great deal more in von Neumann and Morgenstern's classic *Theory of Games and Economic Behavior* than has been presented here. One particularly intriguing section of that book concerns optimal playing in poker. There are 2,598,960 possible

[13]March, J. C. (1972). Model bias in social action. *Review of Educational Research, 42,* 413–429.

poker hands, and because no two of these hands are tied, drawing a particular hand is equivalent to drawing some number between 1 and 2,598,960.[14] Since a hand is won by the person with the highest number, the question is what constitutes good betting strategy. Von Neumann and Morgenstern considered a simplified form of poker in which only two people play. Each person must ante, one person bets, and the other has the opportunity to either match the bet or raise it, at which point the first person may respond by matching the raise. What von Neumann and Morgenstern proved mathematically is that, according to the principle of maximizing expected utility, a player should either bet the maximum amount immediately or fold. (If the player is the first bettor, he or she may "check".) Details of that proof are beyond the scope of this book; what is important is that it is a rigorous demonstration within the context of the theory that hesitant behavior is poor strategy. It implies the exact opposite of obsessing about a decision. In fact, the maximal strategy is to choose some number between 1 and 2,598,960 prior to looking at the value of the hand, bet the maximal amount if the value is above the chosen number, and otherwise not bet at all. In this context, "dynamic decision making" is supported. In fact, absolutely nothing in the theory encourages people to equivocate or postpone.

[14]That is, $\binom{52}{5}$.

CHAPTER

Heads I win; tails you lose.
                                    Anonymous

9

Dominating Strategies

9.1 INTRODUCTION

In Chapter 2, I asserted that attempting to kick an addiction "cannot hurt and might help." That assertion was based on the assumption that the individual is a rational decision maker who would not react to a failure with a self-attribution of weakness but would attempt to learn from it. Moreover, I was assuming that a possible failure would not alter the situation of the decision maker in a way that would significantly lower the probabilities on any future attempts to conquer the addiction (e.g., induce a depressive episode). Finally, I was assuming that the costs of withdrawal would not offset the physical benefits of being free of the addiction for even a limited period of time.

If these assumptions are met, adopting the alternative of trying is what "game theorists" term a *dominating strategy*. If all of the consequences of a particular alternative are superior to those of any other alternatives available to the decision maker, it is termed a *dominating alternative*, and choosing it is a dominating strategy. In the addiction example, failure can result in learning, and success results in freedom. Without an attempt, however, the addict learns nothing and continues to destroy himself or herself. Even if the probability of success is miniscule, trying is clearly preferable to not trying. It dominates (again, granting the listed assumptions).

A dominating strategy is a strategy that is preferable to all others, not necessarily the one that is adopted. In fact, people often do not choose the dominating strategy; the payment of sunk costs, for example is one reason for not doing so.

"Would you rather have 2 cookies and she have 1, or would you rather have 3 and she have 4?" Because most children (and adults) have a profound and abiding preference for 3 cookies over 2, the dominating strategy—if the parent presents the choice—is to opt for 3 cookies for self and 4 for the sibling. Nevertheless, children (and adults) often choose the 2–1 alternative. This choice is based on an invidious *social comparison*, rather than on consequences to the chooser.

Adults? Charles McClintock and Steven McNeel presented Belgian college students with a "game" in which the outcomes were "points" that were converted to money (either .5 franc or .05 franc for each point).[1]

---

[1]McClintock, C. G., and McNeel, S. P. (1966). Reward level and game-playing behavior. *Journal of Conflict Resolution*, *10*, 98–102. See also Messick, D. M., and Thorngate, W. B. (1967). Relative gain maximization in experimental games. *Journal of Experimental Social Psychology*, *3*, 85–101.

Two players, A and B, simultaneously made choices between strategies 1 and 2. The numbers in the cells of Table 9.1 indicate the number of points the experimenter awarded to players A and B, respectively, for each combination of strategies chosen. The choices were repeated.

Table 9.1

<table>
<tr><td></td><td></td><td colspan="2" align="center">**PLAYER B**</td></tr>
<tr><td></td><td></td><td align="center">Strategy 1</td><td align="center">Strategy 2</td></tr>
<tr><td rowspan="2">**PLAYER A**</td><td>Strategy 1</td><td align="center">0, 0</td><td align="center">5, 0</td></tr>
<tr><td>Strategy 2</td><td align="center">0, 5</td><td align="center">6, 6</td></tr>
</table>

Strategy 2 is dominating for both players. Consider player A's payoffs. If player B chose strategy 1, player A received no points. If player B chose strategy 2, player A received 6 points if he chose strategy 2 but only 5 if he chose strategy 1. No assumptions about the psychology of player B were necessary for A to conclude that strategy 2 is the dominating one. As long as there was a chance that player B would choose strategy 2, it was preferable, and if player B never played strategy 2, it wouldn't have mattered what A did. Strategy 2 was preferable for player B for the same reasons.

What do college students do? At least in Belgium in 1965, they chose strategy 1, guaranteeing that they would be no worse off than the other player and that they might be better off (if the other player was a "sucker" who looked after his or her own best interests.) The result was that most students spent their time in this experiment amassing no money whatsoever when they could have been receiving 6 points each time they made a choice. Social comparison can be pernicious.

Perhaps students aren't adults, or perhaps people have matured beyond self-defeating competitiveness since the time of McClintock and McNeel's study. Even from the point of view of the 1980s "me generation," self-defeating social comparisons are "counterproductive." Dominating strategies are, after all, defined in terms of payoff to *self*.

President Ronald Reagan is certainly an adult—and current (as of the time this book is being written). I have twice watched him assert in defense of increased nuclear weapons production that the Soviet economy cannot afford a nuclear arms race *as well* as ours can. The second time, he followed this assertion by a statement that the Soviet economy would be destroyed *first*. Social comparisons can be pernicious.

There is a "way out" of the irrationality of choosing dominated strategies for reasons of social comparisons. Simply define the payoffs *in terms of the comparisons themselves*. Consider, for example, the McClintock and McNeel game, but now define payoffs as the number of points each player gets less the number the other player gets. These payoffs are presented in Table 9.2. In other words, while the experimenters presented numerical payoffs (convertible to money), the *utility* (section 8.1) of these payoffs to the players is a function of the *difference* between the payoffs to the choosing player and the other player. Here, strategy 1 is the dominating strategy.

Table 9.2

		PLAYER B	
		Strategy 1	Strategy 2
PLAYER A	Strategy 1	0, 0	+5, −5
	Strategy 2	−5, +5	0, 0

Thus, choice based on social comparison can be consistent with subjective expected utility theory, but there's a proviso: in order to be rational, the chooser must place a *negative* value on others' welfare. Indifference, which is the basis of capitalist economic theory (by maximizing their own welfare without *any* concerns for others, the butcher, baker, and brewer help others by virtue of the "unseen hand")[2], is unacceptable, as is altruism. If the child in our cookie

[2]Smith, A. (1976). *The Wealth of Nations*. Chicago: The University of Chicago Press. Original work published in 1776.

example is indifferent, then a choice between 2 and 3 cookies is a choice between 2 and 3 cookies irrespective of the number the other child receives. Altruism makes social comparison even less tenable as a reason for choice. An altruistic child would prefer her or his sibling to have 4 cookies rather than 1 and would prefer 3 cookies to 2 for herself or himself. Yet if such a child were then to make a choice based on social comparison, preferring a 2–1 distribution to a 3–4 one, the child would have reversed the choice based on these same outcomes—an irrationality.

Simply put, rationality is the avoidance of a contradiction. It is possible to make a rational choice based on social comparison—but only if one is malevolent. Such malevolence can be quite consistent with the goals of a decision maker—as for example, when one is competing in a football game or against an "evil empire." The alternative explanation is that such choices are a psychological quirk—similar to the quirk involved in honoring sunk costs. They are based on automatic, "thoughtless" responding, and if the choices were presented to people free of the comparison (e.g., "she may have 1 or 4, *and* you may have 2 or 3"), they would not be made.[3] Just as people would prefer paying $100 to be where they want to be rather than where they do not want to be, people generally prefer choices that help both them and others to choices that hurt everyone *when they realize what it is they are choosing*. But dominating strategies are not always obvious.

In addition to hypothesizing malevolence to explain choices based on social comparisons, it is possible to explain them by the revealed preference position described in Chapter 8. If behavior is analyzed within this assumption, it is *by definition impossible* for an individual not to choose a dominating strategy; the mere fact that an individual does not choose a particular alternative demonstrates that it is not dominating for him or her (even though it may appear so to an outside observer). For example, a noted economist once complained about antipollution and wilderness preservation laws in a *Newsweek* editorial. People advocating such laws fail to understand elementary economics, he alleged. That is, the fact that people pollute and destroy the environment means, by definition, that they place a higher value on destruction than on preservation.

[3] For a fuller discussion of the cookie example, see Messick, D. M. (1969–70). Some thoughts on the nature of human competition. *Hypothese, 14e jaargang no. 2,* Tijdschrift voor Psychologie en Opvoedkunde.

The assumption of revealed preference immediately conflicts with common sense, for it implies that for some people psychosis, neurosis, lung cancer, or cirrhosis of the liver are "preferred" to health, that if people destroy their own environment they "prefer" to do so, and that there is no such thing as a "moment of weakness." (For example, the individual "pressing the button" is indicating as valid a preference for death over life as he, or she, would be for life over death if he or she did not.)[4] As pointed out in the previous chapter, the assumption of revealed preference also conflicts with all the theory and empirical findings discussed in Chapters 2 through 7. There is, however, a justification for the assumption: it leads to *a* model of human behavior, just as other assumptions lead to others. The question then is which models are most useful, not one of rationality versus irrationality. The problem with such a model, however, is that it fits any choice ever made. Consequently, no experiment or observation can distinguish between its predictions and those of some other model.

Discussion of the dominance principle throughout history has centered on the desirability of consequences—as opposed to inferring such desirability from the premise that whenever a dominating strategy is present people necessarily choose it. That is, philosophers have examined consequences in particular choice situations and claimed that their examination leads to the conclusion that one alternative rather than another is a dominating one, and that therefore people *should* choose it. The best-known analysis in Western thought is that of Blaise Pascal (1623–1662). In his famous justification of faith in a Christian God, he examined the consequences of believing and not believing. If, indeed, such a God does not exist, Pascal concluded, it makes no difference whether one believes or not; death means personal annihilation. If, however, such a God does exist, then belief results in a positive consequence, whereas lack of belief results in a negative consequence. Therefore, for Pascal belief was a dominating strategy. (What Pascal actually did was to assign probabilities to a Christian God's existence and rough measures of his own "personal values" for believing or not believing. He came to the conclusion that the positive consequences of belief given God exists are so large in comparison to those of being free of belief if God does not that they are

---

[4] Once again, the belief that nuclear war is more apt to start as the result of ignorance than of malevolence, or that people in general are more dumb than vicious, is often regarded as cynical.

quite literally incomparable—in conflict with the Archemedian axiom discussed in Chapter 8. Thus, no matter what probabilities Pascal considered, belief had a higher expectation. It is, of course, the nature of a dominating alternative that such probabilities are irrelevant; if all the consequences of that alternative are better than all of the others available, then the probabilities with which the consequences occur do not matter.)[5] Arnobius of Sicca (also known as Afer ["orator"] or Arnobius the Elder) made roughly the same argument approximately 1300 years earlier:

> Since, then, it is in the nature of things which are still in the future that they cannot be grasped and understood by the touch of anticipation, is it not better reasoning that, of two alternatives which are both uncertain and hang in doubtful suspense, we should believe that one which affords some hopes rather than one which offers none at all? In the former case there is no danger if what is said to be in the future proves vain and idle; and in the latter there is the greatest loss, specifically the loss of salvation, if when the time is come, it be made patent that there was no deceit.[6]

Thus, according to Arnobius (and Pascal) the fact that Christians cannot offer any *proof* of the claims is irrelevant to the *choice* of whether to believe them.[7]

Such analyses depend upon the values that the analyst ascribes to potential consequences. If, for example, we accept the Archemedian axiom and believe that a life free of religious belief in the event it is untrue is superior to one of belief, then there is *some* probability that God does not exist that would lead to a higher expectation for non-belief; belief would not be a dominating strategy. Moreover, there may be disagreement about these values over issues other than whether the Archemedian axiom is satisfied. Consider, for example, the deci-

---

[5] Some theologians have questioned belief made on the basis of decision-theory analysis. Would eternal bliss really be granted to someone who chooses to believe because it is a "good bet." The counterargument is that it is presumptuous to question God's attitude toward such a person.

[6] Arnobius (1949). *The Case against the Pagans*, (H. Bryce and H. Campbell, translators and annotators). Winchester, Maryland: Newman Press, 116–117.

[7] While familiar with some of the history involved, I am indebted to Brown Grier for a particularly lucid description presented at the 1981 meetings of the Mathematical Psychology Association.

sion of a president of the United States of whether to retaliate against a country that has launched a massive and devastating nuclear strike. The purpose of a retaliation policy is to *prevent* an attack, and the occurrence of an attack would show that the policy had failed. The only alternatives available *after* a strike would be to order retaliation, in which case both the United States and the attacking country would be destroyed, and *not* to order retaliation, in which case only the United States would have been destroyed. A president might conclude that restraint was the dominating strategy in such a situation; that is, that nuclear weapons have value only as support for a bluff of retaliation, because at the time of actual decision (and certainly 500 years hence) the world would be better off with less of it destroyed; if the United States were already destroyed, retaliating would be simply honoring a sunk cost of making a threat credible when it no longer mattered. Such an analysis does *not* imply that the president should not threaten previous to the attack. In fact, even if the enemy suspected that such a threat was a bluff, the enemy could not be sure that anger, panic, or irrationality would not negate its implementation, or that the person embracing it wouldn't be replaced—perhaps quite quickly. Thus even if the enemy believed that the probability p of making good on the threat was very low, the expected utility of attack would still be negative.

Before automatically responding to such a no-retaliation strategy as "appeasement" the reader should note that the problem with appeasement prior to World War II was that it led to *future* consequences that were undesirable—not, according to historical accounts, by "whetting the appetite of the aggressor," but by giving up opportunities for a rather quick military victory if in fact war had been declared.[8] The purpose of implementing a threat is to make future threats credible. If some such future threats are irrelevant, so is implementation.

The problem, of course, is that the leader of one *or neither* side may behave rationally. (And how do we know who the leaders will be, say, forty years from now, or even ten?) The solution is to devise a "fail-safe" system, one that is safe against irrationality. No such system is perfect, but we have one good paradigm available. In *constructing* this country, the members of the Constitutional Convention set up an admittedly constipated system of "checks and balances" in

[8]See Speer, A. (1971). *Inside the Third Reich*. New York: Macmillan.

order to guard against abuse of power by future leaders who were *not* always wise and good.[9] In fact, they even placed restraints on their *own* power—in contrast to most revolutionary leaders in history who were so convinced of their own virtue and necessity that they sought to enlarge their power. Moreover, while those founders espoused democracy, they set constraints on its power as well by passing the Bill of Rights. (Recent events have illustrated the wisdom of this restraint as well; opinion polls have indicated that the majority of people in this country do not favor the Bill's specific provisions when they are asked if they agree with them without being informed that the questioner is referring specifically to the Constitutional amendments comprising this Bill.) The solution to the current problem is to set up an international system of laws, armaments, and agreements that would constrain future leaders, regardless of their goals, motives, and irrationalities. (A "star wars" defense that would make one side invulnerable—or worse yet, make the leaders of that side believe it to be invulnerable when it is not—is the antithesis of such a constraint.) For example, dismantling first-strike weapons that could be targets for an aggressive or paranoid enemy would greatly decrease the probability of a unilateral attack by *anyone*. In my view, focusing policy on affecting the thoughts, motives, and feelings of the present leaders of a competing nation is a *mistake*. It is ignoring base rates in favor of dubious individuating information. (See Chapter 5.)

9.2 A CHARACTERISTIC OF SOME DOMINATING STRATEGIES

What strategies are dominating? Often, the answer depends upon the particular situation. A number of generalizations are possible, however. I will discuss one, because it rests on a general principle of choice.

Aristotle urged people to seek "the golden mean" between extremes, "moderation in all things" (which I interpret as including moderation in the pursuit of moderation). But why should this "golden mean" in general be desirable? Clyde Coombs has enunciated a very

---

[9]Wills, G. (1978). *Inventing America: Jefferson's Declaration of Independence.* New York: Random House.

simple principle that implies moderation: *good things satiate and bad things escalate*. This principle has reference to choosing between alternatives that vary in *amount*. Food is an obvious example. After deprivation, an individual derives both important nutritional value and pleasure from initial amounts of food. As amount increases, however, nutritional importance decreases, and the pleasure in each mouthful decreases as well. These "good things" *satiate*. On the other hand, the possibly pernicious effects of calories, additives, processed sugars, fats, and so on, increase as food consumption continues. Moreover, these pernicious effects *escalate*. For example, 500 extra calories per day is more than twice as bad for the eater as 250 extra calories per day (just as being 30% overweight is more than twice as bad as being 15% overweight).

Another of Coombs's examples is the length of a vacation. The first few days of getting "away from it all" are delightful. Soon, however, the vacationer begins to adapt to the new environment, and its positive qualities become less salient. (The 200th view of the mountain or the palace is less thrilling than the third.) In addition, its interesting challenges gradually become hassles. At the same time, the amount of drudgery upon returning home necessary to "make up for lost time" begins to mount. (Even the 9-to-5 worker has a number of outside interests that must be attended to after the vacation is over.) Because drudgery is an escalating phenomenon (i.e., two hours devoted to it is more than twice as bad as one hour), this bad characteristic of vacations also escalates with time. The principle that "good things escalate and bad things satiate" can be visualized with a simple graph; see Figure 9.1.

When the good, satiating characteristics (+) are added to the bad, escalating characteristics (−), the result is a *single-peaked function* that has a maximum value of a moderate amount; see Figure 9.2. Net welfare (positive combined with negative) is maximized at moderate amounts. Coombs and George Avrunin have *proved* that if: (1) good characteristics satiate (the function relating goodness to amount has a slope that is positive and *decreasing*) and (2) bad things escalate (the function relating bad characteristics to amount has a slope that is negative and decreasing—becoming more negative), and (3) the negative function is more rapidly changing than the positive one, then (4) the resulting sum of good and bad "things" (that is, the sum of the good characteristics function and the bad characteristics function) will

Figure 9.1

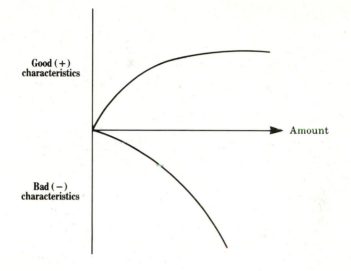

Good (+)
characteristics

Bad (−)
characteristics

Amount

Hypothesized satiation of good and escalation of bad

always be single-peaked.[10] The "flat" nature of this peak in Figure 9.2 is common.

Note that the "good things satiate/bad things escalate" (over amount) principle is in direct conflict with the analyses of prospect theory (Chapter 3), which includes (like Fechner's law and classic economics) a "decreasing marginal returns" principle for negative as

[10]See Coombs, C. H., and Avrunin, G. S. *The Structure of Conflict* (in press). Also, Coombs, C. H., and Avrunin, G. S. (1977). Single peaked functions and the theory of preference. *Psychological Review, 84,* 216–230. As has been pointed out by Coombs and Avrunin themselves, the satiation of good versus escalation of bad principle, while sufficient to yield a single peaked result, is not *necessary*. For example, a linear function over bad added to a marginally decreasing one over good would also yield a single peaked result, as would the addition of another negatively accelerating function that is less "bowed."

Figure 9.2

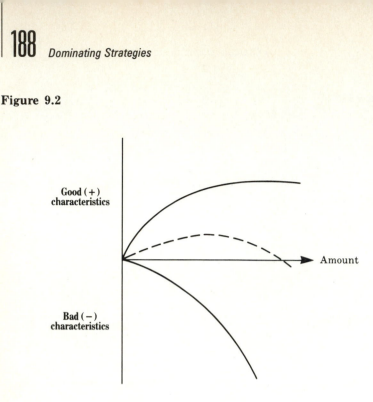

Summation of good and bad

well as positive outcomes. One possible resolution is that the moderation principle is a *realistic* generalization from past experience (although often an implicit one), while the framing effects of prospect theory involve *imagination* of consequences. A nuclear war that killed two-thirds of a population would be more than twice as bad as one that killed one-third, even though an individual decision maker in a particular crisis situation may choose a 50–50 risk of a nuclear war that would kill two-thirds in order to avoid losing one-third for sure. This interpretation is consistent with the irrationality of framing effects—in that a person choosing among alternatives that can equally well be framed positively or negatively cannot consistently frame them both ways according to a negatively accelerating function. (For example, if a person normally sleeps eight hours a night and regards the first four hours as the most important, then the *last* four hours of sleep *lost* must also be the most important; a *positively* accelerating function for the *dis*utility of lost sleep is implied.)

An alternative interpretation is that it's not true in many contexts that "bad things escalate." While this principle is *sufficient* for producing a single-peaked function, it is not *necessary*.

9.3 SOCIAL DILEMMAS

A major problem with choosing dominating strategies is that *individual choices of dominating strategies may have socially disastrous results*. Consider three examples.

1. Those of us who enjoy public television are asked to contribute our "fair share," which is generally *less* than its value to us—apparently a good economic bargain. But ignoring this request is a dominating strategy unless we can contribute a huge amount. If not, our individual contribution (usually $25–$100) will not have a significant effect on the financial status of public television. Our favorite programs will be on the air or off the air depending upon what *others* contribute. Not contributing this money will, on the other hand, make us personally more comfortable. Hence, it is dominating not to contribute. But if every viewer chose this dominating strategy, public television would fold, thereby depriving viewers of a "public good" that is worth more to them than the amount they are asked to contribute.

2. During pollution alerts in Eugene, Oregon, people who can are asked to ride bicycles rather than drive cars. (Industrial pollution is comparatively minimal, but the city often experiences an inverted weather pattern.) The individual complying with this plea has a negligible impact on the general pollution level (what does one car less matter?) but reaps the benefits of the noncompliers' exhausts. Clearly, it is dominating to drive, *especially* during pollution alerts. If other residents comply, the problem will go away. If they don't, the environment of the car is preferable to that of the streets, and the amount of harm done by one car is minimal.

3. Married couples in India are urged by the government to limit the size of their families. Wives, however, generally outlive their husbands by many years, and during their widowhood they have little or no income. By tradition, however, sons are expected to support their widowed mothers. Thus, it is to each woman's per-

sonal benefit to have as many sons as possible. (There are also religious beliefs encouraging motherhood.) The result of women choosing the dominating strategy of large families is, however, a truly "vicious circle"; the widespread poverty resulting from over-population *precludes* the establishment of a social security system, which would in turn reduce the motivation for having large families.

These examples are all dilemmas: while each individual privately has a dominating alternative, *all* individuals would prefer the outcome that would be produced if *all* of them chose the *non*dominating alternative. All public television watchers would prefer contributing their "fair share" to not being able to watch their favorite programs. All residents of Eugene who could ride bicycles would prefer universal compliance, with a consequent dissolution of air pollution, to the situation where no one substituted bicycle for car. All the people in India would presumably prefer population restraint, (with its subsequent diminution of poverty and the possibility of social security) to the situation in which each woman adopted her dominating strategy of having as many children as possible. The problem is that when viewed only in terms of consequences for self, the optimal strategy for each individual decision maker is to choose the dominating alternative, while hoping everyone else involved *will not.*

Such situations are *social dilemmas*. In a social dilemma each individual is confronted with a choice between *dominating* and *dominated* strategies, and everyone involved prefers universal choice of the dominated strategies to universal choice of the dominating ones. Universal choice of the dominating strategies leads to an *equilibrium*, in that no individual has a motive for switching to a dominated strategy—for example, to become the only person in Eugene riding a bicycle. (In fact, no one ever has a motive for switching from a dominating strategy.) This equilibrium is *deficient*, however, because there is another outcome—the outcome that would result from universal choice of dominated strategies—that is preferred by *all*. Thus, a social dilemma is a situation in which all participants have dominating strategies that yield a *deficient equilibrium*.

Economists often define social dilemmas in terms of externalities. Briefly, economic choices are viewed as resulting in payoffs to self—*internalities*—and payoffs to others—*externalities*. When the internalities for a particular choice are optimal, the choice is dominating. If, however, the externalities for a set of dominating choices are *negative, of greater magnitude than the internalities, and shared equally by all*, the result is a social dilemma.[11] If every participant makes the dominating choice, the net result is negative, and because this net result is shared equally by all, each individual's net is negative. Hence, each individual would prefer the outcome in which everyone avoided the dominating choice—that is, the result of universal choice of dominating strategies is deficient. The economic definition of social dilemmas is more complex than the one presented in the preceding paragraph, because it involves *interpersonal comparison* of positive and negative payoffs. The previous definition involves only comparisons within an individual—a preference of each participant for universal choice of dominated strategies over universal choice of dominating ones. The economic definition, however, has the advantage of not involving personal preferences; when some exchangeable form of payoff such as money is available, the pattern of internalities and externalities can lead to a clear understanding of where social dilemmas exist. For example, a purely monetary analysis can establish that gas wars are social dilemmas for retailers, cold wars for nations, and manufacture without constraint on pollution for everyone.

Many analysts believe the nuclear arms race to be a social dilemma. Each side reasons that arming is a dominating strategy. If the other side does not arm, the side that does gains military supremacy, its most preferred outcome (presumably without war, a lose–lose situation). If the other side does arm, arming affords a protection from allowing the other side supremacy, presumably the worst possible outcome. Hence, no matter what the other side does, each is better off arming than refraining from arming. Table 9.3 applies this analysis to the nuclear arms race between the United States and the Soviet Union.

A dilemma exists when each side prefers supremacy to peace and prosperity, and peace and prosperity to the arms race. Advocates of unilateral disarmament argue that the preference for supremacy is a poor one—the extreme of such advocacy being expressed in the old slogan "better Red than dead." As armaments become increasingly destructive to the economies of the U.S. and the USSR, however, a

---

[11]The statement is not "if and only if." All that is necessary for a dilemma to result is that each person's net payoff (positive internality to self minus that person's share of negative externalities from others' defection) is negative. Moreover, there are other dysfunctional situations—"market failures"—in which internalities lead to summed negative results of defection even though some people experience net benefit.

Table 9.3

		USSR	
		Arm	Don't Arm
U.S.	Arm	arms race	U.S. supremacy
	Don't Arm	USSR supremacy	peace and prosperity

compelling argument may be made that the preference for supremacy over peace and prosperity is the poor preference. Perhaps each side eventually will opt for peace and prosperity over supremacy.

Of course this analysis of the arms race between the U.S. and the USSR rests on an assumption of *symmetry*—that is, that the two countries face the same choice and are equally motivated to choose the dominating strategy. If, however, one side is motivated only by a benign desire for self-protection while the other is motivated only by a malevolent desire for supremacy, the result is not a social dilemma, but one of pure offense and defense. The situation becomes more complicated, however, if no matter how malevolent one side is in *fact* its leaders perceive it to be a benevolent power facing a dilemma. Many "hard-liners" appear to eschew even this interpretation. Ours talk, anyway, as if the U.S. is benevolent and the USSR leaders are malevolent *and that the Soviet leaders also believe in their own malevolence and the U.S.'s benevolence.* Thus there is no dilemma at all, but simply a conflict—between unmitigated good and unmitigated evil.

Anatol Rapoport has done extensive empirical and theoretical work on fights, games, and debates. (In fact, he wrote a book of that title.) He has been particularly interested, both scientifically and socially, in conflicts in dilemma situations and has performed an impressive number of studies of two-person social dilemmas.

Such dilemmas are technically termed *prisoner's dilemmas.* This term is derived from an anecdote about obtaining confessions to a bank robbery. According to the story, two men rob a bank. They are apprehended, but in order to obtain a conviction the district attorney needs confessions. He succeeds by proposing to each robber separately that if he confesses and his accomplice does not, he will go free and his accomplice will be sent to jail for ten years; if both confess, both will be sent to jail for five years, and if neither confesses, both will be sent to jail for one year on charges of carrying a concealed weapon. Further, the district attorney informs each man that he is proposing the same deal to his accomplice. Confessing is a dominating strategy. If the accomplice does not also confess, the prisoner who does goes free rather than to jail for a year. If the accomplice does confess, confession means going to jail for five years rather than for ten. But the resulting equilibrium is deficient, because both would go to jail for five years, whereas both would go for only a single year if neither confesses.

This prisoner's dilemma illustrates three important aspects of social dilemmas. First, a dilemma from the participant's perspective may not be a dilemma from others' perspectives. The prisoner's dilemma is purely that of the prisoners. A society member seeking retribution for the robbery might judge the situation to be an example of clever law enforcement (just as a motorist does not view a gasoline price war as a "dilemma"). Second, "honor" (here among thieves) could resolve the dilemma. Paradoxically, in social dilemmas the honorable behavior of choosing the dominated strategy is self-serving if it avoids the deficient equilibrium. But it can do so *only* if it is reciprocated, and in the prisoner's dilemma anecdote the reciprocation must be simultaneous and take place without communication between the participants. Third, what appears to be a dilemma may be embedded in a social structure that is not a dilemma. Confession would no longer be a dominating strategy if, for example, each prisoner were convinced of probable retribution in jail for confessing, or even if each had a stake in his reputation as a "man of honor" that outweighed the possibility of four more years in jail if the other confessed. (Thus, even in the absence of external punishment, honor or concern for reputation can extricate people from dilemmas.)

In the 1950s and early 1960s Rapoport initiated a long investigation of how people (usually college students) behave in repeated ("iterated") prisoner's dilemma situations with payoffs consisting of small amounts of money, or "points." He was particularly interested in determining what strategies would elicit choice of the dominated ("cooperative") strategy from the other participant ("player"). Other investigators quickly became interested in this problem—with its obvious implications for stability or disarmament in a nuclear world dominated by two super powers. (When I was reviewing papers for the *Journal of Abnormal and Social Psychology* in the mid sixties, I half-seriously suggested to the editor that it be renamed the *Journal of Iterated Prisoner's Dilemmas and Rating Scale Behavior.* Fully 60% of the articles published in it at the time involved either iterated prisoner's dilemmas or rating scale measures of attitude change.)

Rapoport himself has devised a good scheme for eliciting cooperation. Called "TIT-FOR-TAT," it consists of first choosing the dominated (cooperative) strategy and then simply choosing the strategy that the other participant has chosen on the previous trial.[12] In Robert Axelrod's computer "tournaments," in which participants submitted programmed strategies for playing repeated prisoner's dilemmas, Rapoport's TIT-FOR-TAT strategy has twice won—that is, accumulated the most points when pitted against forty or so strategies devised by other "experts."[13]

In 1967, however, Amnon Rapoport (no relation), published an article pointing out that *if* people believe that their own behavior can influence the subsequent behavior of the other player (the underlying assumption of the TIT-FOR-TAT strategy) then the iterated prisoner's dilemma is no longer a dilemma.[14] Specifically, if participants expect reciprocity when they choose the cooperative strategy ("reciprocal altruism"), such a choice is no longer dominated. The iterated situation becomes instead a very complicated situation of behavior control in which people reward or punish each other while simultaneously rewarding or punishing themselves (much as a parent who says it "hurts" to punish her or his child with the aim of preventing subsequent undesirable behavior).

In 1968, Garrett Hardin published his famous article entitled "The Tragedy of the Commons."[15] In it he pointed out that the worldwide problems of overexploitation of the environment, pollution, and most particularly, overpopulation (which Hardin views as the source of the other problems) arise from social dilemmas. It is to each individual's personal advantage to exploit, to pollute, and (in "developing"

---

[12]See Rapoport, Anatol, and Chammah, A. M. (1965). *Prisoner's Dilemma.* Ann Arbor: University of Michigan Press.

[13]Axelrod, R. (1984). *The Evolution of Cooperation.* New York: Basic Books.

[14]Rapoport, Amnon (1967). Optimal policies for the prisoner's dilemma. *Psychological Review, 74,* 136–145.

[15]Hardin, G. R. (1968). The tragedy of the commons. *Science, 162,* 1243–1248.

countries) to have children. The title of Hardin's article came from the (proported) overexploitation of common pasture grounds in fourteenth-century England. It was in each herder's best interest to graze more cattle or sheep, because the herdsman's share of the commons depleted by such an addition was less than his increase in wealth derived by adding animals. The result was that the common pastures were overgrazed and eventually had to be abandoned. (The parallel with the current slaughter of whales is clear and chilling.) Similarly, it is to each couple's advantage in an underdeveloped country to add to the "commons" the ultimate exploiting and polluting agent—another human being.

Hardin's solution to this dilemma is to propose "mutual coercion mutually agreed upon." That is equivalent to embedding the dilemma in a social structure of punishments (albeit "mutually agreed upon" ones) *that transform it into a nondilemma.* (Economists and decision theorists term factors such as punishment due to noncooperation "side payments.") This solution is akin to promising subsequent retribution in jail if a prisoner confesses, or a later reward once released if he or she does not; in either case, the strategy of not confessing may then dominate that of confessing purely in terms of its consequences for the prisoner.

The commons situation described by Hardin is different from the two-person prisoner's dilemma in a number of important ways. First, because more people are involved, the harm (negative externalities) resulting from an individual's choice is spread out among many people. Second, each person has only a partial effect on others' outcomes. (Thus, even if the dilemmas are iterated, there may be little possibility of behavior control—hence little opportunity for reciprocal altruism.) Third, both the identity of the participants and the choices they make may be anonymous. (For example, a couple in New Delhi must decide whether to have an additional child without knowing which couples in Calcutta are making the same choice and what they are deciding.)

Do people cooperate (choose the dominating strategy) when embedding the dilemma in a nondilemma and reciprocal altruism are impossible? (This impossibility may arise either because choice is made just once rather than iterated, or because the dilemma involves many people, or both.) In an informal experiment in 1983 Douglas Hofstadter asked twenty eminent colleagues to make a single choice between a C option (cooperative, dominated) and a D one (defecting, dominating) in a monetary dilemma. Each friend was always $19 to $38 better off choosing D rather than C no matter what the others did ($19 if none chose C, $20 if one other did, $38 if 19 others did). Yet if all chose C all received $57, whereas if all choose D, all received $19. (The game was complicated, but it was roughly equivalent to one in which people choose either to receive $25 for themselves or to have $57 distributed among the remaining 19 players at $3 each.) Communication among the players was not permitted. Robert Axelrod, the political science professor who ran the prisoner dilemma computer tournaments, was one of the twenty players; he stated that he saw no reason whatever to cooperate in a one-shot game without communication and chose D "without compunction." In contrast, Daniel C. Dennett chose C, saying, "I would rather be the person who bought the Brooklyn Bridge than the person who sold it. Similarly, I feel better spending $3 gained by cooperation than $10 gained by defection." In all, fourteen of Hofstadter's colleagues chose D while six chose C.[16]

At least some people *do* choose the dominated cooperative strategy in social dilemmas. People contribute to public television, ride bicycles during pollution alerts, and limit the size of their families. Why?

Many systematic studies of why people choose to cooperate or defect in multiperson dilemmas have been conducted at various universities since the early 1970s. Some experimenters have been concerned with how subjects create or use a broader social context of rewards or punishments to extricate themselves from a dilemma. Other studies have involved iterated games with feedback from previous choices. Because both such manipulations may obviate the dilemma nature of the situation, results are not reviewed here. Instead, I will briefly review studies John Orbell, Alphons van de Kragt, and I have conducted in which there were no such "incentive-compatible" reasons for cooperating.

We ran subjects in groups of 5, 10, or 40. A typical experiment is one in which people in a seven-person group must choose between receiving $6 for themselves and having $12 distributed among the six other players, $2 each. The subjects are always $6 better off choosing the money for themselves; yet if all choose that, each will receive $6, whereas if all choose to give away $12, each will receive $12.

What have we found? First, there is a set of "hard-core" cooperators among the subjects, usually college students, who choose the dominated choice even under the most unfavorable circumstances.

[16]Hofstadter, D. (1983). Metamathematical themes. *Scientific American. 248*, no. 6, 14–28.

From 25% to 50% do so depending on the situation.[17] When asked to explain why, they give reasons very much like Dennett's. (Hofstadter terms Dennett's explanation a "wrong reason.")

Second, communication increases cooperation radically, even in situations where choice is anonymous and subjects are paid without ever seeing each other again. There are, however, two provisos: the communication must be about the choice, and the subjects must believe that the benefits of cooperation will go to the people with whom they are communicating. (Without these conditions, the cooperation rate is identical to that found in groups not permitted to communicate; only the "hard core" cooperate.) Communication per se does *not* "raise consciousness" about the ethical value of cooperation. (For example, when the $12 is distributed to people in another room, communication has no effect.) But there is a "carry-over" effect. When people *first* believe benefits will go to other members of their communicating group and are *subsequently* told benefits will go to strangers, they contribute more often than if they did not first believe the benefits would go to their own group members. "Contribution begins at home." What we believe is happening is that communication leads very rapidly to "group solidarity," which elicits both mindless cooperation and trust that others will cooperate.[18]

9.4 THE OBVIOUSNESS OF DOMINATING STRATEGIES

Dominating strategies are usually obvious, but sometimes they are not. For example, some people believe that their contribution to a public good (or voting) will of itself and in some unspecified way lead others to contribute (or to vote—particularly if they are a member of a "swing" group).[19] Moreover, while basing choice on social comparison

---

[17] This rate is virtually identical to that found by Hofstadter among his eminent friends.

[18] For a view of our work and our theoretical interpretation of our results, see van de Kragt, A. J. C.; Dawes, R. M.; Orbell, J. M.; Braver, S. R.; and Wilson, L. A., II (1986). Doing well versus doing good as ways of resolving social dilemmas. In Wilke, H. A. M.; Messick, D. M.; and Rutte, C. G. *Experimental Social Dilemmas*. Frankfurt and New York: Peter Lang, 181–204.

[19] Quattrone, G. A., and Tversky, A. (1984). Causal versus diagnostic contingencies: On self-deception and the voter's illusion. *Journal of Personality and Social Psychology, 46,* 237–248.

may seem to us a mindless form of irrationality, there undoubtedly are spiteful people who experience such discomfort at others' joy that their choice of an apparently dominated strategy (e.g., of "cutting off their noses") is in fact the choice of a dominating strategy.

Occasionally, cognitive limitations may keep us from recognizing a dominating strategy. For example, Tversky and Kahneman have found that a majority of their subjects choose alternative A over alternative B when given the following hypothetical choice, in which a chip is drawn at random from an urn.[20]

A.	Composition of urn	90% white	6% red	1% green	3% yellow
	Payoff	0	+ $45	+ $30	− $15
B.	Composition of urn	90% white	7% red	1% green	2% yellow
	Payoff	0	+ $45	− $10	− $15

After all, alternative A has only one negative outcome associated with it whereas alternative B has two. *But* suppose that there are 100 chips and that you color the center of the single green chip in alternative A red, and that you color the center of the green chip in alternative B yellow. Defining the "color" of a chip as the *color of its center*, each alternative now involves only white, red, and yellow chips. Moreover, there are the same proportion of chips in both alternatives (90% white, 7% red, 3% yellow). If a white chip is drawn, the payoffs are identical for alternatives A and B (0). If a red chip is drawn, alternative A provides *either* $45 or $30; alternative B provides $45; clearly B is better. Finally if a yellow chip is drawn, alternative A provides a loss of $15 while B provides a loss of $15 *or* $10. Once more alternative B is superior; it dominates A.

A subtle example of a nonobvious dominating strategy outside the laboratory may be found in the consequences for a psychologist in a mental hospital who must reach a "clinical" conclusion that a client is either more pathological or less pathological than he or she appears to be. If the psychologist concludes that the patient is "sicker" than is apparent to the other professionals involved, then the staff will tend to

[20]Tversky, A., and Kahneman, D. (1986). Rational choice and the framing of decision. *Journal of Business, 59*, part 2, S251–S278.

feel proud of any progress made and unashamed of its lack. If, however, the patient is pronounced "healthier" than is apparent, the staff will expect progress, and a failure (particularly a dramatic one such as a suicide) could easily be a source of pain to the staff (as well as to the client). Moreover, the psychologist himself or herself may be derogated for having "missed" obvious problems. Viewed purely in terms of the *consequences for the psychologist's reputation and social acceptance*, emphasizing the client's psychopathology is a dominating strategy. Hopefully, such exclusivity of concern is rare, although not—in my experience anyway—nonexistent. ("Pseudoneurotic schizophrenic" was the favorite diagnosis of one such psychologist I knew a few years back. Whatever diagnostic validity this category may have, he used it to indicate that he was not fooled by the client's normal facade and that the other hospital staff members should not be distressed by failing to help the client, since the client was "really" psychotic, underneath. Moreover, this category was a "conceptual sink"; any extreme behavior lent credence to the "schizophrenic" component, while ordinary neurotic behavior was consistent with the "pseudoneurotic" one.) Dominating strategies are compelling.

CHAPTER

. . . [Henry Kissinger] *grasps in a single millisecond the relationship that links the depths of a harbor in South Africa to the harvest of wheat in Ontario, and links these to the distance by armored vehicle, in kilometers, between Luanda and Huambo in Angola, and ties this consideration to the expulsion of a dissident in Moscow and the rise of a senator in Washington.*

James Kilpatrick
July 6, 1980

10

Proper and Improper Linear Models[1]

---

[1]Much of this material was previously published in Dawes, R. M. (1986). Forecasting one's own preferences. *International Journal of Forecasting* *2*, 5–14.

10.1 BEN FRANKLIN

What if there is no dominating strategy? We can attempt a subjective expected utility analysis (Chapter 8), but there is a simpler possibility—one suggested by Ben Franklin in a letter to his friend Joseph Priestley in 1772.[2]

> I cannot, for want of sufficient premises, advise you *what* to determine, but if you please I will tell you *how*. . . . My way is to divide half a sheet of paper by a line into two columns; writing over the one *Pro*, and over the other *Con*. Then, during three or four days' consideration, I put down under the different heads short hints of the different motives, that at different times occur to me *for* or *against* the measure. When I have thus got them all together in one view, I endeavor to estimate the respective weights. . . . [to] find at length where the balance lies. . . . And, though the weight of reasons cannot be taken with the precision of algebraic quantities, yet, when each is thus considered, separately and comparatively, and the whole matter lies before me, I think I can judge better, and am less liable to make a rash step; and in fact I have found great advantage for this kind of equation, in what may be called *moral* or *prudential algebra*.

Franklin's "prudential algebra" involves nothing more than a *weighted average* of reasons for and against a particular course of action. Each positive reason is assigned a score of $+1$, each negative one a score of -1. The scores are then given intuitive *importance weights*. The course of action with the higher resulting sum is judged to be the more desirable one.

Why should this procedure lead to better decisions than making an intuitive judgment at the outset? After all, the weights are intuitive. Doesn't Franklin's method simply substitute one type of intuition for another? Yes, it does, but his method is based on a superior type of intuition. Reasons for adopting a course of action are often *psychologically incomparable*, and research has indicated that people make poor intuitive global judgments when the factors are incomparable. By *poor* I mean they are inferior to those based on intuitive weighting—and nowhere near as good as the judges believe them to be. People tend to have misplaced faith in their global intuitive judg-

---

[2]In Bigelow, J. (ed.) (1887). *The Complete Works of Benjamin Franklin.* New York: Putnam, p. 522.

ments. We are grossly overconfident when we make such judgments, and selective memory for our successes (perhaps a mentally healthy trait) feeds our overconfidence.

What leads me to conclude that intuitive weighting schemes are superior to global intuitive judgment and that people are overconfident? These conclusions are supported by studies in which there are "correct" answers (e.g., medical diagnoses determined after extensive tests or autopsies). When judgment can be compared with such external standards of accuracy, weighting schemes *consistently* are found to be superior to intuitive global judgment, and judges consistently are found to be overconfident in their global judgments. Of course, such studies are relevant only to situations in which a complex (multivariate) strategy or stimulus can be broken down (decomposed) into simpler components—as, in Franklin's example, the probable value of a course of action can be broken down into reasons for pursuing or avoiding it.

Before reviewing this evidence, however, let us consider an example. Imagine that you must select a spy to infiltrate a Spanish-speaking terrorist organization. There are two candidates:

A is a native Spanish speaker, is moderately intelligent, shows no evidence in his past of being particularly trusted or liked by people who know him, and is highly committed to your cause. B speaks fluent Spanish but is not a native speaker (although none of five experts was able to detect an accent), is highly intelligent, and shows evidence in his past of being trusted and liked by people who know him, but you have doubts about the depth of his commitment to your cause.

Now try to make a global judgment. Does A or B "strike" you as more appropriate? Why? A hunch; an intuition? Perhaps A or B reminds you of some *particular* individual who has succeeded or failed at this type of mission in the past or who is stereotypic ("representative," see Chapter 5) of a class of people who have succeeded or failed. Perhaps it is easier to *imagine* (see section 6.3 and Chapter 7) A's or B's succeeding or failing. Perhaps memory, representativeness, and ease of imagination are all factors—conscious or unconscious—influencing your hunch or intuition. But these factors are *poor* predictors. Recall that the ease with which you can imagine events is determined by many variables other than their likelihood.

Instead, consider applying Franklin's prudential algebra—that is, developing a linear model with intuitive weights. If you do that, you will be *forced* to consider the relative importance of the four characteristics: native speech, intelligence, ability to inspire trust, and commitment to cause. There are many ways to construct such a model. Two good ways are (1) to analyze what the mission requires and weight the four characteristics accordingly, and (2) to determine weights by how the four characteristics have correlated with success or failure on similar missions in the past. (This is quite different from "matching" A and B to selected people in the past who happen to come to mind.)

Too many people prefer to make global intuitive judgments based on hunch "hit" or ad hoc choice of variables. Consider for example the judgments about "dyslexic" Amy and the "astrology nut" that were discussed in Chapter 5. Many such "snap" judgments are based on some *plausible* explanation that may or may *not* be valid. For example, J. C. Penney took potential executives to lunch. If they salted their food before tasting it, he concluded that they lacked an "inquiring frame of mind" and rejected them.[3] (Penney did well, but we have no evidence he wouldn't have done equally well had he selected executives at random from among the applicants.) Other snap judgments are based on hunch. But unless the person making such a judgment has some evidence (empirical or theoretical, not just intuitive plausibility) that the hunch is valid, it is in my view arbitrary, stupid, and unethical.

Moreover, intuitive global judgments engender overconfidence. Consider, for example, a letter to "Dear Abby" published in 1975:

DEAR ABBY: While standing in a checkout line in a high-grade grocery store, I saw a woman directly in front of me frantically rummaging around in her purse, looking embarrassed. It seems her groceries had already been checked, and she was a dollar short. I felt sorry for her, so I handed her a dollar. She was very grateful, and insisted on writing my name and address on a loose piece of paper. She stuck it in her purse and said, "I promise I'll mail you a dollar tomorrow." Well, that was three weeks ago, and I still haven't heard from her! Abby, I think I'm a fairly good judge of character, and I just didn't peg her as the kind that would

---

[3]Referenced in Webb, E. J.; Campbell, D. T.; Schwartz, R. D.; and Sechrest, L. (1966). *Unobtrusive Measures: Non-reactive Research in the Social Sciences*. Chicago: Rand McNally.

beat me out of a dollar. The small amount of money isn't important, but what it did to my faith in people is. I'd like your opinion.

SHY ONE BUCK

Note that Shy One Buck did not lose faith in her ability to "peg" people on the basis of almost no information whatsoever; she lost her faith in people. Shy One Buck still believes she is a good "judge of character" based on a single instant's interaction. It is other people who are no damn good. (Note also the gradiosity of this loss of faith—in people in general, not in peoples' memory or their ability to avoid losing loose pieces of paper.)

I cannot guarantee that a choice based on intuitive weighting will necessarily work better than one based on global intuition—just that it *usually* will. This generalization is not a global intuitive judgment of my own; it is based on a large body of research findings.

10.2 THE RESEARCH

The research began by addressing the question of whether trained experts' intuitive global predictions were better than statistically derived weighted averages of the relevant predictors.[4] Such weighted averages are termed *linear models*. This question has been studied extensively by psychologists, educators, and others interested in predicting such outcomes as college success, parole violation, psychiatric diagnosis, physical diagnosis and prognosis, and business success and failure. In all of these studies, the information on which clinical experts based their predictions was the same as that used to construct linear models. Typically, this information consisted of test scores or biographical facts, but some studies included observer ratings of specific attributes as well. All of these variables could easily be represented by (coded as) numbers having positive or negative relationships to the outcome to be predicted. (For example, higher test scores and grade point averages predict better performance in subsequent academic work; higher leucocyte count predicts greater severity of Hodgkin's disease.)

---

[4]The criteria for evaluating the success of prediction was the *product moment correlation coefficient* between prediction and outcome; the weights that optimize this coefficient were determined by *multiple regression*.

In 1954 Paul Meehl published a highly influential book in which he summarized approximately twenty such studies comparing the clinical judgment method with the statistical one.[5] *In all studies, the statistical method provided more accurate predictions, or the two methods tied.* Approximately ten years later, Jack Sawyer reviewed forty-five studies comparing clinical and statistical prediction.[6] Again, there was *not a single study* in which clinical global judgment was superior to the statistical prediction (termed *mechanical combination* by Sawyer). Unlike Meehl, Sawyer did not limit his review to studies in which the clinical judge's information was identical to that on which the statistical prediction was based; he even included two studies in which the clinical judge had access to *more* information (an interview) but did *worse*. (In one of these, the performance of 37,500 sailors in World War II in navy "elementary" school was better predicted from test scores alone than from the ratings of judges who both interviewed the sailors and had access to the scores.[7])

(The near-total lack of validity of the *unstructured* interview as a predictive technique had been documented and discussed by E. Lowell Kelly in 1953.[8] There is no evidence that such interviews yield important information beyond that of in past behavior—except whether the interviewer likes the interviewee, which *is* important in some contexts. Some of my students maintain it is necessary to interview people to avoid choosing "nerds," but they cannot explain how they would spot one, or even what they mean by the term.)

A particularly striking example of clinical versus statistical prediction was conducted by Hillel Einhorn.[9] He studied the longevity of

[5]Meehl, P. E. (1954). *Clinical versus Statistical Predictions: A Theoretical Analysis and Revision of the Literature.* Minneapolis: University of Minnesota Press.

[6]Sawyer, J. (1966). Measurement and prediction, clinical and statistical. *Psychological Bulletin, 66,* 178–200.

[7]Bloom, R. F., and Brundage, E. G. Predictions of success in elementary schools for enlisted personnel. In Stuit, D. B. (ed.). *Personnel Research and Test Development In the Bureau of Naval Personnel.* Princeton, N. J.: Princeton University Press.

[8]Kelly, E. L. (1954). Evaluation of the interview as a selection technique. In *Proceedings of the 1953 Invitational Conference on Testing Problems.* Princeton, N. J.: Educational Testing Service.

[9]Einhorn, H. J. (1972). Expert measurement and mechanical combination. *Organizational Behavior and Human Performance, 13,* 171–192.

patients with Hodgkin's disease during an era when the disease was invariably fatal (prior to the late 1960s). This world expert on Hodgkin's disease and two assistants rated nine characteristics of biopsies taken from patients and then made a global rating of the "overall severity" of the disease process for each patient. Upon the patients' deaths, Einhorn correlated the global ratings with their longevity. While a rating of "overall severity" is not precisely the same as a prediction of time until death, it should predict that. (At least, the world's expert thought it would.) Einhorn found that it does not. (In fact, the slight trend was in the *wrong* direction; higher severity ratings were associated with longer survival time.) In contrast, a multiple regression analysis of the biopsy characteristics scaled by the doctors succeeded in predicting how long the patients lived. The prediction was not strong, but statistically reliable. (See Appendix A.3.)

Another striking example is a study by Robert Libby. He asked forty-three bank loan officers (some senior—in banks with assets up to four billion dollars) to predict which 30 of 60 firms would go bankrupt within three years of a financial report. The loan officers requested, and were provided with various financial ratios—for example, the ratio of liquid assets to total assets—in order to make their predictions. Their individual judgments were 75% correct, but a regression analysis of the ratios themselves was 82% accurate.[10] In fact, the ratio of assets to liabilities *alone* predicted 80% correctly. Both these studies indicate that experts correctly select the variables that are important in making predictions, but that a linear model that combines these variables in an optimal way is superior to the global judgment of these very same experts.

The finding that linear combination is superior to global judgment is strong; it has been replicated in diverse contexts, and *no* exception has been discovered. (A recent study on lie detection alleged that "trained" use of polygraph techniques is superior to linear models,

---

[10]See Beaver, W. H. (1966). Financial ratios as predictors of failure. In *Empirical Research in Accounting: Selected Studies*. Chicago: University of Chicago, Graduate School of Business Institute of Professional Accounting. Duncan, E. R. (1972). A discriminant analysis of predictors of business failure. *Journal of Accounting Research, 10,* 167–179. Libby, R. (1976). Man versus model of man: Some conflicting evidence. *Organizational Behavior and Human Performance, 16,* 1–12.

but it turned out that the statistics had been miscomputed.[11]) As Meehl was able to state thirty years after his seminal book was published, *"There is no controversy in social science which shows such a large body of qualitatively diverse studies coming out so uniformly in the same direction as this one* (italics added).[12]

What effect have these findings had on the *practice* of expert judgment? Almost zilch. Meehl was elected president of the American Psychological Association at a strikingly young age, and the implications of his work were ignored by his fellow psychologists. States license psychologists, physicians, and psychiatrists to make (lucrative) global judgments of the form "It is my opinion that . . .," in other words, to make judgments inferior to those that could be made by a juror with a programmable calculator. For reasons outlined later in this chapter—and interspersed throughout the book—people have great misplaced confidence in their global judgments, a confidence that is strong enough to dismiss an impressive body of research findings and to find its way into the legal system.

My own role in this work was to question whether it is necessary to use statistically optimal weights in linear models for them to outperform experts. I have found that it is not. For years the nagging thought kept coming back to me: maybe *any* linear model outperforms the experts. The possibility seemed absurd, but when a research assistant had some free time I asked him to go to several data sources we had stored in computers and to construct linear models with weights "determined randomly except for sign." (It seemed reasonable that in any prediction context of interest, we would know the direction in which each variable predicted the outcome.) After the first 100 such models outperformed our clinical judges, we constructed 20,000 such "random linear models"—10,000 by choosing coefficients at random from a normal distribution, and 10,000 by choosing coefficients at random from a rectangular distribution. We had three data sets: (1) final diagnoses of neurosis versus psychosis of roughly 860 psychiatric inpatients, predicted from scores on the Minnesota Multi-

---

[11]I admit that I might not have discovered this error as the result of close scrutiny had the outcome been different. Others discovered it as well, and the author subsequently retracted—and has since become an outspoken critic of polygraph testing.

[12]Meehl, P. E. (1986). Causes and effects of my disturbing little book. *Journal of Personality Assessment, 50,* 370–375.

phasic Personality Inventory (MMPI),[13] (2) first-year graduate-school grade point averages (GPA's) of psychology students at the University of Illinois, predicted from 10 variables assessing academic aptitude prior to admissions and personality characteristics assessed shortly thereafter,[14] and (3) faculty ratings of performance of graduate students who had been at the University of Oregon two to five years, predicted from undergraduate GPA's, Graduate Record Examination scores (GRE's), and a measure of the selectivity of their undergraduate institutions. All three predictions had been made both by linear models and by "experts" ranging from graduate students to eminent clinical psychologists. On the average, the random linear models accounted for 150% more variance between criteria and predictions than did the holistic clinical evaluations of the trained judges.[15] For mathematical reasons, *unit weighting* (that is, each variable is standardized[16] and weighted $+1$ or -1 depending on direction) provided even better accountability, averaging 261% more variance.[17,18] Unit or random linear models are termed *improper* because their coefficients

[13] I am indebted to Professor Lewis R. Goldberg of the University of Oregon for sharing this data set.

[14] I am indebted to the late Professor Nancy Hershberg of the University of Illinois for sharing this data set.

[15] I hope that the reader not familiar with the concepts of "normal distribution," "rectangular distribution," and "amount of variance accounted for" will nevertheless appreciate the general conclusion.

[16] All variables are transformed to have an average of zero and a standard deviation of one; this transformation is accomplished by subtracting the average from each untransformed score and dividing by the standard deviation. (See Appendix A2.)

[17] The results when published engendered two responses. First, many people didn't believe them—until they tested out random and unit models on their own data sets. Then, other people showed that the results were trivial, because random and unit linear models will yield predictions highly correlated with those of linear models with optimal weights, and it had already been shown that optimal linear models outperform global judgments. I concur with those proclaiming the results trivial, but not realizing their triviality at the time, I luckily produced a "citation classic"—and without being illustrated with real data sets, the trivial result might never have been so widely known.

[18] My own work is summarized in Dawes, R. M. (1979). The robust beauty of improper linear models. *American Psychologist, 34*, 571–582.

(weights) are not based on statistical techniques that optimize prediction. The research indicates that such improper models are almost as good as proper ones.

The inference is simple. Since random and unit weights predict actual outcomes much better than global judgment, intuitive weighting should also. It is then reasonable to conclude that such weights should also outperform global judgment in situations where there is no outcome to predict. That is, the results in the prediction situations can be used as a guide for preference—assuming that methods that consistently predict better than others when there is an outcome to be predicted will also work better when there is not. Of course, there is no way to check this assumption, because there is no outcome in preference situations. But human intuition would have to have almost magical properties were it to be superior to intuitive weighting when we are making choices of what to do, while simultaneously being consistently inferior when we are trying to predict what will happen. Ben Franklin's advice was wise.

Let us apply my conclusion to an example—to the "desirability" of bullets to be used by police officers in Denver, Colorado—as presented by K. R. Hammond and L. Adelman:[19]

> In 1974, the Denver Police Department (DPD), as well as other police departments throughout the country, decided to change its handgun ammunition. The principle reason offered by the police was that the conventional round-nose bullet provided insufficient "stopping effectiveness" (that is, that ability to incapacitate and thus to prevent the person shot from firing back at a police officer or others). The DPD chief recommended (as did other police chiefs) the conventional bullet be replaced by a hollow-point bullet. Such bullets, it was contended, flattened on impact, thus decreasing ricochet potential. The suggested change was challenged by the American Civil Liberties Union, minority groups, and others. Opponents of the change claimed that the new bullets were nothing more than outlawed "dum-dum" bullets, that they created far more injury than the round-nosed bullets, and should, therefore, be barred from use. As is customary, judgments on this matter were formed privately and then defended publicly with enthusiasm and tenacity, and the usual public hearings were held. Both sides turned to ballistics experts for scientific information and support.

[19]Hammond, K. R., and Adelman, L. (1976). Science, values, and human judgment. *Science, 194*, 389–396.

The disputants focused on evaluating the merits of specific bullets—confounding the physical effect of the bullets with the implications of social policy. Rather than distinguish questions of what each kind of bullet would accomplish (the social policy issue) from questions concerning ballistic characteristics of specific bullets, advocates merely argued for one bullet or the other as a totality. Thus, as Hammond and Adelman pointed out, social policy makers inadvertently adopted the role of (poor) ballistics experts, and vice versa. What Hammond and Adelman did was ascertain the important policy dimensions from the policy makers, and then get professional ratings for each kind of bullet with respect to those dimensions from the ballistics experts. The dimensions identified by the social policy makers were stopping effectiveness (the probability that someone hit in the torso could not return fire), probability of serious injury, and probability of harm to bystanders. The ballistics experts' ratings of the bullets with respect to these dimensions indicated that the last two dimensions were almost perfectly confounded with each other though not perfectly confounded with the first. Bullets do not vary along a single dimension that confounds effectiveness with lethalness. The probability of serious injury *and* harm to bystanders is highly related to the penetration of the bullet, whereas the probability of a bullet's effectively stopping someone from returning fire is highly related to the width of the entry wound. Because policymakers could not agree about the weights to be given to the three dimensions, Hammond and Adelman suggested that they be weighted equally. Combining the equal weights with the (independent) judgments of the ballistic experts, Hammond and Adelman discovered that a bullet not even considered by the disputants "has greater stopping effectiveness and is less apt to cause injury (and is less apt to threaten bystanders) than the standard bullet then in use by the DPD."

It is also possible to modify conclusions, as was done, for example, by David Osborn in choosing Fulbright Professors in the mid 1960's. His method is described as follows:

> One of the most imaginative attempts to evaluate the effectiveness of programs with hard-to-assess objectives is a method devised by David Osborn, Deputy Assistant Secretary of State for Educational and Cultural Affairs. . . . Osborn recommends a scheme of cross-multiplying the costs of the activities with a number representing the rank of its objectives on a scale. For instance, the exchange of Fulbright professors

may contribute to "cultural prestige and mutual respect," "educational development," and gaining "entry," which might be given scale numbers such as 8, 6, and 5, respectively. These numbers are then multiplied with the costs of the program, and the resulting figure is in turn multiplied with an ingenious figure called a "country number." The latter is an attempt to get a rough measure of the importance to the U.S. of the countries with which we have cultural relations. It is arrived at by putting together in complicated ways certain key data, weighed to reflect cultural and educational matters, such as the country's population, gross national product, number of college students, rate of illiteracy, and so forth. The resulting numbers are then revised in the light of working experience, as when, because of its high per capita income, a certain tiny Middle Eastern country turns out to be more important to the U.S. than a large Eastern European one. At this point, country numbers are revised on the basis of judgment and experience, as are other numbers at other points. But those who make such revisions have a basic framework to start with, a set of numbers arranged on the basis of many factors, rather than single arbitrary guesses.[20]

The problem with this procedure is revising "on the basis of judgment." The small amount of research available indicates that linear models modified by reflexive judgment in fact predict more poorly than these same models without modification.[21]

10.3 EXPLANATIONS FOR THE RESEARCH FINDINGS

Why is it that linear models—even random ones—predict better than clinical experts? We can possibly explain this finding by hypothesizing a mathematical principle, a principle of "nature," and a psychological principle.

[20]Held, V. (summer 1966). PPBS comes to Washington. *The Public Interest*, no. 4, 102–115; quotation from pp. 112–113. As cited in Etzioni, Amitai (December 1967). "Mixed scanning: A "third" approach to decision making. *Public Administration Review*, 390.

[21]See Arkes, H. R.; Dawes, R. M.; and Christensen, C. (1986). Factors influencing the use of a decision rule in a probabilistic task. *Organizational Behavior and Human Decision Processes*, *37*, 93–110. Also, Goldberg, L. R. (1968). Simple models or simple processes? Some research on clinical judgment. *American Psychologist*, *23*, 483–496.

The mathematical principle is that monotone ("ordinal") interactions are well approximated by linear models. Such interactions are illustrated in Figure 10.1b. Two factors "interact" in that their combined import is much greater than the sum of their separate imports, but they do not interact in the sense that the *direction* in which one variable is related to the outcome is dependent upon the magnitude of the other variable. It is not, for example, true of monotone interactions that high-highs are similar to low-lows, but that high-highs (or low-lows) are much higher (or lower) than would be predicted by a separate analysis of each variable. If high-highs are similar to low-lows, the interaction is termed *crossed*, illustrated in Figure 10.1a.

For example, a doctoral student subjected identified alcoholic and nonalcoholic prisoners to a benign or stressful experience.[22] He then

Figure 10.1

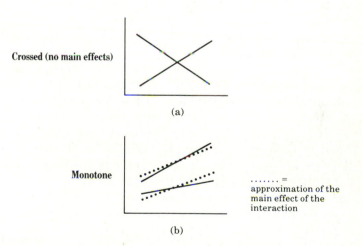

Crossed (a) versus monotone (b) interactions

[22]Glass, L. B. (1967). The generality of oral consummatory behavior of alcoholics under stress. Unpublished doctoral dissertation, University of Michigan.

had them spend 20 minutes in a waiting room before being interviewed by a psychologist about their experience. A nonalcoholic punch was available in the waiting room, and the variable of interest was how much punch the prisoners consumed. The alcoholic and nonalcoholic prisoners drank virtually identical amounts after experiencing the benign situation. After the stressful situation, however, the alcoholic prisoners drank twice as much punch as the nonalcoholics did. Thus, a true interaction was found between stress and drinking behavior of diagnosed alcoholics, but the data analysis indicated that this interaction could *be well approximated* by the two simple main effects: that is, alcoholics drank more punch, and all prisoners drank more punch after being stressed.[23] Another mathematical principle is that coefficients are not as important in linear models as their signs.[24] Thus arbitrary (random) linear models can approximate monotone interaction effects. And, of course, they approximate main effects.

The principle of nature that might explain the finding is that most interactions that exist are, in fact, monotone. It is easy to hypothesize crossed interactions, but extraordinarily difficult to find them, especially in the areas of psychology and social interactions. Because the optimal amount of any variable does not depend upon the value of the others, what interactions there are tend to be monotone. And while a number of crossed interactions have been hypothesized in social interactions (e.g., authoritarian leadership is more effective in some types of situations while "cool" leadership works better in others), they tend to be supported only by verbal plausibility and selective post hoc data analysis. In fact, interactions of *any* sort tend to be ephemeral, as was discovered by Goldberg in his analysis of how the "match" between teaching style and student characteristics predicts student success.[25] Of 38 interactions he thought he had discovered in the first half of an extensive data set, only 24 "cross-validated" *in the right direction* in the second half (not significantly different from chance expectation of 19).

[23]Statistically, the "amount of variance" accounted for by a monotone interaction is *one-ninth* that accounted for in a comparable crossed interaction situation.

[24]Wainer, H. (1976). Estimating coefficients in linear models: It don't make no nevermind. *Psychological Bulletin, 83,* 312–317.

[25]Goldberg, L. R. (1972). Student personality, characteristics and optimal college learning conditions: An extensive search for trait-by-treatment interaction effects. *Instructional Science, 1,* 153–210.

The psychological principle that might explain the predictive success of linear models is that people have a great deal of difficulty in attending to two or more noncomparable ("analyzable") aspects of a stimulus or situation at once. Attention shifts from one to the other and back again. For example, when Roger Shepard asked subjects to make similarity judgments about circles of various sizes containing "spokes" (radii) at various angles, the subjects tended to attend to size *or* angle, but not both.[26] The experience of people evaluating academic applicants is similar. Often they anchor their judgment on a particularly high or low grade point average or test score and then attempt to adjust in light of less vivid information in the applicant's folder. In fact, how *could* an admissions committee member integrate test information and GPA information without knowing something about the distribution and predictability of each within the applicant pool? (Thus, a purely statistical integration will be superior to a global judgment.)

Given that monotone interactions can be well approximated by linear models (a statistical *fact*), it follows that because most interactions that do exist in nature are monotone and because people have difficulty integrating information from noncomparable dimensions, linear models will outperform clinical judgment. The only way to avoid this broad conclusion is to claim that training makes experts superior to other people at integrating information (as opposed, for example, to knowing what information to look for), and there is no evidence for that. There is no evidence that experts *think differently* from others.

10.4 OBJECTIONS

The conclusion that random or unit weights outperform global judgments of trained experts is not a popular one with experts, or with people relying on them. First of all, it is an affront to the narcissism of many of them. One common response is to challenge the expertise of the research experts making the global predictions. "Minnesota clinicians!" snorted a professor of psychology at the University of Michigan. Little did he know that most of the Minnesota clinicians had obtained their Ph.D.'s at Michigan. "Had you used Dr. X," the dean of

[26]Shepard, R. N. (1964). Attention and the metric structure of the stimulus. *Journal of Mathematical Psychology, 1,* 54–87.

a prestigious medical school informed me, "his judgments would have correlated with longevity." In fact, Dr. X was the subject of the study.

Another objection is to maintain that the outcomes better predicted by linear models are all short-term and trivial (like ending up back in jail or flunking out of graduate school). The claim is made that "truly important long-term outcomes" can be predicted better by global judgments. But as Jay Russo points out, this objection implies that the long-term future can be predicted better than the short-term future. Such prediction is possible for variables like death (100 years from now) and rabies (after the incubation period), but those variables, which are very rare, are *not* of the type predicted in these studies. Moreover, as we come to understand processes (e.g., the existence of the rabies or AIDS virus in the blood), "incubation period" becomes nothing more than a manner of speech, and aging is more readily predicted than is death.

A final objection is the "10,000 Frenchmen can't be wrong" one. Experts have been revered—and well paid—for years for their "it is my opinion that" judgments. As James March points out, however, such reverence may serve a *purely social function*. People and organizations have to make decisions, often between alternatives that appear equally good or bad. What better way to justify such decisions than to consult any intuitive expert, and the more money she or he charges, the better. "We paid for the best possible medical advice" can be a palliative for a fatal operation, just as "throwing" the I Ching can relieve someone of regretting a bad marriage. An expert who constructs a linear model is not as impressive as one who gives advice on a "burst" of intuition derived from "years of experience." (One highly paid business expert I know constructs linear models in secret, "bootlegging" computer time from another branch of his company.) So we value global judgment of experts independently of its validity.

But there is also a structural reason for doubting the inferiority of global judgment. It has to do with the bias of available feedback. (See Chapter 6.) When we construct a linear model in a prediction situation, we know exactly how poorly it predicts. In contrast, our feedback about our global judgments is flawed. Not only do we selectively remember our successes, we often have *no knowledge* of our failures—and any knowledge we do have may serve to "explain" them (away). Who knows what happens to rejected graduate school applicants? Professors have access only to accepted ones, and if the professors are doing a good job, the accepted ones will likewise do well—exonerating the professors' judgment. What happens to people misdiagnosed as "psychotic"? If they are lucky, they will disappear from the sight of the authorities diagnosing them; if not, they are likely to be placed in an environment where they may soon become psychotic. Finally, therapy patients who commit suicide were too sick to begin with—as is easily established from perusal of their files.

The feedback problem is well illustrated by an article in praise of "intuition" by Nancy Hathaway that appeared in the October 31, 1984, issue of the *San Francisco Chronicle*. She writes, . . . "Most people rarely receive intuitions so major that they change their lives. From time to time, however, it does happen. There are even legends of people following their intuitions in business decisions: the late Ray Kroc, who bought MacDonald's despite evidence offered by his advisors that it would be a bad investment, did it because 'I felt in my funny bone that it was a sure thing.'" So we know about Ray Kroc. How many investors had "funny bone" feelings that led to ruin? We don't know (absent the type of *prospective* study—similar to those done of linear models). If 36 people have an intuitive feeling that the next roll of the dice will be snake-eyes and are willing to bet even odds on that hunch, on the average one will win. That person is the one most likely to come to our attention; for one thing, the others probably won't talk about it much.

Hillel Einhorn and Robin Hogarth have examined availability of feedback sources, and demonstrated how they *systematically* operate to make intuitive judgment appear valid.[27] Their prototype is of the waiter who decides he can judge whether people tip well from the way they dress. A judgment that some people are poor tippers leads to inferior service, which in turn leads to poor tips—thereby "validating" the waiter's judgment. (Again, not all prophecies are self-fulfilling; there must be a mechanism; intuitive judgment provides one.)

In contrast, the systematic predictions of linear models yield data on just how poorly they predict. For example, in Einhorn's study only 18% of the variance in longevity of Hodgkin's disease patients is predicted by the best linear model (section 10.2), but that is opposed to 0% for the world's foremost authority. Such results bring us abruptly to an unpleasant conclusion: a lot of outcomes about which we care

[27]Einhorn, H. J., and Hogarth, R. M. (1978). Confidence in judgment: Persistence of the illusion of validity. *Psychological Review, 85*, 395–416.

deeply are not very predictable. For example, it is not comforting to members of a graduate school admissions committee to know that only 23% of the variance in later faculty ratings of a student can be predicted by a unit weighting of the student's undergraduate GPA, his or her GRE score, and a measure of the student's undergraduate institution selectivity—but that is opposed to 4% based on judges' global ratings of the applicant. We *want* to predict outcomes important to us. It is only rational to conclude that if one method (a linear model) does not predict well, something else may do better. What is not rational—in fact, irrational—is to conclude that this "something else" is intuitive global judgment.

The point is that many outcomes are not all that predictable. Academic success, for example, is influenced by whom one shares an office with as a graduate student, by which professors happen to have positions available for research assistants, by the person or people with whom one has libidinal involvement (often met on a "chance" basis), by the relative strengths of those with whom one competes for the first job (as judged by the professors who happen to be appointed to the "search committee"), and so on. Moreover, there are clearly self-exacerbating features to an academic career. A "little bit of luck" may lead a new Ph.D. to obtain a position in an outstanding university (or an M.D. in an outstanding hospital or a J.D. in an outstanding law firm), and the consequent quality of colleagues may then significantly reinforce whatever talents the individual brings to the job. (Conversely, a little bit of ill luck may saddle the new Ph.D. with a nine-course per year teaching load, inadequate institutional resources for scholarly or research productivity, and "burnt-out" colleagues. Not many people move from a patent office to a full professorship after publishing a three-page paper, as Einstein did.)

One field in which people find linear models of judgment particularly distasteful is that of *assessing other people*. Is it not important, for example, to *interview* students applying for graduate school? In a word, no. What can an interviewer learn in a half-hour to an hour that is not present in the applicant's record? As Len Rorer points out, belief that one's own interviewing skills provide a pipeline to such information is self-confidence bordering on *hubris*.[28] Moreover, even if

---

[28] Rorer, L. G. A circuitous route to bootstrapping selection procedures. *ORI Research Bulletin, 12,* no. 9.

the interviewer *thinks* he or she has picked up some highly positive or negative quality in the interview, is it really fair to judge applicants *on the impression they make in a single interview conducted by a single interviewer*, as opposed to a record of actual accomplishment (or failure) over a college career? A GPA is a "mere number," but it represents the combined opinion of some fifty or so professors over several years; some professors may be biased for or against particular students, but surely a combined impression based on actual work over time is fairer than one based on a brief interaction with a single person. Furthermore, GPA's predict better than interviews; is it fair to judge someone on the basis of something that does not work? (In contrast, an interview can be used as a recruiting device—for selling the applicant on the school. Again, however, the interviewee would be wiser to make her or his choice on other grounds.)

A colleague of mine in medical decision making tells of an investigation he was asked to make by the dean of a large and prestigious medical school to try to determine why it was unsuccessful in recruiting female students. My colleague studied the problem statistically "from the outside" and identified a major source of the problem. One of the older professors had cut back on his practice to devote time to interviewing applicants to the school. He assessed such characteristics as "emotional maturity," "seriousness of interest in medicine," and "neuroticism." Whenever he interviewed an unmarried female applicant, he concluded she was "immature." When he interviewed a married one, he concluded she was "not sufficiently interested in medicine," and when he interviewed a divorced one, he concluded she was "neurotic." Not many women were positively evaluated on these dimensions, which of course had nothing to do with gender.

10.5 IMPLICATIONS FOR CHOICE

Back to Ben Franklin. The implications of all this research is that if we wish to make choices involving multiple factors we would do well to construct *our own* (improper) linear models. That is in essence what Franklin advised, and the advice is echoed in popular books on decision making that recommend the listing of possible consequences of choices and of our own values (although few such books cite research support for their recommendation). Decision involves predicting our future "states of mind." Given that linear models predict better than intuitive judgment in situations where the accuracy of prediction can be checked, why not this one as well?[29] Of course, there are problems. How do we determine and define the variables)? Might not many of them be related? For example, in assessing a possible job, should we list "money," "status," and "autonomy" as separate characteristics? First, how do we know they are important to us? Secondly, aren't they related? Isn't it true that "high-level" jobs tend to be high on all three while "low-level" jobs are low on all? If so, shouldn't we just list "job level" rather than its separate components?

The answer to the question of importance is rather easy. It is *our* decision. In constructing a weighting scheme, we will list the variables that are important *to us*. If, for example, we think of "job level" in a global and amorphous way, then we should list it. If, on the other hand, money, status, and autonomy each strike us as psychologically salient, distinct, and important, then we should list them separately. Franklin advised his friend not *what* to decide but *how* to decide it. When suggesting a list he was not advising what should be on it, but rather how to become explicit about what is important to the decision maker. Research indicates that when specific variables are known, a linear model predicts better than global judgment. (Often, in fact, simply determining the variables makes the choice obvious.) Moreover, the weights assigned to the variables are those of the individual making the choice. If, for example, sexual compatibility is more im-

---

[29] A colleague has suggested that our intuitive judgments may be valid because we have feedback from our satisfaction or regret after making various choices. This explanation presents a number of problems: (1) We don't know how satisfied we would feel if we had chosen something else (see section 6.4). (2) Aside from the "choices" we make habitually in everyday life, few of our "choices"/judgments are repeated without change—and we are least apt to modify habitual choices. (3) We have difficulty assessing the role of factors over which our choice had no effect in determining the outcome. (4) In fact, all the objections to "learning from experience" (section 6.4) apply to intuitive learning as well as explicit learning. (5) What I suspect we regret in such cases is not the choice itself given the information we had available, but the "failure to put forth the effort" to gather more information or to consider the problem more carefully.

portant to a person choosing a mate than is character, altruism, or sanity, then there is no reason the person should not choose on that basis—and live with the consequences. (Some of my colleagues would disagree.) Again, the point of this chapter is not what, but how. Thus, the answer to the related variables question may be found in a distinction made by Wendell Garner.[30] The fact that two dimensions are correlated in nature (such as height and weight) does not imply that they are not psychologically independent and distinct for the perceiver or judge. If they are distinct, specify them as such.

Once we have determined the variables, we face the problem of evaluating and weighting them. To do so, we must assume that we have *some* insight into our values and "value systems"—and in particular into how we compare conflicting values. My own work has demonstrated that this insight need not be total or profound; evaluations and weights that are "reasonable" provide outcomes very close to those based on optimal ones. Granted these assumptions, the decision is then *decomposed* so that each variable can be considered separately, and the results are combined according to a linear weighting scheme. The reason—once again—for believing that such decomposition can work well in a choice situation that lacks a criterion for evaluating the outcome is that it works in situations where one is present.

Of course, it is not always a simple matter to determine values, and the applied decision experts referred to in section 8.3 may be helpful. In fact, there are systematic cognitive biases in achieving valid decomposition, just as there are governing automatic choice. Thus, Tversky has shown that when matching procedures are used to determine the relative importance of identified variables, the result is that a systematic underestimation of the degree of discrepancy is inferred from choice situations.[31] For example, most baseball experts consider batting average to be more important than home run hitting. Their implicit weighting of the two variables can be determined by asking them to match two players by assigning a value to one of the two variables so that the two players have equal value in their judgment. This could be done, for example, by deciding on the number of

---

[30]Garner, W. R. (1970). The stimulus in information processing. *American Psychologist, 25,* 350–358.

[31]Tversky, A. N. (1986). Paper presented at the 1986 convention of the American Psychological Association, Washington, D.C.

home runs a player with a batting average of .310 would have to hit per year to be of the same value as a player who has a .334 batting average and hits 15 home runs per year. Such matching judgments *systematically underestimate* the importance these judges ascribe to batting average relative to home runs when they are asked to choose the more valuable player among pairs.

Which procedure is better for determining "true" value? For that matter, what *is* such value? This chapter—and indeed this book—is not addressed to those very difficult questions. What *can* be concluded is that the procedure of looking first *within* each variable and then comparing across by some weighting system is superior to that of making global intuitive judgments *across* variables regarding each choice in isolation.

10.6 RELATION TO THE KANTIAN PRINCIPLE AND THE VON NEUMANN AND MORGENSTERN SYSTEM

Using a linear model for decisions guarantees that each decision can serve as a policy for making all other decisions. The reason is simple: all decisions using the same model weigh the same factors the same way. The decision is still the decision maker's responsibility; the decision maker determines the model. What the linear model guarantees is that choices are consistent. Thus, the use of linear models follows Kant's *ethical* dictate that a decision should be made as if it is the choice for all people in that context. Moreover, for reasons to be presented in Chapter 12, while ethical principles may not be derivable from the "principle" of "doing the greatest good for the greatest number" throughout "the long run," they tend to be consistent with that principle. Thus, systematic use of linear models enhances pursuit of that goal as well.

In addition, decision making on the basis of a linear model (proper or improper) satisfies the axioms of the von Neumann and Morgenstern system. For the reasons outlined in section 8.3 for at least *considering* this system when making a choice (recall the diagnosis problem), the use of linear models should be considered as well. In fact, the linear model is an explicit statement of utility.

10.7 APPLICATION TO AFFIRMATIVE ACTION[32]

Consider an affirmative action program for selecting applicants for some program, perhaps a graduate school program or an executive training program. While we may disagree about which programs are most fair (just as we may disagree about which applicants are most talented, or which bullets are most desirable), we generally agree that a program is fair to the degree to which it achieves five goals:

1. Results in a proportional representation among people chosen of underrepresented ethnic or gender groups

2. Treats all applicants uniformly

3. Evaluates applicants on the basis of characteristics predictive of success

4. Evaluates applicants on the basis of meritorious characteristics

5. Maximizes the talent available in the pool of those chosen

Other things being equal, a program that is superior on achieving one of these goals is fairer. Conflicts between potential programs arise, of course, because other things are *not* equal; in fact, some of these goals conflict. For example, if past discrimination has affected people's ability to develop their talents as well as their qualifications (a premise on which the *need* for affirmative action is based), then a procedure that is based purely on the evaluation of talent may be quite fair on dimensions 2, 3, and 5 but unfair on dimension 1 and of dubious fairness on dimension 4. Conversely, a lottery that guaranteed a desired representation of underrepresented groups would be fair on dimension 1 but unfair on all others—as would a quota system (although within each group, applicants could be chosen on the basis of talent and merit, so that a quota system would be *less* unfair than a lottery on dimensions 2, 3, 4, and 5).

What to do?

One solution is to select a goal based on a single dimension and claim that it alone constitutes fairness—perhaps fairness to "underprivileged groups" (goal 1), "fairness to the individual applicant"

---

[32]This section is based on a presentation at a November 1984 symposium at Northwestern University, which was organized by Reid Hastie and Gary Wills and supported by the Exxon Foundation.

(goals 2, 3, and 4), or "fairness to the stockholder" (goal 5). Thus, for example, Lyndon Johnson attempted to impose "fairness" on our war in Vietnam by defining it with respect to the way in which people were selected to die in it—a Fair And Impartially Random (FAIR) draft lottery.

A far more common solution is to pretend that there is no inherent conflict between the dimensions on which the goals are based (as, for example, between a bullet's ability to incapacitate crime suspects and the probability that it will not seriously harm suspects or bystanders). This pretense is expressed in a *purely verbal* assertion that such a procedure will maximize fairness according to all goals at once. For example, the policy of choosing a person from an underrepresented category only when two or more applicants are "substantially equal" *sounds* as if it will eventually result in proportionate representation, while simultaneously treating people uniformly on the basis of their merits and talents and not diminishing the "quality" of those chosen (because the organization is indifferently affected by choosing be-tween those that are "substantially equal"). But—to be redundant— the need for affirmative action is that past discrimination has had a real effect on people, not just on their credentials and test scores, and consequently those from groups already underrepresented due to this treatment are less likely to be "substantially equal" than are those from more privileged groups. Moreover, the "substantial" in "substan-tially equal" allows a great deal of latitude in interpretation. How may faculty members, for example, ever view two job candidates as "sub-stantially equal"? And even though disagreement between some fac-ulty members may arise about *which* candidate is superior, academic in-group influence and bandwagoning typically assure a low proba-bility of a perfectly split vote.

The basic problem with these two approaches is that they don't work. A goal based on maximizing on one dimension does not assure a desirable position on others. In fact, it generally results in an unfavor-able position for those that are negatively correlated. And pretending that the negative correlations do not exist is not a rational premise.

What I am proposing in contrast is an improper linear model system that slightly violates all five criteria of rationality. I call it the *systematically unfair approach*. First, construct the best possible linear weighting system that predicts success without any reference to minority or majority status. Then compute the average linear composite score of the majority-group applicants and the average of each minority ("protected") class from which proportional representation is desired. Then simply *add* to the score of each minority applicant the difference between her or his group mean and the majority group mean. Evaluate all applicants on the basis of such adjusted scores. This procedure assures selection of the most qualified persons *within* groups. Moreover, unlike a quota system this approach does not imply that a minority-group member is automatically chosen in preference to a majority-group member (once the majority quota is filled)—irrespective of qualifications. Only the least qualified majority-group members are subject to "reverse discrimination," and it is their success and contribution that are most problematic.

Does this approach result in proportional representation? It does not assure proportional representation for any particular set of applicants, but the *expected* representation is proportional—provided the variances on the scores for majority and minority groups are equal. Empirical studies have not discovered systematic differences in these variances.

This procedure involves "doctoring" prediction. I use this term deliberately to emphasize that the systematically unfair approach involves a procedure we would not endorse in the best of all possible worlds. Is this procedure even legal? Yes and no. In the Bakke decision, the Supreme Court held that it is *not* legal to "doctor" test scores on the basis of ethnicity but *is* legal to add a factor for ethnicity, *for the good of the institution* (as opposed to society as a whole).[33] This judgment appears to contradict the belief held for millenia that addition is associative. (It is.) So add the factor later. Further, a good institutional case can be made for achieving proportionate representation among selected applicants. (And unlike premeditation in murder—which is established on the basis of behavioral acts *implying* forethought rather than by asking the defendant what he or she had in mind—the demonstration that someone was selecting applicants "for society's sake" rather than "for the sake of the institution" would be difficult indeed, especially if we accept the psychologists' view that the mind is not a unitary entity naked to introspection.) This proposal does, in contrast, contradict the Supreme Court ruling in Griggs versus Duke Power (1972, case no. 124 heard on March 8, 1971, that

[33] For a discussion of the Bakke decision, see McCormack, W. (ed.) (1978). The Bakke decision: Implications for higher education admissions. Report of the American Council on Education and American Law Schools.

criteria for admission to a program be: (1) relevant, (2) nondiscriminatory, and (3) applied in a "color-blind" manner. *But if past discrimination has had a negative effect,* then any relevant criteria applied in a color-blind manner will be discriminatory, any nondiscriminatory criteria applied in a color-blind manner will be irrelevant, and any relevant criteria that are nondiscriminatory can be so only if they are *not* applied in a color-blind manner.

In addition to the policy reasons for considering this systematically unfair proposal, there is a psychological one. In section 8.3 I mentioned the Tversky, Sattath, and Slovic finding that people tend to give more weight to more important aspects of complex alternatives when they choose between them than when they make explicit judgments about desirable weighting.[34] The procedure for eliciting desirable weight was to require matching judgments. (Whether judges "overweight" these more important aspects in choice or "underweight" them in matching cannot be determined—because the research did not include an independent criterion of how people "should" assign weight.) The relevance of this finding for affirmative action programs is that selection decisions are usually made in contexts where meeting affirmative action goals is <u>not</u> the judges' primary concern. Consider, for example, the approach of choosing affirmatively only when applicants are "substantially equal"; here, clearly, the primary aspects on which applicants are evaluated are qualifications predicting performance; race, ethnicity, and gender are secondary. One possible implication of the research is that there is a discrepancy between how much judges weight affirmative action goals when they make an explicit judgment of their importance (high) as opposed to the implicit weighting that occurs when these same judges make actual choices (low). I don't wish to push the implications of a single finding too far, even though it has been replicated.[35] In general, however, affirmative action programs have not worked, at least not in universities, and this discrepancy between actual choice and explicitly derived weighting may be a factor. Judges selecting people are gener-

---

[34]Tversky, A.; Sattath, S.; and Slovic, P. Contingent weighting in judgment and choice. *Psychological Review* (in press).

[35]Fischer, G. W., and Hawkins, S. A. (1987). Riskless preference reversals and information processing strategies. Working paper, Department of Social and Decision Sciences, Carnegie Mellon University.

ally asked to "keep in mind" affirmative action goals; that request may well be for a cognitive feat that is not possible for a judge making choices where qualifications unrelated (or negatively related) to these goals are predominant. In contrast, the systematically unfair approach—by making actual choices automatically once policy is determined—would not allow underweighting of these goals in actual practice.

10.8 MERE NUMBERS

The philosophy presented in this chapter is based on the premise that "mere numbers" are in fact *mere*—neither good nor bad. Just as numbers can be used to achieve either constructive or destructive goals in other contexts, they can be used for good or ill in decision making. *Research* indicates that numbers in a linear model can be well used in making predictions. The implication that they can serve well also in choice and preference contexts is immediate. Using them, however, requires us to overcome a view (*not* supported by the research) that the "mysteries of the human mind" allow us to reach superior conclusions without their aid. The mysteries are there, but not in this context. To do well by ourselves and to treat other persons fairly, we must overcome the hubris that leads us to reject adding numbers to evaluate them, and to experience no more shame when we do so than when we use numbers in determining how to construct a bridge that will not collapse.

CHAPTER

Quitters never win and winners never quit.

11

Giving Up

11.1 GIVING UP STRATEGIES

While I was attending a meeting in Kyoto in 1975, I met a Japanese man with whom I had shared an experience at the University of Michigan in 1960. Late one night outside the Student Union, we both heard the campaign speech in which John F. Kennedy proposed the establishment of a Peace Corps. (A small plaque by the door of the Union commemorates the speech.)

My Japanese friend and I talked about the importance of speeches, and he said he had also heard Emperor Hirohito's speech on August 15, 1945, in which he told the Japanese people that Japan was surrendering. My friend was a boy of nine at the time. He said that he and his family had assumed that the Emperor would tell them that American soldiers would soon invade and that every man, woman, and child in Japan had the duty and honor to fight until all were dead. Instead, the Emperor said: "The war situation has developed not necessarily to Japan's advantage. . . . In order to avoid further bloodshed, perhaps even the extinction of human civilization, we shall have to endure the unendurable, to suffer the insufferable." My friend and his family were prepared to obey the Emperor. Just as my friend had been prepared to die before the speech, afterwards he believed it was his duty to surrender. He told me, "We never questioned. No one questioned the Emperor." This Emperor who quit now (1987) presides over what may be the most prosperous country in the world.

The point of this anecdote is to illustrate that a person (or a nation) that reverses a policy in order to abandon a sunk cost need not suffer the scorn of others. The Emperor was *not* derogated for having "spent lives in vain." Was that due wholly to belief in the Emperor's divinity? President Truman, whom no one regarded as divine, reversed the policy he had proclaimed months earlier (June 26, 1945) at Potsdam by allowing the Japanese to impose as a condition of their surrender that the Emperor be allowed to live and maintain his status. Few in this country faulted Truman for this reversal; moreover, there was little if any discussion of his inconsistency. Reaction was purely that of relief and glee that the war was over, without the massive casualties anticipated from an invasion of the Japanese mainland. Both President Truman and Emperor Hirohito paid dearly for the war, but neither paid dearly for his sudden reversal of policy.

A reviewer of an earlier version of this book challenged the relevance of the quotes about the Tennessee–Tombigbee project to sunk costs (section 2.1). The reviewer maintained that the two senators were probably most interested in obtaining government funds for their state, and that the reference to not "wasting" money already spent was "rationalization" meant to be politically persuasive. The problem with this criticism is that the senators' *motivation* is irrelevant to the rationality (irrationality) of their argument. Moreover, as pointed out earlier, their motive may have been their belief that the argument would "work." By far a more common criticism of assertions about the irrationality of honoring sunk costs is that abandoning them fails to take into account the deleterious effects of "loss of face." It seems especially ironic that the concepts of "face" and "loss of face" were introduced to the American culture during the Second World War—with specific reference to our supposed understanding of the "Oriental mind"—when the Emperor of Japan himself provided us with a most instructive example of how beneficial it can be to abandon sunk costs! But he is not alone. Charles DeGaulle, John F. Kennedy, Anwar Sadat, and Ronald Reagan are among the most admired political figures in our century; DeGaulle reversed French policy in Algeria, Kennedy reversed his Caribbean policy in the Bay of Pigs, Sadat reversed his policy toward Israel, and Ronald Reagan withdrew from Lebanon after the Marine barracks bombing—despite prior repeated assurances that the United States would "never" do such a thing. In contrast, few political decisions are considered as loathsome as Adolph Hitler's decision to flood the crowded Berlin subway system in order to slow the inevitable advance of the Russian armies. People who waste resources or the lives of others by refusing to quit when the cause is hopeless are often termed "criminals"; those who waste themselves rather than attempt to change are called "cowards." (I am not referring to suicide in the absence of a reasonable expectation of a positive life in the future.)

Keeping promises is another matter. When asked to evaluate the desirability of personality and character traits, people typically rate "honesty" highest. Keeping promises is an integral part of being honest. There are, however, three important reasons for keeping promises; one is to satisfy an internal ethical commitment to do so; the second is that most promises are made with an intention to help another person, and reneging on a promise will change the consequences for the other person; a third is to develop a reputation for "trustworthiness" in order to make future promises creditable. As discussed in section 9.1, this consideration may be especially important when the promise is one of harm—that is, a threat. None of these reasons apply to honoring sunk costs per se. There are certainly no mandates to do so, when people are consequently harmed, and if the negative consequences of changing outweigh the positive benefits, then the decision not to change is not based on honoring the sunk costs but on the consideration of future consequences (the decision is rational). What we must question is the automatic assumption that such consequences will be negative. Perhaps, this assumption is often nothing more than a rationalization for attempting to impose an irrational coherence on human existence. (Some people occasionally make promises to God, which raises issues with which I am not competent to deal.)

How are sunk costs best abandoned? Again, the "trick" is to frame the problem with the present situation, rather than the point at which the investment was made, as the status quo. One way of helping to frame the problem in the current context is to discuss the problem with someone who is *not* knowledgeable about the past—except insofar as it may be communicated by the person who could abandon the cost. Such an observer can see much more clearly the irrationality involved in honoring a particular sunk cost, an irrationality that may be obscured by having encumbered the cost in the first place, or perhaps by having paid it bit-by-bit until such payment had become an automatic and habitual (non)decision. In addition, such an observer is not emotionally committed to honoring the cost. In fact, the commitment of such observers as psychotherapists and business consultants is the precise opposite—that of helping their clients change their behavior and attitudes.

The justification that "This is what I've always done" or "This is the way we do it here" has little impact on someone experiencing a new situation. In fact, such a person may experience an "Alice-in-Wonderland" feeling. For example, when I was head of the psychology department at the University of Oregon, the department had a master's degree program in organizational psychology. The students were mainly people with experience in business or governmental organizations who wished to develop skills that would enhance their careers. They tended to be older than the typical graduate student and less academically oriented. A major part of the program consisted of a practicum in which they engaged in supervised consulting work for various community organizations. An organization would select a problem with which its management was concerned, and a group of two to five students would work on it. At one point, I attended a ceremony at which one of these organizations was making a donation to the program. The representative of the organization was quite enthusiastic about the students who had helped his company. He explained that the students had investigated the problems of accidents at a particular mill and that the year after the company accepted their recommendations the money lost at that site due to accidents was decreased by a half-million dollars. What had the students done? They had persuaded management people to talk to workers who had been involved in accidents to get their opinion of why the accidents had occurred and how such accidents might be avoided in the future. This "solution" would seem obvious to most people, but this company had had a long-standing policy of not encouraging interaction between management and labor. Interviewing the workers rather than blaming accidents on "human error" involved a considerable change of attitude and approach.[1] The real skill of the students had not been so much in realizing that the accident rate could be reduced by obtaining the workers' opinions, but in helping the management overcome its own internal barriers to change. Once these had been overcome, there was, of course, no regret for having changed.

11.2 GIVING UP CHERISHED IDEAS

One of the most dearly (expensively) held beliefs of many clincial psychologists is the belief in the validity of Rorschach inkblot interpretation. While this belief may be common in the general American population, it is particularly strong among clinical psychologists, many of whom still give Rorschachs despite the consistent research findings—of literally thousands of published studies—that the Rorschach interpretation is unreliable and invalid. The plausibility of Rorschach interpretation is so compelling that it is still accepted in

---

[1]"A common sign of insensitivity is using the term 'operation error' to describe problems arising from the interaction of operating a system. A rule of thumb might be that human problems seldom have purely technical solutions, while technical solutions typically create human problems." —from Fischhoff, B. "Nuclear Decisions: Cognitive Limits to the Thinkable." Manuscript in preparation.

court proceedings involving involuntary commitment and child custody, with psychologists who offer such interpretations in these hearings being duly recognized as "experts."[2]

American Psychological Association rules of ethics prohibit my presenting an example of a Rorschach inkblot. (Presumably, prior exposure to these blots would contaminate the validity, if there were any, of any subsequent use.) Suffice it to say that there are ten blots on cards roughly the size of regular typing paper. Six of these are black and various shades of gray; the remaining four have color. The blots themselves cover roughly half the area of the cards on which they are reproduced, in a horizontal orientation—that is, the position of a sheet of typing paper turned on its side. These blots are symmetric around a vertical axis in the middle of the card. They were developed by the psychiatrist Herman Rorschach (1884–1922), for purposes totally unrelated to assessing character structure and personality problems.

The subject is asked to say what the cards look like to him or her. The instructions are purposely vague, allowing subjects to make associations from the form, shading, color, or texture of the blots. Moreover, the subject can respond to each blot in its entirety, to major portions of the blot ("large details"), or to small details in the blot's structure; subjects are also free to make use of the white spaces surrounding the blot or within it. Finally, the subject is free to rotate the cards from the positions in which they are presented—and even to turn cards over and look at the back of them.

After the subject gives a response, the examiner asks him or her to explain it with such questions as "Why does it look like a bat?", "What in the blot makes it look like your grandfather drunkenly falling off his chair at his fifty-fifth wedding anniversary celebration?", or simply, "Tell me more." Moreover, subjects are urged to see more than one percept per blot with queries such as "Anything else?"

[2]Now that I am no longer a member of the American Psychological Association Ethics Committee, I can express my personal opinion that the use of Rorschach interpretations in establishing an individual's legal status and child custody is the single most unethical practice of my colleagues. It is done, widely. Losing legal rights as a result of responding to what is presented as a "test of imagination," often in a context of "helping," violates what I believe to be a basic ethical principle in this society—that people are judged on the basis of what they do, not on the basis of what they feel, think, or might have a propensity to do. And being judged on an *invalid* assessment of such thoughts, feelings, and propensities amounts to losing one's civil rights on an essentially random basis.

The theory behind the test is simple. The world contains ambiguity; people respond to the ambiguity in habitual ways, and the more ambiguous the situation in which they find themselves the more important these habitual response styles become. An inkblot, being the ultimate of ambiguity, should be an ideal way to "tap into" such habitual responses. Moreover, the content that people see may give valuable clues about the types of materials they "have on their mind" in that these are free to be *projected* into the stimulus situation, because it in fact has no structure of its own. Hence, the Rorschach is termed a *projective* test. Moreover, as Freud has suggested, the content of dreams and fantasies is particularly indicative of our unconscious needs and conflicts, because there is no external stimulus to which we are responding. By virtue of being a stimulus with minimal structure, the Rorschach inkblots elicit projections of internally generated "percepts"—which can then be used to make inferences about unconscious needs and conflicts.

The theory is not only plausible but compelling. For example, I recall testing a very depressed individual who immediately responded to a blot by saying, "It looks like a bat that has been squashed on the pavement under the heel of a giant's boot." What response could possibly be more "one-down?" The fact that the individual was obviously depressed led to my belief in the validity of the Rorschach. (Note that my observation can be reframed to indicate that his response provided me with no information that I did not already have.) Of course, if he had been obviously psychotic, I could have noted that his percept concerned material not present in the blot (e.g., the giant and the boot). That would have also impressed me, because that response would indicate how he attended to stimuli not present in the environment—virtually the definition of psychosis. Or, if he had suffered from aggressive outbursts, I would have noted the hostility in the response.

I also recall testing a homosexual male nurse (at the time, homosexuality was termed a "disease") who gave approximately forty "vista" responses—for example, vistas of Chinese junks on lagoons with mountains in the background. At the time, the prevailing theory about the etiology of male homosexuality was that it was due to childhood withdrawal of feelings from an overpowering mother who aroused incest fantasies and identification with a weak, passive father—who had to be weak and passive or the mother would not have been that way. How clearly these vista responses indicated the man's pathological tendency to distant himself from emotionally threatening material!

The compelling plausibility of Rorschach interpretation should now be apparent. Clearly, for example, responding to the blots in their entirety would seem to indicate a tendency to search for the "big pictures" in life—even when they aren't there; motion responses must indicate an active imagination; the use of white spaces, a tendency toward oppositionality and perverseness, et cetera, et cetera. Moreover, seeing something that the examiner cannot see must indicate very poor "reality testing"—most probably psychosis. (At one staff meeting I attended, the head psychologist successfully lobbied to have someone labeled "schizophrenic" after waving a Rorschach blot in front of the group and demanding, "Does this look like a bear to *you*?") Like the unstructured interview (see section 10.4), the Rorschach inkblot test is a major technique used by many clinical psychologists.

In contrast to the compelling plausibility of the inkblot test, what does the research show? Based on thousands of studies addressed to this question, the answer is simple: damn little support for the *projective* hypothesis. For example, one consistent finding is that the number of responses the subject makes correlates with scores on intelligence tests. But then again the amount a subject talks in *any* situation may have such a relationship, and intelligence tests are better measures of intelligence than is the Rorschach test.[3] There are also certain intriguing findings, such as that concerning the "index of existential pathology." This index refers to the tendency to see part-human, part-nonhuman things—for example, cartoon characters, elves, satyrs, and witches. One study indicated that "neurotics" have a much higher tendency than do "normals" or "eminent physical scientists" to see such things.[4] This finding appeared, however, at the end of a long paper on the "psychodynamics of eminent physical scientists" in which none of the other hypotheses tested was supported—for example, the hypothesis that eminent physical scientists should have a greater tendency than others to refer to "mother nature." Moreover, the scores on this index were trichonomized in a post hoc manner into 0–3, 3–6, and 6 or more. Perhaps this categorization was made to maximize the value of the statistic used to assess "signi-

[3] A very eminent psychologist once proposed that "intelligence is whatever it is that is measured by intelligence tests."

[4] McClelland, D. C. (1962). On the psychodynamics of creative physical scientists. In Gruber, H.; Terrell, G.; and Wertheimer, M. (eds.). *Contemporary Approaches to Creative Thinking*. New York: Atherton, 141–174.

ficance." (See Appendix A3.) Moreover, there is no mention in the literature of replicating this difference. I mention this finding because it is typical of intriguing findings involving the Rorschach. They appear and then disappear from our body of knowledge.

What about the *basic* dimensions of personality and psychopathology that the Rorschach purports to assess as a projective device? Does it work? The answer to this question—at least up until 1978—may be found by reading the reviews of the Rorschach in the *Mental Measurement Yearbook*. First published in 1938, the *Yearbook* was the work of Oscar K. Burros, who edited it until his death. Beginning as a modest compilation of reviews of intelligence, aptitude, interest, and personality tests, it became the major source of information about all the tests in psychological literature—until its last publication in 1978, which consisted of two volumes of roughly 1,000 pages each. It was not truly a "yearbook," since it was published only every five years or so.

The Rorschach, and other projective tests, were first reviewed in the third volume in 1949. There were two reviews, one favorable and one unfavorable. The unfavorable one was by J. R. Wittenborn, who wrote (page 133):

> What passes for research in this field is usually naively conceived, inadequately controlled, and only rarely subjected to the usual standards of experimental rigor with respect to the statistical tests and freedom from ambiguity. Despite these limitations, the test flourishes, its admirers multiply, and its claims proliferate.

The favorable review was by Morris Kruguman (page 132):

> The Rorschach withstood the clinical test well throughout the years and has come out stronger for it; on the other hand, attempts at atomistic validation have been unsuccessful and will probably continue to be so.

Note that *neither* reviewer cited any studies that demonstrated validity. The favorable one views these as "attempts at atomistic validation"—which the author derogates. (But what could be more "atomistic" than a psychological diagnosis presented in a custody dispute? Such a diagnosis is a qualitative characterization, and if attempts to validate such characterizations on the basis of the Rorschach have been unsuccessful, how can they be made on the basis of this test?) The unfavorable reviewer's characterization of the research as shoddy left open the possibility that good research might show the Rorschach to have some validity.

But if it does have validity, it is not reported in the next *Yearbook*. The favorable review by Helen Sargent asserts instead (page 218) that "the Rorschach test is a clinical technique, not a psychometric method."

By the time the fifth *Yearbook* was published in 1959, the world's leading expert on psychological testing, Lee Cronbach, is quoted in a review: "The test has repeatedly failed as a prediction of practical criteria. There is nothing in the literature to encourage reliance on Rorschach interpretations."[5] In addition, major reviewer Raymond J. McCall writes (page 154): "Though tens of thousands of Rorschach tests have been administered by hundreds of trained professionals since that time [of a previous review], and while many relationships to personality dynamics and behavior have been hypothesized, the vast majority of these relationships *have never been validated empirically*, despite the appearance of more than 2,000 publications about the test." (Italics are in the original.) The other major reviewer, Hans J. Eysenck, was even more negative. After presenting the Cronbach quote, he reiterated again that there is absolutely no evidence for any of the claims of the people using the Rorschach test.

In the sixth *Mental Measurement Yearbook* published in 1965, Arthur R. Jensen wrote (page 509):

> Many psychologists who have looked into the matter are agreed that the 40 years of massive effort which have been lavished on the Rorschach technique have proved unfruitful, at least so far as the development of a useful psychological test is concerned.

And later,

> The rate of scientific progress in clinical psychology might well be measured by the speed and thoroughness with which it gets over the Rorschach.

In the seventh *Yearbook*, John F. Knudsen, a professor of clinical psychology and a practicing clinician, wrote (page 440): "The Rorschach has continued to be characterized by numerous scoring systems and an overwhelming amount of negative research."

Finally, in the eighth *Yearbook* (1978), Richard H. Davis (page 1045) concluded: "The general lack of predicted validity for the

---

[5]Cronbach, L. J. (1958). Assessment of individual differences, *Annual Review of Psychology*, 7, Stanford, Ca.: Annual Reviews, Inc., 448.

Rorschach raises serious questions about its continued use in clinical practice."

Are there not other reviewers in these same volumes who support the test? Yes, but none of them refer to any research results. Instead, they justify use of the Rorschach on the basis that it is a "very novel interview," a "behavior sample," or "source" or that it is a type of "structured interview" with which many clinical psychologists have become comfortable. These claims somewhat vaguely reference "experience" (see section 6.4); in addition there are a few suggestions that appear once and then disappear for using the Rorschach in a novel manner—such as having each member of a distressed couple take the test separately and then requiring the couple to reach a joint conclusion about what the blots look like. The problem, of course, is that there is no evidence that this particular form of "structured interview" is more effective than any other, and as pointed out in section 10.4, only interviews structured to elicit certain specific information are valid. Even if it were demonstrated that this type of interviewing does provide valid information, there is still the question of whether any of it has *incremental validity* (see section 10.4)—that is, whether it provides any information that cannot be obtained from simpler and more reliable sources, such as the history of past behavior. Why then does the Rorschach continue to be used?

The answer may be found in the review of A. G. Bernstein in the seventh *Mental Measurement Yearbook* in 1972. He wrote (page 434): "the view that recognition, the act of construing an unfamiliar stimulus, taps central components of personality functions is one that will remain crucial in any psychology committed to the understanding of human experience." Despite his misuse of the term *recognition* (which means noting that a stimulus has appeared before in one's experience—the exact opposite of "construing an unfamiliar stimulus"), I agree with Bernstein. He refers to a *view*, a *plausible assumption*. If we adopt this assumption, the Rorschach *should* work. The overwhelming evidence that it does not work is ignored. Perhaps some other test works, but this particular one fails. (One really interesting question is why the *same* ten blots have been used for over fifty years, given the failure of the technique and the simultaneous belief in the underlying "theory." The best hypothesis I can provide is that of "institutional inertia.") What I believe is "crucial in any psychology," however, is not a belief in the validity of the Rorschach, but an understanding of *why* people believe it. The fascinating question is, who's projecting what and why?[6] In contrast, a popular new scoring system ("the Exner system") has empirical validity. The major variables in this system that correlate with behavior, however, are based on assessing the *quality* ("form level") of the responses. Such assessment is based on the assumption that parts of the blots *do* resemble some shapes more than others, an assumption totally counter to the "projective" one that it is the *lack* of structure in the blots that leads to valid interpretations of subjects' responses.

Graphology (handwriting analysis) is an even older "art" than Rorschach interpretation. It, also, is highly plausible—for many of the same reasons. Like structuring ambiguous situations, writing is something most of us do all the time; moreover, aside from the rules of penmanship we are taught in grade school, there are no "correct" choices of stylistic details—just as there are no correct interpretations of what Rorschach inkblots look like. Finally, while the content of our handwritten work is conscious, its physical style is not. (In fact, many of us just write as quickly as possible to get it over with, because we already know what we want to say.) What follows is the highly plausible hypothesis that physical characteristics of handwriting convey a great deal of information about personalities. This plausibility is so strong that almost all European firms employ people who claim to be experts in graphology, as do a majority of banks in this country. In fact, my European students inform me that filling out job application forms on a typewriter is not allowed. Of course, the next question is, does graphology "work"?

To my knowledge, the most positive findings concerning handwriting analysis have been presented by Goldberg.[7] He has demonstrated that it is possible to distinguish between the handwriting of males and females, and that of Europeans and Americans. He also speculates that "although the link between handwriting and personality is proba-

---

[6]The materials in this section have been taken from the third through the eighth *Mental Measurement Yearbooks*, all edited by Oscar K. Burros. The third was published in New Brunswick, New Jersey, by the Rutgers University Press, the fourth through the eighth were published in Highland Park, New Jersey, by the Gryphon Press; the years were 1953, 1959, 1965, 1972, and 1978.

[7]Goldberg, L. R. (1986). Some informal explorations and ruminations about graphology. In Nevo, B. (ed.). *Scientific Aspects of Graphology: The Handbook*, Springfield, Ill.: Charles C. Thomas Press, 281–293.

bly very weak, it is not zilch. There is probably a low-magnitude relationship between our handwriting and such broad traits as introversion/extroversion. By 'low' I mean that if we can accurately classify people as introverts and extroverts, and if we have half introverts and half extroverts in the sample, our predictions about them for their handwriting would probably be correct by 70% of the time or less. Not 50%, but not 100%."

There is an important qualification, however. People socially identified as graphology experts are no better than naive individuals at such classification. Moreover, the one expert that Goldberg studied in great depth was able to predict nothing at all. Goldberg collected extensive personality measures on roughly 1,000 students in introductory psychology classes. He and the expert went through these measures to determine exactly which the expert felt she would be able to predict from handwriting samples. She then looked at writing samples drawn from the students' final examinations and attempted to make predictions about the variables she believed she could predict. The results were totally negative.

An apologist for graphology in general (or for this graphologist in particular) might argue that it is the criterion that was flawed, not the handwriting analysis. After all, personality measures are not perfect; perhaps the handwriting analysis predicted better than the tests. It is also possible that Goldberg failed to specify exactly the personality variables the tests assessed, and consequently the expert was in fact making valid predictions about personality variables as she understood them. There is a reason, however, why none of these rationalizations are valid. When presented with the very same handwriting samples twice, the graphologist made totally inconsistent judgments. To quote Goldberg (pp. 287–288):

> Now, psychologists are not only crabby and grumpy, but they are also shady. After the graphologist had completed her analysis of a dozen or so handwriting specimens, I began to start giving back to her the same samples again on a random basis, always correctly identified in terms of sex, but now with a new code number. So, handwriting specimen 007-M might come back to her on some subsequent occasion—like a month later—as handwriting specimen 039-M. For 21 of the essays, I correlated her judgments on two occasions, thus enabling an analysis of intrarater reliability.
>
> After nearly a dozen of these test–retest protocols had been re-rated by the graphologist, she came into my office, quite excitedly, and

said "I've seen this handwriting before." I replied, as calmly as I could, "Of course. I wanted to see how reliable you are, and therefore I have to give you from time to time the same specimens on a second occasion." Then she said, "Oh, that's fine. I just didn't want you to think that you would fool me, because I never forget a handwriting specimen. . . ."

. . . Reliability constrains validity; it provides an upper limit to accuracy. If one says on one occasion that this person is dominant and on another occasion [that] this person is submissive, regardless of whether the person is dominant or submissive, one is going to be right half the time and wrong half the time. So, if one is *completely* unreliable, one cannot have other than a validity coefficient of zero.

And, it turned out that, across all her judgments on repeated occasions, she had stability coefficients near zero. . . .

A recent publication in the *Journal of Applied Psychology* is even more negative.[8] The authors are five Israeli psychologists (Ben-Shakhar, Bar-Hillel, Bliu, Ben-Abba, and Flouga) who tested whether handwriting analysts could predict important characteristics of job applicants. The investigators computed correlations between the judgments of graphologists hired by particular firms and later supervisor ratings of people hired by those firms. Most importantly, the authors compared the graphologists' judgments with judgments made on other bases to determine whether there was *incremental* validity to the graphologists' judgments (again, see section 10.4). While the judgments did not show absolutely no correlation with supervisor ratings, they predicted no better—and often worse—than some other predictors, obvious ones. For example, naive judges' evaluations of the "aesthetic pleasingness" of the handwriting samples predicted equally well. Moreover, both the psychological tests given to the applicants and an "improper linear model" (section 10.2) based on an ad hoc weighting of other cues easily attainable from the handwriting samples outpredicted the graphologists. In fact, this improper model was the best predictor of supervisor ratings—even though it weighted

[8]Ben-Shakhar, G.; Bar-Hillel, M.; Bilu, Y.; Ben Abba, E.; and Flouga, A. (1986). Can graphology predict occupational success? Two empirical studies and methodological ruminations. *Journal of Applied Psychology*, 645–653. See also, Bar-Hillel, M., and Ben-Shakhar, G. (1986). The *a priori* case against graphology, methodological and conceptual issues. In Nevo, B. (ed.). *Scientific Aspects of Graphology*, Springfield, Ill.: Charles C. Thomas Press, 263–279.

one cue in the wrong direction; in constructing the model—which was necessarily specified prior to examining the data (see Appendix A3)—the researchers assumed that married people would be better workers than single people, but actually workers who were single got slightly higher evaluations.

In a subsequent study, the authors investigated the ability of five graphologists thought to be among Israel's best, to judge the occupations of 40 people who had achieved distinction in particular fields. All of these people copied a Hebrew phrase, and the graphologists were told exactly how many were leaders in exactly which fields. The graphologists attempted to match each handwriting sample with the writer's field of achievement. Their performance was at the chance level.

It is not surprising that handwriting is related to certain obvious characteristics, but the point is—as illustrated by the study just cited—that these characteristics can be assessed in much simpler ways. It may well be, for example, that females are differentially rewarded for neat handwriting, and hence that the "graphologists"—expert or naive—can differentiate between males' and females' handwriting at an above-chance level. It is also not surprising that people trained to write in different cultures write differently; therefore, it is not surprising that national origin can be differentiated. Goldberg informs me that the basis of his conjecture about distinguishing introverts from extroverts is a knowledge of the general literature concerning handwriting analysis, but he believes that a simple measure of the size of the writing could also differentiate between introverts and extroverts.

The problem is that studies such as those done in Israel have no impact on the use of graphology. Recall that *none* of the reviews of the Rorschach inkblot test offered empirical support for its validity prior to 1964. (Those that were favorable simply referred to it as a type of clinical tool, one that practitioners believed they could use effectively, and presented no evidence for their conclusions.) Nevertheless, an estimated six million Rorschach inkblot tests were given in 1964. The number of handwriting specimens analyzed each year is probably far greater. Again, the power of plausibility—that is, an easily imagined mechanism by which something may occur—is illustrated. As I will point out in the last section of this chapter, the most effective method of attacking a belief based on plausibility is not presenting disconfirming evidence, but rather providing a *new* plausible hypothesis.

Another example of a dearly held hypothesis may be found in a totally unrelated field—estimating enemy intentions.[9] Egypt and Syria attacked Israel on the afternoon of October 6, 1973. The result was a series of stunning military defeats for Israel, which managed to reverse the military tide only after several desperate battles to achieve a stalemate along lines much closer to the state of Israel than those established after Israel's total military victory in 1967. Subsequently, Egypt and Israel signed a peace treaty, by which much of the territory Israel had seized from Egypt in 1967 was returned.

In 1973, Israel's leaders based their entire strategy on the assumption that they would have at least forty-eight hours' warning of an impending attack. In fact, they had ten. Even then, they thought they had between twelve and fourteen hours to prepare their defense, and they spent three precious hours in Cabinet debate after intelligence chief Ze'ira's "certain warning," because they had no plans for dealing with an attack for which they had less than two days' warning. (On October 3 and 4, Ze'ira had persisted in his estimate that the probability of war was "lower than low.") The Egyptians themselves, who had taken every precaution possible to make their attack unanticipated, were surprised by how unprepared the Israelis were; for example, the Egyptians had expected *fifty times* as many casualties as they actually suffered when crossing the Suez Canal.

What went wrong? Could it be that the Israelis overestimated their confidence in their *intelligence-gathering* capacities? According to Frank Stech of MITRE Corporation, the answer is no. All the information necessary for the anticipation of the attack was in fact gathered by the various branches of Israeli intelligence. Was there, then, some political or personal decision to suppress information? (That possibility is particularly salient in light of the shuttle *Challenger* disaster after suppression of the reports that the O-rings on the booster might not function in cold weather.) There was a bit of political in-fighting over the possibility of war, and there were some instances of mishandling of information and "self-censorship," but the conclusion of Stech and others is that the most important information was readily available to the central decision makers in the Israeli Cabinet. But

[9]Stech, F. Political and military intention estimation: A taxonometric analysis. This is a report prepared for the Office of Naval Research under the auspices of Mathtech, Inc., and it is quoted and discussed with the permission of the author.

were they unaware of it? Did they, for example, "selectively inattend" to important chunks of information?

The answer to this question also appears to be no. As far back as June, the Cabinet had known about the "operation badr" plan for the October Egyptian attack, courtesy of the United States Central Intelligence Agency. Moreover, the United States intelligence community gave the Israeli Cabinet a specific warning approximately three days before the attack. The head of Israel's naval intelligence concluded that war would occur. The unusual Egyptian military movements along the canal in late September and early October were noted, although the predictions of war made by several junior intelligence officers who observed them were excised from the final reports. One basis for this conclusion was that the Soviet Union had begun removing its ships from the Egyptian port of Alexandria and had stepped up control by intelligence-collecting trawlers off the Israel coast; that was well known to the Cabinet at Tel Aviv. Finally, Prime Minister Golda Meir herself noticed the similarity between the departure of Soviet advisors and families on the fourth of October and a similar exodus prior to the 1967 war.

Why, then, did the members of the Israeli Cabinet not reach the "obvious" conclusion? One explanation for which a great deal of evidence can be found is that the Cabinet members were convinced that "it wouldn't make sense" for Sadat to attack Israel. They knew, and they assumed that Sadat knew as well, that the Egyptians could not achieve a total victory. Why, then, would Sadat attack only to lose? Consequently, it was not that information was unavailable, but rather that the overall goal of the Egyptians, particularly Sadat, was misunderstood. Sadat's goal, essentially political rather than military, was to establish an Egyptian stronghold on the East Bank of the Suez Canal.[10]

One reason for this misperception was that Sadat's real purpose appeared to be implausible to Dayan and other Israeli leaders; given the situation of the two countries and their history of conflict, it was difficult to believe that the Egyptians would plan to fight a war that they could not win. Further, sometime during 1971 or 1972 Israeli intelligence sources had obtained authoritative information about the planning and thinking of Egyptian War Minister Sadeq, who believed

[10]Perlmutter, A. (1975). Israel's Fourth War, October 1973: Political and military misperceptions. *Orbis, 19*, 451.

that Egypt should never engage in another war with Israel unless it could achieve a total victory. As noted earlier, this was not the thinking of Sadat, who according to Dupee, "came to the conclusion that it would be better and more satisfactory for the Egyptian people to fight a war and lose, than not to fight at all simply because defeat was likely. . . .[11] Honorable peace was a preferable alternative to an inglorious peace." *The fact that Sadat fired Sadeq in 1972 apparently had very little effect on the thinking of the Israeli Cabinet members*; Sadeq's view of the situation was more plausible to them than Sadat's.

There was another factor besides plausibility. It is what Irving Janis has termed *groupthink*.[12] Some members of the Israeli Cabinet held each other in high regard, and—as representatives of a small and vital state whose existence was continually threatened—may have experienced high morale. As Janis points out, it is *precisely* such otherwise positive qualities of a group that lead its members not to question each other's assumptions and conclusions. An indication that groupthink may have reinforced the plausible inferences on the part of Meir and the others is that the Israeli navy was prepared for an attack from October first onward. Both the admiral and the intelligence officers "knew" an attack was coming, basing their conclusion on very much the same evidence that led the members of the Israeli Cabinet to believe that one was not. Being physically distant from Tel Aviv, however, the naval people were not subject to such groupthink.

11.3 RATIONAL REASONS FOR GIVING UP BELIEFS

The three examples in the previous section have a common characteristic: lack of alternative hypotheses. No one has proposed a rationale other than the "projective" one for explaining how people respond to the Rorschach inkblots. In contrast, many, if not most, clinical psychologists have given up using the "draw a person" text as a projective assessment device. (Disproportionate body parts, choice of clothes or lack thereof, and so on, were thought to be related to "deep" psychological conflicts.) One reason for the abandonment is that research has demonstrated that clinical judgments of types and extent

[11]Dupee, T. (1978). *Elusive Victory: The Arab–Israeli Wars, 1947–1974.* New York: Harper and Row.
[12]Janis, I. (1972). *Victims of Groupthink.* Boston: Houghton Mifflin.

of psychopathology based on the drawings is reflected to the drawings' artistic quality; thus, lack of artistic ability is an alternative explanation to suffering from psychological problems for drawing out-of-proportion figures. I am aware of no hypotheses about the determinants of the stylistic characteristics of handwriting—such as that it is related to the shape of people's hands or hand muscles and not to personality factors. Given their belief that Sadat could not win a total victory, the Israeli Cabinet did not seriously consider that his military preparations were more than a bluff. The old saying "you can't replace something with nothing" appears to apply to such reliance on dearly held hypotheses that are no longer useful. *Logically, however, it is more likely that a hypothesis is not true than that a conflicting one is true.* Thus it is irrational to continue to rely on a hypothesis of unsupported validity until a conflicting one is known to be true.

Let us work out this assertion in detail. Let h_1 refer to a hypothesis, and let h_2 refer to a conflicting one—that is, one that cannot be true if h_1 is true. The relationship between h_1 and h_2 is symmetric: if h_2 is true, then by virtue of h_2's being true, h_1 cannot be true—they contradict. Hence, the probability that both h_1 and h_2 are true is 0. It follows that there are three mutually exclusive possibilities: either h_1 is true and h_2 is not, or h_1 is not true and h_2 is, or neither is true. The latter two possibilities are both negations of h_1, which can be symbolized $\overline{h}_1$. But since h_2 is *equivalent* to h_2 *and* $\overline{h}_1$, it is *one of the two* possible ways in which h_1 can be false; hence, its probability must be less than the probability that h_1 is false. Logically, *no matter what evidence is considered*, it is more probable that one hypothesis is false than that a conflicting one is true. The problem is that without a conflicting hypothesis, however, we tend to minimize the impact of evidence against a hypothesis we have held on the grounds of previous belief or plausibility. That tendency constitutes an irrational use of evidence, because it conflicts directly with the laws of probability theory.

One method for avoiding this irrational tendency is to evaluate evidence as specifically as possible—that is, to try to determine $p(h/e)$ where h is the hypothesis to be evaluated and e is the evidence. That can be quite complex, because it involves some evaluation of the probability of the evidence e independent of the hypothesis h. One "trick" is to determine the *ratio* of the probability that the hypothesis is true given the evidence, to the probability that it is false—that is, to determine the odds of the hypothesis from the given evidence. This can be done quite simply. First, we know that $p(h \text{ and } e)=p(e \text{ and } h)$. Expressing the left-hand term as $p(h/e)p(e)$ and the right as $p(e/h)p(h)$, we conclude:

$$p(h/e) = \frac{p(e/h)p(h)}{p(e)} \tag{11.1}$$

By similar reasoning, we conclude:

$$p(\overline{h}/e) = \frac{p(e/\overline{h})p(\overline{h})}{p(e)} \tag{11.2}$$

where $\overline{h}$ refers to the negation of the hypothesis. Dividing equation 11.1 by equation 11.2, we obtain:

$$\frac{p(h/e)}{p(\overline{h}/e)} = \frac{p(e/h)p(h)}{p(e/\overline{h})p(\overline{h})} \tag{11.3}$$

This equation is termed the *odds ratio* form for evaluating the impact of evidence e. It can be reconceptualized as:

$$\frac{p(h/e)}{p(\overline{h}/e)} = \frac{p(e/h)}{p(e/\overline{h})} \times \frac{p(h)}{p(\overline{h})} \tag{11.4}$$

To use equation 11.4 we first evaluate the probability of hypothesis h without any reference to evidence e. That yields the odds ratio $p(h)/p(\overline{h})$. We multiply this by the fraction $p(e/h)/p(e/\overline{h})$, termed the *likelihood ratio*, to obtain a new odds ratio that our hypothesis h is true given that we have collected evidence e. The point is that if e is more likely given h than given $\overline{h}$, then the odds ratio for h is *increased*; if it is less likely, the odds ratio is *decreased*. In all three examples in the previous section, the accumulating evidence was much more likely given that the hypothesis was not true than that it was. The problem is that without the explicit type of analysis outlined here, the evidence did not lead to decreased belief in the dearly held hypotheses, as it should rationally from equation 11.4. This equation is derived directly from the basic *rules* of probability theory, not from any particular set of beliefs about how evidence should be evaluated in a particular situation; nevertheless, it is generally termed a *Bayesian analysis*. (See Appendix A3.)

Without such controlled thinking, however, we often do not evaluate evidence rationally. In particular, we fail to appreciate the impact of evidence in the absence of a specific hypothesis that conflicts with the one we should reject, or at least believe in less and less as the evidence accumulates. Let me illustrate this point. Recall the finding of the lack of a "hot hand" among basketball players discussed in Chapter 5. The author theorized that the reason people—including the players themselves—believe in the "hot hand" is that they fail to realize that there are often clusters of repetitions of repeated events in purely random sequences. When I tell friends and colleagues of the "hot hand" finding, they don't believe it. Neither, incidentally, did the coach or players of the Boston Celtics. What most people do first is suggest some factor that the researchers might have overlooked. The most common one brought up is the possibility that people who are experiencing a "hot hand" attempt more difficult shots, and if this difficulty had somehow been taken into account in the analysis (i.e., if the percentage of successes "had been controlled" for the prior likelihood of success), then a "hot hand" (positive recency) would have emerged. In fact, the researchers checked out that possibility and found that it did not account for the results. The next response is that there must be some other flaw; doubters say they need "time to think about it."

The two objections I have never heard are those based on doubting the data itself ("Let me look, because they may have miscomputed something") or doubting the qualifications of the researchers to analyze it correctly. In fact, the data were most carefully analyzed, and the researchers are highly qualified. I have discovered, however, a way to convince people that the data are correct—a way that has nothing to do with the data or the qualifications of the researchers. I argue that the whole point of *professionalism* is automating performance. Note, for example, television commercials in which Larry Byrd—the most outstanding player in the National Basketball Association at the time the study was done—was shown spending hours and hours taking the simplest of shots. Practice, I argue, not only makes perfect, but makes behavior automatic as well. In fact, I continue, this is the whole point of "overlearning" through practice. It naturally follows that automatic behavior will not be affected by the emotional components that we believe allow success to breed success and failure to breed failure.

At that point, most people to whom I have talked accept the data as real! Of course, I have no idea at all whether my "plausible explanation" is correct. In fact, from my own tangential experience lecturing in public and playing the piano at informal concerts, I suspect that this explanation is not at all correct. Emotion—provided it is not fear—appears to be an important facilitator of performance. (But maybe my ad hoc plausible explanation is true—for true "professionals.") The point is that I have established the validity of an empirical finding not by urging an examination of the evidence, but rather by providing an alternative hypothesis that is readily available to the imagination of the skeptic. Unfortunately, that is not a rational way to refute a hypothesis. An argument based on equation 11.4, in contrast, is.

One help in evaluating evidence rationally is to decide what its impact will be—if indeed it turns out to be true—*in advance* of observing it. That is, try to make some evaluation of $p(e/h)$ and $p(e/\overline{h})$ prior to deciding whether e is true. Do not simply attempt to "fit" e in a post hoc manner to h. In fact, it is out of efforts to avoid this after-the-fact fitting of data to hypotheses that many of the "rigidities" of "social science research" arise. Investigators are not only urged to specify their hypotheses as precisely as possible in advance, but also to state exactly the kind of data that would lead them to accept or reject these hypotheses prior to collecting the data. (This procedure conflicts with the image of the social scientist as a "wise person" who examines reams of data in order to make some insightful generalization about them.) It is all too easy to fit evidence once obtained to one's dearly held ideas. Evidence that the projective features of Rorschach's responses do not predict anything of interest is thus assimilated in the conclusion that the Rorschach is an excellent "clinical tool." Evidence that handwriting analysis does not predict variables that graphologists claim it does is assimilated in the conclusion that these variables have been poorly defined and evaluated by the psychologists evaluating them. (Evidence of total unreliability—making different inferences from the same evidence on different occasions—is more difficult to explain away.) Each new preparation of Sadat was explained as his putting more energy into his bluff. In like fashion, the "hot hand" might be regarded as just a more subtle phenomenon than the researchers realize.

In fact, this post hoc fitting of evidence to hypothesis was involved in a most grievous chapter in United States history: the internment of

Japanese-Americans at the beginning of the Second World War. When California governor Earl Warren testified before a congressional hearing in San Francisco on February 21, 1942, a questioner pointed out that there had been no sabotage or any other type of espionage by the Japanese-Americans up to that time. Warren responded, "I take the view that this lack [of subversive activity] is the most ominous sign in our whole situation. It convinces me more than perhaps any other factor that the sabotage we are to get, the Fifth Column activities we are to get, are timed just like Pearl Harbor was timed. . . . I believe we are just being lulled into a false sense of security." Surely, if there had *been* sabotage, that *also* would have been used as evidence for the necessity of internment.[13] In such situations, either evidence *or* lack of that evidence is interpreted as supporting the hypothesis. This is not rational.[14] The fact that this variety of irrational thinking can be publicly espoused by someone who otherwise was known for a highly rational—and philosophically "liberal"—approach to social problems illustrates that we are neither consistently rational nor consistently irrational.[15] (A colleague on an ethics committee once pooh-poohed the declaration of innocence on the part of someone charged with child abuse on the grounds that "a particular characteristic of child abusers is that they are prone to massive denial.") The irrationality of the internment was compounded when Japanese-Americans were urged to go voluntarily to the concentration camps in order to "prove" their innocence—in this nation that proclaims the ideal of "innocent until proven guilty."

In all of these examples of not giving up, $p(e/h)$ is insufficiently weighted because evidence e is simply reinterpreted to be consistent with a dearly held hypothesis h. The extreme is an increased belief in h when either e or its negation is observed (such as when the lack of

---

[13] I am indebted to a term paper of March 9, 1984, by Teresa Brougher for the Warren quote and a particularly succinct and persuasive discussion of the "doublethink" involved in the decision. Her paper is entitled "The Decision to Intern Japanese-Americans."

[14] $p(h)=p(h \text{ and } e)+p(h \text{ and } \bar{e})=p(h/e)p(e)+p(h/\bar{e})p(\bar{e})$. If *both* $p(h/e)$ and $p(h/\bar{e})$ are greater than $p(h)$, then $p(h)>p(h)p(e)+p(h)p(\bar{e})=p(h)[p(e)+p(\bar{e})]=p(h)$, a contradiction.

[15] The human individual is *not* a "fairly tight-knit pattern of consistency." See footnote 2 in Chapter 6.

sabotage was thought to be a reason to fear it). As pointed out in the algebraic development of this section, however, there is a perfectly rational way of integrating $p(e/h)$ with the prior probability of h, $p(h)$. It follows that errors can be made not only by holding onto hypotheses despite evidence, but by giving insufficient weight to hypotheses independent of evidence, weight that is captured by the $p(h)$ term in equations 11.1 through 11.4. Does that happen? Yes. Let me give an example.

Several years back, a university sponsored an education program for prisoners who were first-time offenders and who otherwise qualified for admission. The prisoners lived in a "half-way house" near campus and took regular academic courses. Although they were not supposed to frequent the local taverns, many of them did. I met one there who after several beers began talking about how he had ended up in prison. A bartender in an establishment that offered illegal gambling, he had also been involved in collecting gambling debts, at gunpoint if "necessary." One day a man from faraway Nevada had come to the bar and lost a substantial amount of money, for which he had written IOU's, on which he subsequently reneged. My friend had been sent down to Reno to collect the money. He tracked down the man and demanded the money—at gunpoint. The man promised to have it that afternoon, and when my friend returned and drew out his gun again "there were cops behind every chair in the apartment." After expressing his moral outrage that someone would renege on a debt and con the police into helping him, my friend announced that he will never end up in jail again "because I'll never go to Nevada again."

People laugh when I tell that story, but viewed in nonprobabilistic terms, the bartender's inference is reasonable. After all, he had collected debts at gunpoint many times without being arrested, and he had been to Nevada only once. Why not ascribe the "cause" of his arrest and jailing to something special about Nevada rather than to his own activities? Equations 11.1 through 11.4 indicate that there is a crucial problem with this inference. The hypothesis that there is something special about collecting debts at gunpoint in Nevada as opposed to other places is extremely improbable prior to the evidence of an arrest in Nevada. That is, $p(h)$ is very low. Then, even granting that $p(e/h)$—the probability of an arrest in Nevada given there is something special (and dangerous to an enforcer) about that state—is high, $p(h/e)$ remains low.

In fact, I question making any causal attribution at all to "explain" the arrest following that particular incident as opposed to others. (See section 2.2.) One possible noncausal interpretation is that if one goes around collecting money at gunpoint there is always some probability of being arrested each time. And it happened. The way to avoid being arrested for collecting money at gunpoint is to stop doing it, rather than to try to figure out what led to an arrest on one occasion. Certainly, a *sequence of events* preceded that incident that did not precede the others, but a *"cause"*? In fact, this attempt to discover such causes may contribute to the maintenance of behavior that is self-defeating or socially pernicious, for once we decide "why" the behavior led to bad consequences on one occasion but not others, we may feel confident in repeating it. I made the same argument in section 7.6 concerning the possibility of nuclear war. Rather than one superpower trying to figure out exactly what will "cause" the other to react this way or that, each might be better off adopting policies that lead to a lessening of the probability of nuclear confrontation occurring *one way or the other*. That problem's solution is not as simple as my friend's; the best solution is to stop collecting money at gunpoint anywhere. The principle, however, is the same. By acknowledging *uncertainty*—as opposed to irrationally accepting a causal hypothesis—we are often better off. This principle will be discussed in Chapter 12.

CHAPTER

*I returned, and saw under the sun,
that the race is not to the swift, nor
the battle to the strong, neither yet
bread to the wise, nor yet riches to
men of understanding, nor yet favor
to men of skills; but time and chance
happeneth to them all.*

Ecclesiastes

PROMETHEUS: *I stopped mortals
from foreseeing their fate.*
CHORUS: *What sort of remedy did
you find for this plague?*
PROMETHEUS: *I planted in them
blind hopes.*
CHORUS: *This was the great advantage you gave mortals?*
PROMETHEUS: *And besides I gave
them fire.*

Aeschylus,
Prometheus Bound

*Doubt is not a pleasant state but
certainty is a ridiculous one.*

Voltaire

The Value
of Uncertainty

12.1 UNCERTAINTY AS NEGATIVE

We often dread uncertainty. A common way of dealing with our knowledge of the uncertainty in life is to ignore it completely, or to invent some "higher rationale" to explain it, often a rationale that makes it more apparent than real. Thus, the observations of the preacher in Ecclesiastes stand in marked contrast to the narratives in the remainder of the Old Testament, where people generally "get what they deserve." The Old Testament Israelites, for example, lose battles when they turn away from Yahweh to worship graven images or to adopt the policies of neighboring tribes; when they mend their ways, they win. False prophets are put to death; true ones triumph— although the heads of some of them end up on a platter first. The battle "is" to the moral—if not to the strong; bread is supplied to the wise, and riches to men of understanding—although they may, as Job, suffer first. Uncertainty, randomness, lack of fit between deserving- ness and dessert are all apparent, not real. (Admittedly, exactly what members of Job's first family—or the people of Jericho other than the traitorous prostitute—did to deserve their fates is not entirely clear.)

Many who have abandoned traditional religion manifest the same dread of uncertainty in a belief in some "higher order"; astrology, scientology, tarot cards, and innumerable other systems help many people "make sense" of life's uncertainty and vicissitudes, which are believed to be part of some deep underlying structure that they strive to understand. (There *is* structure in the universe, but is it related to the course of an individual life?) Shaking off the dread of uncertainty in our lives and the need for denying its existence is extraordinarily difficult; even those who have a profound and compelling *intellectual* belief that the world is not constructed according to human needs typically wonder what they "did wrong" when their children develop leukemia.

In fact, we even tend to deny the random components in trivial events that we *know* to be the result of chance. In a brilliant series of essays and experiments, Ellen J. Langer demonstrated that—often without any conscious awareness—*we treat chance events as if they involve skill and are hence controllable*.[1] For example, gamblers tend

[1]Langer, E. J. (1975). The illusion of control. *Journal of Personality and Social Psychology, 32*, 311–328. Also see Langer, E. J. The psychology of chance. *Journal of Social Theory and Behavior, 7*, 185–207.

to throw dice with greater force when they are attempting to roll high numbers than when they are attempting to roll lower numbers. A much more striking example concerns beliefs in winning lotteries. Langer conducted a lottery in which each participant was given a card containing the name and picture of a National Football League player; an identical card was put into a bag; the person holding the card matching the one drawn from the bag won the lottery. In fact, Langer conducted two lotteries. In one, the participants chose which player would constitute their ticket; in the other, players were assigned to the participants randomly. Of course, whether or not the entrants were able to choose their own players had no effect on the probability of their winning the lottery, because the cards were drawn at random from the bag. Nevertheless, when an experimental collaborator ("stooge") approached the participants offering to buy their card, those who had chosen their own player on the average demanded *more than four times as much money* for their card as did those with randomly assigned cards. Upon questioning, no one claimed that being allowed to choose a player influenced his or her probability of winning. The participants just *behaved* as if it had.

In another striking experiment, Langer and Roth were able to convince Yale undergraduates that they were better or worse than the average person *at predicting the outcome of coin tosses.*[2] The subjects were given rigged feedback that indicated they did not perform any better than at a chance level—that they were correct on 15 of 30 trials. What the experimenters did was manipulate whether the subjects tended to be correct toward the beginning of the 30-trial sequence or toward the end. Consistent with a "primacy effect," those subjects who tended to be correct toward the beginning were apt to think of themselves as "better than average" at predicting, while those who did not do well at the beginning judged themselves to be worse. (Of course, due to random fluctuations, the probability of success in predicting the outcome of coin tosses cannot be expected to be invariant across a sequence as short as 30 trials.) In addition, "over 25% of the subjects reported that performance would be hampered by distraction. In the same vein, 40% of all the subjects felt that performance would improve with practice."[3] Thus, not only do people behave as if

[2]Langer, E. J., and Roth, J. (1975). Heads I win, tails is chance: The illusion of control is a function of the sequence of outcomes in a purely chance task. *Journal of Personality and Social Psychology, 32,* 951–955.

[3]Langer and Roth, *Ibid.*, p. 954.

they can control random events, they also express the conscious belief that doing so is an ability, which like other abilities is hampered by distractions and improves with practice. It is important to remember that these subjects were from one of the most elite universities in the world, yet they treated the prediction of coin tosses as if it involved some type of skill.

Treating chance events in which we have some input (e.g., choosing a lottery ticket or picking numbers in lotto) as if they involved an element of skill is, of course, the basis of superstitious behavior. Superstitions are particularly likely to develop when the outcomes of behaviors involve components of both skill and chance (e.g., making a hit in a baseball game) because it is easy to confuse factors based on skill with those based on chance. In fact, if we were to evaluate these behaviors mindlessly by simply noting what we did and what outcome followed, there would be little way of distinguishing between chance and skill components—short of deliberately varying our behavior in a systematic fashion and then conducting a statistical analysis to determine which behaviors are associated with success and which with failure. Neither people nor rats do that, however; instead, both humans and rats have a strong tendency to adopt a "win-stay-lose-switch" strategy, repeating whatever preceded success and changing whatever preceded failure (e.g., swinging the bat precisely 5 times in the on-deck circle). Such a strategy has two *logical* consequences: first, it is impossible to evaluate the chance component in success versus failure, and second, the distinction between adaptive and superstitious behavior becomes meaningless. (One simply "did" X, and Y "followed.") As pointed out in Chapter 1 and emphasized in Chapter 6, decisions based purely on the basis of the outcomes ("reinforcements") of past experience do not satisfy our criterion of rationality, because they are not made with regard to probable consequences.

A much-trumpeted success of Skinnerian behaviorism was its ability to "explain" superstitious behavior. If the analysis just proposed is correct, this success is based on the fact its principles do not distinguish between adaptive and superstitious behavior. Moreover, even a pigeon or rat with expert statistical skills and training would tend to behave superstitiously when its total environment consisted of a Skinner box. Given that nothing can be done in such an environment other than press a bar or refrain from doing so, and that the only environmental variability involves the appearance of food, a desperately hungry animal (the animals in Skinner's experiments were kept at 75% of normal body weight) would experience an overwhelming temptation to adopt a "win-say-lose-switch" strategy, and hence never learn. (I certainly would.) Moreover, the problem is confounded by the experimenter's deliberate reinforcement of superstitious behavior, thereby further blurring the distinction between superstition and adaptation.

Often, however, we even fail to understand the probabilistic nature of events in which we have no involvement whatsoever. For example, many psychological experiments were conducted in the late 1950s and early 1960s in which subjects were asked to predict the outcome of an event that had a random component but yet had base-rate predict-ability—for example, subjects were asked to predict whether the next card the experimenter turned over would be red or blue in a context in which 70% of the cards were blue, but in which the sequence of red and blue cards was totally random. In such a situation, the strategy that will yield the highest proportion of success is to predict the more common event. For example, if 70% of the cards are blue, then predicting blue on every trial yields a 70% success rate. What subjects tended to do instead, however, was match probabilities—that is, predict the more probable event with the relative frequency with which it occurred. For example, subjects tended to predict 70% of the time that the blue card would occur and 30% of the time that the red card would occur. Such a strategy yields a 58% success rate, because the subjects are correct 70% of the time when the blue card occurs (which happens with probability .70) and 30% of the time when the red card occurs (which happens with probability .30); $.70 \times .70 + .30 \times .30 = .58$. In fact, subjects predict the more frequent event with a slightly higher probability than that with which it occurs, but do not come close to predicting its occurrence 100% of the time, even when they are paid for the accuracy of their predictions.[4,5] Despite feedback through a thousand trials, subjects cannot bring themselves to believe

[4]They *do* predict the more frequent event more frequently when they are given a monetary incentive to do so, but not nearly as frequently as they should to maximize their payoffs. For example, subjects who were paid a nickel for each correct prediction over a thousand trials in which the more probable event occurred with a 70% frequency on a random basis predicted that that event would occur 76% of the time.

[5]Tversky, A., and Edwards, W. (1966). Information versus reward in binary choice. *Journal of Experimental Psychology, 71,* 680–683.

that the situation is one in which they *cannot* predict. (Rats do the same thing when food is randomly placed on the left or right side of a T-maze.) Apparently, the uncertainty inherent in this experimental situation is simply unacceptable, even though failing to appreciate it results in reduced payoffs to the subject. (And, once again, it appears to be unacceptable to those of us who develop arthritis or cancer—or lose children.)

As demonstrated by Langer, when there is a chance component in the outcomes of our own behavior, we tend to treat the chance component *as if* it involves skill. In the probability matching experiments, subjects responded to a purely probabilistic outcome beyond their control *as if* it were deterministic. (There "must" be some pattern there.) Einhorn has suggested that the crucial distinction between "clinical" and "probabilistic" approaches to prediction and control is whether or not the individual treats probabilistic events as if they were deterministic.[6] Regarding probabilistic events as deterministic in fact makes the rules of probability theory—such as the necessary consideration of base rates—irrelevant. For example, if the sequence of events in a probability-matching experiment really were deterministic, the prediction of the low-probability event would be neither "counterinductive" nor silly. It is precisely such counterinductive judgments made by his colleagues that led Meehl—a psychoanalyst as well as a leading researcher in the area of clinical judgment—to express strong concern about their reasoning capacities, as in the article "Why I Do Not Attend Case Conferences."[7] A simple explanation is that, like subjects in probability-matching experiments, these colleagues do not regard the outcomes in the world as inherently probabilistic.

Einhorn goes on to argue that the probabilistic approach is *superior* to the clinical one, as evidenced, for example, in the studies conducted by Meehl and others summarized in section 10.2. I concur. Even if the world has some underlying deterministic structure, we do not (yet?) understand it, and in particular we do not comprehend it

[6]Einhorn, H. J. (fall 1986). Accepting error to make less error. *Journal of Personality Assessment, 50,* no. 3, 387–395.

[7]Meehl, P. E. (1973). Why I do not attend case conferences. In *Psychodiagnosis: Selected Papers.* New York: Norton.

with respect to the events in human life about which we are most concerned. Moreover, subjects' inability to appreciate the probabilistic nature of the probability-matching experiments even after as many as 1,000 trials indicates that the tendency to reject probabilism is a strong bias—not a generalized consequence of adaptive learning from experience.

Could treating chance as skill be explained on a motivational basis? For example, does the belief that we cannot predict the outcome of coin tossing or batting somehow threaten our ability to cope with the world? Or is it cognition itself so inextricably bound with our attempts to predict and control, that our judgments about events in the world— no matter how clearly they are randomly determined—implicitly assume predictability? I do not know the answer.

Clearly, there are contexts in which lack of predictability involves threat. For example, Cable News Network presented an interview with three "experts" while the jury was deliberating during the New Bedford rape trial in 1984. One of these, a psychologist named Lee Salk, proclaimed that one of the worst aspects of such victimization is that the experience undermines the three beliefs on which our ability to cope with the world is based: the belief that we are superior, the belief that we are invulnerable, and the belief that the world is just, and that "it takes several years to reestablish these beliefs."[8] In contrast, Lord Acton observed in 1887 that "history provides neither compensation for suffering nor penalties for wrong."

12.2 THE PRICE OF DENYING UNCERTAINTY

The most extreme denial of uncertainty with which I dealt in my aborted training to be a clinician was that of someone I'll call Harold, a patient in a mental hospital where I did volunteer work. About six

---

[8]What total nonsense! The fact is that almost all of us are superior in some ways and inferior in others, that we are not invulnerable, and that the world is not just. If, as Salk and others maintain, a "mentally healthy attitude" is based on these three illusions, then it is time to question quite seriously whether such a concept of "mental health" should not be abandoned in favor of a more realistic one.

months before I met him, he had a shaky marriage held together by concern for his two-year-old son, and he was doing badly at a job he disliked. One morning he was fired from his job and he went home. When he arrived the police were there and his wife was hysterical. His son had run into the street and been killed by an automobile. After his wife had been sedated, he wandered back to his former workplace which was nearby, and into the canteen. An attractive woman motioned him to join a group she was with for a cup of coffee. Drinking coffee was strictly forbidden by his religion. He suddenly realized that this woman was trying to *liberate* him from his compulsive adherence to his religious teachings and that she might be trying to liberate him sexually as well. His boss had liberated him from his unpleasant job, and the motorist had liberated him from his bad marriage. All of these people had formed a conspiracy to *help* him! He ended up in the hospital when he mistook strangers for members of that conspiracy. His belief was unshakable; for example, protestations by the hospital staff members that they were trying to help him with his problems were met with simply a knowing smile.

Psychiatrist Silvano Arieti maintained that it is not uncertainty (or pain) per se that creates psychotic disorders, but rather the attempt to "make sense" out of it in a way that does not make sense to others—the "psychotic insight."[9] Of course, not all attempts to reduce uncertainty are pathological. We all attempt to reduce uncertainty. Organizations do it; political decision makers do it; uncertainty reduction is essential to science, if not all knowledge. It can become pathological, however, if it becomes too important. Such pathology is not limited to those of us socially identified as "sick."

There must, for example, be some explanation for a plague. "The Jews are poisoning the wells," some unenlightened people of the thirteenth century concluded. In fact, such explanations have been resurrected in the lifetime of many of us to explain such other phenomena as a worldwide economic depression. These "explanations" led to vicious programs. It is not pathological to seek to reduce uncertainty. Such a quest may even lead to knowledge allowing us to understand things that puzzle us today. It *is*, however, pathological to conclude

[9] Arieti, S. (1974). *Interpretation of Schizophrenia*, 2nd edition. New York: Basic Books.

that we *must know now* in situations containing inherent uncertainty, at least when analyzed in terms of our present knowledge.

A belief that if I am successful, I must somehow have "deserved it" can make me into a pompous ass. A belief that if I am not, I must have done something very bad in the past can make me into a depressed masochist. There is evidence, due mainly to the work of Bernard Weiner, that most people tend to ascribe their successes to their own characteristics and their failures to factors beyond their control, such as plain bad luck. Depressed people's thinking does not follow this pattern; if anything, it reverses it. Many of my colleagues have subsequently made the inferential leap that it is therefore mentally healthy to ascribe success to oneself and failure to circumstances—and that distressed people should be trained to make these self-serving but logically unjustifiable attributions. Of course, all outcomes are due to some combination (though not necessarily "interaction"—see section 10.3) of personal and situational factors, which are extraordinarily difficult to unravel, particularly for a single result. An automatic bias for weighting the type of factors to explain particular outcomes is unjustifiable.

By derogating the role of chance in life, we all lose. (Again, while certain phenomena that we now attribute to chance may eventually be predictable to controllable, they remain chance ones from our current perspective.) Many of us know people who have suffered some great misfortune who appear to *prefer* believing they did something to bring it about to believing that it was something that just "happened." Thus, beliefs that "poor psychological attitudes" precede cancer or arthritis are prevalent, despite a lack of evidence that psychological distress precedes *physical* disease.[10] In fact, an editorial in the *New England Journal of Medicine* was even "ethically condemned" by the American Psychological Association for challenging the belief.[11] The price of achieving such illusory control is, however, the labeling of ourselves or others as "cancer personalities," just as people derogated themselves

---

[10] This is based on current research. My authority is Sheldon Cohen, whose area of research is the role of social factors ("social support") in ameliorating or exacerbating stress.

[11] Council condemns journal editorial (1985). *American Psychological Association Monitor, 16,* no. 10, 6.

and others who had tuberculosis for possessing a troubled and frail soul prior to the discovery of the tuberculosis bacterium.[12]

The price of our retreat from uncertainty is often paid by others. Some individuals believe that if people are poor, or are on the street or addicted or ill, they must somehow have done something to deserve that fate. In the face of such deservingness, help is futile. Moreover, given the biasing effects of retrospective memory (see section 6.4), these people themselves may accept that judgment; for if they, too, believe in "just desserts," that could play a crucial role in determining their recall of what it is they *did*.

A gross misunderstanding of the role of chance in evolution can lead to cruelty as well as to failure to help. Consider "social Darwinism." Even the strongest "adaptationists" maintain that it is a *slight* genetic advantage that leads to a slight increase in the probability of success in the "struggle for existence," which over *many* generations can lead to genetic change. But to claim, as some social Darwinists did, that a single individual's poor situation implies the lack of genetic capacity viciously underestimates the role of chance in life, viciously because it leads to the conclusion that it is "nature's way" to let such people suffer and die—"in order to" let good genes multiply. While the threat of uncertainty may cause pain, its denial can be cruel.

Such costs of denying uncertainty are high—too high to justify any feeling of security that this denial may offer. In particular, the pathological consequences of believing in a *just world* are severe—both for others and for oneself. They have been documented more extensively than here by Melvin J. Lerner.[13] An essential part of wisdom is the ability to determine what is uncertain; that is, to appreciate the limits of our knowledge and to understand its probabilistic nature in many contexts. It follows that an essential part of bravery is eschewing a false sense of security—for example, not believing we are invulnerable or superior, or that the world is just.[14]

---

[12]Sontag, Susan (1978). *Illness as Metaphor*. New York: Farrar, Straus and Giroux.

[13]Lerner, M. J. (1980). *The Belief in a Just World: A Fundamental Delusion*. New York: Plenum Press.

[14]It is symptomatic of the unity of the field of psychology that what an academic psychologist (Lerner) studies as a "delusion," a practicing one (Salk) maintains to be a cornerstone of mental health.

Some psychologists, however, urge people to develop these beliefs—as part of a general effort to reinforce belief in "internal control" of outcomes, since belief in such control is supposed to be a motivator for desirable choice and putting forth effort. It is true that parents attempt to reward good behavior and punish bad so that their children learn to behave in ways that the parents wish; moreover, children who see little contingency between their own behavior and their rewards and punishments often behave badly—at least we can *improve* their behavior by increasing the contingency.[15] In addition, employees who believe that they have control over the rewards they receive for their work are motivated to work hard and be productive. Consequently, employers and supervisors are well-advised to establish within their organizations a contingency between employee accomplishments and rewards. Global, diffuse control is another matter. If we have "put away childish things" when we are no longer children, we understand that we have more or less control over outcomes depending on the particulars of the situation. Illusory control can have the pernicious effects discussed above. Some "control theorists," nevertheless, claim that belief in control, illusory or real, is a mentally healthy motivator.

Rationally, it often doesn't matter how much control we have over outcomes—so long as we have some. For example, various alternatives will still have the same ranking in expected value (see Chapter 8) even if a large random component determines the actual outcome. Understanding the wisdom of Ecclesiastes should in no way inhibit us from choosing the best possible alternative and pursuing it with all our energy. To maintain that it is necessary or desirable to overestimate the amount of control we have is to maintain that we can function only as children or employees of someone else, not as autonomous adults. Unfortunately, some of my colleagues treat their adult clients as if they really were children, and give advice to the entire population on the same basis. (Striking examples of treating the adults as adults may be found in some of the rhetoric of John F. Kennedy. In one speech, he stated bluntly that life is not fair—and gave the example that during wartime some people are shot on battlefields while others sit at desks. In his famous American University speech shortly before

[15]Patterson, G. R. (1986). Performance models for antisocial boys. *American Psychologist, 41*, 432–444.

his assassination he proclaimed that this country, comprising 6% of the world's population, cannot control everything that happens on the globe, and that it would be a tragic mistake to equate national security with such control.)

One of the most extreme examples of overestimation of degree of control can be found in the work of Taylor, who refers to herself as a "control theorist." In an article otherwise arguing that belief in control is adaptive to adjusting to threatening situations, Taylor presents the following anecdote about a woman with breast cancer.[16]

> One of the women I interviewed told me that after detection of her breast tumor she believed that she could prevent future recurrences by controlling her diet. She had, among other things, consumed huge quantities of vitamin A through the singularly unappetizing medium of mashed asparagus. A year and a half later, she developed a second malignancy. This, of course, is precisely the situation all control researchers are interested in: a dramatic disconfirmation of efforts to control. I asked her how she felt when that happened. She shrugged and said she guessed she'd been wrong. She then decided to quit her dull job and use her remaining time to write short stories—something she had always wanted to do. Having lost control in one area of her life, she turned to another area, her life work, that *was* controllable."

Taylor presents no evidence whatsoever that her subjects who attempted to achieve illusory control over recurrence of breast cancer were better off than those who did not, although the article itself contains throughout the clear implication that attempting such control is psychologically valuable. Her anecdote, however, can be interpreted in the precisely opposite way she interprets it; it can be interpreted as an example in which *giving up* the attempt to control is valuable. Exactly why devoting oneself to one's "life work" should be interpreted as an effort at "control" is unclear. In contrast, "shrugging" is clearly a communication that one does *not* have control. Perhaps if the shrug had occurred a year and a half earlier, a year and a half of the woman's life (and all our lives are finite) would have been devoted to the work she desired rather than to a dull job and mashed asparagus.

---

[16]Taylor, S. E. (1983). Adjustment to threatening events: A theory of cognitive adaption. *American Psychologist, 38,* 1161–1173, quote on p. 1170.

12.3 UNCERTAINTY AS POSITIVE

Imagine a life without uncertainty. Hope, according to Aeschylus, comes from the lack of certainty of fate; perhaps hope is inherently "blind." Imagine how dull life would be if variables assessed for admission to a professional school, graduate program, or executive training program really *did* predict with great accuracy who would succeed and who would fail. Life would be intolerable—no hope, no challenge.

Thus, we have a paradox. While we all strive to reduce the uncertainties of our existence and of the environment, ultimate success, that is, a total elimination of uncertainty, would be horrific. In fact, it may be that such procedures as testing for AIDS antibodies and predicting the recurrence of breast cancer on the basis of hormonal analysis are the results of long medical marches that have taken us to a place we do not wish to be. I can imagine the horror I would feel at being notified that I had received blood tainted with AIDS, or that I possess a gene that invariably leads to Alzheimers disease. I have no way of knowing whether that would be worse than learning I have a terminal illness. At least in the latter situation most people feel sick.[17] Knowing *pleasant* outcomes with certainty would also detract from life's joy.[18] An essential part of knowledge is to shrink the domain of the unpredictable. But while we pursue this goal, its ultimate attainment would not be at all desirable.

12.4 UNCERTAINTY AND ETHICS

If there were no uncertainty about the consequences of behavior, ethics and morality would not exist. If we *knew* which alternative in each decision-making situation would benefit us the most, we would choose it. Such total knowledge would, of course, include any benefit

---

[17]It is true that in the Middle Ages the first symptoms of plague—green discoloration of the lymph nodes on the groin—occurred before the person felt sick. But sickness followed within a day, and death shortly thereafter.

[18]Wouldn't perfect predictability with control be desirable? The problem is that perfect predictability would entail knowledge of what we were *bound* to do.

that we derive from behaving in a manner that we now term "ethical," perhaps even punishment or reward after death. But it would not be an ethical choice; it would simply be a self-interested one. In fact, there would be no choice at all. We could not even suffer from "weakness of the will" or satisfy an addiction if we were *fully* aware of the degree to which subsequent pain would outweigh momentary pleasure. Even if we took some joy in the joy of others or pain in their pain, total knowledge of how our behavior would affect them as well as ourselves would once again dictate what to choose. Trying to decide in a way that maximizes the utility of consequences would not be a problem. It would not even be a mandate. It would happen automatically, which means there would be no decisions at all. Hence, there would be no ethical concerns for the decision maker.

I am not proposing that ethics can be *derived* from uncertainty, but rather that uncertainty is a necessary *precondition* for the existence of ethical choice. To a large degree, an individual concerned with ethics wishes to do "the right thing" because the consequences of choice are *not* immediately obvious. Moreover, I am not proposing that the ethical choice is one that maximizes the utility of pleasure for oneself or others in a probabilistic sense, although that certainly is *one characteristic* of most decisions that people regard as ethical. Nevertheless, one conclusion that can be drawn by studying the *history* of ethical thought is that there is a general consensus that "ethical" decisions overlap to a large extent with those that benefit *others*—and the decision makers *themselves* "in the long run"—however much philosophers have disagreed throughout the ages about what actions are good or bad, or about what people "mean" by such terms, or even whether ethical imperatives are "facts" (or even "pseudoconcepts"). I am not claiming that this correlation *defines* what we mean by "good," or that the concept of "benefit" is not as ambiguous as the ethical terms themselves in many situations, or even that ethical rules must be "consequentialist." For example, it is possible to suppose that ethical rules consist of a set of "categorical imperatives" irrespective of consequences, as Immanuel Kant did. Nevertheless, the consequences of such imperatives tend to be beneficial; for example, "Act as if each decision is a rule to be followed by all mankind."

Admittedly, there is ambiguity in ethical systems. For example, if I believe in imperatives, how might I decide which imperative is relevant to each situation—or even what policy should be adopted by "all mankind" in *this* situation, which is also ambiguous. (In fact, the essential difference between "act utilitarian" and "rule utilitarian" may not be so much one of basic position as one of disagreement about the degree to which "a situation" can be defined in general terms.) If I believe in "the greatest good for the greatest number," I am faced with the problem of maximizing two functions at once, even if I steadfastly ignore the circularity of defining ethical action in terms of "good." And so on.

There is, however, some structure in ethical thought—just as there is statistical structure in many contexts of uncertainty. "Is" may or may not imply "ought," but it is clear that "ought" implies "is." We do not define or mandate ethics without reference to the capabilities of human beings. No ethicist demands, for example, that people should not fear death or pain or should know the consequences of all their behaviors. Most ethical systems, moreover, maintain that the ethics of a decision can be most clearly judged by considerations at the time the decision is made, *a belief that presupposes that consequences are uncertain*. This general principle may appear trivial, but it is not. It implies that ethics are judged in terms of *rules* about decision, such rules being found in virtually every human society. The ethics of decision are not judged on the basis of the consequences that *happen* to follow. For example, a doctor who has skillfully and conscientiously treated a patient in the manner best indicated by the current state of medical knowledge is not condemned if the patient subsequently dies. Nor is a doctor who botches an operation due to drunkenness commended if the patient survives the operation and lives to age 96 without any further medical problems. Nor are professors who never prepare for classes but yet can lecture in a brilliant or entertaining fashion regarded as paragons of virtue by their colleagues, even if they get higher student ratings than those who conscientiously attempt to teach as well as possible. (The former are faulted for not having done as well as they could with preparation.) If I rob a bank that subsequently defrauds an insurance company that is exploiting a number of people, and it just happens to turn out that the insurance company's loss is the straw that leads to the dismissal of a nonethical chief executive, with the overall result that the insurance company starts treating its clients more fairly, neither I nor the bank defrauding the company is congratulated for an ethical coup. Like the drunken surgeon, my behavior and the behavior of the bank are judged in terms of the decisions themselves. And there is a strong *correlation* between such decisions and their *probable* consequences for our own and others' "long-term" best interests. (In the long run, we all are dead—but others live.)

The result, as pointed out, is the establishment of ethical *rules*, as opposed to judging the moral quality of the behavior purely in terms of its consequences. Rule based systems are consistent with the general philosophies of attempting to maximize—or satisfice—in the face of uncertainty and of making each judgment a policy one, as well as consistent with the empirical findings presented in section 10.2 that decisions based on a systematic consideration of the *components* of complex situations tend to be superior to those based on an attempt to grasp such situations in their entirety. In fact, a good rebuttal to "situation ethics" is that it is impossible to grasp most situations in their totality, even though it is distressingly easy to delude ourselves into thinking we can. The conclusion that "ordinarily I wouldn't do this, but in this situation I understand that . . ." is often a precursor to immorality or disaster. Even from a purely egotistic point of view, such exceptions can be disastrous. For example, as Senator Sam Ervin pointed out, people who are ordinarily truth tellers must be possessed of a perfect memory for what they said when they start to lie. None of us has such a memory.

Both from a research point of view and from a normative ethics point of view, we must conclude that what we "ordinarily" believe to be valuable or ethical behavior in such situations is what we should decide to do in *this* situation. (I grant again that it can be very difficult to determine the boundaries of the class of situations encompassing this particular one.) Thus, for example, it is *unethical* for psychologists who know that unstructured interviews are generally not predictive of future behavior to decide to base a personnel or legal decision on a *particular* unstructured interview or set of interviews. It is—in my view—even unethical for a psychologist involved in such decision making to remain ignorant of the research literature concerning the invalidity of unstructured interviews—through intellectual laziness or a defensive attribution that the research is somehow "irrelevant" to his or her particular practice. (The most common justification of such irrelevance judgments is that personal experience has led the clinician to believe that his or her particular judgment is valid irrespective of the general findings—a justification based on denial or ignorance of all the problems of "learning" from such unstructured experience.) To quote Paul Meehl: "If I try to forecast something important about a college student, or a criminal, or a depressed patient by inefficient rather than efficient means, meanwhile charging him or the taxpayer ten times as much money as I would need to achieve greater predictive accuracy, that is not a sound ethical practice. That it feels good, more warm and cuddly, to me as the predictor is a shabby excuse indeed."[19]

The views expressed in the preceding paragraphs conflict directly with the philosophy presented in the major reference book used by the American Psychological Association's Ethics Committee.[20] On page 14 of that book the authors express the view that people who are high on idealism and low on relativism "assume that the best possible outcome can always be achieved by following the universal moral rules." The analysis just completed on the role of uncertainty and ethics indicates that the rationale for rejecting situationalism is that outcomes are *not* certain, and that it is empirically obvious that following universal moral rules (or any rules at all, or intuitions, or gut feelings, or anything) does not "always" lead to the achievement of "the best possible outcome." It is because there *is* a probabilistic relationship between action and outcome that rules are so important. If, in contrast, the relationship were not probabilistic, then there would be no reason *not* to be a situationalist—or, in fact, a total egotist without any ethical concerns whatsoever. Believing that rules lead to "the best possible outcomes" also distorts ethical judgment of behavior—particularly the behavior of others, whose situations and alternatives available at the time of choice are not readily appreciated by the judge. For if following ethical rules leads invariably to good outcomes, then the existence of a bad outcome can be used to infer violation of the rules. It is bad enough to attempt to infer motivation from behavior, but to infer it from consequences is an absolutely irrational procedure, and a Draconian one as well. We are *not* omniscient. As I have tried to point out in this section, it is this very lack of omniscience that mandates us to consider the ethical implications of our choices.

[19]Meehl, P. E. (1986). Causes and effects of my disturbing little book. *Journal of Personality Assessment*, *50*, 370–375, quote on p. 374.
[20]Keith-Spiegel, P., and Koocher, G. P. (1985). *Ethics in Psychology: Professional Standards in Cases*. Hillsdale, N. J.: Lawrence Erlbaum Associates. I served on the committee; this book was referenced often.

Of course, rules as the *sole* source of ethical mandates and judgments can "run amok." For example, Rudolf Hoess, the commandant at Auschwitz, wrote in his autobiography (smuggled out of a Polish prison before he was hanged) that he was emotionally appalled at what he had to do "as a good national socialist." His rationale or rationalization, for killing 2,900,000 people was that he followed "principles" (much as Plato and others would have us do) rather than "feelings." For example:

> I nodded to the junior non-commissioned officer on duty and he picked up the screaming, struggling children in his arms and carried them into the gas chamber, accompanied by their mother who was weeping in the most heart-rending fashion. My pity was so great that I longed to vanish from the scene; yet I might not show the slightest trace of emotion.[21]

Hoess may have been lying, just as the Tennessee senators quoted in section 2.1 may have been rationalizing. That is not the point. It is the implicit validity of the argument that such "stifling of all softer emotions" is the cornerstone of ethics that calls into question mindless adherence to rules. Clearly, feelings as well as rules are important in determining ethical judgments and choice. (Once again the use of the concept of "rationality" in this book is quite different from the neo-Platonic, hierarchical use in such dictums as "Reason should rule emotion." Rationality does not dictate what to decide, only *how*. In fact, rationality per se dictates only how *not* to decide. Abandoning the basic principles of rationality leads to contradiction, hence fruitless behavior once she [rationality] "raps . . . on the knuckles.")

12.5 APPRECIATING UNCERTAINTY

Without uncertainty, there would be no hope, no ethics, and no freedom of choice. It is only because we do not know what the future holds for us (e.g., the exact time and manner of our own deaths) that we can have hope. It is only because we do not know the consequences of our actions (e.g., the exact effect of our treatment of others) that we face ethical choice. It is only because we do not know exactly the results of

[21]Hoess, Rudolf (1959). *Commandant at Auschwitz: Autobiography*. London: Weidenfeld and Nicholson.

our choices that our choice can be free. Moreover, most of us are aware that there is much uncertainty in the world, and one of our most basic choices is whether we will accept that uncertainty as a fact or try to run away from it. Those who choose to deny the reality of uncertainty invent a stable world of their own. Such people's natural desire to reduce uncertainty, which may be basic to the whole cognitive enterprise of understanding the world, runs amok to the point that they come to believe uncertainty does not exist. The "statistician's definition of an optimist" as "someone who believes that the future is uncertain" is not as cynical as it may first appear to be.[22]

[22]Kish, L. (March 1978). Chance, statistics, and statisticians. Presidential Address to American Statistical Association. *Journal of American Statistical Association, 73*, no. 361, 1–6.

A P P E N D I X   A1

Basic Principles of Probability

DEAR ABBY: *My husband and I have just had our eighth child. Another girl, and I am really one disappointed woman. I suppose I should thank God she was healthy, but, Abby, this one was supposed to have been a boy. Even the doctor told me that the law of averages were [sic] in our favor 100 to 1.*

June 28, 1974

A1.1 THE CONCEPT OF PROBABILITY

The bulk of this book deals with the evaluation of the likelihood, or probability, of consequences of choice. All such future consequences are viewed as uncertain. Moreover, there is empirical evidence that those of us who believe in the uncertainty of the future underestimate it (section 10.4). Thus, an absolute essential of rational decision making is to deal constructively with this uncertainty. Irrationality, for reasons pointed out in section 1.3, is not constructive; at least the conclusions that follow from it cannot be true of the world. Thus, the "bottom line" is that likelihoods and probabilities must be assessed rationally.

Likelihoods are commonly expressed in terms of probabilities, or odds. The *odds* of an event equal the probability of its occurrence divided by one minus the probability; for example, a probability of 2/3 equals odds of 2 to 1, that is, (2/3)/(1/3). A *set* of probabilities (or odds) is consistent if and only if it satisfies *four broad algebraic rules*. Otherwise, it is contradictory. These rules, which are really quite simple, are formally termed the *principles of probability*, or of "probability theory." This appendix will explain each of these principles. The method of presentation is first to discuss probabilities relevant to the principle in the context of equally likely outcomes—most commonly illustrated by coin tosses and dice rolls, then to present the principles both algebraically and verbally, and then to discuss them in more general contexts.

Because we evaluate and discuss uncertainty in terms of probabilities, it follows that our view of uncertainty is rational if and only if the probabilities we assign to possible events satisfy the four rules. If the rules are satisfied, our view of uncertainty is termed *coherent*, otherwise it is *incoherent* (read "irrational").

Before proceeding, however, four caveats are in order. First, our discussion of probability will be limited to numerical (or vaguely numerical) judgments about *future* events. For the decision maker, events in the past either have occurred—and thus are not uncertain—or have not occurred—in which case they cannot have probabilities assigned to them. We speak loosely, of course, of the probability of past events. For example, we might speak of the probability that Lee Harvey Oswald was the assassin of John F. Kennedy (or the lone assassin), the probability that a defendant "actually" committed a crime, or even the probability that a hypothetical coin has rolled off a table and landed heads up. For the purposes of this book, however, such statements about the probability of past events can be interpreted as the probability that we would reach certain conclusions *were* we to learn the truth, which of course is a possible future event. Sometimes probabilities are interpreted as "degree of belief"—or as "objective" frequencies over a large number of repetitions. Nevertheless, all students (and developers) of probability theory agree that the four basic rules must be satisfied. (In fact, as an abstract branch of mathematics, probabilities are *defined* as numbers that follow these rules, and concrete interpretations and other meanings assigned to probabilities are not considered.)

This appendix also includes beliefs about probabilities that order them or categorize them. Such beliefs, as well, may or may not reflect coherent judgment because such beliefs *can* in fact either satisfy or violate the principles. For example, the belief that the world's best tennis player is more likely to lose the first set of a championship match *and* win the match than he is to lose the first set alone (a purely ordinal belief) contradicts the principles of probability theory—as does the belief that the probability of a disease given a symptom is necessarily equal to the probability of the symptom given the disease (a belief of equivalence with no specific number proposed).

Only *sets* of (two or more) probabilistic beliefs may be irrational (except for the trivial constraint that a probability less than zero or greater than one is irrational). Probabilities cannot be evaluated for rationality in isolation. For example, it is not necessarily "irrational" (as defined here) to believe that the sun will not rise tomorrow with probability .9. It would be irrational, however, to hold that belief *and* the belief that you will go to work tomorrow with probability .8 *and* the belief that you will go to work only if the sun rises—all simultaneously.[1]

[1]What is "simultaneous"? One explanation for irrationality in assessing probabilities—and in decision making in general—is that people fluctuate between different "states of mind" when viewing different parts of a problem and that conclusions reached in one state are not compared with those reached in another.

A1.2 HISTORY: FROM GODS TO NUMBERS

How did probability theory begin? By evaluating gambles.

In Robert Grave's *I, Claudius*, Caligula and Claudius are playing dice prior to Caligula's assassination (and watching bloody games with just enough attention so that Caligula could order losers—and occasionally winners—to be put to death).[2] The four dice they used (termed *astragali*) were made from ankle bones of dogs or sheep and had four faces, each with a different number: 1, 3, 4, 6. The winning throw is a "Venus roll," a roll in which four different numbers are face up. Claudius is winning—a possibly mortal situation for him given Caligula's outbursts of pathological anger. Fearful, Claudius hands Caligula beautiful new astragali that are loaded to yield Venus rolls. When Caligula wins back his money, he is especially delighted, *because he interprets his success as a sign that the goddess Venus is favorably disposed toward him that day*. In his euphoria, he fails to take the usual precautions departing from the games and is assassinated.[1]

According to historian Florence N. David, belief that the outcome of games was due to the influence of gods or goddesses, or of supernatural forces ("destiny"), was common in the ancient Egyptian, Greek, and

---

[2]Graves, R. (1943). *I, Claudius*. New York: Penguin Books.

[3]How would we determine the probability of a Venus roll? Consider the order of the astragali reading from left to right (from any perspective). The "1" may be in any of the four positions, the "3" in any of the remaining three, the "4" in any of the remaining two, and the "6" in a position then determined. Hence, there are $4 \times 3 \times 2 \times 1 = 24$ possible ways of obtaining a Venus roll. The total number of possible rolls, however, is 4^4, because any of the four numbers in the first position, in the second, and so on. Thus, we conclude that the probability of a Venus roll is 24/256, or approximately .094.

There is another way of reaching the same conclusion. Consider the four positions in sequence. Any number face up in the first position is compatible with a Venus roll. *Given* the number appearing in the first position, the number in the second can be any of the three remaining; the probability of that is 3/4. Given that the numbers in the first two positions are different, the number in the third position must be one of the two remaining; the probability of that is 2/4=1/2. Finally, if the numbers in the first three positions are all different, the probability that the number in the last position is the remaining one is 1/4. "Chaining" these probabilities yields $1 \times (3/4) \times (2/4) \times (1/4) = 6/64 = 24/256$, or approximately .094. (Because not all outcomes are equally likely, the actual probability is lower, approximately .04.)

Roman civilizations. (And in its implicit—unconscious?—form may still be common today among compulsive gamblers.) Moreover, different gambling outcomes were often associated with different gods. In fact, these beliefs about gambling apparently were one reason for its being outlawed by the Roman Catholic Church in the Middle Ages. A monotheistic God did not "play at dice"—and gambling was a catalyst to polytheism.[4]

(Most of us now would regard Caligula as superstitious and silly. There is, however, the alternative interpretation. By giving Caligula loaded dice, Claudius inadvertently deceived him into believing Venus was favorably disposed when in fact she wished him ill—as demonstrated by Caligula's earlier losses. Thus Claudius's deception made him partially responsible for the assassination and his own ascension to the throne.)

Of course, not all ancient Greeks and Romans believed that gambling outcomes were influenced by the gods. In Book II of *De Devinatione*, Cicero wrote:

> Nothing is so unpredictable as a throw of the dice [modern translation], and yet every man who plays often will at some time or other make a Venus-cast; now and then indeed he will make it twice and even thrice in succession. Are we going to be so feeble-minded then as to aver that such a thing happened by the personal intervention of Venus rather than by pure luck?[5]

Cicero believed "luck" determined the success of gambling with essentially random devices. He also apparently understood that there was a relationship between the luck (odds) on a particular throw or set of throws and long-term frequencies. The major modern development he

[4]But John Wesley was a monotheist. The following excerpt is from his journal of March 4, 1737, and refers to his decision to remain single: "At length we agreed to appeal to the Searcher of Hearts. I accordingly made three lots. In one was writ 'Marry.' In the second 'Think not of it this year.' After we had prayed to God to 'give a perfect lot,' Mr. Delamotte drew the third, in which were the words, 'Think of it no more.' Instead of the agony I had reason to expect, I was enabled to say cheerfully 'Thy will be done.'" A counting approach to this procedure leads us to conclude that Wesley had arranged for 2 to 1 odds mandating bachelorhood. His subsequent lack of agony over the result is understandable.

[5]Cicero was later executed, illustrating that rationality does not guarantee success, only increases its likelihood. In fact, as pointed out earlier, opting for rationality when others do not can lead to social ostracism.

did not foresee is that of *determining* the odds by counting. (And counting was possible only after the development of arithmetic procedures that made complex computation possible; despite the Greeks' skill in geometry and logic, arithmetic was not developed in the Western world until the Renaissance.)

Such counting was first systematically proposed by Cardano (1501–1576)—a Renaissance man who was simultaneously a mathematician, physician, accountant, numerologist, and inveterate gambler (who *lost*, for while he understood his own principle of counting outcomes, he had a distressing habit of counting incorrectly). He was a man whose stormy life included watching his son hanged for allegedly poisoning his wife (Cardano never believed it) and being charged as a heretic for reading Christ's horoscope.[6] Here is how counting leads to the principles of probability theory:

> Tossing a coin results in one of two possible outcomes: heads (H) or tails (T).
>
> Tossing a coin twice results in one of four possible outcomes: HH (two heads), HT (a head followed by a tail), TH, or TT. See figures A1.1 and A1.2.
>
> Tossing a coin three times results in one of eight possible outcomes: HHH, HHT, HTH, HTT, THH, THT, TTH, or TTT.
>
> And so on.

Outcome is a technical term in probability theory. It refers to a specific result of an *experiment* such as tossing a coin a certain number of times. An *event* is a collection of outcomes. This concept is crucial to probability theory, and the term "event" will be used throughout this and subsequent chapters—even when less stilted English would require another word. "Collection" in this definition does not necessarily mean more than one outcome; that is, an event may consist of a single outcome. Moreover, a collection may consist of all outcomes; that is, the event consisting of all outcomes is a well-defined one. It is symbolized S.

Tossing a coin twice results in one of a number of possible events. For example:

A. The event *two heads* consists of the single outcome HH. (It is equivalent to the event *no tails*.)

---

[6] Being an "intellectual" was more exciting in the Italian Renaissance than it is for many people now.

Figure A1.1

		SECOND TOSS	
		H	T
FIRST TOSS	H	HH	HT
	T	TH	TT

Table illustrating the possible outcomes of two tosses

B. The event *exactly one head* consists of the outcomes HT and TH. (It is equivalent to the event *exactly one tail*.)

C. The event *at least one head* consists of the outcomes HH, HT, and TH. (It is equivalent to the events *at most one tail* and *not two tails*.)

And so on.

In fact, there are 15 ($=2^4-1$) events consisting of at least one outcome:

Events consisting of a single outcome,

> HH
> HT
> TH
> TT

Events consisting of pairs of outcomes,

> HH, HT
> HH, TH
> HH, TT
> HT, TH
> HT, TT
> TH, TT

Figure A1.2

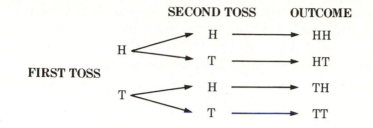

"Tree" diagram of the possible outcomes of two tosses

Events consisting of triples of outcomes,

HH, HT, TH
HH, HT, TT
HH, TH, TT
HT, TH, TT

And the event consisting of all four outcomes,

HH, HT, TH, TT

A verbal description may be given to each event. (Try it.)

Note that as a result of tossing a coin *twice* there are *four* possible outcomes and *fifteen* possible events consisting of one or more outcomes. Actually, mathematicians define *sixteen* possible events, because for the sake of completeness, they also consider the event consisting of *no* outcomes. It is termed the *null* event ("nothing happened"), and it is symbolized ∅. Is the null event nothing but the (null) result of an obsessive-compulsive frame of mind? No. The concept of the null event has had the same salutary effect on the development of probability theory that the concept of zero had on the development of our number system. (The concept zero was not introduced into computation in Western culture until about A.D. 900. Prior to that there was one Roman symbol for ten (X), another for twenty (XX), and so on, with the result that it was much more difficult to add and subtract than it is using zeros. For example, X+XXX=XL, rather than 10+30=40, which is obtained in part by adding 0 to 0 to obtain 0.)

I will first illustrate how probabilities are assigned to events by considering equally likely outcomes, and then generalize to other events. Consider two tosses of a "fair" coin. By *fair*, I mean that

1.   heads or tails are equally likely on each toss, and

2.   there is no relationship between the results of successive tosses.

"Fairness" resides in both the coin and the coin tosser. The first condition states that the coin has no *bias* and that the coin tosser cannot or does not control the outcome. The second condition states that the coin "has no memory" (or if it does, its muscles are too weak to control its landing), and once again that the coin tosser cannot or does not control it. (Many "subjectivist" statisticians allege that fairness resides in the *beliefs* of the *observer* that the coin and coin tosser satisfy these conditions.) Under these conditions, there are four equally likely outcomes: HH, HT, TH, and TT.

The probability of an event when outcomes are equally likely is equal to the number of outcomes in the event divided by the number of possible outcomes. The number of outcomes is 4 when a coin is tossed twice.

A.   The event *two heads* consists of only the outcome HH; therefore its probability is 1/4.

B.   The event *exactly one head* consists of the outcomes HT and TH; therefore, its probability is (1+1)/4=1/2.

C.   The event *at least one head* consists of the outcomes HH, HT, and TH; therefore, its probability is (1+1+1)/4=3/4.

And so on.

Following standard notation, events are symbolized by capital letters and their probability by p. For example, if A is the event *all heads or all tails*, it consists of the outcomes HH and TT; hence,

$$p(A) = (1+1)/4 = 1/2$$

A1.3 THE PRINCIPLES OF PROBABILITY THEORY

It should be clear now that probabilities are numbers between 0 and 1. Moreover, $p(\varnothing)=0$, because there are no outcomes in the null set. Thus, the following principles are true for probabilities assigned to events consisting of equally likely outcomes:

Principle I: $0 \leq p(A) \leq 1$

Principle IIa: $p(S) = 1$

Principle IIb: $p(\varnothing) = 0$

Events can also be combined. The event (*A and B*) (termed their *intersection*) consists of all outcomes common to both. For example, the event *at least one head* consists of the outcomes HH, HT, and TH, while the event *at least one tail* consists of the outcomes HT, TH, and TT. Thus the event *at least one head and at least one tail* consists of the outcomes HT and TH. (Note that this event is equivalent to the event *one head and one tail*.) Such an event is termed a *compound event* and the probability of such an event is termed a *compound probability*. (Note that any one event may be considered to be a compound event; for starters, each event is equivalent to the intersection of itself and S.)

Another type of combination involves outcomes in *either* of two events. The event *A or B* (termed their *union*) consists of all the outcomes in either. (Any overlapping outcomes are included; logically *or* means "in either singly or in both.") For example, the event *at least one head* consists of the outcomes HH, HT, and TH, while the event *at least one tail* consists of the outcomes HT, TH, and TT. The event *at least one head or at least one tail* consists of HH, HT, TH, and TT; that is, it is S (because there must be at least one head or at least one tail).

In these two examples, the two events of the intersection or union were partially overlapping. That need not be so (as was indicated, for example, by taking the intersection of an event with S, or its union with $\varnothing$). We may take the intersection or union of totally disjoint events—that is, those that have no outcomes in common. Or one event may be a distinct part of another—that is, all the outcomes comprising the first are in the second as well or the events are identical. An event is a set of outcomes. Linking *any* two events by *and* or *or* defines a new set of outcomes, an event.

When two events have no outcome in common, they are *mutually exclusive*. For example, the event *two tails* and the event *at least one head* are mutually exclusive.

Mathematicians and statisticians make use of the null set to express the fact that two events are mutually exclusive—that is, have no outcomes in common. Briefly, when two events *A* and *B* are mutually exclusive, the compound event consisting of their intersection is the null set (is devoid of outcomes). Thus A and B are mutually exclusive whenever

$$(A \text{ and } B) = \varnothing$$

which by Principle IIb means that

$$p(A \text{ and } B) = 0$$

Again, consider tossing a fair coin twice. Let A be the event *two tails* and B be the event *exactly one head*. These events are mutually exclusive (the first consisting of the outcome TT and the second of the outcomes HT and TH). Moreover, the probability of A is 1/4 while that of B is 2/4=1/2. The probability of A *or* B is 3/4, because there are three outcomes in A or B (TT, HT, and TH). Thus, $p(A \text{ or } B)=p(A)+p(B)$.

Whenever any two events A and B are mutually exclusive, the number of outcomes in A *or* B must equal the sum of the number of outcomes in each. If there are n equally likely outcomes in S, m in A and m' in B, then if A and B are mutually exclusive

$$p(A \text{ or } B) = \frac{m+m'}{n} = \frac{m}{n} + \frac{m'}{n}$$
$$= p(A) + p(B)$$

This observation yields a general principle:

Principle III: If $p(A \text{ and } B) = \varnothing$ (equivalently, $p(A \text{ and } B)=0$), then $p(A \text{ or } B) = p(A) + p(B)$

(Does this principle work backward? That is, if $p(A \text{ or } B)=p(A)+p(B)$, does it necessarily follow that $(A \text{ and } B)=\varnothing$? This question may be answered by noting that if A and B have at least one outcome in common, $p(A \text{ or } B)$ is *less* than $p(A)+p(B)$.)

The introduction of two more concepts completes this sketch of probability theory. The first is that of the *complement* of an event. Specifically, the *complement of an event A consists of all the outcomes in S that are not in A*. The complement of A is often symbolized $-A$ or $\overline{A}$. For example, consider a coin tossed twice:

1. If A is the event *two heads* (consisting of HH), the complement of A is the event consisting of HT, TH, and TT—the event *at least one tail*.

2. If A is the event *exactly one head* (consisting of HT and TH), then the complement of A is the event consisting of HH and TT—the event *all heads or all tails*.

3. If A is the event *at least one head*, then $\overline{A}$ is the event *all tails*.

And so on.

Relationship I: If $\overline{A}$ is the complement of A, then $p(\overline{A}) + p(A) = 1$.

This relationship is established by noting that A and $\overline{A}$ are mutually exclusive; hence by Principle III, $p(A \text{ or } \overline{A}) = p(A) + p(\overline{A})$. But $(A \text{ or } \overline{A})$ is equal to S, because $\overline{A}$ by definition consists of all those outcomes in S not in A. Therefore, $p(A) + p(\overline{A}) = p(S)$, which equals 1 by Principle IIa.

Note that Principle IIb, that $p(\varnothing) = 0$, was not used in establishing Relationship I; it was established entirely from Principles IIa and III. In fact, Principle IIb itself can be shown to follow from Principles IIa and III via Relationship I. For since $\varnothing$ is the complement of S, $p(\varnothing) + p(S) = 1$; but since $p(S) = 1$ from Principle IIa, it follows that $p(\varnothing) = 0$. (That is a rigorous proof that the probability of nothing is nothing—zero.)

Finally, it should be noted that the implication in Relationship I cannot be reversed, unlike that in Principle III. That is, it does *not* follow that if the sum of the probabilities of two events is 1, they are complements of each other. For example, the event *exactly one head* resulting from two coin tosses has probability 1/2 when outcomes are equally likely, as does the event *exactly one tail*. But the probability of either exactly one head or exactly one tail does not equal 1 (1/2+1/2); they are not complementary events. In fact, they are identical, both consisting of the outcomes HT and TH.

The final concept is that of *conditional probability*. It can be easily defined by a formula, but that can wait. The essential idea is that the probability of an event A is assessed differently *conditional upon* knowledge of whether another event has or has not occurred. For example, if the events A and B are mutually exclusive, then an outcome in A *cannot* be in B; thus, the probability of A given B's occurrence is 0. At the other extreme, if all the outcomes in B are also in A, then the probability of A given B is 1.

The conditional probability of *A* given *B* is symbolized $p(A|B)$; it can be expressed verbally in a variety of ways:

1. the probability of *A* conditional upon *B*'s occurrence
2. the probability of *A* conditional upon *B*
3. the probability of *A* given *B*
4. the probability of *A* if *B* occurs

If outcomes are equally likely, the probability of *A* given *B* is equal to the number of outcomes in *both* events (their intersection) divided by the number of outcomes in *B*. In effect, having been "given" *B*, we know that the actual outcome must be selected from it, and the probability that an outcome from *A* occurs is therefore equal to the relative number of outcomes in *B* that are also in *A*. The event *B* now defines the number of possible outcomes; it has, in effect, replaced S.

Let m' be the number of outcomes in *A* and *B* (their intersection), and let m be the number of outcomes in *B*. Then, given equally likely outcomes,

$$p(A|B) = m'/m$$

Now divide the numerator and denominator of the fraction m'/m by n to obtain

$$p(A|B) = \frac{m'/n}{m/n}$$

But since $p(A \text{ and } B)=m'/n$ while $p(A)=m/n$, we conclude:

$$\text{Principle IV: } p(A|B) = \frac{p(A \text{ and } B)}{p(B)}$$

This principle constitutes the formal definition of conditional probability.

Now let's look at some examples of conditional probabilities resulting from tossing a fair coin twice. The probability of the event *two heads* given the event *at least one head* is 1/3. (HH is the only outcome in the event "two heads," while the event "at least one head" consists of the outcomes HH, HT, and TH.) Occasionally, this probability is mistakenly believed to be 1/2 rather than 1/3; for example, some people think the probability of a two-child family having two daughters when at least one child is a daughter is 1/2.

In contrast, probability of the event *two heads* given the event *the first toss is a head* is 1/2. The common event is again HH, but here the event that is given has only the two outcomes HH and HT. The probability a two-child family consists of two daughters when the first is a daughter is 1/2, because boys (B) and girls (G) have (roughly) equal probabilities of being born. In contrast, there are *three* ways to have "at least one girl": GG, GB, BG; in only one of these—GG—is the other child a girl. Again, the probability of two girls given at least one girl is 1/3, not 1/2.

Principle IV may be reformulated by "multiplying through" by $p(B)$. That is,

$$p(A|B)p(B) = p(A \text{ and } B), \text{ or}$$

Principle IV′: $p(A \text{ and } B) = p(A|B)p(B)$

When expressed in the manner of Principle IV′, the conditional probability definition constitutes a *chaining principle* for obtaining the probability of compound events. (Remember the Venus roll example.) For example, the probability that both coin tosses are heads (the event *both heads*) is equal to the probability that the first one is a head multiplied by the probability that the second one is a head given the first one is a head. The reader should verify that both these latter probabilities are 1/2, so that the desired probability of the compound event is 1/4. The probability of drawing two spades randomly without replacement from a deck of cards is equal to the probability that the first draw is a spade (=13/52, because there are 52 cards in the deck, 13 of which are spades) multiplied by the probability that the second is a spade given the first is a spade (=12/51, because there are 51 cards left of which 12 are spades). The desired probability of this compound event is (13/52)(12/51)=3/51. We could also derive this probability by dividing the number of pairs of spades (=78) by the number of pairs of cards (=1346), again obtaining 3/51.

Chaining may take place in either direction; $p(A \text{ and } B)$ equals both $p(A|B)p(B)$ *and* $p(B|A)p(A)$. Sometimes it is more convenient to chain in one direction than in the other—such as when there is a natural sequence from earlier to later.

Finally, *independence* between events can now be defined. The intuitive definition is that A and B are independent if $p(A|B)=p(A)$. Accepting this definition, we can multiply both sides by $p(B)$ to obtain:

Independence: $p(A \text{ and } B) = p(A)p(B)$

since $p(A|B)p(B)=p(A$ and $B)$ by Principle IV'. Moreover, dividing by $p(A)$, we can infer that $p(B|A)=p(B)$; hence, independence is symmetric. The definition that $p(A$ and $B)=p(A)p(B)$ is the one used by mathematicians, because the concept should also be valid if $p(A)$ or $p(B)$ equals 0, in which case division and multiplication would be inappropriate.

Probability theory can, now, be applied in much broader contexts. For example, the designs of dikes and dams are based on estimates of the probability that rivers will reach certain flood levels. Engineers clearly don't believe that all flood levels are equally likely, but rather have reference to the frequencies with which certain water levels have occurred in the past. We also may speak of the probability that the Yankees will defeat the Pirates in the World Series, or the probability of an atomic holocaust prior to the year 2000. In such cases, there is no relative frequency to use, but rather a rough, "educated" estimate based on knowledge of baseball, politics, technology—or perhaps on our level of pessimism. When there are neither equally likely outcomes nor frequencies on which to rely, probabilities are often related to "fair" betting odds. For example, if you believe that the probability is 1/3 that the Yankees defeat the Pirates, you should be barely willing to bet \$2 on the Pirates against \$1 on the Yankees; that is, you should be willing to accept all bets in which you must bet less than \$2 to \$1 and reject all those in which you must bet more than \$2 to \$1. That's an assessment of your *personal probabilistic belief*, and in fact a school of philosophers of probability known as *personalists* or *subjectivists* have argued that *all* probability is ultimately based on personal belief. (Isn't, for example, the assertion that all outcomes are "equally likely" one of belief?)

Actually, there has been considerable debate throughout the centuries about whether probability statements refer to facts, individual beliefs (coherent ones) about the world, or logical relationships between evidence and belief—or between different beliefs. It is not clear how important this debate is to probabilistic reasoning; however, it *is* clear that people with different understandings about the "meaning" of the term *probability* reach the same conclusions about particular probabilities.

For example, consider an experiment in which one of two dice is drawn at random from a bag. One of them has four green and two red faces and the other has four red and two green faces. Without examining the die drawn, the experimenter rolls it. What is the probability of a red face showing as a result? All agree it is 1/2. And all agree that the reason is that the probability of drawing each particular die is 1/2.

Some people argue that this latter conclusion follows because we have no reason to believe that we have drawn one particular die or the other; some argue that 1/2 reflects their belief that each die is equally likely; some argue that the concept of "randomness" logically entails a probability of 1/2 that we have drawn either; and still others argue that the equal probability of drawing either is based on a hypothesis about an "objective" fact whose validity could be assessed by repeated draws. It is even possible to argue that the "real" probability of drawing whichever is actually drawn is 1, because nothing ever really occurs at random in the world, but that in our ignorance of all the factors involved and their interaction we must opt for 1/2. All conclude, however, that the probability of drawing either die is 1/2. Then, the probability that a red face shows is the sum of the probabilities that the predominantly red-faced die is drawn and that a red face shows, plus the probability that the predominantly green-faced die is drawn and that a red face shows (by Principle III). The first probability is $(1/2) \times (2/3)$, and the second is $(1/2) \times (1/3)$ (both by Principle IV'). Hence, the probability of a red face is $2/6 + 1/6 = 1/2$. Agreed.

So what, in general, is a *probability*? First, probabilities refer to *numbers assigned to well-defined events*. A "well-defined event" is one that can be unambiguously interpreted as occurring or not occurring in the future. Second, probabilities must satisfy the basic principles, reiterated here:

I. $0 \le p(A) \le 1$

II. $p(S) = 1$

III.   If the intersection $(A \text{ and } B) = 0$, then $p(A \text{ or } B) = p(A) + p(B)$

IV. $p(A|B) = p(A \text{ and } B)/p(B)$

Without demeaning the philosophers who attempt to find an additional meaning for "probability" we can accept the *structural* ("formal") meaning of probability as numbers that satisfy these four principles. For purposes of this book, I have added the additional meaning that events shall be in the future.

Note that a *single* probability cannot violate the principles unless it falls outside the interval between 0 and 1. Thus, probabilities refer to *sets* of numbers describing relationships between *sets* of events. Of course, people may assert probabilities that violate the principles and insist that they are discussing "probabilities" in the usual sense of the term. But *rational* (or *coherent*) probabilities must satisfy the principles, which is the only type of "probability" a mathematician or statistician would accept.

What is an example of a common probabilistic belief that violates these principles? Consider these sequences of events:

1. A star athlete becomes a drug addict, enters a treatment program, and wins a championship.

2. A star athlete becomes a drug addict and wins a championship.

When one or another such sequence of events is presented to subjects, many judge the first to be more probable than the second. But by the principles of probability it *cannot* be. To understand why, break the sequences into their constituent events:

A. The athlete becomes an addict.

B. The athlete becomes a champion.

C. The athlete enters a treatment program.

(It is not necessary to label events in the order in which they occur in time.) Now the belief is that

$$p(A \text{ and } B \text{ and } C) > p(A \text{ and } B)$$

But that is not rational, which we can demonstrate in two ways:

First demonstration. By the chaining principle (IV′), it follows that

$$p(A \text{ and } B \text{ and } C) = p(C|A \text{ and } B)p(A \text{ and } B)$$

because the intersection (A and B) is just another event. But since $p(C|(A \text{ and } B)) \leq 1$ by Principle I,

$$p(A \text{ and } B \text{ and } C) \leq p(A \text{ and } B)$$

Second demonstration. (A and B)=(A and B and C) joined with (A and B and $\overline{C}$). But (A and B and C) and (A and B and $\overline{C}$) are mutually exclusive. Therefore by Principle III,

$$p(A \text{ and } B) = p(A \text{ and } B \text{ and } C) + p(A \text{ and } B \text{ and } \overline{C})$$

which means it must be greater than or equal to the first term. (The point is that the athlete could have won the championship by some route *other* than entering a treatment program. The athlete could have quit drugs for other reasons, the athlete could have been so extremely talented and lucky that it didn't matter, the championship could have been rigged, and so on.)

The belief that the likelihood of an unlikely event, or combination of events, is enhanced by adding plausible additional events to it is termed the *scenario effect*; such effects have been extensively investigated by Daniel Kahneman and Amos Tversky. These added events can yield a "good" (believable) story, even though they in fact *restrict* the number of possibilities that can lead to the original event, or combination. For example, when anthropologists reconstruct from a few bones the nature of a particular prehistoric culture, their reconstructions often seem more believable when they supply details about which they couldn't possibly have any knowledge, as pointed out by Paul Washburn. And we all know that telling people only known facts is not as persuasive as embellishing our story (for example, courtroom summations). It is well documented by cognitive psychologists that the scenario effect results in irrational probability judgments. (See Chapter 7.)

I would like to end with a discussion of two probabilistic beliefs that are wrong but not irrational. Their combination, however, is irrational.

1. The gambler's fallacy. The more often a coin falls heads (tails) the more likely it will be to fall tails (heads) on the next toss. Thus, HT is more likely than HH, HHT is more likely than HHH, and so on. (As noted earlier, such a belief would be correct only if the coin had both memory and muscle—or if the person tossing it can control it.)

This fallacy occurs in contexts other than coin tossing. Consider the example, the doctor's proported advice in the letter to "Dear Abby" at the beginning of this appendix. The probability of bearing 8 consecutive daughters is (roughly) $1/2^8 = 1/256$. But the probability of bearing a daughter *after* seven other daughters have been born is about 1/2. Like coins, sperm have no memories, especially not for past conceptions of which they know nothing. The principle is the same as that in the solution to the game of balla referred to in section 2.3.

2. Distributing ignorance equally across verbally defined categories (rather than across concrete outcomes). Since a coin tossed twice can yield 0, 1, or 2 heads, this pseudo principle states that each such result occurs with the probability 1/3.

Suppose that someone believes in *both* the gambler's fallacy and in distributing ignorance. By the gambler's fallacy,

$$p(HT) \geq p(HH)$$

But by the distribution of ignorance fallacy,

$$p(HH) = 1/3$$

Therefore, $p(HT) \geq 1/3$, and by a similar argument, $p(TH) \geq 1/3$. Hence, their sum is greater than or equal to 2/3, but their sum must simultaneously equal 1/3 by the distribution of ignorance fallacy.

Such *combinations* of belief are irrational. Yet people hold them. Choices based on such incoherent probabilistic assessments must themselves be incoherent—and may lead to personal and social harm. The inverse conclusion, that probabilities satisfying Principles I–IV *cannot* lead to a contradiction, is also true, but proving it lies beyond the scope of this book.

A P P E N D I X   A2

DISTRIBUTIONS AND THE LAW OF LARGE NUMBERS

Celtics Try "Struggling Man" to Beat Lakers 104–102   Boston — Kevin McHale [the Celtics' highest-percentage shooter] was having a terrible game. But, with fourteen seconds left and the score tied, Boston coach K. C. Jones called a play for him to shoot.
   "I think K. C. figured I might be due," McHale said after the game.

Associated Press
January 17, 1985

A2.1 OVERVIEW

Appendix A1 presented the basic concepts of probability theory in the form of a few simple principles. Appendixes A2 and A3 will outline some concepts that are necessary for understanding the relationship between coherent probability beliefs and the data on which they are based. Thus, these two appendixes present principles of *statistics*. Most dictionaries give two definitions of *statistics*, one as an abstract system for dealing coherently with uncertainty, the other as a collection of numerical information, such as batting averages. A good definition for our purposes is that statistics as a field consists of specifying the *relationships* between data collected and coherent probabilistic inferences—or, as will be explained in Appendix A3, between samples and populations.

A2.2 RANDOM VARIABLES

As has been pointed out, when a fair coin is tossed twice, there are four equally likely outcomes: HH, HT, TH, and TT, each occurring with probability 1/4: there are two heads with probability 1/4, one head with probability 1/2, and no heads with probability 1/4. Let us define X as a *variable* whose values, labeled x, equal the number of heads obtained. Then, when the event consisting of the outcome HH occurs, $x=2$; when HT or TH occurs, $x=1$, and when TT occurs, $x=0$. The probability that $x=2$ can be expressed as $p(x=2)=1/4$; further,

$p(x=1)=1/2$, and $p(x=0)=1/4$. We know these things already, but this new notation is necessary for introducing the concept of *random variable*.

First, note that when a fair coin is tossed, it is possible to determine the probability that $x \le a$ (x is less than or equal to a) for any number a. In our coin tossing example the probability that $x \le 1$ (that it equals 0 or 1) is 3/4, which is the sum of the probability that it equals 0 (which is 1/4) plus the probability it equals 1 (which is 1/2). The probability that $x \le 2$ is 1, and the probability that $x \le 0$ is 1/4.

The number a need not correspond to a particular value of x. For example, the probability that $x \le -2$ is 0. Continuing the examples, the probability $x \le 1.5$ is equal to 3/4 (again, because that occurs when $x=0$ or $x=1$). The probability that $x \le 3.7$ is 1, the probability that $x \le -17$ is 0, and the probability that $x \le 1001$ is 1. Why do we bother with such values of a? Because they lead to a perfectly general definition of *random variable*. Specifically, when it is possible to determine (or define) the probability that the value of a numerical variable describing events is less than or equal to any given number, then that variable is referred to as a *random variable*. This definition can be stated in more precise language.

Definition: Let X be a numerical variable describing events. X is a *random variable* if for any arbitrarily chosen number a there is a well-defined probability that the value x of X is less than or equal to a; $p(x \le a)$.

Why do we bother with the "less than or equal to"? In the coin toss example, after all, the variable x (number of heads) had values that were specific, discrete numbers (0, 1, and 2). The answer is that the "less than or equal to" definition allows us to deal with *any* random variables, not just discrete ones. For example, suppose that a point is chosen with equal probability at any position on a one-inch line, and consider the experiment to be an idealized one in which points have no width, length, or thickness—and lines have only length. The probability of choosing a line corresponding to *exactly* ½ inch from the left is effectively zero. Nevertheless, it is clear that the point is equally likely to fall in the first or the last half-inch of the line; hence, the probability is 1/2 that its distance from the left is less than or equal to ½ inch. It has probability 3/4 of being located in the first ¾ inch, and so on. Thus the distance from the left is a random variable.

We can also infer the probability that the point is between two locations. In the example with the one-inch line, the probability is 1/2 that the point is located between the first quarter-inch and the last.

This probability is obtained by subtracting the probability that the point is located in the first quarter-inch—which is 1/4—from the probability it is located in the first ¾-inch, which is 3/4; 3/4−1/4=1/2.

In general, if we wish to determine the probability that a random variable has a value between a and b (a less than b), we subtract the probability that is less than or equal to a [$p(x \le a)$] from the probability that is less than or equal to b[$p(x \le b)$]. That is, subtracting $p(x \le a)$ from $p(x \le b)$, we get the probability that $a < x \le b$. For example, the probability that a river crests between two and four feet above flood level is equal to the probability that its crest is less than or equal to four feet above flood level minus the probability that its crest is less than or equal to two feet above flood level.

A2.3 AVERAGES OF NUMBERS AND EXPECTATIONS OF RANDOM VARIABLES

The *average* of a set of n numbers is equal to their sum divided by n. For example, the average of the set of four numbers 1, 7, 9, and 11 is 7; (1+7+9+11)/4.

Note that the average is the *center of (numerical) gravity*. That is, the sum of the positive discrepancies from the average equals the sum of the negative discrepancies. In the example, 1 has a negative discrepancy of 6, 7 has no discrepancy, 9 has a positive discrepancy of 2, and 11 has a positive discrepancy of 4; 6=2+4. If we were to place equal weights on a ruler at 1″, 7″, 9″, and 11″, the ruler would balance on a fulcrum underneath it at 7″, the average. No other number than the average is a center of gravity; it is unique. If, for example, we had miscomputed the average and believed it to be 8″, the sum of the negative deviations would be −8—that is, (1−8)+(7−8),—and the sum of the positive deviations would be 4—that is, (9−8)+(11−8). If we placed the ruler on a fulcrum at the 8″ mark, it would immediately tilt to the left.

Thus the concept of average of a set of numbers is straightforward. What is not always clear, however, is exactly what we wish to average. The following example of such ambiguity is pirated from Leslie Kish.

A small graduate school offering professional doctorates in astrology states in its brochure that the average class in its program has twenty students in it, an attractive number for students interested in personalized instruction and close interaction with skilled astrologers. In fact, the school offers five classes. The first class, in basic astrology, is required of all entering students; it has eighty students in it. It is given in a lecture format with multiple-choice exams. The other four classes are five-student seminars—in clairvoyance, telepathy, psychokinesis, and tarot—taken by students who have passed the first class. The five classes thus have 80, 5, 5, 5, and 5 students in them, and the average of these five numbers is indeed 20; 100/5. Moreover, if only twenty students passed the first class and all passed the seminars, the respective passing rates would be .25, 1, 1, 1, and 1, for an average of .85, a fact also emphasized in the brochure.

If we compute not the size of the average class but the average size of each student's classes, however, we get a number much different from 20. Eighty students are in a class of size 80 and 20 students are in classes of size 5. When we average across those 100 *students*, we compute an average of 65; [(80×80)+(20×5)]/100. Moreover, 80% of the students flunk out of the institution. Most students entering the program with the expectation of finding small classes and passing them will be disappointed. (But, as the president of the institution may be quick to point out, people with real skill in the area should not be surprised at what they find.)

An example that is not hypothetical was available every day in 1984 on the CNN television news network (or at least on every morning that I watched). Danny Thomas is walking in a park, and he says, "Whenever we senior citizens come together, the topic of medical care is bound to come up." (He walks, facing the screen.) "Did you know that today, Medicare pays less than half the average hospital bill, leaving *you* responsible to pay the rest? Less than half? That means you could wind up paying thousands of dollars. The deductible is now over $350, and you could pay that for one day in the hospital." (Think about that last sentence. What happens after the deductible is applied to the bill?) He goes on to sell insurance "for which you cannot be turned down for any reason" to cover that vanishing deductible. (Given the premium rates and the amount of the deductible—$358 in 1984—there would be no reason to turn anyone down.)

The message is that a senior citizen covered by Medicare could be stuck with 50% of a huge hospital bill. Of course, that's not true. Medicare pays only half the average hospital bill because most hospital bills are (relatively) small. Take all those hospital bills, most of which are under $1,000, compute the percentage paid by Medicare, and average these percentages. The number is less than 50. That does not imply that a patient with a large bill will pay over 50%, or anything near that.[1]

A final example. About ten years ago, a study of sex discrimination at the University of California at Berkeley found that while, *overall*, women applicants to graduate school had a lower probability than men of being admitted, within each department the probability for women was higher. The reason? Women tended to apply to departments with low admission rates overall; for example, English as opposed to electrical engineering.

The examples are of *Simpson's paradox*. Grouping numbers (e.g., into departments, income brackets, classes, or individual bills), obtaining a sum or an average for each group, and then averaging these individual sums or averages yields a different result than averaging overall. It's not really a "paradox," because it is easily understood (or, at least, understandable).

Thus, even simple averages can result in misleading inferences. An average may *sound* as if it conveys the information in which one is interested, but yet fail to do so. There is no simple "rule of thumb" for deciding which average is the important one. Such a decision involves thought, and skepticism. Succeeding steps depend on the context. In the hypothetical astrology school example, the potential applicant who understands that it is *classes* that are being averaged might ask himself or herself, "Am I interested in being a *student* or a *class* at that institution?" The answer is obvious, and the applicant *should* then understand that the relevant information is obtained by averaging across students, not classes. The senior citizen should be concerned about the percentage of large bills that is covered by Medicare, not the percentage of the average bill or the average percent.

Mean is sometimes used synonymously with *average*, and sometimes with *expectation*, the concept explained now. The *expectation* of

[1]One of my fonder fantasies while writing this book is that people who read it will subsequently laugh at such deceptive commercials and have nothing to do with the respective companies. Actually, the Danny Thomas commercial is not as bad as one of Mobil Oil's that chronically advertised to its stockholders that it made only $0.01 on each gallon of gasoline sold. That is less than 1%! Of course, the profit margin of a company is not based on the percentage of the *sales* price going to profit, but on the amount of profit in the sales relative to the *cost of production*. As a starter, national and state taxes included in the sales price of gas are totally irrelevant to profit margin. (Exactly why Mobil wished to downplay its profits to its stockholders in this deceptive manner is unclear.)

a random variable is analogous to the average of a set of numbers—
only whereas an average is determined by weighting each number
equally, the expectation of a random variable is determined by weighting each value by its probability. Weighting discrete random variables
by probabilities is simple (conceptually, anyway). Just take each
value, multiply it by its probability, and sum. For example, the average number of heads resulting from two tosses of a fair coin is 1; it is
equal to:

$$0 \times [p(x=0)] + 1 \times [p(x=1)] + 2 \times [p(x=2)], \text{ or}$$
$$0 \times (1/4) + 1 \times (1/2) + 2 \times (1/4) = 0 + 1/2 + 1/2 = 1$$

Now suppose, that the variable is not discrete. For each value of a it is
possible to determine $p(x \leq a)$. (This possibility follows from the definition of a "random variable.") This can be plotted as in Figure A2.1.
Usually, $p(x \leq a)$ is plotted from the lowest possible value of a to the

Figure A2.1

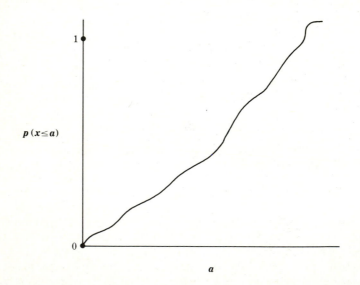

Illustration of a continuous random variable: The cumulative distribution
function

highest within the context, although as pointed out earlier, it could be plotted from negative infinity to positive infinity. Note that such a plot, termed a *cumulative distribution function*, always has an increasing values of a (is "monotone"). Because X is a random variable, we know $p(x \leq a)$ and $p(x \leq b)$ for all a and b. Hence, for $b > a$, $p(a < x \leq b)$ can be inferred by simply subtracting $p(x \leq a)$ from $p(x \leq b)$. The result can be plotted as in Figure A2.2.

In Figure A2.2, $p(a' < x \leq b')$ is represented by the *area* between a' and b'. Note that the total area under the curve in this plot, the *density function*, is equal to 1—just as in the cumulative distribution function values of $p(x \leq a)$ [on the "ordinate"] vary from 0 to 1.[2] As before,

Figure A2.2

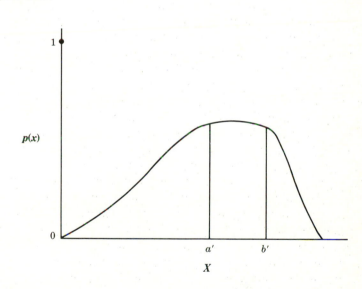

Illustration of a continuous random variable: The density function

[2]The reader familiar with calculus will note that the density function is a derivative of the cumulative distribution function; that is, the cumulative distribution function is the integral of the density function. Moreover, the expectation is the integral over the entire density function of the value multiplied by its probability.

$p(a<x\leq b)$ is usually plotted from the lowest to the highest possible value in the context. The *expectation* of a random variable is the horizontal *center of gravity* of the density function.

When the random variable consists of a finite number of discrete values, its cumulative distribution function consists of a number of points and its density function consists of a number of straight lines. As an example, consider tossing a fair coin *three* times and define a random variable of the number of heads. Then:

$p(x\leq0)$ = 1/8 (TTT)
$p(x\leq1)$ = 1/2 (TTT, HTT, THT, TTH)
$p(x\leq2)$ = 7/8 (TTT, HTT, THT, TTH, HHT, HTH, THH)
$p(x\leq3)$ = 1 (HHH)

The cumulative distribution function is plotted in Figure A2.3.

Figure A2.3

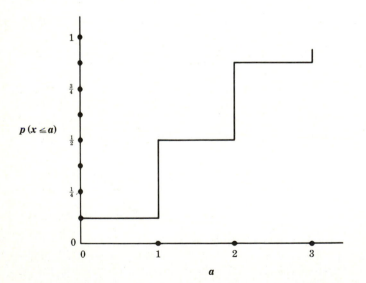

Illustration of a discrete random variable: The cumulative distribution function

Figure A2.4

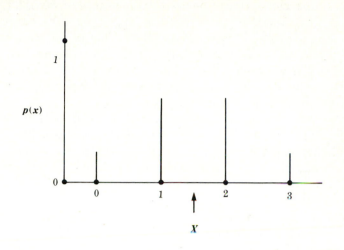

Illustration of a discrete random variable: The distribution function

Figure A2.4 plots the density function (usually termed a "distribution function" when the value of the random variable is discrete). The arrow indicates the expectation of this function (that is, its center of gravity), which is 1½.[3]

Note that it is not necessary to plot these functions to refer to them. The cumulative distribution function is perfectly well defined by $p(x \leq a)$ for all a and the density (or distribution) function by the area between a and $b (b > a)$ corresponding to $p(x \leq b) - p(x \leq a)$.

A2.4 VARIANCES OF NUMBERS AND RANDOM VARIABLES

Let us begin our discussion of variance by looking at numbers, specifically the set 1, 7, 9, and 11. Their average is 7, of course, but what would be a good measure of their variability? As demonstrated earlier, the deviations about the average total zero; that is, the sum of the

---

[3]$p(x=0)=1/8$, $p(x=1)=3/8$, $p(x=2)=3/8$, $p(x=3)=1/8$; thus the expectation $=0(1/8)+1(3/8)+2(3/8)+3(1/8)=0+3/8+6/8+3/8=12/8=1½$.

negative deviations equals the sum of the positive deviations. Thus, the deviations per se cannot be used as a measure of variability. The squares of the deviations, however, are all positive. Their average is termed the *variance* of the set of numbers. That is, *the variance of a set of numbers is the average squared deviation about the mean (average)*. The variance is the standard measure of variability used in statistics. The square root of this average, termed the *standard deviation*, is another commonly used measure.

In the number set 1, 7, 9, 11, the first deviation from the average is -6, the square of which is 36; the second deviation is 0; the third is $+2$, the square of which is 4, and the last is $+4$, the square of which is 16. Hence, the sum of the squared deviations is 56 (that is, $36+0+4+16$), which yields an average squared deviation of 14. The standard deviation is the square root of 14, or 3.78.

For understanding the last part of this appendix it is important to know what happens to the variance when all the numbers in a set are multiplied by the same constant c. Briefly, the effect of this is that the previous variance is multiplied by c^2. This is true whether c is positive or negative, and whether it is greater than or less than 1 in absolute value. Thus, for example, if we measured the lengths of various boards in feet, and then decided to change our measuring scale to inches, the variance in inches would be 144 times the variance in feet.

Why c^2? First consider what happens to the mean. Since every number in the set is multiplied by the same constant c, the mean is c times as large. Now consider the deviation of each number from the mean. Because each number is multiplied by c, the deviation of each number from the mean is simply c times the original deviation. That is, if x is a particular number and $\bar{x}$ the mean of the set from which it is drawn, $cx-c\bar{x}=c(x-\bar{x})$. Squaring yields c^2 times the original deviation squared; that is, $(c(x-\bar{x}))^2=c^2(x-\bar{x})^2$. Hence, since all squared deviations are multiplied by c^2, their average also is—just as the original average was multiplied by c when all numbers were. For example let 1, 7, 9, and 11 be multiplied by -3. The new numbers are -3, -21, -27, and -33. Their average is $-21=-84/4$, which equals (-3×7). The squared deviations from -21 are 18^2, 0, -6^2, and -12^2, which when summed yield 504; $324+0+36+144$. Thus, the average is 126, which is equal to $(-3)^2\times14$.

Because the standard deviation is the square root of the variance, the standard deviation of a set of numbers multiplied by c is multiplied by the square root of c^2, which is the *absolute value* of c. For example, multiplying the standard deviation of a set of numbers by -3 yields a number 3 times as large as the standard deviation—just as if it had been multiplied by $+3$. I used a negative value of c in the example to illustrate this principle. Because c is squared, it has the same effect whether it is positive or negative; hence, the variance and standard deviation are unaffected by the sign of c. Note also, once again, that c need not be greater than one. If, for example, we were to change the measurement of some lengths from inches to feet, the variance in inches would be 1/144th as large as the variance in feet, and the standard deviation 1/12th.

The variance of a discrete random variable is determined by squaring the deviation of each value and then weighting these squared deviations by the probability of the value. That is, the variance, is the *expected squared deviation from the expectation*. Again, consider tossing a fair coin twice, and let the random variable of interest be the number of heads. The expected number of heads is 1, as demonstrated earlier. Because there will be two heads with probability 1/4, 1 with probability 1/2, and 0 with probability 1/4, the variance of this random variable is

$$1/4 \times (2-1)^2 + 1/2 \times (1-1)^2 + 1/4 \times (0-1)^2 = 1/2,$$

and hence the standard deviation is .707.

To determine the variance of *any* random variable X, begin by noting that the square of each value x of X minus the expectation of the distribution is a well-defined random variable itself (because for all a there exists a probability that $(x-\text{expectation})^2 \leq a$). Thus, the density (or for discrete variables, the distribution) function of this squared deviation is well defined. The *variance* is simply the expectation of this (new) function.

Finally, it is often important to determine the means and variances of sums of random variables. For example, the number of heads resulting from two tosses of a fair coin is equal to the sum of the number of heads resulting from the first toss plus the number of heads resulting from the second. As we have determined, the number of heads resulting from two tosses has expectation 1; the expectation of the number of heads resulting from the first toss is 1/2 and that from the second is 1/2 as well; $1=1/2+1/2$. The expectation of the sum of two random variables is *always* equal to the sum of the expectations.

What about the variance? The variance of the number of heads in two tosses is 1/2, as demonstrated earlier. The variance of each *single* toss is determined by noting that the number of heads on a single toss is equal to 1 with probability 1/2 and 0 with probability 1/2. Therefore, the variance is

$$1/2(1-1/2)^2 + 1/2(0-1/2)^2 = (1/2)(1/4) + (1/2)(1/4) = 1/4$$

Again, $1/4+1/4=1/2$. But the variances are added *only because the two tosses are independent* (as defined in Appendix A1). In fact, the variance of a sum of random variables will equal the sum of the variances *only* when the sets of values of the two random variables summed are independent. In this book, we will consider summing only independent random variables. The precise definition of independent random variables is that X and Y with values x and y are *independent* if and only if:

$$p(x \leq a \text{ and } y \leq b) = p(x \leq a)\, p(y \leq b) \text{ for all } x \text{ and } y.$$

If so, the variance of X plus Y equals the variance of X plus the variance of Y. Note that the standard deviations do *not* add, because (variance X + variance $Y)^{1/2} \neq$ (variance $X)^{1/2}$ + (variance $Y)^{1/2}$. In contrast, as pointed out earlier, the expectation of the sum equals the sum of the expectations no matter what.

A2.4 THE LAW OF LARGE NUMBERS AND THE "LAW OF SMALL NUMBERS"

The Law of Large Numbers can be illustrated with coin tosses. For example, imagine that we toss a fair coin 4, 16, 100, or 10,000 times. Now consider a distribution of the *number* of heads and a distribution of the *proportion* of heads. Both the number and the proportion are well-defined random variables.

The expected number of heads on a single toss is 1/2; $0 \times (1/2) + 1 \times (1/2)$. Therefore, because the (random variable) number of heads resulting from n coin tosses is simply that variable added to itself n times, the expected number of heads in n tosses is $n/2 = 2, 8, 50$, and 5000 for 4, 16, 100, and 10,000 tosses, respectively.

What is the variance? Because the tosses are independent, the variance is the sum of the variances, each of which is 1/4; $1/2 \times (0-1/2)^2 + 1/2 \times (1-1/2)^2$. Thus, the variances are 1, 4, 25, and 2,500, respectively, and in general, the variance of the sum of n tosses is $n/4$. *As n increases, the variances get larger.* The distribution function (which, take my word for it, has the same shape irrespective of the number of times the coin is tossed) has more "spread." It is *less* tightly centered around its expectation of $n/2$ as n increases.

Now consider the expected value of the *proportion* of heads. We do not add proportions from each toss. The expected proportion is, rather, the expected value divided by n; that is, $n/2$ divided by n. That is equal to 1/2 irrespective of n. As is intuitively compelling, the expected proportion of heads is *always* 1/2.

To determine the variance of the proportion, again we do not add— in this case—the variances. The proportion of heads is the number of heads divided by n. But dividing by n is equivalent to multiplying by $(1/n)$. We know from the previous section that multiplying a random variable by c multiplies its variance by c^2; hence, the variance of the proportion of heads is the variance of the number of heads multiplied by $(1/n)^2$. We have just seen that the variance of the number of heads is $n/4$. Therefore, the variance of the proportion of heads is $(1/n)^2(n/4) = 1/4n$: 1/16, 1/64, 1/400, and 1/40,000 for 4, 16, 100, and 10,000 tosses, respectively. *As n increases, the variances of proportions decreases.* Because the distribution function of the sum retains the same shape irrespective of the value of n, that of the proportion does also. (It is just the sum divided by n.) It is *more* centered about its expectation of 1/2 as n increases.

Intuitively, as a fair coin is tossed more often, the proportion of heads has a higher and higher probability of being close to 1/2. The *number* of heads, in contrast, has a lower and lower probability of being close to $n/2$.

Stated more precisely, the *Law of Large Numbers* implies that the probability that the actual proportion of heads falls outside any arbitrary small interval around 1/2 can be made arbitrarily small by tossing the coin enough times.

In the coin tossing example, the shape of the distribution function (of *both* the number and proportion of heads) remains constant irrespective of n; hence, the proportion of the distribution within a certain number of standard deviations of 1/2 remains constant. By making this standard deviation (which is just the square root of the variance) arbitrarily small by increasing n, we make any given interval arbitrarily small.

Figure A2.5 illustrates the results of tossing a coin 4, 16, 100, and 10,000 times. The actual number and proportion of heads is discrete, but the results are well approximated by the *normal density function* presented. (Again, to determine the probability that the value x is between points a and b just determine what proportion of that function lies between a and b.)

Does the Law of Large Numbers imply that the actual proportion of heads of an actual coin tossed an arbitrary number of times must approach 1/2? No. What it demonstrates is that *if* the coin is fair, this proportion must approach 1/2. It is the result of pure mathematical (statistical) reasoning about a hypothetical ideal—the fair coin. This ideal has the same philosophical status as the ideals of "point" and "line" in Euclidian geometry. *If* we accept Euclid's axioms, then certain consequences follow. Euclidian geometry does not imply that every time we use a precise measuring instrument to evaluate the sides of what we believe to be a right triangle we will discover that the Pythagorean formula is satisfied exactly. There are no perfect right angles in a room, there is no perfect two-dimensional plane, and even space itself is curved (although not much in a room). Mathematical results are of an if–then variety. The remarkable consequence is that these purely logical conclusions based on hypothetical ideals lead to so much knowledge of the "real" world.[4]

So the genius of James Bernoulli (1665–1705), who first discovered (derived, proved, invented) the Law of Large Numbers, was in specifying the relationship between single probabilities and aggregate probabilities; for example, between the .50 probability a fair coin lands

---

[4] At least it is remarkable to me. In my view, why mathematics is "relevant" to empirical reality is a central philosophical question that has never been adequately answered. The present positions of nominalism, modeling, and formalism fail to account for the *necessity* of mathematical results. When observations do not conform to conclusions, we reject either the observations, the premises leading to the conclusion, or the reasoning itself. We do not conclude that the premises, the reasoning, and the observations are all correct but that in this instance mathematical reasoning does not apply to the world.

Figure A2.5

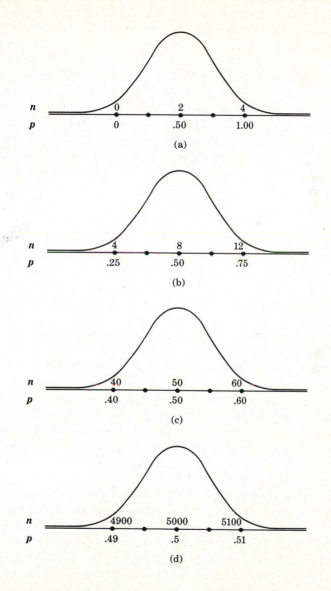

Illustration of the Law of Large Numbers with increasing *n*

heads and the probability that the proportion of heads in n tosses falls outside a given interval around .50. The Law has great applied value in statistics, because it allows us to assess aggregated probabilities in situations where it is not possible to assess single probabilities. For example, it is not possible to assess whether a coin is "fair" by tossing it once; it lands either heads or tails. Observing one single head, for example, we could conclude only that the coin does not have two tails. Now, however, suppose we toss it 100 times and observe 80 heads; that is, the proportion $P=.8$. We know from the algebraic development that if the coin is fair, the expected value of the distribution of proportion of heads is .50 and its variance is $1/400=.0025$ (standard deviation$=1/20=.05$). Thus, the observed proportion, if the coin is fair, is 6.00 $[=(.80-.50)/.05]$ standard deviations above the expected value. The shape of the coin toss distribution (approximately "normal") is one in which only 1/10,000th of one percent lies outside 6.00 standard deviations of its expectation. Observing 80 heads in 100 tosses, we might conclude that the coin was *not* fair—unless we had extraordinarily compelling reasons from other sources to believe it was.

The procedure just outlined is termed *hypothesis testing*, and it is possible as a consequence of the Law of Large Numbers, which yields decreasing variance in the distribution of proportions as a sample gets larger. We *hypothesize* something about a single event or probability (e.g., that the coin is fair). Observation of a single outcome does not allow us to evaluate the hypothesis. The Law, however, allows us to infer a subsequent hypothesis about probabilities of aggregate events. For example, if we believe the outcome of a particular election to be a "toss-up," we cannot evaluate our belief very well by polling a single voter. But by interviewing 100 or 1,000 voters we can evaluate our belief. (In fact, roughly 1,000 television watchers are polled to obtain the Neilson ratings.) This hypothesis-testing procedure is described in greater detail in Appendix A3.

It is crucially important to understand that the Law of Large Numbers applies to the proportion of heads, *not the number* of heads, in our coin tossing example. In fact, the variance of that random variable about its expectation $(n/4)$ *increases* as n gets larger.

The proportion of heads is equivalent to the average number of heads. Does the Law of Large Numbers apply to *all* averages? Yes, if the averages are based on *independent* events. Independence implies that the variance of the sum of n independently repeated experiments is n times the variance of the random variable. The average is the sum divided by n. Hence, the variance of the average is $(1/n)^2$ times the variance of the sum, which is just n times the variance. However, $(1/n)^2 n = 1/n$. Thus the variance of an average based on n independent repetitions is the variance divided by n. It is that simple. And, of course, this variance decreases as n increases.

But what about the shape of the distribution? The Russian mathematician Chebichev (sometimes anglicized *Tchebycheff*, 1821–1894) proved that *no matter what the shape of the distribution*, the probability of a random variable having a value greater than k standard deviations away from its expectation is less than $1/k^2$. He proved this result using only algebra and a simple inequality.[5] Thus, by increasing n to make the standard deviation of the average sufficiently small, the Law of Large Numbers follows.

Again, it is crucial to understand that the law does not apply to sums, but to averages. Nevertheless, people often act and talk as if it applies to sums. For example, people seem to believe that if they gamble often, their "gains and losses will average out." Not so. The variance of the *relative amount* of their wins and losses decreases, but the actual amount of money won minus lost (or vice versa) diverges, because the variance of sums increases—rather than decreases—over trials. If, for example, the gambler tosses a fair coin once for a stake of $10, the standard deviation of the outcome is $10. He or she wins or loses $10 with probability .50. The expected value is 0. The variance is

---

[5]Chebichev's proof, simplified: consider the distribution of a random variable X "standardized" so that it has an expectation of 0 and a variance, hence a standard deviation, of 1. (Any random variable may be standardized by subtracting its expectation from each value and dividing by its standard deviation.) Then the expectation of X^2 is 1 (because it is, by definition, the variance). Now define a *new* variable, X', as equal to 0 if the absolute value x of X is less than or equal to some number k, otherwise equal to k. This new variable X' is a well-defined random variable and X'^2 clearly has an expectation less than that of X^2 (because it equals 0 if the absolute value of X is less than that of k and otherwise equals k, its square is never greater than X's). Its expectation, however, is equal to the probability that the absolute value of X is greater than k multiplied by k^2, plus 0. That is, the expectation of X'^2 equals $p(|x| \geq |k|)k^2$, but this expectation is less than 1. Therefore, $p(|x \geq |k|) \leq 1/k^2$.

$1/2 \times (10-0)^2 + 1/2 \times (0-10)^2 = 100$; hence the standard deviation is \$10. Now the gambler tosses it 25 times for \$10. The expected value is still 0, but the standard deviation is \$50. And, in fact, the probability of winning or loosing as little as \$10 is only .31. It is only the *proportional* amount won or lost that decreases over time.

Daniel Kahneman and Amos Tversky refer to the belief that the Law of Large Numbers holds for inadequate n as belief in the "law of small numbers." A person who is (almost) as impressed by 8 heads out of 10 tosses as by 80 out of 100 is expressing belief in this law. (The actual probability of getting a discrepancy as great as 8 out of 10 tosses of a fair coin is .11, and the probability of 80 out of 100 is .00001.)

Kahneman and Tversky's "law" raises an interesting question: do we recognize random sequences when we see them? As pointed out in section 5.7, the answer is no. As the result of the "law of small numbers," people expect *too much* alternation from random events and consequently identify those that show the most alternation as the truly random ones (the gambler's fallacy). People tend to reject truly random sequences as having too little alternation; truly random sequences are seen as constrained. That presents a field day for hypothesizing constraints to "explain" the groupings in genuinely random sequences—particularly sequences of personal or social outcomes. Such concepts as momentum, karma, motivations, God's will, and so on, are used to account for the perceived groupings in random sequences. And, of course, if the explanation is sufficiently "slippery" that it fits a random pattern to begin with, it is unlikely that further random events will disconfirm it.[6] For example, many observers of basketball games (and players!) note the phenomenon of the "hot hand" in shooting, although Gilovich, Vallone, and Tversky have demonstrated that there is no relationship between success on successive shots; it is just that some players have higher shooting percentages than others.[7] Recall also that Russel Vaught and I showed that commercial airplane crashes (both fatal and nonfatal) between 1950 and

---

[6] Helping others to invent explanations for random patterns of events in their lives can be very lucrative.

[7] See the news item excerpt at the beginning of this appendix. Coach K. C. Jones was wise. It is not that McHale was "due," but that he was the Celtics' highest-percentage shooter, period. Moreover, a belief in the "hot hand" (or, in this case a "cold hand") on the part of the Lakers' players and coach may have made the choice of McHale a surprise.

1970 fit a distribution based on the assumption that they occurred independently of each other.[8]

Perhaps an understanding of coin tossing and the Law of Large Numbers is important to an understanding of the more important things in life—or at least an understanding of which things are not there.

[8] Again, assume that every flight has the same (tiny) probability p of ending in a fatal crash and that such crashes are independent of each other. Consider what happens after a fatal crash. The probability that the next flight is fatal is p, and the probability that it is not is $(1-p)$. Now consider the probability that the next fatal crash occurs on the *second* subsequent flight. That flight will be the next fatal one only if the first subsequent flight is *not* fatal, the probability of which is $(1-p)$, and the second flight *is* fatal (the probability of which is p). Granted the independence assumption, then these two events occur with probability $(1-p) \times p$. Note that this probability is *less* than p. In general, the probability that the first subsequent fatality occurs on the nth subsequent flight is $(1-p)^{n-1}p$. If there is *no* pattern (dependence) between flights and each results in a fatal crash with the same probability, *the most probable flight on which the next fatality occurs is the very next flight.* Of course, it is an extremely low probability, but it is still more probable that the next fatality occurs on the first subsequent flight than on the nth.

People don't understand that this conclusion follows from an assumption of total independence with unchanging probabilities (i.e., total "randomness"). As demonstrated in section 5.7, people instead believe that "randomness" implies (too much) alternation. Thus, when less alternation is discovered than expected on a psychological basis (though not a rational one), the results appear to be "bunched"; for example, "airplane accidents occur in threes."

A P P E N D I X A3

SAMPLING, SIGNIFICANCE, EFFECT SIZE, AND THE SEDUCTIVENESS OF POST HOC ANALYSIS

Isn't that remarkable. Among the five of us here there are three Leos and two Cancers, and President Jerry Ford is a Cancer, which makes three Leos and three Cancers. I bet the probability of that is almost zero. Is that the sort of thing you people could figure out?

—astrologer in a dinner-table discussion
of possible applications of statistical analysis to astrology

A3.1 POPULATIONS AND STATISTICS

The statistic with which many Americans are most familiar is the batting average. It is simply a number between 0 and 1 that summarizes the relative frequency with which a baseball player gets a hit on those occasions at bat when the player does not "walk," get hit by a pitch, or make a "sacrifice." If a hit is assigned the value 1 and an out the value 0, it is the player's average.

This *statistic* is purely a summary of past events. It is not a random variable, it does not in and of itself lead to a probability judgment about future events (e.g., whether the player will make a hit the next time at bat), and it is not part of a probability distribution or density function. It is just a number that has a very precise meaning, much like the number on the page of this book. Often, however, we wish to use such numbers to make a *probabilistic inference*.

Suppose, for example, we were interested in estimating the average weight of males over eighteen years of age in the United States. One possibility would be to weigh every such man. That would be financially and procedurally impossible—by the time we weighed the last man the weights of some of those previously assessed would have changed, and some men would have died. Instead, what we would do is *randomly sample* a set of such men. Then, we would compute the average weight in the sample—a statistic analogous to a batting average (i.e., a well-defined number based on some previous experience, in this case that of having men in our sample stand on an accurate scale). We would then make some *inference* about "United

States men in general." Before discussing how such an inference is made, we need to define a few general terms that are important in understanding it.

The set of objects, events, or observations about which we are interested in making an inference is termed a *population*. Technically, a population can be defined as *any* collection of objects, observations, or events (i.e., any old "set"), but usually there is some *defining characteristic* that describes the set. (The definition of the characteristic must be a precise one that allows us to determine whether each object, event, or observation we consider is or is not in that population; usually a verbal definition will do, but not always.)

We *sample* from the population in order to understand something about it. For example, we may sample weights, which are numbers. We can also sample characteristics that are categorical or that are simply ordered. The point is that we have *one* characteristic that defines a population and we are interested in making a statement about *another* characteristic of that population. (In the example we think of the population as consisting of "men," or alternatively as consisting of "men's weights"; it doesn't matter which.) Thus far, I have made no reference to probability or probability theory.

How do we sample? If we sampled from a professional football team or from a group of winning jockeys, we would have a perfectly legitimate sample of men, but their weights would not be a very good basis on which to estimate the average weight of the U.S. male population. Instead, we should—insofar as possible—collect a *random* sample from that population. What is meant by that is that our sample is drawn in such a way that every *sample* from the male population is equally likely to be drawn. It is not just that all males are equally likely to be drawn. For example, if we were to separate the men into those of above-median height and those of below-median height, then toss a fair coin to decide whether we would sample exclusively from the taller or the shorter group, and then sample randomly within each group, each male would have an equal probability of being chosen. That would not be a very good way of sampling, however, because if we chose a taller man we would be likely to compute an average weight that is greater than the average in the general population, while if we chose the shorter men, our computed average would be "biased low." If each sample is equally likely, each man will be, but *not* vice versa. Thus, any procedure that violates the condition that each object, event, or observation is equally likely to appear in the sample violates random sampling, but, again, not vice versa. What we do with this average is explained in the next two sections.

It should be pointed out that random sampling is defined in probabilistic terms (every sample equally likely) but that actually sampling in such a way to achieve—or approximate—this ideal is no easy matter. In the hypothetical example of weight, it would be extremely difficult for us to contact men with no home addresses or telephone numbers to insure their equal chance at being included in our sample, and such men may tend to be heavier or lighter than other men. Moreover, we have no way of coercing people once selected to agree to be weighed; perhaps obese men would be less willing to participate in the survey. (Of course we could simply *ask* these men about their weights, but then we face the problem of systematic lying; even after assurance of complete anonymity, many people do not like to reveal embarrassing things about themselves such as overweight.) Just like points, lines, and probabilities, a random sample is a *conceptual* entity.

Samples that are not random can lead to very erroneous conclusions. In 1936, for example, the *Literary Digest* poll indicated that Alfred Landon would defeat Franklin Roosevelt in the upcoming election when in fact Roosevelt won all but two states.[1] This sample was drawn from people who owned telephones or automobiles (and hence could be selected from the phone book or registry of motor vehicles). Apparently, such people tended to be wealthier than others in the voting population and hence more favorably disposed toward the Republican candidate. (Note that this is a *plausible* explanation and thus subject to the type of skepticism outlined in section 11.2.) Systematic deviations from random sampling can be even more subtle. For example, if an interviewer is instructed to select a certain house on a street by a means designed to assure random sampling and is told to select another one "at random" if no one is present at the first house, she or he may be drawn to select the most attractive house on the block—with the cumulative result that the households polled tend to be slightly more affluent than was intended by the statistician who designed the random sampling procedure. In fact, human intuition

---

[1]Gallup, George (1978). Opinion polling in a democracy. In Tanur, J. M.; Mosteller, F.; Kruskal, W.; Link, R.; Pieters, R.; Rising, G.; and Lehmann, E. (eds.). *Statistics: A Guide to the Unknown*, 2nd ed. San Francisco: Holden–Day, Inc., 187.

does not yield random samples, or even an individual "random" instance. (As was illustrated in section 5.7, people's intuition about what constitutes randomness is quite poor.) The use of such procedures as random number tables is mandatory, but even then there are severe problems with actually implementing the choice of objects, events, or observations to be studied.

A3.2 SAMPLING DISTRIBUTIONS AND SIGNIFICANCE TESTS

In classic statistical analysis, a population is assumed to have certain characteristics. For example, there is a number corresponding to the average weight of men over 18 in the United States, and a fair coin has a single probability, .50, of falling heads. Uncertainty resides in our *knowledge* of these characteristics.

The classical approach is to express the uncertainty probabilistically in terms of the distribution or density functions of particular characteristics of random samples drawn from the population. For example, we could draw a random sample of men from the United States population and compute an average of their measured weights. This average would not—in general—correspond perfectly to the mean of the population. It would be a random variable, and as a result of mathematical developments in the theory of statistics, we can characterize this variable. For example, if we toss the fair coin 10 times, we observe a certain proportion of heads. In general, it will not be exactly .50 (in fact, the probability that it is exactly .50 given that we are sampling from a population with a value .50 is only .25). We can, however, specify what the distribution of sampled proportions should look like—given the assumption that the coin is fair. In other words, the classic procedure is to *hypothesize* the characteristics of the population we are sampling from and then mathematically *derive* what is termed a *sampling distribution* of the corresponding *statistics* that will result from random sampling. This step is purely mathematical. It does not tell us whether our assumptions about the characteristics of the population are correct; nor does it in itself yield a method for making inferences about the population—which is our ultimate goal. For example, what we want is to be able to say something about the average weight of the U.S. male population or to make some statement of the fairness of the coin we toss. At this point, all we know is that granted certain assumptions about the population from which we are sampling, the corresponding characteristics in our samples constitute random variables.

Suppose, for example, that we are going to toss a coin we hypothesize to be "fair" 10 times. What are the probabilities of obtaining actual proportions of 0, .1, .2, . . ., .9, and 1.0 heads? The answer can be worked out using the principles presented in Appendix A2. If the coin is truly fair (which entails assuming that all tosses fall heads with probability .50 and are independent of each other), then the probability of obtaining no heads is equal to $1/2^{10}=1/1024$. The probability of obtaining exactly 1 head (for a proportion of .1) can be obtained by first considering the probability of obtaining any *particular* pattern of 1 head and 9 tails; that is again just 1/2 multiplied by itself 10 times. Because there are 10 places in which the single head could occur, there are 10 such patterns consisting of the event 1 head and 9 tails; therefore, the probability is 10/1024. And so on. By simple arithmetic, we can obtain the sampling distribution of the proportion of heads. Note that this *proportion* is the random variable; the assumed probability of .5 of the coin's landing heads—the definition of a fair coin—is an assertion (*hypothesis*) about the population from which we are sampling.

Now suppose that we actually toss the coin and observe 9 tails. How can we use this information to make some inference about the population? Our inference is based on observing where in the sampling distribution our actual observation occurs. It is the next to the most extreme point. The probability of observing it is 10/1024, while that of observing the most extreme event is 1/1024. We note that *if* our hypothesis about the population is correct, then the probability of observing something as extreme as what we obtained is only 11/1024. Our observation might make us suspicious of our assertion about the population.

The procedure just described is termed *hypothesis testing*. We hypothesize something about a population, randomly sample from it, and then decide our hypothesis is incorrect if the characteristic we sample falls in the extreme of the sampling distribution of the statistic we are evaluating. That is a very convoluted procedure for "drawing conclusions about populations from samples."[2]

For starters, how do we determine the part of the sampling distribution in which our computed statistic must fall in order for us to *reject*

---

[2]Paul Hoel's definition of *statistical inference*, which appears on page 1 of his book *Elementary Statistics*, 2nd ed. New York: Wiley, 1960, 1966.

the hypothesis that we are sampling from the specified population (technically, the *null hypothesis*)? Falling in any particular 5% or 2% is as improbable an outcome as is falling in any other particular 5% or 2%. Generally, we are interested only in values that deviate from those we would expect on the basis of our hypothesis (or hypotheses) about the population we are sampling; consequently we reject a null hypothesis if we obtain a statistic in the *tails* of the sampling distribution. If we were to operate strictly according to the procedures of the classical theory, we would specify the region in the tails that would lead us to reject the null hypothesis before we collect our sample and compute the relevant statistic; such a region is termed a *rejection region*; the proportion of the sampling distribution in this area is termed the *significance level* of a result. For example, observing 9 tails in 10 tosses of a coin hypothesized to be fair leaves us to reject the null hypothesis at the 11/1024th level of significance. (In general, certain conventions are used—so that we speak of significance as being at the .05, .01, or .001 level.)

Or should we have considered that we would also reject the null hypothesis if we had observed 9 *heads* in 10 tosses? If we had been prepared to do that, then we should also consider the possibility that our proportion of heads falls in the other tail of the sampling distribution (majority of heads). Had we been prepared to reject the null hypothesis in that case as well, our rejection region would have consisted of 2 times (11/1024)th the sampling distribution, or approximately .02 rather than .01. Whether we should use this *2-tailed test* as opposed to the *1-tailed test* described earlier is a matter of our *decision* about how to do the statistical analysis. The observation—the number of heads and tails in 10 tosses—is unaffected by that, but as will be explained in section A3.5, how we view an observation depends upon how we have decided to collect and analyze our data.[3]

Where does all this convoluted logic lead? To the rejection of a very precise hypothesis about a population value. That's all. For example, the statement that there is "overwhelming scientific evidence that a particular chemical is associated with the development of cancer in rats" might mean simply that we can reject the null hypothesis "the

---

[3] For years, there was a "heated controversy" in the psychological literature about whether people "should" use 1-tailed or 2-tailed tests; in my opinion, the roots of the controversy lay in the ease with which one could publish an opinion about this issue—without having to engage in empirical or mathematical work. The issue will not be discussed here.

population of rats given the drug have the same incidence of cancer as the population of rats not given the drug" at a very extreme level of significance. That conclusion may be based on sampling a number of rats given the chemical and a number of rats not given the chemical. The *sampling distribution of the differences* in the cancer rates is then worked out on the assumption that the mean difference in the populations sampled is 0; then, a difference in the proportions in the extreme tail of the sampling distribution is observed. (As will be emphasized in section A3.3, the size of the sample has a great deal to do with the significance of the result.) The statistically defined "significance level" of the effect *in and of itself* does not imply anything about its magnitude.

The sampling distribution was easy to specify in the case of tosses of a fair coin. There are mathematical techniques for specifying the sampling distribution in other situations as well. The most commonly used technique relies on a variant of the *central limit theorem*, which was first proved in 1733 by De Moivre (1667–1754). It states, briefly, that if we are sampling from a distribution with a known mean and variance, then as our sample becomes large, the mean of the sampling distribution of sample means is normally distributed with a mean equal to the population mean and a variance equal to the population variance divided by the sample size. That is, if the mean of the population equals μ and its variance equals σ^2, then the sampling distribution of the mean $\overline{X}$ approximates a normal distribution with mean equal to μ and variance equal to σ^2/n. Such normal distributions were illustrated in Appendix A2; specifying the function that describes them is beyond the scope of this book, and the proof of the Central Limit Theorem is far beyond the scope. The reader unfamiliar with this concept may consult any standard introductory statistics text to see why the sampling distribution of sample means becomes "more normal" with increasing sample size.

How can we apply this result to our example of tossing a coin 10 times? We know that if the coin is fair it has a probability of .5 of landing heads, and we know moreover that the variance is 1/4 (see Appendix A2). Therefore, the mean of the sampling distribution of proportion of heads based on 10 tosses is likewise 1/2, and its variance is 1/40. The standard deviation is therefore .158. A result of 90% tails is therefore $(.1-.5)/.158 = -2.52$ standard deviations away from the mean of the sampling distribution. Actually, we should compute this ratio on the basis of 85%, because .9 is in the middle of the interval .85 to .95, and tossing the coin 10 times, we cannot obtain any result that is not a multiple of .1. Therefore, the number of standard deviations away from the mean is -2.21. The proportion of the normal curve that lies beyond 2.21 standard deviations is .03; therefore, we would conclude that our results are significant at the .03 level.

Actually, the sample of size 10 is not large enough to invoke the Central Limit Theorem; what I have done is use another result that indicates that the normal distribution is a good approximation to the coin tossing one even when the sample sizes are not very large. I use the simple numbers for illustrative purposes. In fact, few researchers and analysts would invoke the Central Limit Theorem without a sample size of at least 30.

There is one additional use for the sampling distribution. Its mean is the best single ("point") estimate of the mean of the population from which we are sampling, and its variance is a slightly biased (low) estimate of the variance in that population. (In fact, the "best"—in several senses—estimate of the population variance is $n/(n-1)$ times the variance in the sample.)

A3.3 SIGNIFICANCE VERSUS EFFECT SIZE

Now suppose we have a coin that we believe is biased to fall heads. We sample an adequate number of tosses to reject the null hypothesis that the probability is .50. What would be a good measure of the *degree* to which the coin is biased?

First, we know from the preceding section that the actual proportion of heads is a good estimate of the coin's bias. But how different is that from .50? If P is the proportion of heads observed, $P-.50$ equals the difference between it and the .50 value hypothesized. But most answers concern the *degree* of bias, not the amount. In many contexts, the actual difference has no meaning unless it is assessed relative to some standard. For example, a difference of 2 implies something quite different if we are talking about centimeters, inches, or feet. While in the coin tossing example $P-.50$ might seem a quite adequate measure of difference, what we need is a general measure.

The usual way of evaluating difference is relating it to the standard deviation of the distribution of the hypothesized population. In this example, we would divide $P-.50$ by the standard deviation of the probability that an unbiased coin lands heads. As demonstrated in Appendix A2, this is just .25. Thus, a standard measure of the degree to which our particular coin differs from a fair one is $(P-.50)/.25$, or

4(P − .25). Dividing by the standard deviation yields a *relative* measure that can be compared across contexts. We simply assert that a particular sample mean is so many standard deviations above or below the hypothesized population mean.[4] (Remember that a proportion is a mean of 0's and 1's.) For example, psychologists who evaluate psychotherapy treatments that use different measures of outcome effectiveness estimate the mean and standard deviation on a measure of some particular distress of (randomly selected) people who have not received the therapy (control group) and assess the mean score of the people who (again, randomly chosen) have received the therapy. They then determine how many standard deviations above the control-group mean the experimental-group mean is. That number of standard deviations is the "effect size." For example, Janet Landman and I reanalyzed data comparing randomly chosen groups of people who received psychotherapy with groups who were randomly denied it.[5,6,7] The average effect size in psychotherapy experiments we studied was about .68.

[4] The reader who perceives a logical contradiction between first rejecting the hypothesis that we are sampling from a population and then defining "effect size" relative to a characteristic of this population is, indeed, being perceptive. The contradiction exists.

[5] Landman, J. T., and Dawes, R. M. (1981). Psychotherapy outcome: Smith and Glass's conclusions stand up under scrutiny. *American Psychologist*, *37*, 117–133.

[6] Smith, M. L., and Glass, G. V. (1977; *American Psychologist*, *32*, 752–760) had previously analyzed a larger set of data in which a third of the studies did not involve true random assignment.

[7] The subjects in both the therapy group and the control group were given tests at the end of the therapy to assess how well they were coping with the problems about which they had indicated a willingness to enter therapy. The average effect size was .68. *Assuming* that the test scores are normally distributed, this effect size can be translated into a statement that a person at the 50th percentile in the therapy group would have been at the 75th percentile (of coping with the problem) in the control group. A different interpretation is that if a person was chosen at random from the therapy group and compared to a randomly chosen person from the control group, the odds are 2–1 that the person in therapy would have had a higher score. It must be remembered, however, that all these numbers refer to scores on behavioral measures or questionnaires designed by the investigators; it cannot necessarily be inferred that as a result of psychotherapy people are happier or "healthier"—and certainly not that they are necessarily better people as a result of it.

How does this statistic of relative magnitude relate to statistics used to assess significance? The latter are typically based on the sampling distribution *of sample means*. The standard deviation of *this* distribution, however, is not that of the population sampled but, rather, this standard deviation divided by the square root of the sample size. That is, as demonstrated in Appendix A2, the variance of means is equal to the variance divided by n. (To recapitulate: the variance of the sum of independent observations is equal to the sum of the variances. Given that we are sampling from the same distribution, all these variances are equal; hence the variance of the sum is n times the variance. An average, however, is $1/n$ times the sum. Therefore, the variance of the average is $(1/n)^2$ times n times the variance, or the variance divided by n.) It follows that the statistics used to evaluate significance are—and I'm speaking "loosely" here—based on standard deviations that are reduced by a factor of $\sqrt{n}$; hence, they augment the effect size by that same factor.

We can be more specific. Suppose that we wish to test whether the mean of a particular population is μ and that we're willing to assume that the standard deviation of that population is σ. We obtain a random sample of 64 observations from the population and compute the mean $\overline{X}$ of the numbers obtained. The standard deviation of the sampling distribution of sample means is equal to $\sigma/\sqrt{n}$. By making use of the Central Limit Theorem, we can consult a table that presents the area in the normal density function beyond that number of standard deviations to determine our "significance level." Our estimate of the effect size, however, is $(\overline{X}-\mu)/\sigma$, not $((\overline{X}-\mu)/\sigma)/(\sqrt{n})$. The statistic used to assess the statistical significance is therefore *larger* than the statistic used to assess effect size by a factor precisely equal to $\sqrt{n}$.

What does all this pure statistics imply for making decisions? It implies that there is a very important relationship between the magnitude of an effect, its significance, and the size of the sample used to establish its existence (i.e., to "reject the null hypothesis"). Effects estimated as being quite small can in fact be highly significant if the sample size is large enough. A result that seems "true beyond any reasonable doubt" can be trivial if it is based on a large sample. Conversely, effects established on the basis of quite small samples can be very important. In order to assess claims that are made in newspapers and other media about effects of drugs, therapies, life styles, and so on, it is necessary to consider the size of the samples on which the claims are based.

Not all conclusions about statistic significance make use of the normal curve, but the general relationship of the square-root magnitude of sample size, effect, and significance still holds. Again, this assertion is not precise, but it is at least approximately correct in the context of the most common tests of significance. To say that something has been proved with great confidence is quite different from asserting that it is a large effect; the mediating variable is sample size.

Occasionally, effect sizes are presented in ways other than differences between means divided by standard deviations. There is no general principle for evaluating such presentations, but it is important to keep in mind exactly what it is that is presented. For example, the studies reviewed in the 1961 Surgeon General's report on smoking and health presented effect sizes in terms of "mortality ratios," the proportion of men with certain characteristics who were heavy cigarette smokers that died in a given period divided by the proportion of men with the same characteristics who did not smoke and died in the same period.[8] A typical ratio compares "age-adjusted" death rates of men with "short-lived parents and grandparents." The age-adjusted death rates per 1,000 are 44.8 for smokers and 21.1 for nonsmokers. The ratio is, therefore, 2.12; 44.8 ÷ 21.1.

The tobacco industry missed a good bet there. When 21.1 die, 978.9 live; when 44.8 die, 955.2 live. The *survival* ratio of smokers to nonsmokers is therefore 955.2/978.9, or .98. Thus, even though the smokers are twice as likely to die, they are 98% as likely to live.

In general, the *simpler* an evaluation of effect size is, the more easily it is interpreted. In the present example, the best would be simply a presentation of the distribution of age at death of smokers compared to the distribution of age at death of nonsmokers. Given such a presentation, it would be possible to compute differences, ratios, and even ratios of ratios as desired. It is not, however, possible to move from such *derived* statistics to simpler ones.

A3.4 AN ALTERNATIVE METHOD OF STATISTICAL INFERENCE: BAYESIAN INFERENCE

Many statisticians and people who must base inferences on statistical analysis are dissatisfied with the classical analysis. This dissatisfaction arises because the very precise information yielded by classical

[8]*Smoking and Health: Report of the Advisory Committee to the Surgeon General of the Public Health Service.* Public Health Service Publication No. 1103 (1964).

analysis is not of the type that those people desire. For example, significance testing does not lead to a probabilistic inference about what *is*—that is, the characteristics of the population sample in which the researcher or decision maker is interested. Rather, hypotheses about what the population *is not* are generated, and then *rejected* by the tests. The null hypotheses tested are that there is "no effect"—for example, that the weights of this particular type of men do not differ from those of the general population, the coin is not biased, the salaries of males and females in a particular position are not different, cigarette smoking has no effect on longevity, and so on. Such hypotheses are rejected. It is tempting to characterize the conclusions of significance testing as "there is not nothing." But even that would be an overstatement. A more accurate characterization would be "if there is nothing, I sampled an unusual amount of it." For many of us, that's not a very satisfactory conclusion for our efforts. Whether we are doing research ourselves or evaluating the research of others in order to make some personal life decision—perhaps about smoking or taking a particular drug—most of us would prefer to have something more.

Estimating means and effect sizes yields somewhat more information. In fact, many casual readers of statistical findings believe the mean of a sample is *identical* to the mean of the population from which it is drawn. Interpretations of effect sizes—as illustrated in the example comparing mortality ratios with survival ratios—are often more ambiguous. Sometimes, however, means and effect sizes can provide valuable information to the decision maker.

Bayesian inference is an alternative to statistical inference. To understand what it is, consider a statement made at the beginning of section A3.2 that a population has whatever characteristics it happens to have, and that the uncertainty in a situation resides in our knowledge of these population characteristics. Classical statistical analysis uses a convoluted method for reducing this uncertainty. Bayesian analysis, in contrast, deals with the uncertainty directly by making reference not to the population itself but to our *beliefs* about the population. These beliefs can certainly be characterized by probability distributions and density functions. For example, while there is truly a mean of the weight of adult men in the U.S. population, which consists of a single point, our belief about this weight can legitimately be considered a random variable. What we then do is collect data in order to modify our belief—that is, to change the shape of the random variable. In the example concerning weight, we would certainly hope that as a result of the data collected, the variance of this variable would be decreased. We would then have less uncertainty about the average weight.

The details of Bayesian analyses are far beyond the scope of this book. What I will do instead of attempting to present them is to discuss a very simplified example, in order to demonstrate some of the reasoning involved. I will then "wave my hand" at a variety of problems. The reader should not infer, however, that Bayesian analysis is in any sense vague. There are no steps in which a Bayesian analyst simply "waves a hand."

Let us suppose that we have two bookbags containing black and red poker chips. Bookbag A contains 70% red poker chips, while bookbag B contains 40% red poker chips. Someone rolls a die. If it comes up 1 or 2, he hands us bookbag B; otherwise he hands us bookbag A. We are allowed to sample 10 poker chips from the bag presented. After each observation, we are required to replace the poker chip before drawing again. We are not, however, allowed to observe the outcome of the roll of the die. Our task is to make a probabilistic inference about which bag we are sampling from.

Suppose that we draw 6 black chips and 4 red ones. That would certainly be more "representative" of bag B than of bag A, but on the other hand, we know that as the result of the roll of the die, it is twice as likely that we have been handed bag A. How can we combine the *evidence* from our sample with our *prior belief* based on the roll of the die?

One way is to use the *Bayes theorem*, a one-step inference from the fourth principle of probability theory attributed to the Reverend Thomas Bayes (d. 1761). Let d stand for the data we have collected—6 blacks and 4 reds. Let A and B refer to the two bags. It is easy enough to determine the conditional probability of the data given that we are sampling from either bag A or bag B. We can then infer the conditional probability that we are sampling from one of the bags *given* the data if we know both the probability we are sampling from that bag at the outset (which we do) and the probability of obtaining the data, which can be computed. Specifically,

$$p(\text{A and } d) = p(d \text{ and A}) \qquad \textbf{(A3.1)}$$

From the fourth principle of probability, we can infer

$$p(\text{A}|d)p(d) = p(d|\text{A})p(\text{A}), \text{ or} \qquad \textbf{(A3.2)}$$

$$p(\mathrm{A}|d) = \frac{p(d|\mathrm{A})p(\mathrm{A})}{p(d)} \qquad \textbf{(A3.3)}$$

Actually, it is simpler to use the ratio rule presented in section 5.3. To recapitulate in this context:

$$\frac{p(\mathrm{A}|d)}{p(d|\mathrm{A})} = \frac{p(\mathrm{A})}{p(d)} \qquad \textbf{(A3.4)}$$

Similarly,

$$\frac{p(\mathrm{B}|d)}{p(d|\mathrm{B})} = \frac{p(\mathrm{B})}{p(d)} \qquad \textbf{(A3.5)}$$

Dividing, we obtain

$$\frac{p(\mathrm{A}|d)}{p(\mathrm{B}|d)} = \frac{p(\mathrm{A})p(d|\mathrm{A})}{p(\mathrm{B})p(d|\mathrm{B})} \qquad \textbf{(A3.6)}$$

As a result of dividing (A3.4) by (A3.5), we eliminated the troublesome term $p(d)$; our result is the ratio of $p(\mathrm{A}|d)$ divided by $p(\mathrm{B}|d)$. Knowing this ratio and that the sum of the two probabilities must equal 1 (we are sampling from just one bag, so, by Principle III, the probabilities sum to 1), we can easily compute both.

In the example, $p(\mathrm{A})=2/3$, and the probability of obtaining the sample of 6 blacks and 4 reds *in the particular order we drew them* is simply $.3^6 \times .7^4$. Similarly $p(\mathrm{B})=1/3$ and the probability of getting the sample in that same order given we are drawing from bag B is $.6^6 \times .4^4$. Thus $p(\mathrm{A}|d)$ divided by $p(\mathrm{B}|d)=.0001167/.0003981$, or .29. Hence, the probability we are drawing from bag A is .22, and from bag B, .78. Note that the evidence in this hypothetical experiment has strongly outweighed the prior odds of 2–1 that we were drawing chips from bag A.

In general, Bayesian analysis consists of specifying *prior beliefs*, by which we mean beliefs that exist prior to the time we sample. In the example, the roll of the die leads to such prior beliefs. Evidence sampled is then amalgamated with prior beliefs according to *Bayes theorem* (equation A3.3), and they are modified by the rules of probability theory. In the men's weights example, our prior beliefs about the mean would be represented not by a single point, but rather by a density function, which would then be modified by the mean weight of a sample.

A3.5 THE POST HOC ANALYSIS OF COINCIDENCE

My older daughter was born on the same day of the year that my mother died, and my younger daughter was born on the same day of the year that my mother was born. What a remarkable coincidence! A totally naive analyst might conclude that the probability of that was $(1/365)^2$, or .0000075. But, of course, the coincidence could have been reversed, and it would be equally remarkable—so perhaps a more appropriate figure is .000015. And, of course, they both could have been born on the same day of the year my mother was, or both born on the same day of the year she died, so perhaps that figure should be doubled to yield .00003. Then again, my older daughter has visual artistic talent and my younger one writes short stories—and their birthdays could, of course, be the same as those of well-known persons in those respective fields. And then there are the birthdays of people we all admire such as George Washington, Abraham Lincoln, Grover Cleveland, Jack Kennedy—not to mention Omar Khayam, Mahatma Ghandi, Bertrand Russell, and whoever it was that wrote Ecclesiastes. The point is that I could go on and on; although *in retrospect* a *particular* coincidence—such as common birthdays—may appear to be very "improbable," it is very highly probable that some—in fact, many—coincidences will occur.

To understand this principle, consider the probability of death. We will make the simplifying assumption that it is equally probable each day. Then, given a life expectancy of 70 years (25,568 days), the probability of dying on *any* particular day is .00004 (take my word for it), but the probability of dying on *some* particular day is 1.00. Or consider another example. Let us select totally at random a number between 1 and 10,000; the probability that any particular number is chosen is .0001; yet the probability that *some* number is chosen is, again, 1.00. Interestingly, some philosophers in the eighteenth century, when probability theory was being developed, equated a probability of .9999 with a "moral certainty." In the death example, that would imply that it is morally certain that we will live through the next day. (Therefore don't buy insurance? Or, at least, don't buy it on any particular day?)

These first two paragraphs of this section are meant to illustrate an important principle: although the probability that a particular event will occur may be close to 0, *the probability that nothing at all will happen is exactly 0.*

How do we decide, therefore, whether a coincidence is "really" evidence of ESP? Or whether the finding in a particular study of helping behavior in a subway that tall people are more helpful than short people indicates that there is a correlation between height and altruism? Or whether the fact that between 1900 and 1968, inclusive, the taller candidate won the presidency indicates an American voter preference for taller men?[9]

The answer to such questions is not easy, but a simplified example might help. Consider, again, drawing a number at random from the numbers 1 through 10,000. If a friend who claims to have ESP tells me in advance that I will sample the number 973 and I do, I am impressed. If, on the other hand, he or she asks me to draw a number and then explains its extrasensory significance *after* I have announced it is 973, I'm not the least bit impressed. Now it's the same number. My awe or lack of it, however, is determined by the procedures leading to the claim that 973 has some special significance—specifically the decision-making procedures employed by my friend, and consequently by me. By announcing the number in advance, he or she would have led me to consider *only* the number 973 as a "success." I can specify that decision prior to drawing the number. When the significance is explained to me after the number is drawn, however, I am forced to decide what credence to give this "significance" subsequent to my observation— and I am sufficiently leery of my friend to realize that there are a great many such numbers to which he or she could ascribe some "significance." This principle is illustrated in Figure A3.1. The figure presents sixteen patterns of heads and tails that can result from six tosses of a coin to which some significance could be ascribed post hoc (all heads, all tails, alternation, alternation by pairs, mirror images, etc.). Once a coin has been tossed six times (or six coins at one time), however, the probability of *one* of these uniquely interesting patterns occurring is not 1/64, but rather 16/64.

Do people make such post hoc judgments? And do people believe such patterns are "significant" not only in the everyday sense of that word but in the technical, statistical sense as well? Yes. One example is the astrologer's quote at the beginning of this appendix. It is the "optional ending point" procedure described in detail by statistician

[9]The figures published by the two campaign staffs in 1972 indicated that Richard Nixon and George McGovern were of exactly the same height; the press corps did not concur.

Figure A3.1

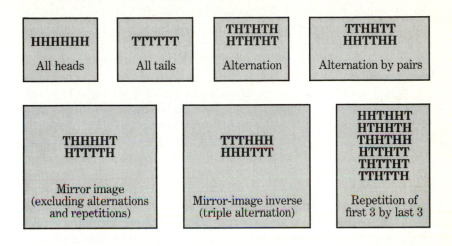

Sixteen apparent patterns that can occur in six random tosses of a coin

Persi Diaconis.[10] This technique, used by many "psychics," involves keeping the naive observer "in the dark" about exactly what is to be accomplished until it is "done." For example, the psychic B. D., whom Diaconis analyzed in some detail, would ask a volunteer to name two cards and then ask two other volunteers to pick small numbers "at random." He would then place two shuffled decks of cards on a table and start turning over the cards in each deck one by one until he reached the larger of the two numbers selected. Of course, if the two cards named happened to appear before he turned over the larger of the two numbers, it was a "successful demonstration." If both cards appeared simultaneously, it was *clearly* a success. If one of the cards named appeared with the larger number, the demonstration was considered a success, also. If nothing "unusual" happened, then the cards of one deck were turned over one by one until the smaller of the two numbers selected was reached. By that time, all sorts of outcomes could have occurred. And so on, and so on. The "optional stopping"

[10]Diaconis, P. (1978). Statistical problems in ESP research, *Science, 201*, 131–136.

trick is not to tell people in advance how you will manifest your "psychic" powers. The probability of a coincidence then becomes remarkably large. It helps also to proclaim, as the psychic Uri Geller does, that your powers "come and go" for reasons that are inexplicable to you. Then, not finding some striking coincidence in a number of attempts—or even in half of your attempts—is readily understood by the observers.

Would "scientists" engage in such nonsense? Yes. A recent president of the American Psychological Association gave as his presidential address a talk on "torque and schizophrenic viability." In it, he presented some absolutely striking data. Of 52 children who had seen him ten years earlier who drew circles clockwise, 11 were later diagnosed as schizophrenic; of the 54 who drew circles counterclockwise, only 1 had been diagnosed schizophrenic. This relationship reached the ".01 level of statistical significance." He related his finding to the fact that "the world turns in a counterclockwise direction with respect to the north–south axis" and that "with some exceptions, this 'left-turning' is characteristic of living cells."

Certainly, a finding of this magnitude—particularly when it related to fundamental properties of the earth and of the very unit of life—should have set the psychological world on its ear. At the least, it might have contributed to our understanding of schizophrenia, which is one of the two mental health problems in this country (along with depression). Figure A3.2 illustrates the number of times the article reporting this research was referenced in the *Social Science Citation Index* in the subsequent eight years.

Why so few citations? Perhaps the researcher will be neglected for fifty years only to be rediscovered as the founder of a modern theory of schizophrenia? I think that a more likely explanation is found in part of his talk: "Subjects for this study were 155 children first seen for psychological evaluation at my private psychological clinic." Children seen for such evaluations are given many tests, each of which can be evaluated on a multiplicity of variables. The researcher reported his findings on only one of these in his presidential address. My educated guess is that that was one out of approximately 200 that he could have easily related to later diagnoses of schizophrenia. (It is important to what follows to note that this guess is based on my knowledge of clinical practice, not on the plausibility that he looked at many. But imagine a scenario in which a child enters a psychologist's office, is asked to draw a circle, and is then told to go away.)

Figure A3.2

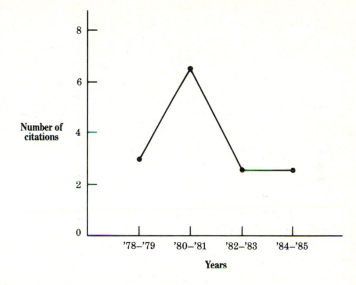

Average yearly citations of "torque" article, 1978–1985

How does one evaluate whether one of these very unusual findings *might* be important? The answer, of course, is to determine whether it can be repeated (replicated). Attempts to replicate such unusual findings in the fields of psychology and other social sciences have had a dismal history.

If we look hard enough we're bound to "find" something, because the probability that exactly nothing will happen is indeed exactly zero. Both classical and Bayesian analyses are addressed to questions asked beforehand. In evaluating research findings in order to reach rational decisions it is crucial to determine whether they were hypothesized in advance or simply picked out post hoc—from the "booming, buzzing experience" of the person proporting to have discovered them.

BIBLIOGRAPHY

Arkes, H. R., and Blumer, C. (1985). The psychology of sunk cost. *Organizational Behavior and Human Performance*, *35*, 129–140.

Arkes, H. R., and Hammond, K. R. (eds.) (1986). *Judgment and Decision Making: An Interdisciplinary Reader*. New York: Cambridge University Press.

Axelrod, R. (1984). *The Evolution of Cooperation*. New York: Basic Books.

Bartlett, F. C. (1958). *Thinking: An Experimental and Social Study*. New York: Basic Books.

Bar-Hillel, M., and Ben-Shakhar, G. (1986). The a priori case against graphology: Methodological and conceptual issues. In Nevo, B. (ed.). *Scientific Aspects of Graphology*. Springfield, Ill.: Charles C. Thomas Press, 263–279.

Ben-Shakhar, G.; Bar-Hillel, M.; Bilu, Y.; Ben Abba, E.; and Flouga, A. (1986). Can graphology predict occupational success? *Journal of Applied Psychology*, 645–653.

Brickman, P., and Campbell, D. T. (1971). Hedonic relativism and the good society. In Appley, M. H. (ed.). *Adaptation-Level Theory: A Symposium*. New York: Academic Press.

Coombs, C. H., and Avrunin, G. S. (1977). Single-peaked functions and the theory of preference. *Psychological Review*, *84*, 216–230.

Cyert, R. M., and March, J. G. (1963). *A Behavioral Theory of the Firm*. Englewood Cliffs, N. J.: Prentice-Hall.

David, Florence N. (1962). *Games, Gods, and Gambling*. London: Charles Griffin, chapter 4.

Dawes, R. M. (1976). Shallow psychology. In Carroll, J., and Payne, J. (eds.). *Cognition and Social Behavior*. Hillsdale, N. J.: L. Erlbaum Associates.

——— (1979). The robust beauty of improper linear models. *American Psychologist*, *34*, 571–582.

Diaconis, P. (1978). Statistical problems in ESP research, *Science*, *201*, 131–136.

Edwards, W. (1954). The theory of decision making. *Psychological Bulletin*, *51*, 380–417.

Einhorn, H. J. (1972). Expert measurement and mechanical combination. *Organizational Behavior and Human Performance*, *13*, 171–192.

Einhorn, H. J., and Hogarth, R. M. (1978). Confidence in judgment: Persistence of the illusion of validity. *Psychological Review*, *85*, 395–416.

Fischhoff, B. (1980). For those condemned to study the past: Reflections on historical judgment. In Schweder, R. A., and Fiske, D. W. (eds.). *New Directions for Methodology of Behavioral Science: Fallible Judgments in Behavioral Research.* San Francisco: Jossey–Bass, 79–93.

Furby, L. (1973). Interpreting regression toward the mean in developmental research. *Developmental Psychology, 8*, 172–179.

Gilovich, T.; Vallone, R.; and Tversky, A. (1985). The hot hand in basketball: On the misperception of random sequences. *Cognitive Psychology, 17*, 295–314.

Grether, D. M., and Plott, C. R. (1979). Economic theory of choice and the preference reversal phenomenon. *American Economic Review, 69*, 623–638.

Hammond, K. R., and Adelman, L. (1976). Science, values, and human judgment. *Science, 194*, 389–396.

Hardin, G. R. (1968). The tragedy of the commons. *Science, 162*, 1243–1248.

Inhelder, B., and Piaget, J. (1958). *The Growth of Logical Thinking from Childhood to Adolescence.* New York: Basic Books.

Janis, I. (1972). *Victims of Groupthink.* Boston: Houghton Mifflin.

Jones, E. E., and Nisbett, R. E. (1972). The actor and the observer: Divergent perceptions of the causes of behavior. In Jones, E. E.; Kanouse, D. E.; Kelley, H. H.; Nisbett, R. E.; Valins, S.; and Weiner, B. (eds.). *Attribution: Perceiving the Causes of Behavior.* Morristown, N. J.: General Learning Press.

Kahneman, D., and Tversky, A. (1979). Prospect theory: An analysis of decision under risk. *Econometrica, 47*, 263–291.

Kahneman, D.; Slovic, P.; and Tversky, A. (eds.) (1982). *Judgments under Uncertainty: Heuristics and Biases.* Cambridge, England: Cambridge University Press.

Lerner, M. J. (1980). *The Belief in a Just World: A Fundamental Delusion.* New York: Plenum Press.

Luce, R. D., and Raiffa, H. (1957). *Games and Decisions.* New York: Wiley.

March, J. C. (1972). Model bias in social action. *Review of Educational Research, 42*, 413–429.

McKean, K. (1985). Decisions, decisions. *Discover,* June, 22–31.

Meehl, P. E. (1954). *Clinical versus Statistical Predictions: A Theoretical Analysis and Review of the Evidence.* Minneapolis: University of Minnesota Press.

————— (1986). Causes and effects of my disturbing little book. *Journal of Personality Assessment, 50*, 370–375.

Nisbett, R., and Ross, L. (1980). *Human Inference: Strategies and Shortcomings of Human Judgment*. Englewood Cliffs, N. J.: Prentice-Hall.

Orbell, J. M.; van de Kragt, A. J. C.; and Dawes, R. M. (in press). Explaining discussion-induced cooperation. *Journal of Personality and Social Psychology*.

Posner, M. I. (1973). *Cognition: An Introduction*. Glenview, Ill.: Scott, Foresman.

Rapoport, A., and Chammah, A. (1965). *Prisoner's Dilemma*. Ann Arbor: University of Michigan Press.

Savage, L. J. (1954). *The Foundations of Statistics*. New York: Wiley.

Simon, H. A. (1979). Rational decision making in business organizations. *American Economic Review, 69*, 493–513.

————— (1985). Human nature in politics: The dialogue of psychology with political science. *American Political Science Review, 79*, 293–304.

Slovic, P.; Fischhoff, B.; and Lichtenstein, S. (1982). Responsibility, framing, and information-processing effects in risk assessment. In Hogarth, R. (ed.). *New Directions for Methodology of Social and Behavioral Science: Question Framing and Response Consistency*, No. 11. San Francisco: Jossey–Bass.

Staw, B. M. (1982). Counterforces to change. In Goodman, P. S. (ed.). *Change in Organizations*. San Francisco: Jossey–Bass, 87–121.

Stech, F. (1979). Political and military intention estimation: A taxonometric analysis. Report prepared for the Office of Naval Research under the auspices of Mathtech, Inc., Bethesda, Maryland.

Thaler, R. (1985). Mental accounting and consumer choice. *Marketing Science, 4*, 199–214.

Tversky, A., and Kahneman, D. (1974). Judgment under uncertainty: Heuristics and biases. *Science, 185*, 1124–1131.

————— (1983). Extensional versus intuitive reasoning: The conjunction fallacy in probability judgment. *Psychological Bulletin, 90*, 293–315.

————— (1986). Rational choice and the framing of decision. The *Journal of Business, 59*, part 2, S251–S278.

Tversky, A.; Sattath, S.; and Slovic, P. (in press). Contingent weighting in judgment and choice. *Psychological Review*.

van de Kragt, A. J. C.; Dawes, R. M.; Orbell, J. M.; Braver, S. R.; and Wilson, L. A., II (1986). Doing well versus doing good as ways of resolving social dilemmas. In Wilke, H. A. M.; Messick, D. M.; and Rutte, C. G. *Experimental Social Dilemmas*. Frankfurt and New York: Peter Lang, 181–204.

von Neumann, J., and Morgenstern, O. (1944). *Theory of Games and Economic Behavior*. New York: Wiley.

von Winterfeldt, D., and Edwards, W. (1986). *Decision Analysis and Behavioral Research*. Cambridge, England: Cambridge University Press.

NAME INDEX

SUBJECT INDEX